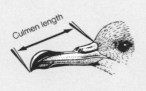

54 Black Petrel

Sea-bird bill profiles: albatrosses, petrels, shearwaters

Use these life-size bill profiles together with the field information for the accurate identification of dead birds washed up on the beach.
• Compare the bill shape of your specimen with the drawings.
• Take precise measurements (using calipers) of *culmen length* and *bill width* (see diagram). If you think the bird is rare or unusual, take it to the museum.

55 Westland Petrel

• Prion identification is very difficult. Our drawings are guides to average specimens only. Prion bills vary greatly. Some are virtually impossible to identify because species and racial clines are probably operating. Take all difficult prions to the museum.

56 White-chinned Petrel

47 Broad-billed Prion
Length 31.5-38 mm
Width 18-25 mm

48 Lesser Broad-billed Prion
Length 26.5-34 mm
Width 12.5-20.5 mm

49 Antarctic Prion
Length 25-30 mm
Width 12-16 mm

50 Slender-billed Prion
Length 23-27.5 mm
Width 9-12 mm

51 Fulmar Prion
Length 19-25 mm
Width 10-14.7 mm

52 Fairy Prion
Length 19.5-26 mm
Width 10-12.5 mm

57 Flesh-footed Shearwater

FIELD GUIDE
TO THE
BIRDS OF AUSTRALIA

*The most complete one-volume
book of identification*

SIMPSON & DAY

VIKING

Contents

Viking
Penguin Books Australia Ltd
487 Maroondah Highway, PO Box 257
Ringwood, Victoria 3134, Australia
Penguin Books Ltd
Harmondsworth, Middlesex, England
Viking Penguin, A Division of Penguin Books USA Inc.
375 Hudson Street, New York, New York 10014, USA
Penguin Books Canada Limited
10 Alcorn Avenue, Toronto, Ontario, Canada M4V 3B2
Penguin Books (N.Z.) Ltd
182-190 Wairau Road, Auckland 10, New Zealand

First published by Lloyd O'Neil Pty Ltd in 1984 as
The Birds of Australia
Second edition 1986
First published in this format in 1989 (third edition) by
Penguin Books Australia Ltd as *Field Guide to the Birds of Australia*
Fourth edition 1993

10 9 8 7 6 5 4

Designed by Zöe Gent-Murphy
Printed and bound by Southbank Book, Melbourne

National Library of Australia
Cataloguing-in-Publication data

Field guide to the birds of Australia

4th ed.
Includes indexes
ISBN 0 670 90478 3.

1. Birds — Australia — Identification. 1. Simpson, Ken. 1938- . II. Day, Nicolas, 1955-

598.2994

Introduction

Writers
Tom Aumann
David Baker-Gabb
Kevin Bartram
Simon Bennett
Ron Brown
Margaret Cameron
Mike Carter
Andrew Corrick
Stephen Debus
Denise Deerson
Xenia Dennett
Peter Fell
Kate Fitzherbert
Cliff Frith
Geoff Gayner
Belinda Gillies
Marc Gottsch
Murray Grant
John Hatch
Victor Hurley
Jack Hyett
Andrew Isles
Angela Jessop
Jaroslav Klapste
Peter Klapste
Tess Kloot
Brett Lane
Alan Lill
Gordon McCarthy
Ellen McCulloch
Peter Mason
Peter Menkhorst
Clive Minton
Mick Murliss
Ian Norman
Richard Noske
David Paton
Paul Peake
Trevor Pescott
Des Quinn
Pat Rich
Bruce Robertson
Len Robinson
Tony Robinson
Ken Simpson
Lance Williams
John Woinarski
Richard Zann

Ornithologists and bird-watchers alike are anticipating a new, official check-list of Australian birds from the Royal Australian Ornithologists Union, but it is a long time in coming.

We are in a state of transition between two scientific nomenclatures. The importance of molecular biology studies over the last 20 years, using a range of new DNA-DNA hybridisation techniques, by Charles Sibley and Jon Ahlquist and associates, cannot be overstated. Their results, coupled with all the previous anatomical, fossil and behavioural studies, have provided another 'giant step' to understanding the evolutionary relationships, the phylogenetic tree, so far as birds are concerned, and the official checklist will have to be changed to include this information.

Much of the research is still being checked, but enough has already been discovered to solve some knotty problems as to where various bird species, genera or families should be placed in relation to each other. Here are just a few examples. The Plains-wanderer is a wader, not a button-quail. Vultures of Central and South America are allied to storks, not other birds of prey. The Spangled Drongo and the Australian Magpie-lark are monarch fly-catchers. Australian chats are honeyeaters ... the list goes on.

We begin to introduce some of these changes by keeping the Field Information part of the book as it was, but we take a 'middle path' in the Handbook, where we constantly refer to Sibley & Ahlquist's work, but do not adopt all their rearrangements. Instead we have a Family presentation sequence based on a modern interim List of Bird Families (unpublished) which will be the basis for a forthcoming volume of the Australian Biological Resources Study, Bureau of Fauna and Flora, Canberra.

Ken Simpson and Nicolas Day, April 1992

Acknowledgements

We very sincerely thank the following people who have contributed in varying ways to the fourth edition of this book: Felicity Anderson, Jim Bannan, Mike Carter, Dr Les Christidis, Clare Coney, Alistair Coutts, Gil Davidson, Jeff Davies, David Eades, Belinda Gillies, Jack Hyett, Andrew Isles, Ellen McCulloch, Dr Keith McDougall, Noreen and Norman McKendrick, Ian Mason, Dr Peter Menkhorst, Dr Bob Parsons, Bernie Ryan, Dr Richard Schodde, Fred Smith, Bob Swindley, Philip Veerman, Andrew Wegener and Zoe Wilson.

Additionally, we are grateful for the assistance of staff and librarians at The Museum of Victoria, Arthur Rylah Institute, Bird Observers Club of Australia, Royal Australasian Ornithologists Union and Australian National Parks and Wildlife Service.

Editor
Ken Simpson

Illustrator
Nicolas Day

Art Director
Peter Trusler

Field Consultants
Kevin Bartram
Len Robinson

Publisher's Editor
Robyn Carter

Publisher's Reader
Walter Boles

Designer
Zoë Gent-Murphy

Designer's Assistant
Heather Jones

Typesetter
Tricia Randle

Contents Illustrator
Jeremy Boot

Contributing Illustrators
Black and white:
Kevin Bartram
Alistair Coutts
Nicolas Day
Annette Dowd
Graham Milledge
Alison Titchen
Peter Trusler

How to use this book to identify a bird

Step 1 Key to Families (pages 6-15)
By using the illustrations and text in the **Key to Families** try to work out which Family your bird belongs to. For example: does it look like a gull, a kingfisher, or an owl?

Step 2 Field Information (pages 16-275)
● When you think you know which Family your bird belongs to, turn to the **Field Information** section. The appropriate pages are indicated in bold type in the **Key to Families**.
● Look for the bird on the colour plate(s). The number beside the illustration refers you to the text for that species. All the field information for the species appears on the facing page, under the same number. Read the text carefully, then check the map (see **Legend for distribution maps** on this page) to make sure the bird you have seen is likely to be found in the area you have seen it. Remember, the maps are only a general guide to distribution. If you require a more detailed map reference see *The Atlas of Australian Birds* (Royal Australasian Ornithologists Union) under the RAOU number given beside each map.
● If all the information provided corresponds with what you have seen, then you have probably identified your bird correctly. You may wish to record it in the ticking boxes beside the map. If not sure of your identification, recheck the illustrations and text, or refer back to the **Key to Families** again.

Step 3 The Handbook (pages 276-378)
If you want to read more about the taxonomy, behaviour, feeding and breeding habits (see breeding bar legend below) of the bird, the second page reference in the **Key to Families** will refer you to this information.

The indexes of Latin and common names should be used if you know the name of the bird you wish to look up.

Legend for distribution maps
▨	Breeding
▨	Non-breeding and vagrant
▶	Offshore islands where birds have been recorded
→	Migration trends

Legend for breeding bars in The Handbook
▨	Main breeding season
▨	Casual breeding and breeding in response to unseasonable rainfall

Parts of a bird's body

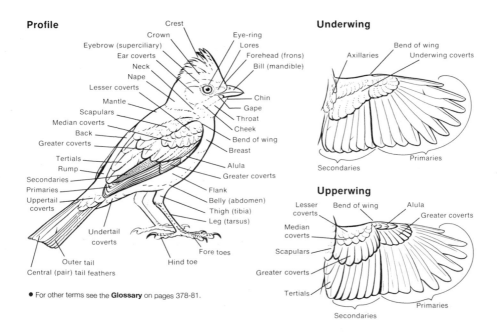

Profile

Crest
Crown
Eyebrow (superciliary)
Ear coverts
Neck
Nape
Lesser coverts
Mantle
Scapulars
Median coverts
Back
Greater coverts
Tertials
Rump
Secondaries
Primaries
Uppertail coverts
Undertail coverts
Outer tail
Central (pair) tail feathers

Eye-ring
Lores
Forehead (frons)
Bill (mandible)
Chin
Gape
Throat
Cheek
Bend of wing
Breast
Alula
Greater coverts
Flank
Belly (abdomen)
Thigh (tibia)
Leg (tarsus)
Fore toes
Hind toe

Underwing

Bend of wing
Axillaries
Underwing coverts
Primaries
Secondaries

Upperwing

Lesser coverts
Bend of wing
Alula
Greater coverts
Median coverts
Scapulars
Greater coverts
Tertials
Primaries
Secondaries

● For other terms see the **Glossary** on pages 378-81.

Preface to the Fourth Edition

For this edition — the fourth overall, and the second of the *Field Guide* — we have replaced 11 colour plates, making improvements and adding more images. Some 52 extra or replacement black-and-white drawings are included, and there are changes to 93 distribution maps. Field information entries have been rewritten or modified for 160 species. Resequencing and some renumbering in both text and plates has been necessary in the presentation of certain species.

A new section, **Rare bird bulletin**, contains some 16 rare or new species for Australia and nearby regions, and miniature colour plates depict these occasional stragglers and vagrants. We had previously referred to some of these birds but now they are illustrated.

The entire **Handbook** section has been rewritten, and expanded by 40 pages. Additional space has been allocated for the **Habitats of Australia**, **Prehistoric birds** and **DNA-DNA hybridisation**. This exciting recent research in molecular biology and the consequent reinterpretation of the evolution of birds is explained by constant reference to Sibley & Ahlquist's pioneering work in this field.

An innovation is the section, **Australian island territories' checklists**, which introduces a list of the many species recorded from six of the major islands scattered about the oceans and for which the Australian government is ultimately responsible. Many bird-watchers visit Lord Howe and Norfolk islands, and a lucky few make it to Christmas Island. Generally only research personnel manage to find their way to Cocos (Keeling) Island, or to the subantarctic islands of Macquarie and Heard. Appropriate references have been added for each island account.

The **Glossary** has been enlarged by about 50 entries. The book has been re-referenced and re-indexed. This is a true new edition of *The Birds of Australia, A Book of Identification*, in both the physical and bibliographic senses.

Your ideas for further line drawings, confirmed extensions of range for our maps, and any well-intentioned criticisms to improve this book will always be welcomed.

Ken Simpson and Nicolas Day

Stop Press: New Bird for Australia

Red-throated Pipit *Anthus cervinus*

RAOU Atlas

Vagrant to Broome, NW Aust. from the Eurasian Holarctic area, Scandinavia to E Siberia; winters to tropical Africa and Asia, reaching Borneo. Recorded/photographed on 6-9/1/1992; four observers. **Breeding** (N Hemisphere) variably red or reddish about eyebrow, crown, throat, breast. Strongly black-striped crown, nape, flanks, rump. Breast heavily streaked/blotched black. Legs pinkish. **Non-breeding** less or no reddishness about throat. Eyebrow may retain faint colour. All body stripes remain prominent; pale to white belly. **Size** 14.5 cm. **Voice** distinctive; melodious; also sharp calls; some are disyllabic. **Habitat** seen in short, wet grass with animal footprints breaking surface (Broome). Identify from Richard's Pipit (larger, paler, flanks not striped); Singing Bushlark (smaller). Bird stands 'more horizontally' than Richard's Pipit; is shorter-tailed, darker-backed.

Non-br.

Br.

Reading

Carter, M. J., 1992, 'A new bird for Australia: Red-throated Pipit *Anthus cervinus*', *Bird Observer* no. 717, March 1992, p. 2;

Heinzel, H., Fitter, R. & Parslow, J., 1972, *The Birds of Britain and Europe with North Africa and the Middle East*, William Collins Sons & Co., London, pp. 208-9.

Key to Families

Emus   Family Dromaiidae   **16-17**, 294

Australia's national emblem and largest endemic bird.
Flightless, fast-running, strong-legged, stands two metres
high. Loose, grey, shaggy plumage.   Species: World 1; Australia 1.

Cassowaries   Family Casuariidae   **16-17**, 293

Stocky and flightless, this large ratite has black, hair-like
plumage, a helmeted head, a bright face and distinctive neck
wattles.   Species: World 3; Australia 1.

Mihirungs (Extinct)   Family Dromornithidae   288-9

Huge runners with heavy bills, hoof-like toes, tiny wings.
Miocene-Pleistocene fossils. Not illustrated here.

Ostriches   Family Struthionidae   **16-17**, 293

The plumage of the Ostrich is black and it is the world's
largest living bird. Each foot has two toes — the only bird
with fewer than three.   Species: World 1; Australia 1.

Grebes   Family Podicipedidae   **18-19**, 299-300

Sharp-billed diving birds with legs far back on the body;
feet have lobed toes. Grebes cannot walk well on land.
Species: World 20; Australia 3.

Penguins   Family Spheniscidae   **20-1**, 298-9

Plump, small to large sea-birds with upright stance. Dense,
waterproof plumage. Wings modified as flippers for sustained
swimming, diving.   Species: World 18; Australia 11.

Albatrosses   Family Diomedeidae   **22-7**, 294-5

Medium to very large, long-winged, gliding, oceanic sea-
birds. Small tubular nostrils at side of large, hook-tipped
bills; webbed feet.   Species: World 13; Australia 10.

Petrels, Shearwaters
Family Procellariidae   **28-39**, 296-7

Small to medium, long-winged, gliding, oceanic sea-birds.
Tubular nostrils on top of stout, hooked bills; webbed feet.
Species: World approx. 66; Australia 41.

Storm-Petrels   Family Oceanitidae   **40-1**, 297

Tiny, blackish or grey, long-legged petrels with rapid
swooping flight. Feed by fluttering or pattering over wave
surfaces.   Species: World 20; Australia 7.

Diving-Petrels   Family Pelecanoididae   **40-1**, 298

Tiny, dumpy, short-winged, resembling Northern Hemisphere auks. Fly between waves with rapid wing beats; dive
and swim well.   Species: World 4; Australia 2.

Pelicans   Family Pelecanidae   **42-3**, 303

The large Australian Pelican has a spectacular long bill and loose pouch. All four toes are linked by webbing.
Species: World 8; Australia 1.

Gannets, Boobies   Family Sulidae   **42-3**, 301-2

Stout-billed sea-birds which indulge in spectacular plunge-diving. Feet fully webbed. Gannets frequent colder seas; boobies more tropical seas.   Species: World 9; Australia 5.

Darters   Family Anhingidae   **44-5**, 301

Darters lunge with snake-like necks and slender bills to spear fish under water. Resemble cormorants but larger, slimmer, broader-winged.   Species: World 4; Australia 1.

Cormorants,
Shags   Family Phalacrocoracidae   **44-5**, 301

Cormorants swim and dive for fish. Like darters, their feet are fully webbed. They often perch with outstretched wings.
Species: World 29-33; Australia 5.

Frigatebirds   Family Fregatidae   **46-7**, 300

Large, dark sea-birds with long, hooked bills and long, deeply forked tails. Soar on long pointed wings over tropical seas. Feed on the wing.
Species: World 5; Australia 3.

Tropicbirds   Family Phaethontidae   **46-7**, 300

Stout, white-plumaged sea-birds with two long, central tail streamers. Plunge-dive for food; strong direct flight; soar in updrafts.   Species: World 3; Australia 2.

Herons, Egrets,
Bitterns   Family Ardeidae   **48-53**, 303-4

Slender, long-legged, long-necked, aquatic birds with bills like daggers.   Species: World 61; Australia 14.

Storks   Family Ciconiidae   **54-5**, 304

Large waterbirds with long, stout bills. During flight or soaring, their broad wings, extended neck and long trailing legs are distinctive.   Species: World 17; Australia 1.

Ibises, Spoonbills   Family Plataleidae   **54-5**, 304-5

Diagnostic bills distinguish these from similarly built herons. They feed by touch: probing (ibises), sweeping through shallow water (spoonbills).   Species: World 32; Australia 5.

Flamingos (Extinct)   Family Phoenicopteridae   288-9

Tall, long-limbed, filter-feeding, aquatic birds. Miocene-Pleistocene fossils. Not illustrated here.

Palaelodids (Extinct)   Family Palaelodidae   288-9

Large, tall, probably straight-billed, aquatic birds. Miocene fossils. Not illustrated here.

Geese, Swans, Ducks   Family Anatidae   **56-65**, 308-10

Birds of the wetlands with dense waterproof plumage, webbed feet and flattened bills. Most fly strongly. Important game birds.   Species: World 145; Australia 23.

Osprey   Family Pandionidae   **66-7**, 305

A fishing hawk with broad wings, strong legs and talons to seize slippery prey. Nest is a large, conspicuous stick platform.   Species: World 1; Australia 1.

Kites, Goshawks, Eagles, Harriers   Family Accipitridae   **66-75**, 305-7

Birds of prey with short heads, broad wings, hooked bills and large talons. Females larger than males. Often seen soaring.
Species: World approx. 219; Australia 18.

Falcons   Family Falconidae   **74-7**, 307-8

Predatory birds with 'toothed' upper bill, a dark cap or tear-drop cheek mark, long pointed wings and swift flight.
Species: World 61; Australia 6.

Mound-builders (Megapodes) Family Megapodiidae   **78-9**, 310

Large, strong-legged, dark or spotted, ground birds. Some have bare heads and bright wattles. Eggs incubated in soil mounds.   Species: World 12; Australia 3.

Quails, Pheasants   Family Phasianidae   **80-1**, 311

Small and striped to large and long-tailed, bright ground birds.   Species: World approx. 211; Australia approx. 7.

Button-quails   Family Turnicidae   **82-3**, 312

Resemble true quails (Phasianidae) but lack a hind toe. Females larger, brighter and polyandrous — mate with several males each breeding season.   Species: World 14; Australia 7.

Plains-wanderer   Family Pedionomidae   **82-3**, 315

Like button-quails but have a hind toe. Weak, fluttering flight.   Species: World 1; Australia 1.

Rails, Crakes, Swamphens, Coots   Family Rallidae   **84-9**, 313

Small to large, long-toed, stout-billed, skulking, aquatic birds.   Species: World 123; Australia 16.

Cranes   Family Gruidae   **90-1**, 312

Tall, elegant, upright birds with red heads, grey bodies. Sharp bill longer than head. Elaborate dancing displays. Soaring flight.   Species: World 16; Australia 2.

Bustards   Family Otididae   **90-1**, 314

Stately, heavy, grassland-dwelling birds with long legs, pointed bills.   Species: World 24; Australia 1.

Jacanas (Lotusbirds)   Family Jacanidae   **92-3**, 314-5

Rail-like in appearance, jacanas are waders with specialised long toes and hind claws for running over floating freshwater plants.   Species: World 8; Australia 1.

Thick-knees (Stone Curlews)
Family Burhinidae   **92-3**, 317

Tall, large-eyed, plover-like, bush- and beach-dwelling waders. Both species are widespread but relatively uncommon.   Species: World 9; Australia 2.

Painted Snipe   Family Rostratulidae   **92-3**, 315

Long-billed, strikingly patterned waders. Female brighter. May 'freeze' when disturbed.   Species: World 2; Australia 1.

Oystercatchers
Family Haematopodidae   **92-3**, 316

Black or pied coastal waders.   Species: World 7; Australia 2.

**Lapwings, Plovers,
Dotterels**   Family Charadriidae   **94-9**, 317-18

Short-billed, round-headed, large-eyed, plain or camouflaged waders.   Species: World 64; Australia 16.

Stilts, Avocets   Family Recurvirostridae   **98-9**, 317

Medium-sized, distinctive waders with very long legs. Bills slender: straight (stilts), upturned (avocets). Often in large flocks. Yapping calls.   Species: World 13; Australia 3.

**Curlews, Sandpipers, Snipes,
Godwits**   Family Scolopacidae   **100-9**, 318-20

Large Family of usually long-billed, longish-legged, migratory waders. Smallest are the stints; largest the Eastern Curlew. Species: World approx. 85; Australia approx. 43.

Phalaropes   Family Phalaropodidae   **110-11**, 320

Boldly marked, fast-flying waders. Feed by spinning when swimming.   Species: World 3; Australia 3.

Pratincoles   Family Glareolidae   **110-11**, 321

Fork-tailed, long-winged, brownish waders of inland and barren areas.   Species: World 16; Australia 2.

Skuas, Jaegers   Family Stercorariidae   **112-13**, 321-2

Piratical sea-birds with variable plumage, elongated central tail feathers and white wing flashes.   Species: World 6; Australia 5.

Gulls, Terns   Family Laridae   **114-23**, 322-6

Solid and medium-winged, gulls have white, grey and dark plumages, heavy bills, webbed feet. Terns and noddies are similar, but slender, thin-billed and narrow-winged. They stand horizontally. Some are crested. Dive into water for food or pick it off the surface.
Species: World approx. 88; Australia 28.

Pigeons, Doves

Family Columbidae   **124-31**, 326-8

Plump, plain or colourful, fast-flying fruit- or seed-eaters. Some have crests. Stout bill; some drink by sucking. Tail medium to long, square or pointed. Build frail stick nests.
Species: World approx. 297; Australia 25.

Cockatoos

Subfamily Cacatuinae (see below)   **132-5**, 328-32

Medium to large parrots with prominent erectile crests. They have a complete orbital ring. Plumages range from black to white. Tail long, or short and square. Loud, often raucous voices. Feed on roots, seeds, blossom; some eat insects. Recent work has clarified the identification of corellas and black-cockatoos in Western Australia.

'True' Parrots   Family Psittacidae   **134-5**, 328-32

All parrots are 'true' parrots: stocky-bodied; medium-sized wings; stout, hooked bills; two toes forward and two back. In this book, all parrots are regarded as one Family with several well-defined Subfamilies (see above and below).
Species: World approx. 332; Australia 52.

Lorikeets   Subfamily Loriinae   **136-7**, 328-32

Noisy, fast-flying, forest-dwelling parrots. They are small, with short, pointed tails, or medium-sized, with long pointed tails. Three Australian genera; all eat nectar, pollen and fruit.

Fig-Parrots

Subfamily Opopsittinae   **136-7**, 328-32

The smallest Australian parrot. Tail is short, rather rounded. Predominantly green, the three isolated populations (races) may be identified from each other by facial markings.

'Long-tailed' Parrots

Subfamily Polytelitinae   **138-9**, 328-32

Tails are long and graduated, each narrow tail feather with a fine tip. Wings are long and pointed. Fast-flying birds. Bills are small. Male and female plumages differ. Large flocks of a couple of the species may frequent grain crops in arid areas.

'Broad-tailed' Parrots

Subfamily Platycercinae   **140-7**, 328-32

A 'grab-bag' of assorted parrots. Tails medium to long in proportion to body length and frequently fanned in display. Taxonomic fluctuations affect the total number regarded as 'full species' — rosellas, ringnecks, hooded parrots are all under consideration at present.

Parasitic Cuckoos,

Coucals   Family Cuculidae   **148-51**, 332-3

Slender, small to large, plain or barred, long-tailed birds with narrow wings, fast undulating flight and ventriloquial calls. All but the Pheasant Coucal are parasitic on other bird species.   Species: World 127; Australia 13.

Hawk Owls   Family Strigidae   152-3, 334-5

Small to large nocturnal birds, usually with yellow irises and large eyes set in an indistinct facial disc. Females generally larger (except in Australia). Often heard giving monotonous territorial calls.   Species: World 135; Australia 5.

Barn Owls   Family Tytonidae   154-5, 333-4

Small to large, slender-legged, nocturnal birds with all dark eyes set in a distinctive facial disc. Females larger. Usually silent. Hunt largely by listening for rodents, reptiles, large insects.   Species: World 12; Australia 5.

Frogmouths   Family Podargidae   156-7, 335

Small to large nocturnal birds with weak feet, longish tails, rounded wings and massive, broad bills. Males larger. Plumage grey or brown. Resemble dead branch stubs while perched. Active in open forests and rainforests at late dusk.   Species: World 13; Australia 3.

Owlet-nightjars   Family Aegothelidae   156-7, 336

Very small, delicate, grey, nocturnal birds. Small, broad bill edged by prominent bristles. Large, forward-facing eyes, weak feet, rounded wings and long, broad tail. Almost no reflective eye shine.   Species: World 8; Australia 1.

Nightjars   Family Caprimulgidae   156-7, 336

Small to medium nocturnal birds with long tails, small broad bills and long pointed wings which, in flight, are stiff and irregular in movement. Very reflective eye shine in light. Normally roost by day on the ground. Nest amid leaf litter. Camouflaged plumage provides marvellous protection.   Species: World 75; Australia 3.

Swiftlets, Swifts   Family Apodidae   158-9, 336-7

Quick-flying, dark-coloured insectivores with long, swept wings, square or forked tails, large eyes, a small bill but wide gape. Large swifts are migratory; resident swiftlets breed in caves.   Species: World 84; Australia 6.

Kingfishers   Family Alcedinidae   160-3, 337

Usually brightly coloured, kingfishers have stout bodies, large heads, long heavy pointed bills and small feet. Fast, direct flight. Nest in holes in trees, banks, termite mounds.
Species: World 91; Australia 11.

Bee-eaters   Family Meropidae   162-3, 338

Vocal, gregarious, migratory and brightly coloured birds. Bill long and down-curved; legs small. Hawk aerial insects. Nest in a burrow.   Species: World 24; Australia 1.

Rollers   Family Coraciidae   162-3, 338

Known for their habit of rolling during aerial display flights. The Dollarbird has a red bill and stout body. When it hawks insects from exposed perches, white 'silver-dollar' wing spots become visible.   Species: World 11; Australia 1.

Pittas Family Pittidae   **164-5**, 338-9

Plump, medium-sized, brightly coloured birds with short tails and long legs. Upright stance. White wing patches in flight. Secretive, ground-dwelling, in rainforests, tropical scrubs and mangroves. Usually located by loud, distinctive calls, often given while perched high.
Species: World 26; Australia 3.

Lyrebirds Family Menuridae   **164-5**, 339-40

Large, predominantly brown forest birds with long tails, legs and toes. They forage on the ground and fly only weakly. Breeding males have a loud, protracted song including much mimicry given during spectacular displays on prepared dancing mounds.   Species: World 2; Australia 2.

Scrub-birds Family Atrichornithidae   **164-5**, 340

Considered to have close affinities with lyrebirds (Menuridae). Plumages are dark rufous and dark brown, with fine vermiculated patterns. Sexes differ. Birds are retiring, remain near ground, rarely fly. Loud, ventriloquial voice, containing much mimicry. The Noisy Scrub-bird is an endangered species.   Species: World 2; Australia 2.

Old World Larks Family Alaudidae   **166-7**, 366

Small, streaked, grassland songbirds. Hind toe long, sharply clawed. Erectile head feathers as short crest. Endemic Bushlark and introduced Skylark both have aerial display flights. Identify them from Richard's Pipit (Motacillidae).
Species: World 82; Australia 2.

Swallows, Martins
Family Hirundinidae   **166-7**, 363-4

Small songbirds which hawk aerial insects. They have long, straight, pointed wings and either forked or square tails. Most are migratory or nomadic.   Species: World 78; Australia 6.

Old World Pipits,
Wagtails Family Motacillidae   **168-9**, 367

Slender birds which often wag their long tails up and down. Pipits resemble larks (Alaudidae) but have yellow legs and *no* crest. The vagrant wagtails have pied plumages, plus yellow, green or grey.   Species: World 54; Australia 5.

Cuckoo-shrikes,
Trillers Family Campephagidae   **170-1**, 357

Insectivorous, arboreal birds with slender bodies, long pointed wings and graduated tails. Plumages black, grey, brown and pied combinations; some have barrings. They have undulating flight and trilling voices.
Species: World 72; Australia 7.

Bulbuls Family Pycnonotidae   **172-3**, 364

Generally small Old World birds. Brown to olive-green, often crested with decurved notched bills and distinctive head marks. Two introduced species; one survives about Sydney and Coffs Harbour, NSW.   Species: World 118; Australia 1.

Old World Thrushes, Flycatchers and allies
Family 'Muscicapidae'   172-93, 350-2, 354-6

A varied group of small to medium-sized insectivorous birds, often taking their prey on the wing. Usually excellent songsters. Pronounced sexual differences in some. Some juveniles are spotted. A taxonomically complex group.
Species: World approx. 400; Australia 54-6.

Chowchillas, Whipbirds, Wedgebills, Quail-thrushes   Family Orthonychidae   194-7, 352

Four genera of rather secretive, long-tailed songbirds which live on or close to the ground, although in diverse habitats. Most are camouflaged; some are crested; some are mimics.
Species: World 11; Australia 10.

Babblers   Family Pomatostomidae   198-9, 352-3

Noisy, gregarious, mainly ground-feeding birds with plump brownish bodies, longish tails and pointed, down-curved bills. Territorial groups build several prominent dome-shaped stick nests for nesting and communal roosting.
Species: World approx. 255; Australia 4.

Old World Warblers   Family Sylviidae   200-3, 364-5

A Family whose membership often changes with the vagaries of taxonomists. Currently includes small, brownish, grass- and reed-dwelling, heavily streaked, strong-voiced song-birds. Some have aerial display flights.
Species: World approx. 400; Australia 8.

Fairy-wrens   Family Maluridae   202-9, 342

Three genera of small, cocked-tailed, insectivorous 'wrens' (warblers). Breeding males are brilliant; non-breeding and young males, and females are brown (fairy-wrens). Both sexes generally similar to the streak-plumaged grasswrens, and the emu-wrens, which have modified tail feathers.
Species: World approx. 23; Australia approx. 18.

Bristlebirds, Scrubwrens, Gerygones, Thornbills
Family Acanthizidae   210-21, 348-50

Large Family of small to tiny dull birds. Active and with pleasant voices, they are mainly ground-dwelling or foliage-foraging insectivores. All build dome-shaped, sometimes pendant, nests. Only females incubate.
Species: World approx. 72; Australia approx. 41.

Sittellas   Family Neosittidae   222-3, 353-4

These birds climb on tree-trunks and branches. They are small, social, grey and black-and-white with orange to white wing bars, slightly upturned bills, yellow legs and feet. One variable species.   Species: World 1; Australia 1.

Treecreepers   Family Climacteridae   222-3, 341

These birds climb up tree-trunks and branches; some also hop on the ground. They are small and brownish with pale fawn wing bars, slightly down-curved bills, strong legs, long toes. Sexes are different.   Species: World 6; Australia 6.

13

Honeyeaters
Family Meliphagidae   **224-43**, 343-6

Honeyeaters have brush-tipped tongues, decurved bills (1-3 cm long), are mainly dull green or brown with patches of brighter plumage or skin around face, and are slim (10-15 cm long).   Species: World 171; Australia 68.

Chats   Family Ephthianuridae   **244-5**, 347

Bright males and similarly coloured but duller females and juveniles typify these often nomadic and flocking small birds of the inland plains and coastal salt marshes.
Species: World 5; Australia 5.

Sunbirds   Family Nectariniidae   **246-7**, 367

Small, brightly coloured, slender-billed, quick-flying, nectar and insect feeders. At times are like honeyeaters and hummingbirds in behaviour and flight mannerisms. Build pendulous nests with side entrances.   Species: World 117; Australia 1.

Flowerpeckers   Family Dicaeidae   **246-7**, 367-8

Tiny, short-billed and short-tailed, Mistletoebirds spread the parasitic plant on which they largely depend for food.
Species: World 58; Australia 1.

Pardalotes   Family Pardalotidae   **246-7**, 347-8

Tiny birds restricted to Australia. Mostly spotted and colourful with short tails, and short, broad bills. Feed on insects on tree foliage; breed in hollows or burrows, sometimes in colonies.   Species: World 5; Australia 5.

White-eyes   Family Zosteropidae   **248-9**, 365

Small greenish or yellowish birds with divided, extensible brush-tipped tongues. Most have a white eye-ring of tiny feathers. Migratory and nomadic. Build small, suspended, cup-shaped nests. Piping calls.   Species: World 84; Australia 3.

True Finches   Family Fringillidae   **250-1**, 370

Small to large seed-eaters with stout conical bills for cracking seeds and nuts. Plumages vary from camouflaged to brilliantly coloured. The nest is cup-shaped. Two species introduced into Australia.   Species: World 440; Australia 2.

Old World Sparrows
Family Passeridae   **250-1**, 368

Small, compact, brown-plumaged seed-eaters with 17 tail feathers and thick conical bills. Sexes rather similar. They build roofed, spherical nests. Often classified with weavers (Ploceidae).   Species: World 37; Australia 2.

Weavers, Waxbills, Grass-Finches, Mannikins
Family Ploceidae   **250-7**, 368-70

Two groups of small, colourful seed-eaters. Weavers construct beautifully woven grass nests with roofs. Estrildids are long-tailed and smaller with peculiar palate patterns. Their nests are bottle-shaped.   Species: World 120; Australia 22.

Starlings, Mynahs Family Sturnidae **258-9**, 366

Solid, sharp-beaked, dark-plumaged (iridescent in two species), strong-legged birds. They are vocal, aggressive, nomadic or migratory colonists. Species: World 108; Australia 3.

Orioles, Figbirds Family Oriolidae **258-9**, 357-8

Both sexes of Australian orioles and Figbird females are similar, resembling the duller streaked females of some brighter foreign species. Species: World 25; Australia 3.

Drongos Family Dicruridae **258-9**, 355

Gleaming black, fish-tailed and red-eyed, the Spangled Drongo is distinctive. Species: World 20; Australia 1.

Bowerbirds Family Ptilonorhynchidae **260-1**, 358-9

Males have bright crests, capes or iridescent plumage; females are drab and camouflaged. Males clear courts or construct bowers.
Species: World 18; Australia 8.

Birds of Paradise
Family Paradisaeidae **262-3**, 359-60

Adult sexes are different. Males are spectacular in colour and feathering; females and immature males are drab and camouflaged. Rainforest birds. Mainly fruit-eaters.
Species: World 43; Australia 4.

Australian Mud-nesters
Family Corcoracidae **264-5**, 363

Large black, or small grey birds which live in sociable groups, build solid mud nests and assist each other in breeding. Species: World 2; Australia 2.

Magpie-larks Family Grallinidae **264-5**, 355-6

Black and white (plover-like), long-legged, vocal, mud-nest building birds. Pairs often seen on roadsides. Flocks in winter. Species: World 2; Australia 1.

Woodswallows Family Artamidae **264-5**, 360-1

Small, robust, mostly nomadic songbirds with bluish, black-tipped bills. Distinctive 'batwing' shape (in flight), rotate tails (when perched); may huddle together.
Species: World 10; Australia 6.

Butcherbirds,
Currawongs Family Cracticidae **266-9**, 361-2

Solid, arboreal, strong-flying birds. Black, or black, grey and white. Large, robust, hooked bills; loud voices, harsh and/or melodious. Species: World 10; Australia 8.

Ravens, Crows Family Corvidae **270-1**, 362-3

Uniform, glossy black birds with minor physical differences. They have stout, rather long bills. Plumage is often reflective. Calls are 'cawing'. Species: World 112; Australia 6.

World species numbers based on Howard & Moore, 1984, *Birds of the World*, Macmillan, New York.

Field Information

Ostrich, Cassowary, Emu

1 Ostrich *Struthio camelus**

Distinctive. **Male** plumage black, long, soft and loosely webbed. Bill broad and flat. Head, neck and upper legs grey. White plumes in wings and tail. Lower legs and feet grey-brown; two toes — only bird in the world with fewer than three. Breeding males develop reddish colour on gape, edge of upper mandible, feet. A red, protrusible hemi-penis may be apparent at times. **Female** lighter brown body plumage, off-white plumes. **Size** up to 2.4 m; the world's largest living bird species. **Hatchlings** downy, dark stripes on neck. **Juv.** brownish; black stripes on head, neck. **Imm.** mottled brown, grey plumage, darkening with age. Race *australis* often mentioned but precise genetic composition not known. **Habitat** open mulga woodlands, bluebush plains and sandhills. Flightless. Runs with vestigial wings held out, at up to 55 km/h. Farmed S Aust. population mostly controlled; may be a few feral birds. More farms setting up in some States.

Ostrich plume

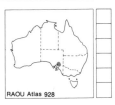
RAOU Atlas 928

2 Southern Cassowary *Casuarius casuarius*

Distinctive. Tall, greyish casque (helmet) on both sexes. Skin on head pale blue, becoming darker down neck. Some red lateral skin on neck. Two long red-to-crimson free-swinging fleshy wattles originate at front of neck. Body black. Feathers coarse, hair-like with shaft, aftershaft. Short, stout green-grey/brown/grey legs; feet same colour; three toes. Inner toe-nail an elongated spike up to 120 mm. **Female** slightly larger, brighter coloured. **Size** to 1.75 m approx. **Hatchling** downy; striped yellow, black to about 3 months. **Juv.** brown-bodied, head, neck pattern as adult but duller; smaller wattles; no casque. **Imm.** similar, but body blacker with increased age. Aust. race *johnsonii*. **Habitat** tropical rainforests, preferring stream banks, clearings. Adults aggressive, kick; approach with care.

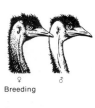
Double-shafted feather

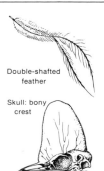
Skull: bony crest

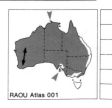
RAOU Atlas 002

3 Emu *Dromaius novaehollandiae*

Distinctive. General plumage dark brown to grey-brown. Feathers have shaft, aftershaft; plumage long, thick, drooping, soft, appears shaggy. Skin of head, throat blue. Long legs and feet dark grey-brown; three toes. Body plumage of breeding female darkens; black feathers cover head and neck. **Size** stands to 2 m. **Hatchling** crown spotted; body downy with dark brown to black body stripes. **Juv./Imm.** dark head; plumage even-coloured, less mottled. Smaller than adults. Three races: *novaehollandiae* (SE Aust.) whitish ruff when breeding; *woodwardi* (N Aust.) slender, paler; *rothschildi* (SW Aust.) darker, no ruff during breeding. **Voice** deep drumming. **Habitat** varies widely: arid inland plains, tropical woodlands, heaths, coastal dunes; not rainforests. Flightless. Runs with a bouncy, swaying motion. May be solitary, in family groups or in large flocks. North-south migrant in W Aust.

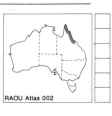
♀ ♂
Breeding

RAOU Atlas 001

Tracks

Hard Surface   Soft Surface

Double-shafted feather

* Introduced

3

1 ♂   1 ♀

1 chicks

3 Imm.

3 ♀

3 ♂   3 chick

2 1st year   2 ♀

2 chick

N.DAY.

4 Great Crested Grebe *Podiceps cristatus*

Distinctive. Dagger-like bill. Eye red. Black line from gape to eye. Cheeks and throat white. Has pointed black ear tufts on dark brown head. Neck encircled with rufous, black-tipped ruff. Silky-white underparts gleam snow-white in sunlight. In flight, conspicuous white margins on dark grey wings. **Non-breeding** ruff and tufts greatly reduced or absent in winter. **Size** to 50 cm.
Downy young dark brown with white stripes on head and body. **1st year** retains some stripes on head. **Imm.** without ear tufts or ruff; many resemble wintering adult. Race in Aust. is *australis*. **Voice** barking and rattling. **Habitat** pairs in breeding season on freshwater lakes with aquatic and marginal vegetation. Gregarious at other times, on fresh or saline waters — lakes, lagoons, estuaries, bays. Winter flocks may appear unexpectedly. Dives for food and to escape from danger; average duration less than 30 seconds.

Diving

Hatchling

RAOU Atlas 060

5 Hoary-headed Grebe *Poliocephalus poliocephalus*

Bill dark, tipped cream. Eye pale. Head black with white plumes. Back dark grey, occasionally brownish. Breast pale buff. Underparts silky white. **Non-breeding** pale grey body. Head without white facial plumes, or with only a few. **Size** 25-30 cm. **Juv.** head striped black and white. **Voice** normally silent; soft churrings near a nest. **Habitat** lakes, swamps; frequently on brackish water or on sea off estuaries. Often seen to fly away from danger or observer. Also dives to escape and for food. Has a long splashing take-off from water surface; quick wing beats in flight; white wing bar shows. Nomadic. Identify from non-breeding Australasian Grebe.

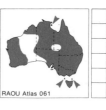

Head shaking

Courtship behaviour

RAOU Atlas 062

6 Australasian Grebe *Tachybaptus novaehollandiae*

Bill dark, tipped cream. Eye yellow. Head and neck black. Bare skin forms a pale yellow face spot. Richly coloured chestnut stripe extends back on to side of neck. Back dark brown. Underparts silver-grey. **Non-breeding/Imm.** duller; facial spot whitens; may be barely visible. These, and Hoary-headed Grebes in breeding plumage, may easily be confused with one another. **Size** 25-27 cm; fractionally smaller than Hoary-headed Grebe. **Juv.** face striped black and white. **Voice** shrill and chittering. **Habitat** generally on fresh water; may join Hoary-headed Grebes in mixed flocks during winter but less gregarious. This species is more likely to dive than to flee danger (or bird-watcher) by flying.

Hatchlings
5

6

RAOU Atlas 061

4: Great Crested Grebe

Courtship behaviour

'Advertising' call.

Head shaking

'Penguin' posture

4

6

5

4
Breeding

4
Non-breeding

4 Imm

5
Breeding

5
Non-breeding

6
Breeding

6
Non-breeding

6 Juv.

N. Day

7 King Penguin *Aptenodytes patagonica*

Distinctive. Steel-blue on back. Prominent ear patch orange (adult), to pale (juv./imm). **Size** 80-92 cm.

RAOU Atlas 927

8 Gentoo Penguin *Pygoscelis papua*

Distinctive. Bill, feet orange. White patches over eyes just meet on crown. Head speckled white. **Size** 71-76 cm.

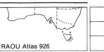

RAOU Atlas 926

9 Chinstrap Penguin *Pygoscelis antarctica*

Distinctive. Bill black. White face; black line slanting under chin diagnostic. **Size** 69-77 cm.

RAOU Atlas 925

10 Adelie Penguin *Pygoscelis adeliae*

Distinctive. White eye-ring diagnostic. **Size** 60-79 cm. **Juv./Imm.** chin whitish; black about eye.

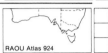

RAOU Atlas 924

11 Magellanic Penguin *Spheniscus magellanicus*

Distinctive. Two white bands of about equal width, each *above* similar blackish bands on throat and breast, diagnostic. **Size** 68-72 cm.

RAOU Atlas 858

12 Royal Penguin *Eudyptes schlegeli*

Golden frontal crest; white to grey face diagnostic. **Size** 65-76 cm. **1st to 4 years** crest shorter.

Imm: 1-2 yrs

RAOU Atlas 968

13 Rockhopper Penguin *Eudyptes chrysocome*

Distinctive. Position of front end of lateral eye-stripe/crest diagnostic. Dull black cheeks. **Size** 45-60 cm. **1st year** eye-stripe not defined; chin whitish; dark bill, horn-tipped. Race *mosleyi* visits Aust. regularly; *filholi* one record.

RAOU Atlas 003

14 Fiordland Penguin *Eudyptes pachyrhynchus*

Distinctive. Back bluish. White streaked, dull blackish cheeks. Position of each end of lateral eye-stripe/crest diagnostic. **Size** 54-71 cm. **1st year to imm.** eye-stripe defined; chin whitish.

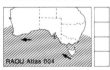

RAOU Atlas 004

15 Erect-crested Penguin *Eudyptes sclateri*

Distinctive. Shape and position of front end of lateral eye-stripe/crest diagnostic. Cheeks glossy black. **Size** 67-74 cm. **1st year** chin, throat pale; eye-stripe defined.

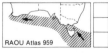

RAOU Atlas 959

16 Snares Penguin *Eudyptes robustus*

Position of front end of lateral eye-stripe/crest diagnostic. Cheeks glossy black. **Size** 67-74 cm. **1st year** eye-stripe defined.

RAOU Atlas 923

17 Little Penguin *Eudyptula minor novaehollandiae*

Smallest penguin. Greyish face; back dark blue. Trailing edge of flipper white. **Size** 32-34 cm. **1st year** chin, throat greyish. Bill blackish.

Metal flipper band

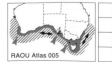

RAOU Atlas 005

9

11

8

7
Imm.

10

16

15

12

13
Imm.
1st yr

13

14
Moulting

17
Chick

17

14 Imm.
1-2 yrs

18 Wandering Albatross *Diomedea exulans*

Note: plumage varies widely; amount of white developed by an individual depends on its sex, age (generally whiter with age) and population characteristics at its breeding island. **Male** powerful pink bill, tipped yellow. White above and below, including crown. White upperparts; breast has varying densities of fine black wavy lines (vermiculations). Tail white, sometimes tipped black. Outer wing and trailing edge black. Underwing white, extreme tips *always* black; pattern constant, little variation with sex or age. Legs, webbed feet pale flesh. **Female** like male, but *always* has brown speckles or striations on crown. **Size** 80-135 cm; wingspan 260-350 cm. **Imm.** (and some darker breeding adults) widely varying (see diagrams). Upperparts with varying black chequered patterns. Upperwing shows increasing white with age, spreading outward from body along *centre* of wings, typically with white patches. Tail white, black terminal band. **Juv.** completely chocolate-brown except for white face and virtually white underwing. Tail black. Body becomes paler, until most of brown replaced by white. A dark to pale brown collar and breast band are last traces of juv. plumage. **Voice** croaking, guttural cackles; bill clappering. **Habitat** oceanic, coastal seas. Habitually follows ships, fishing boats. Most common great albatross in Aust. seas. 'Domed' crown, 'humped' back give 'angular' appearance. Identify from Royal Albatross and from much smaller Australasian Gannet.

Aging:
Imm. (top)
to
Adult (bottom)

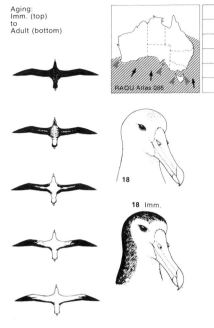

18

18 Imm.

19 Royal Albatross *Diomedea epomophora*

Note: white develops along the leading edge of the upper wing only in race *epomophora*. Where the white merges with black tips and along trailing edge, it appears as a dusting or speckling, *not* chequering as in Wandering Albatross. Powerful bill flesh-coloured, less pink than Wanderer, usually longer. Crown less domed, forehead gently sloped. Diagnostic black cutting edge along upper bill visible at close range. Race *epomophora* 'Southern Royal Albatross'. **Breeding** wholly white above and below (no vermiculations). Underwing like Wandering Albatross. Tail wholly white. Old adults resemble the whitest 'Wanderers'. Legs, feet fleshy-white. Race *sanfordi* 'Northern Royal Albatross' smaller than *epomophora*. Upper wing wholly black; pincer-like extensions on to the back formed by black tips to long scapular feathers. Underwing has broader black mark along outer wing adjacent to the carpal — *diagnostic* of this race. **Size** 76-130 cm; wingspan 305-350 cm. **Imm.** both races resemble adult *sanfordi* but females of *epomophora* have a sprinkling of white along leading edge of inner upperwing. **Juv.** both races generally similar to adult *sanfordi* but few black flecks on crown, back, rump. Tail has narrow black sub-terminal band or spots. **Voice** coarse croakings, guttural sound; bill clappering.
Habitat oceanic, more so than Wanderer. Attends fishing boats; less inclined to follow ships. More 'rounded', less 'angular' appearance than Wanderer. Identify from Wanderer and much smaller Australasian Gannet. Check underwing of White-capped Albatross; backs of all mollymawks for *sanfordi*.

Aging:
Imm. (top)
to
Adult (bottom)

Race *sanfordi*:

Race *sanfordi*:

Race *epomophora*

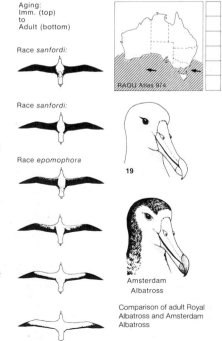

19

Amsterdam
Albatross

Comparison of adult Royal
Albatross and Amsterdam
Albatross

19 Race *sanfordi*

19 Race *epomophora*

18

18

18

19 *pomophora* Juv.

19 Race *epomophora*

19 Race *sanfordi*

18 Juv.

18 Juv.

18

18

19 Race *epomophora*

18 Juv.

18

19 Race *sanfordi*

20 Black-browed Albatross *Diomedea melanophrys*

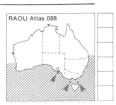

Bill base
from above

RAOU Atlas 088

Race *melanophrys:* Bill yellow-orange. Head white except black brow. Iris black. Rump, underparts white. Upperwing, mantle, tail black. Underwing white; has broad black leading edge, occupying a third or less of wing breadth, widening at 'elbow' and past the carpal joint. Primaries, secondaries black. Legs flesh-white. **Sub-adult** more black on underwing. Bill browner, tipped black. **Juv./Imm.** bill blackish-brown, *or* dull yellow at base with a black tip. Usually grey on collar, sometimes extending to crown with increasing age. Underwing changes from all dark with pale grey centre, to a white centre. Race *impavida:* Like Black-browed adult but has pale honey-coloured iris; more black in eyebrow. Underwing has black streaks on axillaries, and on carpal to primary covert region. **Juv.** like *melanophrys* juv. but iris dark honey. **Size** 85 cm; wingspan 240 cm. **Habitat** oceanic, coastal; follows ships.

21 Buller's Albatross *Diomedea bulleri*

Bill base
from above

RAOU Atlas 931

Bill like Grey-headed Albatross, but yellow, broader along top ridge of bill (culmen). Hood dark grey with white cap. Underwing has narrower black borders than Black-browed, which are parallel to leading edges. Black primaries with white bases, secondaries black. Feet flesh-pink. **Size** 80 cm; wingspan 220 cm. **Juv.** like adult; bill dark horn-brown, darker on sides, tip. **Habitat** oceanic, coastal.

22 Grey-headed Albatross *Diomedea chrysostoma*

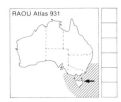

Bill base
from above

RAOU Atlas 090

Yellow along top ridge (culmen) of black bill; small pink mark on bill tip. Yellow or pink *also* on basal edge of lower bill to half-way along its length. Uniform pearl-grey hood, slightly paler cap. Black eye-ring. Otherwise like Black-browed adult, including underwing. **Sub-adult/Imm.** like adult; bill duller. Head varies from white with grey nape, to grey with white cheeks, front and crown. Underwing has broad black edges. At sea, identify from sub-adult Black-browed Albatross by black (*not* pale) bill, combined with white centre in black-edged underwing. **Size** 85 cm; wingspan 240 cm. **Juv.** head dark grey; *may* have white throat, cheeks. Bill black with very faint colour areas; tip black. Underwing dark, pale grey in centre. **Habitat** oceanic.

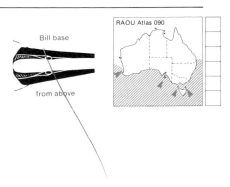

23 Yellow-nosed Albatross *Diomedea chlororhynchos*

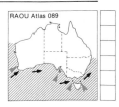

Bill base
from above

RAOU Atlas 089

Race *bassi:* Smallest mollymawk. Bill long, slender, black; yellow only on top ridge (culmen), pink tip. Head white, *sometimes* with grey cheeks. Underwing like Buller's Albatross, but primaries black; black along leading edge of wing narrower. Race *chlororhynchos:* Probably also occurs off Aust. Like *bassi* but grey hood with a white cap. **Size** 75 cm; wingspan 200 cm. **Juv.** bill black; yellow being faint or absent. Head white. **Habitat** coastal, oceanic.

Note Laysan Albatross, normally central and north Pacific Ocean, has rather similar underwing pattern to Black-browed Albatross (see p. 272 for further details).

22
Juv.

22

20
Race *melanophrys*
Juv.

20
Race *melanophrys*

22 Imm.
Pale head form

22

20
Race *impavida*

20
Race *melanophrys*

23
Race *bassi*

21

21

20
Race *melanophrys*
Imm.

3
bassi

21

23

17

N.B.

24 Shy Albatross *Diomedea cauta*

Largest mollymawk. Three races. Race *cauta:* Bill grey on sides, with yellow tinge and tips. Cap white. Black line from eye to bill. Head either white, grey-cheeked, *or* grey-hooded, cut off by a white collar. Mantle grey. Wings, tail grey-black. Rump, underparts, underwing white except for thin black borders. Primaries white at base, black outer half. Small, black triangle at leading base of wing. Feet pale blue-grey. **Imm.** bill greyer, small black spot at tip. Head white *or* with a strong collar. **Juv.** head moults progressively from all-grey with white cheeks, frons and caps to collared appearance. Bill grey, whole tip black. Underwing with slightly broader borders. Primaries about two-thirds black.

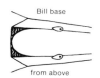

Bill base / from above

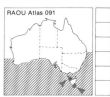

RAOU Atlas 091

Swimming

   Race *salvini:* Like nominate but has yellower bill, with small black spot on lower tip. Head, neck grey, forming a hood. Cap white. Underwing like nominate but primaries all black; only a faint ghosting of white at their bases. **Imm./Juv.** bill like imm./juv. of nominate. Head similar to nominate, normally greyer. Sometimes only pale frons, lores and throat. **Imm.** collar like nominate; underwing like adult *salvini.*
   Race *eremita:* Bill bright yellow, small black spot on lower tip. Head all leaden-grey; cap slightly paler. Underwing like *salvini.* Feet bright orange-pink. **Juv.** bill olive-brown, with black tip; plumage like adult; grey sometimes extends over upper breast.
   Size 95-100 cm; wingspan 240-260 cm. **Habitat** oceanic, coastal. Race *cauta* common; *salvini* uncommon; *eremita* few Aust. records.

25 Sooty Albatross *Phoebetria fusca*

Small albatross. Appears all-dark at sea. Warm chocolate brown; slightly paler across wings, mantle (our plate may show head and mask as too prominent). Eye-ring white, black gap in front. Bill black with cream to orange sulcus (line along lower bill). Tail very long, wedge-shaped. Pale shafts to primaries. Legs, feet pale grey with flesh tones. **Size** 85-90 cm; wingspan 185-215 cm. **Juv.** like adult but grey sulcus, grey eye-ring, buffy 'scales' may show across neck, collar, mantle and breast; primary shafts may be dark. **Habitat** oceanic. Graceful gliding flight on long wings. Rises and falls in flight more than other albatrosses (except Light-mantled). Identify from Light-mantled Sooty Albatross; Giant-Petrels; procellariiform petrels (p. 34).

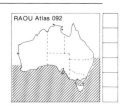

RAOU Atlas 092

26 Light-mantled Sooty Albatross *Phoebetria palpebrata*

Like Sooty Albatross but has a frosty grey mantle, belly and rump which contrast with a black face and wings. Bill has a blue line (sulcus). Legs, feet pale grey with flesh tones. **Size** 85-90 cm; wingspan 185-215 cm. **Juv.** like adult but has buffy scales on back, neck and breast. **Habitat** oceanic. Flight like Sooty Albatross.

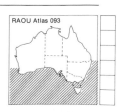

RAOU Atlas 093

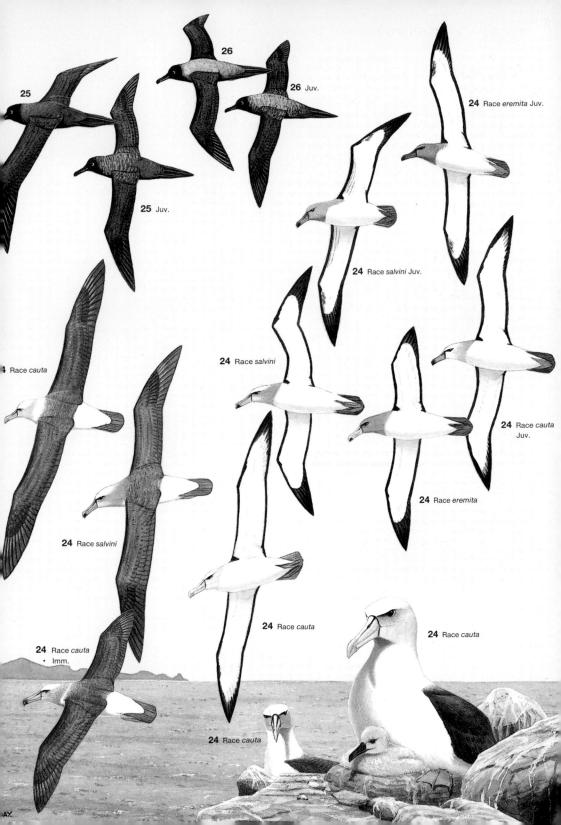

25

26

26 Juv.

25 Juv.

24 Race *eremita* Juv.

24 Race *salvini* Juv.

4 Race *cauta*

24 Race *salvini*

24 Race *cauta* Juv.

24 Race *salvini*

24 Race *eremita*

24 Race *cauta* Imm.

24 Race *cauta*

24 Race *cauta*

24 Race *cauta*

AY.

27 Southern Giant-Petrel *Macronectes giganteus*

Albatross-sized petrel with a bulbous bill. **Dark morph** (adults rare in Aust.; juvs common). Bill horn. tipped green. Nostrils extend far along bill. Brown or grey eyes. Dark brown body. White head. White mottling down neck and leading edge of wing to carpal. Tail medium length with a shallow wedge. Feet fleshy-grey. **Juv./Imm.** all dark; face whitens with age. Sometimes green tip on bill duller. **White morph** white, a few spots on body and wings. **Size** 85-90 cm; wingspan 200-220 cm. **Habitat** oceans, bays. Follows ships, scavenging. Identify from Sooty Albatross by short, less pointed tail, pale bill; Wandering Albatross juv. is larger and has white underwing.

Head markings

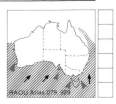

RAOU Atlas 079 929

28 Northern Giant-Petrel *Macronectes halli*

Identical to Southern Giant-Petrel except bill tipped reddish-brown. Iris grey or grey brown. White about bill and face, mottled at borders. Eye, throat, rest of head dark. *No* white leading edge of wing. *No* white phase. **Juv.** all dark. Bill often duller red than adult. **Size** and **Habitat** like Southern.

Flight profile

Head markings

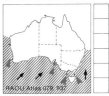

RAOU Atlas 079 937

29 Southern Fulmar *Fulmarus glacialoides*

Pink bill; black tip; blue nostrils. Eye dark. Face, underparts white. Silver-grey from behind eye to tail. Primaries and their coverts black; large white primary patch; covert bases grey. Secondaries black. Underwing white; edge of primaries to carpal black, thin grey trailing edge. Feet blue, webs pink. **Size** 50 cm. **Habitat** oceans. Flight stiff-winged; quick flapping then gliding. Varying numbers reach Aust.

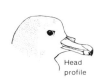

Head profile

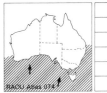

RAOU Atlas 074

30 Antarctic Petrel *Thalassoica antàrctica*

Like Cape Petrel, but browner or greyer, with a broad unbroken white stripe through centre of wings; all dark mantle and rump. Bill longer than Cape; brown on sides. Feet greyish-flesh. **Size** 45 cm. **Habitat** oceans. Flight stiff-winged; quick flapping then gliding. Vagrant.

Head profile

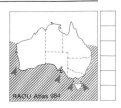

RAOU Atlas 949

31 Cape Petrel *Daption capense*

Black and white petrel. Soft parts black. Race *capense:* Blackish head, hind neck, upperback. Lower back and rump white, spotted black. Upperwing black with two large separate white patches, one at primary bases, the other at secondary bases. Throat white, mottled black. Underparts white. Underwing white, edged black. Race *australis* (doubtful): Black more extensive on back and wings; many intermediate individuals. **Size** 35-45 cm. **Habitat** oceans, bays, follows boats. Flight stiff-winged; quick fluttering, flapping and then gliding.

Head profile

RAOU Atlas 984

32 Snow Petrel *Pagodroma nivea*

All white. Short, stout black bill. Eyes, legs black. Long wings. Slightly wedge-shaped tail when fanned. **Habitat** oceans. Flight erratic; gliding and fluttering. Rare vagrant.

Head profile

RAOU Atlas 080

29

30

27 Juv

31

32

31
Race australis

31

27 White morph

27 Dark morph

28 Juv

28

29

31

N.H.Day.

33 Great-winged Petrel *Pterodroma macroptera*

Dark brown. Reflective dark underwing. Pale face
(race *gouldii*); darker (race *macroptera*). **Size** 41 cm.
Habitat oceanic. Wheeling flight, wings held forward.

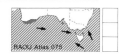

34 White-headed Petrel *Pterodroma lessonii*

Whitish head, black eye patch. White below. Dark
reflective underwing; white basal leading edge. **Size** 43 cm.

 Underwing pattern

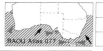

35 Providence Petrel *Pterodroma solandri*

Brown head, grey body. White primary bases separated
from black-tipped white greater coverts. **Size** 40 cm.

36 Kermadec Petrel *Pterodroma neglecta*

Upperwing pattern

Dark morph all dark underwing like Providence, with white
basal leading edge. **Pale morph** white head and body.
Variable intermediate phases. **Size** 38 cm. **Habitat** oceanic.

37 Herald Petrel *Pterodroma arminjoniana*

Colour phases like Kermadec, but white stripe through
centre of underwing; smaller. **Size** 36 cm. **Habitat** oceanic.
Flight arcing and wheeling, typical of other *Pterodromas*.

38 Tahiti Petrel *Pterodroma rostrata*

Bulbous bill. Brown, white belly. **Size** 38 cm.
Habitat oceanic.

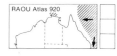

Underwing pattern

39 Kerguelen Petrel *Pterodroma brevirostris*

Dark grey. Large head. Stiff wings. Dark reflective
underwing, white basal leading edge. **Size** 33 cm.

40 Soft-plumaged Petrel *Pterodroma mollis*

Like White-headed Petrel but much smaller, with darker
head and tail, sometimes collared. **Size** 33 cm.

41 Mottled Petrel *Pterodroma inexpectata*

White below; grey belly. Underwing white, primaries
tipped black. Black from base of primaries to carpal. Broad
line extends into central median coverts. **Size** 33 cm.
Habitat oceanic.

 Head pattern

42 Gould's Petrel *Pterodroma leucoptera*

Dark head. Pale below. Underwing white; primaries,
secondaries mostly black. Primaries to carpal edge black.
Line extends from carpal into central median coverts.
Size 29 cm. **Habitat** oceanic.

 Head pattern

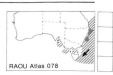

43 Black-winged Petrel *Pterodroma nigripennis*

Like Gould's but head pale grey with black eye patch.
Underwing borders broader. **Size** 29 cm. **Habitat** oceanic.
Typical flight of 'cookalarias' (includes Gould's, Cook's)
is rapid and strong, wheeling in great arcs.

 Head pattern

39

35

35

33

40

40

45
White-necked Petrel

37

34

37

33

41

43

43

36
Pale morph

36
Pale morph

36
Dark morph

38

41

42

42

N. Day

44 Cook's Petrel *Pterodroma cookii*

Pale grey cap to mantle. Dark upperwings. Underparts, underwing white, a narrow black line along trailing edge to primary/carpal region into centre of secondary median coverts. **Size** 28 cm. **Habitat** oceanic. Rare.

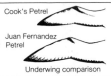

Cook's Petrel

Juan Fernandez Petrel

Underwing comparison

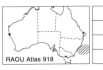

RAOU Atlas 918

45 White-necked Petrel *Pterodroma cervicalis*

Black cap on white head. Broad white collar. Blue-grey above; broad black 'M' across wings. Underparts, underwings as Cook's; black margins a little broader. **Size** 40-43 cm. **Habitat** oceanic. A few sightings.

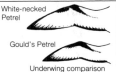

White-necked Petrel

Gould's Petrel

Underwing comparison

46 Blue Petrel *Halobaena caerulea*

Bill slender, black. Blue line on lower bill. Frons white. Cap black. Blue-grey above, faint 'M' across wings. Dark tail band; *white* tail tip. White below. **Size** 28 cm. **Habitat** oceanic. Long-winged graceful flight.

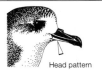

Head pattern

RAOU Atlas 081

47 Broad-billed Prion *Pachyptila vittata*

Huge, bowed (boat-shaped) black bill; extensive exposed lamellae; small nail. Blue line on lower bill. Head, frons dark grey. Thin white eyebrow. Large dark collar. Blue-grey above; strong 'M' marking. White below. Narrow black tail tip. Undertail barred grey, white; black centre. Feet blue; webs yellow. **Size** 27 cm; folded wing 19-23 cm. **Habitat** oceanic. Rare. Glides, banks; flutters on surface.

Head pattern

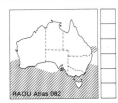

RAOU Atlas 082

48 Lesser Broad-billed Prion *Pachyptila salvini*

Like Broad-billed; bill generally smaller, narrower; distinctly bowed; sides bluish; less lamellae but obvious; nail small. Head *paler; frons paler* grey. **Size** 26 cm; folded wing 17-21 cm. **Habitat** oceanic.

Head pattern

RAOU Atlas 941

49 Antarctic (Dove) Prion *Pachyptila desolata*

Identical at sea to Lesser Broad-billed. In hand, bill generally narrower; *larger* nail; sides usually straight; little lamellae. **Size** 26 cm. **Habitat** oceanic.

Head pattern

RAOU Atlas 064

50 Slender-billed Prion *Pachyptila belcheri*

Like Antarctic Prion (some individuals indistinguishable at sea) but bill *thinner* (no lamellae). Frons white; eyebrow broad. The prion with greyest back. Faint 'M' marking. **Size** 25 cm. **Habitat** oceanic.

Head pattern

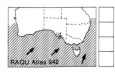

RAOU Atlas 942

51 Fulmar Prion *Pachyptila crassirostris*

As Fairy Prion; bill more robust. Aust. record suspect.

52 Fairy Prion *Pachyptila turtur*

Bill short; nail large. Eyebrow faint. 'Bluest' prion (except Fulmar Prion); bold black 'M' on wings. Tail band *twice as broad* as Antarctic Prion. Undertail broadly tipped black; *no* central black. **Size** 25 cm. **Habitat** oceans, coastal breeding islands.

Head pattern

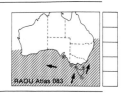

RAOU Atlas 083

Note The Juan Fernandez Petrel, recently recognised in Australian seas, is described on p. 272. It is now considered by some to be a new species; others still regard it as a race of (and thus conspecific with) the White-necked Petrel *Pterodroma cervicalis*.

53 Grey Petrel *Procellaria cinerea*

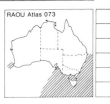

RAOU Atlas 073

Bill greenish or greyish-flesh coloured. Grey upperparts; darker on wings, crown and tail; often appears uniformly dark. Dark crown extends well below eye. Throat, breast and belly white. Undertail coverts, underwings dark. Prominent wedge-shaped tail. Legs like bill. **Size** 50 cm. **Habitat** oceanic. High, wheeling flight with much gliding and shallow dives, and submerged swimming. Often described as duck-like in flight. Generally solitary or in small flocks; known to follow ships.

54 Black Petrel *Procellaria parkinsoni*

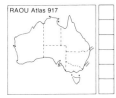

RAOU Atlas 917

Dark-tipped pale bill; otherwise completely black, including feet. In practice, very difficult species to identify. Distinguished from Flesh-footed Shearwater by heavier bill and black rather than pale feet; from Great-winged Petrel (both races) by relatively short, pale bill and lack of face colour; from White-chinned Petrel (both races) by dark bill tip and lack of chin colour. Most problems occur with the closely related Westland Petrel from which it can only really be differentiated by its smaller size. **Size** 46 cm. **Habitat** oceanic. Buoyant flight and dives.

55 Westland Petrel *Procellaria westlandica*

RAOU Atlas 916

Dark-tipped pale bill. Otherwise completely black, including feet. In all respects a larger version of the Black Petrel from which it cannot be readily distinguished. Differentiate from similar species by using same criteria as for the Black Petrel. Its greater size differentiates it further from the Great-winged Petrel but makes confusion with the White-chinned Petrel more likely. **Size** 53 cm. **Habitat** oceanic.

56 White-chinned Petrel *Procellaria aequinoctialis*

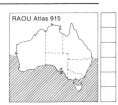

RAOU Atlas 915

All dark except for a rather variable white chin patch. This feature is not always prominent and thus confusion with Black and Westland Petrels is possible. The conspicuously large all pale bill, distinguishes it from these species. Distinguished from Flesh-footed Shearwater by black *not* pale feet; from Great-winged Petrel (both races) by bill colour and body size. A South Atlantic race *conspicillata* (illustrated) is relatively rare (only a small breeding population on Tristan da Cunha) and may be wholly sedentary. These birds have extensive white on face and chin giving a dramatic spectacled appearance. Local race *aequinoctialis* might be confused with juvenile Giant Petrels but much smaller size and complete *absence* of white in plumage *except* on the chin should differentiate it. **Size** 56 cm. **Habitat** oceanic. Generally solitary or in small groups. Known to be aggressive when feeding and a regular ship follower. Flight like that of a small albatross with slow, deliberate wing beats and glides.

53

53

55

54

33
Great-winged Petrel

25
Sooty Albatross

28
Northern Giant Petrel
Imm.

56
Race *aequinoctialis*

60
Sooty Shearwater

56
Race *conspicillata*

N.K.T.Day

57 Flesh-footed Shearwater *Puffinus carneipes*

Large chocolate-brown shearwater. Bill horn, tipped black. Underwing dark; reflective coverts and primaries. Feet flesh-pink; do *not* trail beyond tail. **Size** 47-48 cm. **Habitat** oceanic, coastal. In flight holds wings straight; tail rounded.

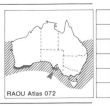

Black Petrel

Flesh-footed Shearwater

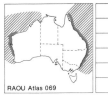

RAOU Atlas 072

58 Wedge-tailed Shearwater *Puffinus pacificus*

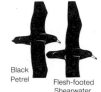

Wedge-tailed Shearwater

Smaller than Flesh-footed. Bill leaden-grey, tip black; looks pale in distance. **Dark morph** all dark; paler non-reflective centres to underwings. Tail long, wedge-shaped. Legs flesh-white. **Light morph** paler above; faint 'M' mark. Throat to vent white. Underwing white, but black primaries, secondaries; some grey blotching on axilla, leading edge. **Size** 45-47 cm. **Habitat** oceanic, coastal. Holds wings well forward, glides low over water.

Pink-footed Shearwater

RAOU Atlas 069

59 Buller's Shearwater *Puffinus bulleri*

Buller's Shearwater

Bill blue-black. Cap black, contrasts with blue-grey upperparts which have a strong 'M' marking. Underparts, underwing white. Narrow black trailing edge to underwing. Tail slightly wedge-shaped. Feet pink. **Size** 45-46 cm. **Habitat** oceanic, coastal. Gliding graceful flight.

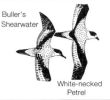

White-necked Petrel

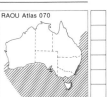

RAOU Atlas 975

60 Sooty Shearwater *Puffinus griseus*

Wing moult

All dark. Wedge-tailed Shearwater size. Dark grey, large, long bill. Underwing may vary: (a) greyish centre, streaked black; (b) white on primary coverts extends down wing through median coverts; some black streaking; (c) mostly white, faint streaking. Tail short, rounded. Feet trail. Outside surface of legs black, inside surface flesh-pink. **Size** 45-47 cm. **Habitat** coastal, oceanic. Flies with rapid wing beat and gliding. In summer, southern birds are visibly in heavy wing moult; gaps appear in wings.

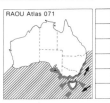

RAOU Atlas 070

61 Short-tailed Shearwater *Puffinus tenuirostris*

Juv.

Like Sooty but much smaller; shorter-billed. Usually has darker underwing than Sooty; variable gradings: (a) all dark silvery-grey; (b) grey; white central streak, faint black streaks; not usually white on primary medians or greater coverts; (c) all white in centre (rare). Short, rounded tail. Feet trail. **Size** 41-43 cm. **Habitat** coastal, oceanic. Flight like Sooty but more rapid. From January to April birds do *not* moult on wings; no gaps appear.

RAOU Atlas 071

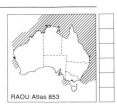

62 Streaked Shearwater *Calonectris leucomelas*

Largest shearwater *consistently* to visit Aust. Very large pale bill with dark tip. Head white. Black streaks on crown (variable). Black nape. Upperparts grey-brown with pale scalloping. Indistinct 'M' across back. White tips to upper tail coverts. Underparts white. Underwing white with black primaries, secondaries. Some fine streaking on axilla, leading wing edge. Tail rounded. Feet pink. **Size** 48-50 cm. **Habitat** coastal, oceanic. Straight-winged; glides like an albatross. Identify from Buller's Shearwater and rare vagrants.

Gliding

RAOU Atlas 853

59

57

58
Dark morph

58
Dark morph

9

62

57

58
Light morph

60a

60c

62

61

61a

61c

60

60b

60

N. Day.

63 **Manx Shearwater** *Puffinus puffinus*

Nominate race smaller than Short-tailed Shearwater. Bill larger and more robust than Fluttering or Hutton's Shearwater. Upperparts black. Underparts from throat to tail white. Underwing including axillaries white, but primaries black. Thin black leading edge. Legs light pink but outer surfaces black. **Size** 36-40 cm. **Habitat** coastal, oceanic. One Aust. record. Flies like Short-tailed Shearwater but faster wing beats.

RAOU Atlas 914

64 **Fluttering Shearwater** *Puffinus gavia*

Most are slightly smaller than Hutton's Shearwater. Black above, including slight collar, ear coverts and below eye. Underwing white, but dark axillaries tipped white. Central shafts of feathers on leading edge of wing dark; appears streaked (a variable feature). Undertail coverts white. **Size** 31-36 cm. **Habitat** nearly always coastal, occasionally oceanic. Flies with rapid, whirring wing beats close to the sea, banks only in strong wind. Note: some *gavia* and *huttoni* are so similar that they may not be distinguished at sea.

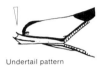

Undertail pattern

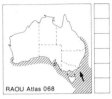

RAOU Atlas 068

65 **Hutton's Shearwater** *Puffinis huttoni*

Like Manx Shearwater, but smaller. In body size and bill length, most are larger than Fluttering Shearwater. Collar usually very prominent; at sea gives a hooded effect. Underwing varies: (a) grey with faint white centre and dark streaking, or (b) extensive white centre, strongly streaked; axillaries black. Undertail coverts vary from heavily flecked black to white. Sides of undertail usually flecked. **Size** 35-38 cm. **Habitat** prefers coast, also oceanic. Flies like Fluttering Shearwater.

Undertail pattern

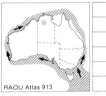

RAOU Atlas 913

66 **Little Shearwater** *Puffinis assimilis*

Smaller than Fluttering Shearwater. Bill very short. Eye-ring, ear coverts white. Underwing white except for black outer half of primaries and thin leading edge. Feet blue. **Size** 25-30 cm. **Habitat** coastal, oceanic. Fastest wing beats of any shearwater.

Head pattern

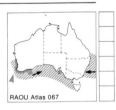

RAOU Atlas 067

67 **Audubon's Shearwater** *Puffinus lherminieri*

Like Fluttering Shearwater, with a shorter bill, longer tail. Underwing like Little Shearwater, but broader black margins. Undertail coverts black. **Size** 30-35 cm. **Habitat** oceanic, coastal. Vagrant. Several recent sightings. Glides close to the water.

Undertail pattern

RAOU Atlas 912

64 Fluttering Shearwater
Underwing pattern

65 Hutton's Shearwater
Underwing pattern

68 Wilson's Storm-Petrel *Oceanites oceanicus*

Sooty-black; white rump. Wings rounded; pale greyish crescent on greater upperwing coverts. **Size** 15-19 cm. **Habitat** oceanic. In flight, long legs and yellow webbed feet project beyond square tail.

Rump pattern

RAOU Atlas 063

69 Grey-backed Storm-Petrel *Oceanites nereis*

Head to chest brown-black. Pale ashy-grey back; paler grey rump, tail. Upperwings dark grey; pale grey upper coverts; black primaries. Underwing white, except thin leading edge. Wide black band on square tail. White belly, underwings. **Size** 16 cm. **Habitat** oceanic.

RAOU Atlas 064

70 White-faced Storm-Petrel *Pelagodroma marina*

White frons, eyebrow. Dark grey crown; broad eye-stripe. Grey shoulders, back. Rump pale grey. Black primaries. White below. Underwing white, dark-bordered. Square dark tail. **Size** 20 cm. **Habitat** oceanic. Yellow webbed feet project in flight.

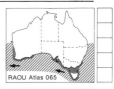
RAOU Atlas 065

71 Black-bellied Storm-Petrel *Fregetta tropica*

Black above. Throat usually white. Grey on greater upperwing coverts. Black 'V' on chest leads to narrow central stripe; some lack this but broad 'V' usually present. Rest of underparts white; underwing white, bordered black. White rump. **Size** 20 cm. **Habitat** oceanic. Feet project beyond square black tail.

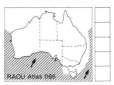
RAOU Atlas 066

72 White-bellied Storm-Petrel *Fregetta grallaria*

Like Black-bellied but black chest cuts straight off from white belly. Black throat. Some have dark rump, *or* streaked, dusky or dark underparts. Shorter legs than Black-bellied. **Size** 20 cm. **Habitat** oceanic. Feet do *not* extend beyond square tail.

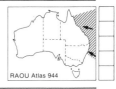
RAOU Atlas 944

73 Matsudaira's Storm-Petrel *Oceanodroma matsudairae*

Sooty-brown. Forked tail. Long wings; paler crescents on coverts; quill bases show as white patches. **Size** 24 cm. **Habitat** oceanic.

74 Leach's Storm-Petrel *Oceanodroma leucorhoa*

Brownish-black. Rump usually white (can be black) with complete or broken black line. Paler grey-brown greater upperwing coverts. Deeply forked tail. **Size** 20 cm. **Habitat** oceanic.

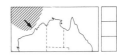
Rump pattern

RAOU Atlas 911

75 Common Diving-Petrel *Pelecanoides urinatrix*

Tiny, dumpy petrel. Bill sides parallel. Black above; white below; silvery underwing. **Size** 20-25 cm. **Habitat** oceanic. Quail-like flight, neck out.

Bill

Oblique view

RAOU Atlas 085

76 South Georgian Diving-Petrel
Pelecanoides georgicus

Like Common Diving-Petrel. Bill sides rounded. Some have white scapular bands. **Size** 18-21 cm. **Habitat** oceanic.

Bill

Oblique view

RAOU Atlas 910

77 Australian Pelican *Pelecanus conspicillatus*

Large black, white bird. Long pink bill. Distensible throat pouch; red when courting. Primaries, shoulders, rump, tail, upperwing except centre, black; otherwise white. Head, neck can be greyish. Legs grey. **Size** 160-180 cm. **Juv.** smaller; grey-brown where adults black. **Voice** grunting. **Habitat** open fresh and salt water. Flies in lines or 'V's; soars in graceful circles. Swims in flocks.

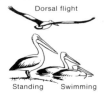
Dorsal flight

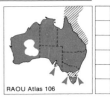
Standing   Swimming   RAOU Atlas 106

78 Australasian Gannet *Sula (Morus) serrator*

Bill grey; edges of plates (sheaths) bordered black. Short black stripe in centre of throat. Black line through gape. Eye-ring dark blue; iris grey. Head buff-yellow. Rest of body white, with black primaries, secondaries. Black centre to tail (edges white). Black feet, green on toes. **Size** 90-95 cm. **Juv.** grey-brown including hood. Spotted white upperparts; white underparts. **Imm.** brownish, head, upperparts spotted white. Patchy black feathers on wings, mantle with age. Tail *can* be *all black*. **Habitat** oceans, bays.

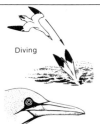
Diving

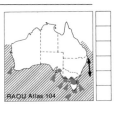
RAOU Atlas 104

79 Cape Gannet *Sula (Morus) capensis*

Like Australasian Gannet, but always *black* tail, *longer* black stripe down throat, brighter blue eye-ring, white eyes; broader black margins around face, on bill. **Size** 85-90 cm. **Juv./Imm.** similar to Australasian Gannet, but long black gular stripe. **Habitat** oceans, bays; one resident on Wedge Light, Port Phillip Bay (Vic.) from 1981; still present 1992. Three at Lawrence Rocks (W Vic.), early 1992.

80 Red-footed Booby *Sula sula*

White morph blue-grey bill, eye-ring. Pink mask. Yellow head. White body. Black primaries, secondaries. Red legs. **Dark morph** all brown. **Intermediate morph** brown with white rump, tail, abdomen. **Size** 75 cm. **Juv./Imm.** brown, mottled white. Bill black, may be tinted dull blue. Legs, feet dark grey. **Habitat** oceans; the most pelagic booby.

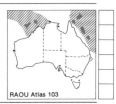
RAOU Atlas 103

81 Masked Booby *Sula dactylatra*

Largest booby. **Male** yellow bill. Black mask. Yellow eye. Body white with black primaries, secondaries. Tail black. Legs grey. **Female** green base to bill. Race *dactylatra* (N Aust.); race *fullagari* breeds Norfolk, Lord Howe islands. **Size** 80-85 cm. **Juv./Imm.** head, neck brown; white collar. Upperparts grey-brown. Narrow white rump. Underwing white with band from carpal to axillaries. Plumage whitens with age: upperparts whiten from rump; upper wing becomes white; collar extends more. Identify from young gannets by more striking head pattern; darker mask; longer tail; bird 'dumpier'. **Habitat** oceans, reefs.

Eye colour:
race *personata* (above)
race *fullagari* (below)

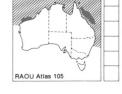
RAOU Atlas 105

82 Brown Booby *Sula leucogaster*

Male yellow bill; bluish base. Upperparts, breast dark brown. Belly to vent white. Underwing white with broad dark brown borders. Legs yellow. **Female** bill all yellow. **Size** 75 cm. **Juv./Imm.** belly, underwing dull brown, contrasting with otherwise dark brown pattern of adults. **Habitat** oceans, reefs.

Body pattern

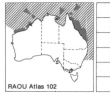
RAOU Atlas 102

82 ♀

82 Juv.

81 ♂

Abbott's Booby ♂

81 Juv.

♀ 81

Abbott's Booby ♀

82 ♂

78 Juv.

78 Sub-adult

78

79

80 White morph

80 Juv.

80 White morph

77

80 Intermediate morph

80 Dark morph

78

80 Intermediate morph

80 Dark morph

83 Darter *Anhinga melanogaster*

Long pointed bill. Snake-shaped neck. Long rounded tail. **Male** dark grey to glossy black with a white stripe bordered by black, from bill to first bend in neck. Wings iridescent with cream streaks. **Female** grey-brown above; pale grey below; also has white neck stripe. **Size** 90 cm. **Juv./Imm.** like female, but stripe less distinct and body paler. **Voice** clicking sounds. **Habitat** lakes, rivers, swamps; rarely coastal. Often immerses in water up to neck. Holds wings out 'to dry' when perched. In flight, cream upperwing streaks form a wing bar; soars.

Drying wings

♂

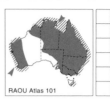

RAOU Atlas 101

84 Black-faced Shag *Leucocarbo fuscescens*

Non-breeding black bill, facial skin, cap (*no* white over eyes), back of neck, wings, tail and thigh patch to legs. Black-edged feathers glossed green. Eye aqua-green. White below. **Breeding** short white nuptial plumes on hind-neck, rump, thighs. **Size** 65 cm. **Imm.** browner above; face paler grey; eye brown. **Voice** grunts, hissing. **Habitat** rocky sea coasts. At various times shags and cormorants spread wings out when perched.

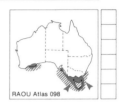

RAOU Atlas 098

85 Pied Cormorant *Phalacrocorax varius*

Like Black-faced Shag but larger. Longer, dark horn bill. Orange facial and throat skin. Blue eye-ring. Side of neck *all* white. Belly sometimes rusty. **Size** 70-75 cm. **Juv./Imm.** browner; face duller. **Voice** grunts. **Habitat** prefers large areas of water, coastal or inland lakes, rivers. Regularly flies in 'V' formation.

'V' flight

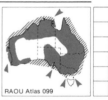

RAOU Atlas 099

86 Little Pied Cormorant *Phalacrocorax melanoleucos*

Small version of the Pied Cormorant. Short, yellow bill with black borders; *no* bare throat skin. Face blackish. White goes *over* eye to bill base. A short crest of black feathers before bill. Side of neck *divided* black and white. No black leg stripe. **Size** 50-55 cm. **Juv./Imm.** black feathers above eye and on thighs. **Voice** short croak. **Habitat** most aquatic habitats. Flies separately, *not* in 'V' formation.

Typical cormorant foot

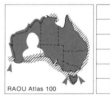

RAOU Atlas 100

87 Great (Black) Cormorant *Phalacrocorax carbo*

The largest Aust. cormorant. All black with yellow facial skin and throat pouch. **Breeding** white nuptial plumes on neck, plus white chin and thigh patch, otherwise black. **Size** 80-85 cm. **Juv./Imm.** dirty blackish-brown; facial skin duller. **Voice** croaks, grunts, hisses. **Habitat** most aquatic habitats. Flies in 'V' formation.

Flight line

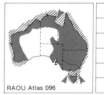

RAOU Atlas 096

88 Little Black Cormorant *Phalacrocorax sulcirostris*

Small, slender black cormorant. All black (including dark slender bill) except for glossy green back. More bronzed when breeding. **Size** 60-65 cm. **Voice** male makes ticking sounds. **Habitat** most aquatic habitats. Flies in 'V' formation. Congregates in larger flocks than do other cormorants.

Feeding flock

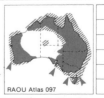

RAOU Atlas 097

89 Christmas Frigatebird *Fregata andrewsi*

Male black. Red throat pouch which expands into a balloon during courtship (as in all other male frigatebirds). White abdominal patch. Brown wing panels.
Female similar to Least Frigatebird female, but white on belly leads to abdomen, and conspicuous black 'spur' markings on upper breast. **Size** 89-100 cm. **Juv.** difficult to separate from other juv. frigatebirds. **Habitat** tropical NW seas. Once recorded in Darwin. Breeds on Christmas Is.

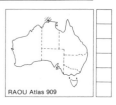

90 Great Frigatebird *Fregata minor*

Male black. Red throat pouch. **Female** white chest; pale grey throat. Brown wing bars. Eye-ring, feet reddish. **Size** 86-100 cm. **Juv./Imm.** begins with tawny-coloured head, gradually gets darker all over (males) or gets a black cap (female). **Habitat** tropical seas.

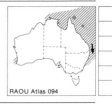

91 Least Frigatebird *Fregata ariel*

Male black. Red throat pouch. Thin white markings from flanks on to wings. **Female** like female Great Frigatebird, but with a black throat, white collar, and markings on underwings. **Size** 71-81 cm. **Juv./Imm.** difficult to distinguish from other frigatebirds. **Habitat** tropical seas. Often seen soaring high during cyclonic weather.

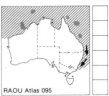

92 Red-tailed Tropicbird *Phaethon rubricauda*

Race *westralis* (tropical, temperate seas off WA): **Breeding** body white; some tinted pink. Race regarded as having two colour morphs. Pointed, stout, tern-like, scarlet to orange bill. Black crescent patch before and through eye. Black primary shafts; broader black marks on tertiary feathers. White tail with two long (40-43 cm), red, central tail streamers. Legs, feet black. Race *roseotincta* (E Aust. seas): Larger. **Size** 86-90 cm. **Juv.** bill black. Lacks tail streamers. White body with strongly black-barred area of dorsal surface — inner wings, mantle, back, rump, upper tail. **Imm.** far fewer black marks on dorsum; red tail streamers appear. **Voice** clamorous rattles, screams. **Habitat** tropical, subtropical seas. Soars, glides, hovers, flies high and fast, dives into sea; swims with tail feathers cocked up.

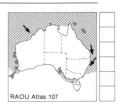

93 White-tailed Tropicbird *Phaethon lepturus*

Race *fulvus* ('Golden Bosunbird', northern seas off WA): **Breeding** body brilliant white; some tinted apricot-yellow. Race regarded as having two colour morphs. Bill yellow to orange. Black crescent patch before and through eye. Black central wing bar; primary bases black. White central tail streamers long (40 cm), black at base. Legs, feet blue-grey to off-white; webs black. Birds in E Aust. seas smaller, have no gold tint. **Size** 72.5 cm. **Juv.** numerous narrow, black, crescentic dorsal barrings from crown to rump, and on inner wings. Dark tail margins; no white tail streamers or golden tint. **Imm.** presumably as for Red-tailed Tropicbird. **Voice** harsh rattles, screams. **Habitat** tropical, subtropical seas. Flight like Red-tailed but quicker, more graceful, pigeon-like.

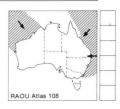

89 ♀

91 ♀

89 ♂

91 Juv.

90 ♀

90 Juv.

91 ♂

♂ 90

♂ 91

Pink morph **92**

93 Golden morph

92 White morph

93 White morph

N.H.J. Day.

94 Great-billed Heron *Ardea sumatrana*

Bill long, stout and dark brown; paler at base of lower mandible. Entire plumage bronzy-brown with nuchal crest, hackles on foreneck and lanceolate plumes on back. Belly creamy-brown. Legs dark grey. **Size** 100-110 cm. **Juv.** more rusty brown; no crest, hackles or plumes. **Voice** penetrating (and to the inexperienced), frightening calls including loud guttural roars and groans given by day and night. **Habitat** mangrove-fringed tidal channels of tropical Aust.; occasionally recorded upstream along major rivers.

RAOU Atlas 184

95 Pacific (White-necked) Heron *Ardea pacifica*

Bill dark grey. Head and neck white except for a line of brown and back spots down the foreneck. Back and wings sooty-black with a bluish sheen. Maroon lanceolate plumes on back and upper breast. Prominent white patch on shoulder of wing. Breast and belly grey-brown, streaked white. Legs dark grey. **Non-breeding** plumes reduced or absent. **Size** 76-107 cm. **Juv.** neck has greyish wash; the foreneck is more heavily spotted and lanceolate plumes are absent. The white shoulder patch, visible both at rest and in flight (looks like headlights on flying bird), distinguishes this from juv. of much smaller Pied Heron. **Voice** harsh croaks. **Habitat** moist pasture, floodwaters and shallows of freshwater wetlands.

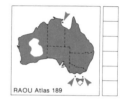

RAOU Atlas 189

96 White-faced Heron *Ardea novaehollandiae*

Bill dark brown, paler at base of lower mandible. Face to just behind the eye, white. Upperparts and wings grey. Belly paler grey. Flight feathers dark grey. Pale chestnut hackles on lower neck. Lanceolate plumes on back. Legs yellow. **Non-breeding** plumes and hackles reduced or absent. **Size** 60-70 cm. **Juv.** face grey or with white only on chin. Dull brown wash on plumage, particularly on belly. **Voice** harsh croaks. **Habitat** pasture, farm dams, parkland, most wetlands including intertidal flats. Often perches on trees and posts.

96 Adult

96 Imm.

102 Grey phase

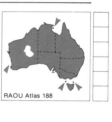

RAOU Atlas 188

97 Pied Heron *Ardea picata*

Bill yellow. Head and nuchal plumes dark blue-grey. Neck white. Body and wings dark blue-grey. Both blue-grey and white hackles frill the lower neck and there are lanceolate plumes on the back. Legs yellow. **Non-breeding** plumes and hackles reduced. **Size** 45-50 cm. **Juv.** both head and nuchal crest white; hackles and plumes absent; back tinged brown. Belly grey-brown streaked with white. **Voice** harsh croaks. **Habitat** near coastal swamps, rubbish tips, sewage-works and intertidal flats.

Roosting

RAOU Atlas 190

97

96

94
Juv.

96
Juv.

95
Juv.

95

94

96
Juv.

96
Breeding

95
Breeding

97
Juv.

97
Breeding

98 Cattle Egret *Ardea ibis*

Bill yellow or pinkish-yellow. Long loose rusty-brown plumes on head. Neck, breast and back rusty-brown; remaining plumage white. Legs greenish-grey. Bill, face and legs may become red briefly prior to egg laying. **Non-breeding** plumage snowy white. Rusty plumes are progressively acquired from mid-August and traces may remain until May. Short stocky appearance, rounded forehead and prominent feathers under the lower mandible distinguish it from other egrets. **Size** 46-54 cm. **Voice** harsh croaks. **Habitat** pasture; among stock; occasionally shallows of wetlands.

Feeding amongst cattle

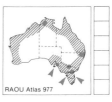

RAOU Atlas 977

99 Great Egret *Ardea alba*

Bill usually black; facial skin green. Body and wings white as are the long lacy scapular plumes. Legs dark grey or black; slightly paler on tibia. **Non-breeding** bill usually yellow; facial skin yellow; plumes fewer or absent. Distinguished from other egrets, particularly the Intermediate Egret, by long bill and low flat forehead, long neck with prominent kink (neck = 1.5 times length of body). **Size** 90-103 cm. **Voice** harsh croaks. **Habitat** floodwaters, rivers, shallows of wetlands, intertidal mud-flats. Legs extend well beyond tail in flight.

Stalking

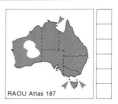

RAOU Atlas 187

100 Little Egret *Ardea garzetta*

Bill black. Facial skin yellow to orange; varies in courtship. Entire plumage white; two long thin nuchal plumes; lacy plumes on upper breast, wings, mantle. Legs black; soles of feet yellow. **Non-breeding** facial skin yellow; plumes few or absent. Small size, black bill, yellow soles, slender build distinguish it. **Size** 55-65 cm. **Voice** harsh croaks. **Habitat** shallows of wetlands, intertidal mud-flats.

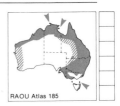

RAOU Atlas 185

101 Intermediate Egret *Ardea intermedia*

Bill orange or red; facial skin green. Plumage white with long lacy plumes arising from the upper breast and scapulars. Tibia red; tarsus black. **Non-breeding** bill orange-yellow; face yellow. Few or no plumes. Legs black. Distinguished from the Great Egret by proportionately shorter and thicker bill; higher forehead; shorter, thicker and less-kinked neck (neck = length of body). Legs appear shorter in flight. **Size** 56-70 cm. **Voice** harsh croaks. **Habitat** shallows of wetlands, intertidal mud-flats.

99   96   101

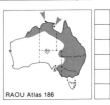

RAOU Atlas 186

102 Eastern Reef Egret *Ardea sacra*

Bill comparatively long and thick. Legs shorter, thicker than other egrets; appear very short in flight. Two colour morphs. **Grey morph** bill grey. Plumage dark sooty-grey except for some white on throat. Hackles on lower neck; lanceolate plumes on back. Legs yellowish-grey. Identify from White-faced Heron by darker plumage, *no* white on face. **Juv.** brownish-grey, slightly brown cap; identify from Striated Heron, juv. White-faced Heron. Grey morph commoner in south of range. **White morph** bill pale horn to yellow. Entire plumage white; legs yellow. **Size** 58-75 cm. **Voice** harsh croaks. **Habitat** intertidal zone: rocks, coral reefs, mangroves, mud-flats. Roosts communally.

White morph: stalking

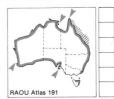

RAOU Atlas 191

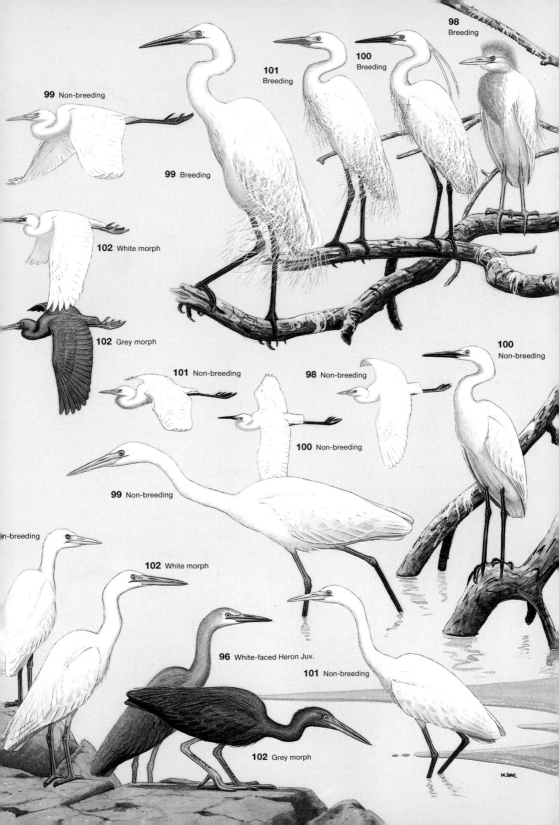

99 Non-breeding

101 Breeding

100 Breeding

98 Breeding

99 Breeding

102 White morph

102 Grey morph

101 Non-breeding

98 Non-breeding

100 Non-breeding

100 Non-breeding

99 Non-breeding

n-breeding

102 White morph

96 White-faced Heron Juv.

101 Non-breeding

102 Grey morph

N. DAY.

103 Striated Heron *Ardeola striatus*

Five Aust. races have in common: glossy black crown, nuchal crest; body darker above than below; metallic sheen on back; throat, foreneck streaked black and dark brown. Races are *macrorhynchus*, E Aust., dark-olive above, dusky-brown below; *litteri*, NE Aust. and PNG, dark grey-green; *stagnatilus*, N Aust., browny-grey; *cinereus*, NW Aust., pale grey; *rogersi*, WA, rufous. **Size** to 49 cm. **Voice** variety of sharp calls. **Habitat** mangroves, intertidal flats. Crouches low with neck extended or retracted; adopts head-up posture of bitterns when disturbed.

Crouched stalking posture

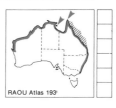

RAOU Atlas 193'

104 Rufous Night Heron *Nycticorax caledonicus*

Breeding bill, crown black; two slender white nuchal plumes. Upperparts, wings, rufous. Belly white. **Non-breeding** lacks plumes. **Size** to 59 cm. **Juv.** mottled and streaked brown on white. **Imm.** mottled rufous; black cap. **Voice** deep croaks. **Habitat** swamps, intertidal flats, estuaries, rivers, creeks, large ornamental ponds. Feeds nocturnally; roosts in trees close to water by day; also under wharves (e.g. Port of Melbourne).

Imm.

Dorsal flight

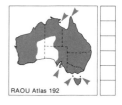

RAOU Atlas 192

105 Little Bittern *Ixobrychus minutus*

Male crown, back, tail black; hind-neck deep reddish-brown. Wing black; large pale-buff wing patches. Breast, flanks white, streaked dark and light brown. Belly, undertail white. **Female** black replaced by brown; underside more heavily streaked; wing patch brown-buff. **Size** to 30 cm. **Juv.** browner and streaked overall. Wing patch not obvious. **Voice** deep repetitive croaks. **Habitat** reedbeds, dense vegetation of freshwater swamps, watercourses. Very secretive.

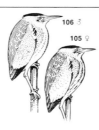

106 ♂
105 ♀

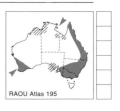

RAOU Atlas 195

106 Yellow Bittern *Ixobrychus sinensis*

Like male Little Bittern but *no* black on back; differs from female Little Bittern by black wings, less obvious wing patches. **Juv.** heavily streaked. **Size** to 30 cm. **Habitat** as for Little Bittern. Only one Aust. record.

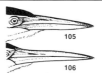

105

106

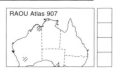

RAOU Atlas 907

107 Black Bittern *Ixobrychus flavicollis*

Male bill black above, yellow below. Upperparts sooty-black; side of neck yellow. Underparts white; prominent brown and black streaks down neck. Dark brown blotches on breast, belly. **Female** upperparts brown, *not* black. **Size** to 66 cm. **Juv.** like female; buff feather edges. **Voice** deep repetitive notes. **Habitat** mangroves, streamside vegetation including small creeks in forests.

♂   ♀

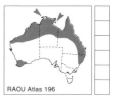

RAOU Atlas 196

108 Australasian Bittern *Botaurus poiciloptilus*

Adults/Juv. similar. Upperparts brown; mottled cream and buff; more so on wing coverts. Brown stripe down side of neck edges the white throat. Underside cream-buff, streaked and barred dark brown. **Size** to 72 cm. **Voice** male call low-pitched boom. **Habitat** reedbeds, swamps, streams, estuaries. Secretive, flies heavily when disturbed.

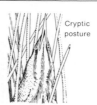

Cryptic posture

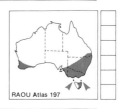

RAOU Atlas 197

Note   Recent opinion reduces Aust. races of Striated Heron to two: *A.s. stagnatilis*, including former races *rogersi* and *cinereus* (W, NW and N of Aust., to Gulf of Carpentaria), and *A.s. macrorhynchus* (perhaps G. of C.; and from Cape York, N Qld, to Mallacoota, Vic.).

108

104

104
Breeding

104
Juv.

103 Race *stagnatilus*
Grey morph

103
Juv.

103 Race *stagnatilus*
Rufous morph

107

103 Race *macrorhynchus*
Rufous morph

105

♂ **105**

105
Juv.

106
Juv.

107 ♂

108

107
Juv.

109 Black-necked Stork *Ephippiorhynchus asiaticus*

Black, thick, straight bill. Head, neck, tail, broad wing-stripe glossy black. Body, remainder of wings, white. Very long red legs. **Size** 112-115 cm; stands to 120 cm; wingspan to 200 cm. **Juv.** dull brown. **Voice** not adequately described; clappers with bill. **Habitat** river pools, swamps, intertidal flats. Soars expertly with neck extended and legs trailing; at height check Australian Pelican.

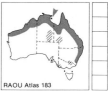

RAOU Atlas 183

110 Glossy Ibis *Plegadis falcinellus*

Bill olive-brown. Reddish-brown body; back, wings have purple-green sheen, changing with light and distance; may appear black. Legs variable, olive to dark brown. **Size** 50-53 cm. **Juv.** duller; white, brown streaks on head, upper neck. **Voice** soft calls. **Habitat** freshwater wetlands, pasture. Distinctive; in flight check Little Black Cormorant.

Nestling

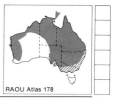

RAOU Atlas 178

111 Australian White Ibis (Sacred Ibis)
Threskiornis molucca (recently *T. aethiopica*)

Sexes similar. **Male** longer bill. Black bill and naked skin on head, upper neck. Some pink bands across nape. Body, wings white (but often stained dirty brown). Black inner secondary plumes give appearance of 'black tail'. Wings tipped black. Red naked skin under wing to sides of breast. Yellow upper tail when breeding; otherwise white. Legs reddish brown. **Size** 65-75 cm. **Juv.** head duskier; bill shorter. **Voice** drawn-out croaks. **Habitat** all but most saline of wetlands and pasture; tidal flats; rubbish dumps. In flight note black head, white body and wings; soars, often with other ibis. Roosts in trees, mangroves.

Breeding colony

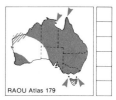

RAOU Atlas 179

112 Straw-necked Ibis *Threskiornis spinicollis*

Bare head, bill, upper neck black. Back, tail and wings black with metallic sheen. Belly, neck white; yellow straw like breast plumes not visible at distance. Legs black. **Size** 65-70 cm. **Juv.** bill shorter. **Voice** drawn-out croaks. **Habitat** shallow freshwater wetlands and pasture, rarely intertidal flats. In flight note white body and black wings. Soars in thermals; flies directly in 'V' formation.

'V' flight

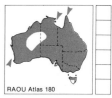

RAOU Atlas 180

113 Royal Spoonbill *Platalea regia*

Bill black, distinctive. Black skin on head to just behind eye. Small patches of red on forehead and yellow above each eye. White erectile nuchal plumes. Body, wings white. Legs black. **Non-breeding** lacks plumes, coloured patches on face. **Size** 70-76 cm. **Habitat** shallows of fresh and saltwater wetlands including intertidal flats. Feeds by sweeping submerged bill from side to side.

Bill from side

Bill from above

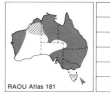

RAOU Atlas 181

114 Yellow-billed Spoonbill *Platalea flavipes*

Bill yellow, distinctive. Grey facial skin edged black. Body creamy-white except for black lace-like plumes on inner secondaries. Hackles on upper breast. Legs yellow. **Non-breeding** face yellow, without black edge. Hackles, plumes reduced or absent. **Imm.** birds show black markings on tertials. **Size** 80-90 cm. **Voice** soft calls: bill clattering. **Habitat** shallows of freshwater wetlands, occasionally on dry pasture. Often roosts in trees.

Bill from side

Bill from above

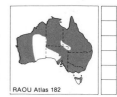

RAOU Atlas 182

Note Recent studies indicate that the names 'Australian White Ibis *Threskiornis molucca*' are better applied to the species than is 'Sacred Ibis *Threskiornis aethiopica*'.

88 Little Black Cormorant

111

110

112

♂ 109

113

111
Juv.

112

112
Juv.

114

110
Imm.

110

111

111

109
Imm.

♀ 109

113
Non-breeding

113
Breeding

111
Stained Plumage

114
Non-breeding

Nicolas Day.

115 Magpie Goose *Anseranas semipalmata*

Head black with distinct knob in older birds. Hooked bill. Face skin yellow to flesh in colour. Neck to upper breast black. Mantle, upperwing coverts, rump and belly white. Upperwing black with white coverts. Underwing black with white wing linings. Tail black. Legs long and yellow. Partly webbed toes. **Size** 71-92 cm; wingspan 150-160 cm approx. Distinguished from all other species by pied plumage and long yellow legs; from Black Swan in flight by short neck, lack of white flight feathers. **Imm.** as adult but white parts mottled grey or brown. **Habitat** rush and sedge-dominated swamps, flood plains.

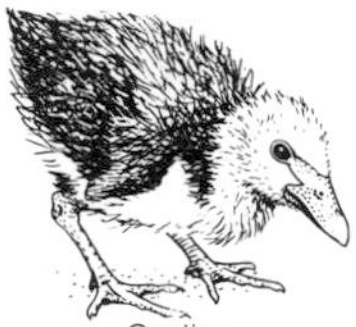

Gosling

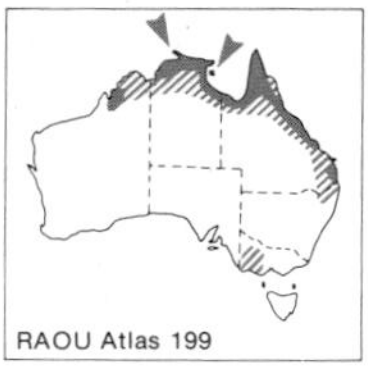
RAOU Atlas 199

116 Wandering Whistling-Duck *Dendrocygna arcuata*

Blackish crown and hind neck contrasting with uniform buff face and foreneck. Bill black. Upperparts brownish-black, feathers edged chestnut. Shoulders chestnut. Undertail white. Flank plumes white, edged chestnut. Legs and feet black. Race in Aust. and New Guinea is *australis*. **Size** 54-60 cm. Distinguished from Plumed Whistling-Duck by darker body plumage and shorter flank plumes. **Imm.** similar to adults but duller. **Voice** distinctive; shrill and whistling. **Habitat** deep vegetated lagoons and swamps, flooded grasslands. In flight has short rounded wings, trailing legs.

Duckling

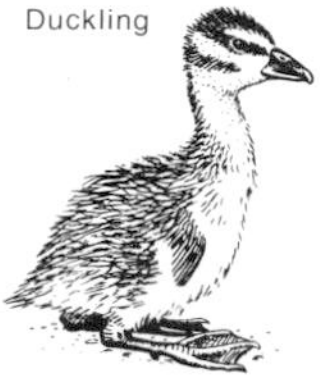

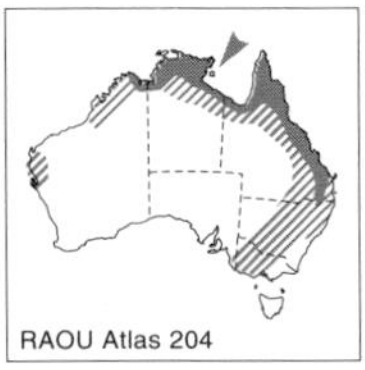
RAOU Atlas 204

117 Plumed Whistling-Duck *Dendrocygna eytoni*

Pale brown on crown and hind neck. Face and foreneck whitish-buff. Bill pink. Upperparts brown, feathers of upper back edged yellow. Wings above brown; paler below. Breast pale chestnut, finely barred in black. Long buff flank plumes, edged black. Abdomen pale buff. Tail and rump darker brown with upper tail coverts buff, spotted darker brown. **Size** 42-60 cm. Conclusively identified by the long flank plumes which extend over back. **Imm.** paler than adults; indistinct breast markings. **Habitat** tropical grasslands.

Duckling

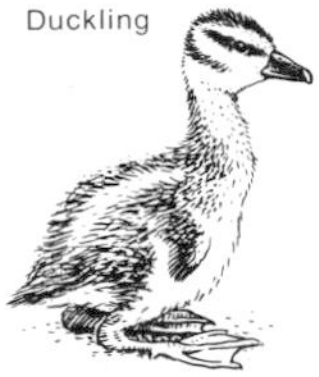

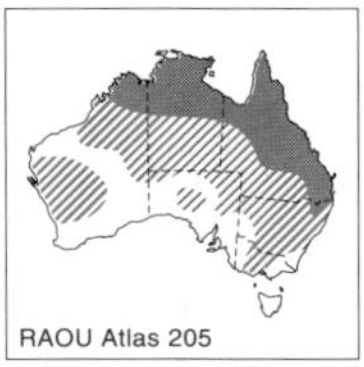
RAOU Atlas 205

118 Black Swan *Cygnus atratus*

Very large black bird with long slender neck and white tipped wings. Bill orange and dark red with white bar near tip, nail whitish. Legs and feet black. **Female** slightly smaller; bill and iris paler. **Size** 106-142 cm; wingspan 160-200 cm approx. **Imm.** grey-brown with paler feather edgings; white flight feathers tipped black. **Voice** musical trumpeting calls. **Habitat** large expanses of open water, fresh through to salt, with abundant aquatic vegetation; pasture, crops and mud-flats. Frequently heard flying overhead at night.

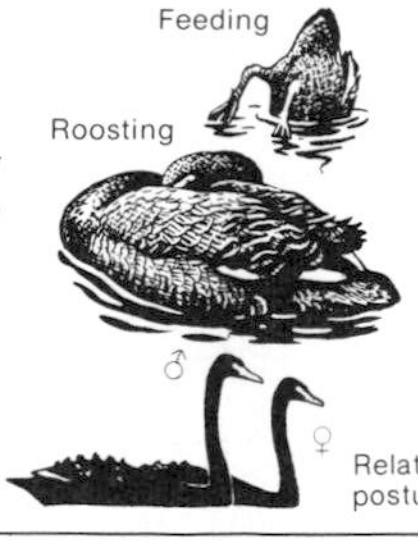
Feeding
Roosting
♂
♀

Relative size and posture of mated pair

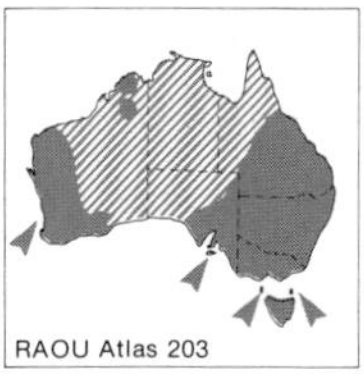
RAOU Atlas 203

119 Mute Swan *Cygnus olor**

Huge, entirely white swan with loud musical wing beat. **Female** smaller. Bill orange with black knob at base, larger in breeding males. Legs and feet black. **Size** 127-156 cm; wingspan 220-240 cm approx. **Imm.** grey-brown (except for white 'Polish' phase) with grey knobless bill. **Habitat** rivers and ornamental lakes.

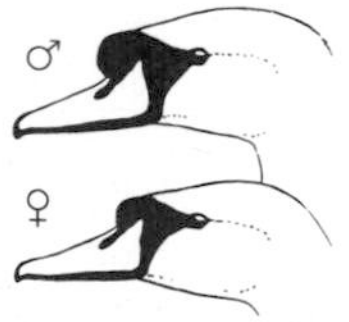
♂
♀

Head comparison (adults)

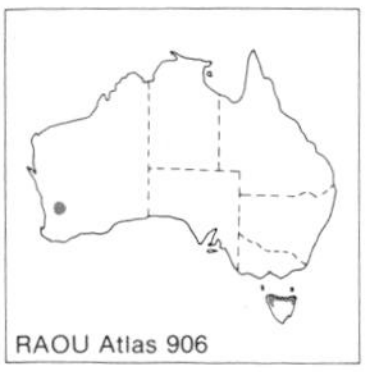
RAOU Atlas 906

* **Introduced**

120 Freckled Duck *Stictonetta naevosa*

Duckling

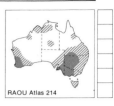

RAOU Atlas 214

Uniformly coloured with large (crested) head and dish-shaped bill. **Male** uniform dark brown to black head covered in small white or buff freckles. Bill slate to dark grey; red to orange base when breeding. Body dark brown with uniform freckling. Abdomen to undertail paler with white freckles. Upperwing dark brown; coverts freckled. Underwing light brown; white wing linings mottled pale brown. Distinguished from Pacific Black Duck in flight by hunched appearance and lack of bright white underwings. **Female** paler; obscure freckling. **Size** M 52-59, F 48-54 cm. **Imm.** pale brown; deep buff freckles. **Habitat** breeds in heavily vegetated permanent fresh swamps; disperses to fresh and saline permanent open lakes, especially during drought. Usually seen loafing in daytime on fallen trees or sand spits in small or large groups. Distinctive 'peaked' appearance to back of head often visible on roosting birds.

Roosting

121 Cape Barren Goose *Cereopsis novaehollandiae*

Gosling

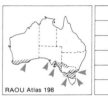

RAOU Atlas 198

Distinctive. Pale grey with small head and short triangular-shaped bill. Pale grey head with white crown. Bill black with prominent greenish cere. Body pale grey, dark spots on scapulars and wing coverts. Legs pink to deep red; feet black. In flight black wing tips, undertail coverts and tail are diagnostic. **Size** 75-100 cm. **Imm.** paler cere; duller body. **Habitat** breeds on small offshore islands with tussocks, grassland and scrub. Disperses to open improved pasture on breeding and other islands, also mainland.

122 Australian Shelduck *Tadorna tadornoides*

Duckling

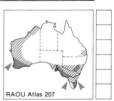

RAOU Atlas 207

Large-bodied, brightly-coloured duck with small head and bill. **Male** head and neck black, tinged green. White ring around base of neck and occasionally around black bill. Upperparts mainly black; underparts dark brown with cinnamon breast. Upperwing coverts white; primaries black; large green speculum. White underwing linings with black flight feathers. Legs, feet dark grey. **Male eclipse** yellowish-brown breast with less defined neck ring. In flight large white panel on forewing contrasts with dark body. **Female** eye-ring and base of bill white, sometimes merged; chestnut breast. **Size** M 59-72, F 56-68 cm. **Imm.** white flecking on front of head; white areas of plumage flecked grey; otherwise body duller. Unlike other Aust. ducks, often flies in long lines or 'V' formation when travelling. **Habitat** large open brackish or fresh lakes; pastures and open woodlands.

Alert posture

123 Radjah Shelduck *Tadorna radjah*

Duckling

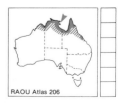

RAOU Atlas 206

Striking white duck with chestnut breast band. Head pure white with pink bill. Body white except for dark back, black rump and tail. Undertail and flanks black. White upperwing coverts; black primaries. Legs, feet pink. Black wing-tips visible in flight. The Aust. race is *rufitergum*. **Size** M 50-56, F 49-61 cm. **Imm.** white areas flecked grey-brown. **Voice** very vocal, often utters harsh rattling call whilst flying through thick timber. **Habitat** coastal wetlands and rivers; mud-flats, paperbark swamps.

121

121

121
Imm.

122 ♂

122 ♂

♀ **122**

122 ♂

♀ **122**

123

123

123

123

120

120

120

♀ **120**

120 ♂
Breeding

♂ **120**
Non-breeding

N. Day

124 Pacific Black Duck *Anas superciliosa*

Crown blackish, face white to buff with two black stripes. Body plumage dark brown. Upperwing has purplish-green speculum. Legs, feet yellow-green. Distinguished from Freckled Duck and Mallard in flight by dark body plumage contrasting with white wing linings and dark-striped pale face. Aust. race is *rogersi*. **Size** 47-60 cm. **Habitat** usually deep, permanent, heavily vegetated swamps, but also more open waters.

Duckling

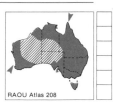
RAOU Atlas 208

125 Mallard *Anas platyrhynchos**

Male green head and white neck ring. White underparts. Legs, feet orange. In eclipse, as female but bill dull green. **Female** mottled and streaked dusky-brown; distinguished from Pacific Black Duck by lighter plumage, pale (not bright) underwing and lack of striped face pattern. Introduced; many domestic forms. Hybridises with Pacific Black Duck. **Size** 52-68 cm. **Habitat** mainly lakes in town parks, dams and larger lakes.

Domestic varieties

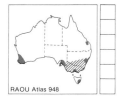
RAOU Atlas 948

126 Grey Teal *Anas gibberifrons*

Mottled grey-brown duck. In good light, a white throat and paler face distinguish it from darker female Chestnut Teal; from other species by narrow white wing-stripe and thin white wedge down centre of underwing. Aust. race is *gracilis*. **Size** 37-48 cm. **Imm.** paler. **Habitat** any available water, including floodwaters, tanks and dams. More coastal during dry periods.

Duckling

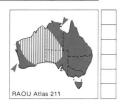
RAOU Atlas 211

127 Chestnut Teal *Anas castanea*

Male dark iridescent green head, chestnut underparts and distinctive white patch on flank. Can be confused with male Aust. Shoveller unless lack of white face crescent and smaller bill is noticed. Eclipse, if occurring, probably not distinguishable from imm. male. **Female** similar to Grey Teal but darker, lacking the pale throat. **Size** 38-48 cm. **Imm. male** duller, blotchier body plumage, dark patchy head pattern. **Habitat** breeds in brackish to fresh coastal swamps. Disperses to fresh water, tidal mud-flats, inlets.

Duckling

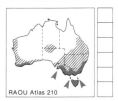
RAOU Atlas 210

128 Australasian Shoveller *Anas rhynchotis*

Heavy spatulate black bill, low sloping forehead diagnostic. **Male** head blue-grey with vertical white crescent. Body plumage similar to male Chestnut Teal. Upperwing coverts pale blue-grey. Legs, feet bright orange. In eclipse, duller. **Female** bill dark. Body mottled brown with paler chestnut underparts, blue forewing duller. Aust. race is *rhynchotis*. **Size** 46-53 cm. **Habitat** heavily vegetated swamps, floodwaters. Only Aust. duck with noisy, whirring flight.

Duckling

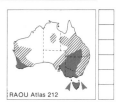
RAOU Atlas 212

129 Northern Shoveller *Anas clypeata*

Male differs from Australasian Shoveller by the uniform green head, pure white breast and sides of back. **Female** bill flanges orange; check is not a Mallard or Mallard-cross. White tail edges visible in flight, on water; female Aust. Shoveller has brown tail edges. **Size** 46-55 cm. **Habitat** mainly vegetated freshwater swamps. Vagrant.

128
129
Head comparison of females

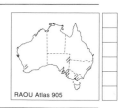
RAOU Atlas 905

* **Introduced**

127 ♂
126
128 ♂
124
127 ♀
126
128 ♀
128 ♂
125
124
125 ♂
129 ♂
124
125 ♀
♂ 128
♀ 128
127 ♂
♀ 127
126
124/125
Hybrid
124

130 Garganey *Anas querquedula*

Grey Teal-sized duck with striking blue-grey forewing.
Male rich brown head, neck and breast with prominent
white stripe over eye. Upperparts blackish-brown with
long drooping black and white scapulars. Underparts
white with fine black wavy lines. In eclipse, similar to
female, but forewing blue-grey. **Female** distinguished from
Grey Teal by dark crown and eye-stripe contrasting with
pale face. Belly white and forewing pale grey. **Size** 38-
41 cm. **Voice** a distinctive harsh rattling call.
Habitat shallow swamps with dense cover. A long-
distance migrant from N Hem. to N Aust. Rare.

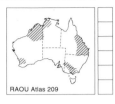
RAOU Atlas 209

131 Pink-eared Duck *Malacorhynchus membranaceus*

Distinguished by striking 'zebra' striped plumage and
large, square-ended spatulate bill. Head has large brown
eye patch on white, finely-barred face. Small pink patch
behind eye. Bill grey with skin flaps either side of tip.
Upperparts brown. Underparts white, barred dark brown.
Undertail buff. Upperwing brown with white trailing
edge. Underwing linings white, finely-barred brown.
Rump has distinctive white crescent. Tail brown with
white tip. **Size** 36-45 cm. **Imm.** paler, with less distinct
pink ear patch. **Voice** can be located in mixed flocks of
ducks by distinctive chirruping call. **Habitat** breeds
inland, on temporary floodwaters; in periods of drought
occurs on more permanent open waters including sewage
farms near the coast.

Bill profile
Duckling

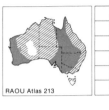
RAOU Atlas 213

132 Hardhead (White-eyed Duck) *Aythya australis*

Male large, rounded head rich dark brown. Bill black with
blue bar near tip. Eye white. Rest of body plumage as head,
except for white, mottled brown lower breast. Undertail
coverts white. Upperwing brown with broad white bar
across secondaries. Underwing white, bordered dark
brown. Diagnostic, broad, white wing bar in flight. **Female**
paler; iris brown. **Size** 42-49 cm. **Imm.** uniform yellow-
brown; eye dark. **Voice** nasal 'mow'. **Habitat** deep
vegetated swamps and other large open waters when not
breeding. Diving habits, sloping 'stern' (which can obscure
the white undertail), and large head can lead to confusion
of this species with Blue-billed Duck male.

Duckling

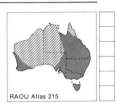
RAOU Atlas 215

133 Maned (Wood) Duck *Chenonetta jubata*

Land-dwelling duck of fine goose-like proportions with
dark head and pale body. **Male** head and neck brown with
short dark mane. Bill small blackish. Body mainly grey
with speckled brown breast and black lower belly and
undertail. Upperwing diagnostic with pale grey forewing
contrasting with black wing-tips. Noticeable white panel
along rear edge of secondaries. **Female** whitish line above
and below eye; grey-brown body plumage with white
lower belly and undertail. **Size** 44-50 cm. **Imm.** lighter than
adults. **Voice** a distinctive drawn-out mournful 'now' with
a rising inflection. **Habitat** lightly timbered areas near
water with access to short pasture or herbage; inland tanks
and dams. Often perches in trees.

Perched in tree
RAOU Atlas 202

132 ♂

132 ♀

133 ♂

133 ♀

130 ♂

130 ♀

133 ♂

130 ♂

131

131

131

132
Imm.

2 ♀

132 ♂

130 ♂

131

131

130 ♀

♂ 133

♀ 133

N. Day

134 Cotton Pygmy-Goose
Nettapus coromandelianus

Duckling

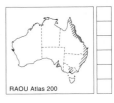

RAOU Atlas 200

A tiny duck with white face and neck. White on primaries (male) and thin white trailing edge to wing (female) distinguish this species from Green Pygmy-Goose in flight. **Male** basically white. Short black bill. Upperparts blackish, glossed green. Underparts white; narrow black breast band. **Female** more dusky with noticeable white eyebrow and dark line through eye. Aust. race *albipennis* is slightly larger than the Asiatic race *coromandelianus*. **Size** M 35-38, F 33-38 cm. **Imm.** as female but lacks green gloss. **Habitat** deep lagoons, swamps and dams particularly with waterlilies and other floating vegetation. A surface feeder; not known to dive.

135 Green Pygmy-Goose *Nettapus pulchellus*

Duckling

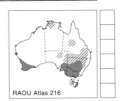

RAOU Atlas 201

Distinguished in flight from Cotton Pygmy-Goose by large white wing panels on rear edge of wing next to body. **Male** head, neck and upperparts blackish, glossed green with bright white face patch. Underparts off-white. **Female** duller, flanks and neck have more grey-brown mottling than Cotton Pygmy-Goose and the white eyebrow is more obscure. **Size** M 30-36, F 30-34 cm. **Imm.** as female. **Voice** male has a distinctive shrill 'pee-whit' call. **Habitat** as for Cotton Pygmy-Goose but will also utilise shallow, spike-rush dominated swamps in the wet season. Tends to dive on occasion, unlike Cotton Pygmy-Goose.

136 Blue-billed Duck *Oxyura australis*

Duckling

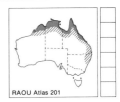

RAOU Atlas 216

Dark, compact diving duck with short 'dished' bill. **Male** head black. Bright blue bill. Body deep chestnut. Tail black with stiff, pointed feathers, usually carried below the water surface but sometimes erected and fanned. Eclipse plumage becomes duller and feathers are broadly edged pale brown. Bill is then slate-grey. **Female** head dark brown, paler on throat and below eye. Bill dark grey. Body finely barred and freckled buffish. Paler below. **Size** 35-44 cm. **Imm.** paler, barring more distinct. Distinguished in all plumages from the Musk Duck by 'dished', *not* triangular bill, also by more rounded head and smaller size; from Hardhead by *lack* of white undertail and broad white wing bar. **Habitat** deep freshwater marshes with dense vegetation; more open waters in non-breeding season. Flight rapid and low on short narrow wings. Floats higher than Musk Duck.

♀ with duckling

137 Musk Duck *Biziura lobata*

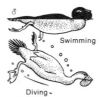

Swimming

Diving

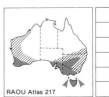

RAOU Atlas 217

A powerful, bizarre-looking duck that often swims partially submerged. **Male** large. Heavy thickset head. Stout, dark-grey triangular bill with a large black lobe of skin hanging below. **Female** smaller. Very small bill lobe. **Size** M 60-73, F 47-60 cm. **Imm.** as female but tip of lower mandible yellow. **Habitat** permanent swamps with dense vegetation. Large open lakes, inlets and bays. When disturbed thrashes across water in a cloud of spray; not often seen in flight. Spectacular splashing displays by courting males. An expert diver.

134 ♂

134 ♀

135 ♀

135 ♂

136

137 ♂

137 ♂
Displaying

134 ♀

134 ♂

135 ♂

135 ♀

♀ 136

♂ 136

136
Imm.

137 ♂

♀ 137

138 Osprey *Pandion haliaetus*

Dark brown upperparts; white head and underparts. Brown streak through eye and down sides of neck. Band of brown mottling across chest. Barring on underwings and tail. **Female** larger. **Size** F 60-66, M 50-55 cm. **Juv.** rufous markings on upperparts; heavier chest band than adults. **Voice** plaintive whistles. **Habitat** mangroves, rivers and estuaries, inshore areas, coastal islands. Soars on long, angled, bowed wings. Patrols over water; hovers, plunges feet-first. Identify from imm. White-bellied Sea-Eagle, 1st-year Brahminy Kite.

Gliding head-on

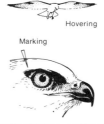

Ventral pattern

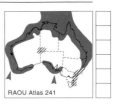

RAOU Atlas 241

139 Black-shouldered Kite *Elanus notatus*

Body white with grey and white wings; prominent black shoulders. **Male** slightly smaller. **Size** F 35-38, M 33-36 cm. **Juv.** spotted to golden-tan on head, neck, breast and back. **Voice** harsh 'kar'; quiet 'chep'. **Habitat** hunts from perches in open woodlands or by hovering over tall grasses. Often a dawn and dusk hunter; hovers with faster wing beats than Letter-winged Kite; soars with elevated wings. Perches singly or in family groups in top branches of dead trees.

Hovering

Marking

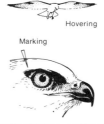

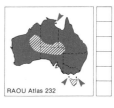

RAOU Atlas 232

140 Letter-winged Kite *Elanus scriptus*

Large eyes surrounded by black patch give an 'owl-like' appearance. Body white with prominent black bar along undersides of grey and white wings. **Male** slightly smaller. **Size** F 35-38, M 33-36 cm. **Juv.** white with mottled brown to tan-orange on head, back, breast. **Voice** harsh 'kar-kar' or 'chip-chip'. **Habitat** desert grasslands and timbered watercourses. Preys on rodents and especially relies on plagues of them to boost its own population numbers. Hunts at night — the only Aust. hawk to do so. Roosts communally in daylight. Soars with elevated wings; wingbeat is slower than Black-shouldered Kite; hovers. Identify from Barn Owl, Eastern Grass Owl at night.

No marking

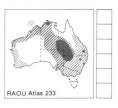

RAOU Atlas 233

141 Pacific Baza (Crested Hawk) *Aviceda subcristata*

Slate-grey upperparts and chest. Short crest. Belly whitish with bold dark bars. Thighs and vent pale rufous. Underwings have pale rufous lining; boldly barred 'fingers'. **Female** slightly larger. **Size** F 43-46, M 35-40 cm. **Juv.** much browner upperparts. Race *njikena*, NT and Kimberley, WA, is smaller and darker. Recent texts ignore races, which may therefore be considered a cline in size across the north of the continent. **Voice** shrill double whistle, rising and falling; quieter whistles and trills. **Habitat** coastal and subcoastal closed and open forests; urban trees and parklands. Flight buoyant, leisurely; hovers around tree canopies; hangs from foliage with beating wings. Soars on flat or slightly drooped wings; performs undulating diving display flight with wings held in a stiff 'V'. Identify from imm. Brown Goshawk.

Gliding head-on

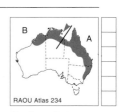

Juv.

RAOU Atlas 234

A = Race *subcristata*
B = Race *njikena*

Osprey Adult

Juvenile

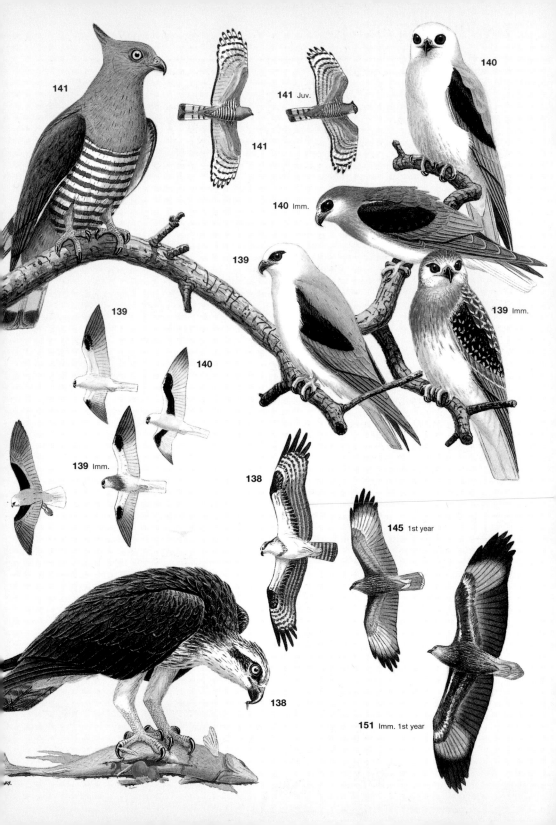

141

141 Juv.

141

140

140 Imm.

139

139

140

139 Imm.

139 Imm.

138

145 1st year

138

151 Imm. 1st year

142 Black Kite *Milvus migrans*

Uniformly dark brown, appearing black in strong light.
Pale shoulder bar. **Male** slightly smaller. **Size** F 50-55, M
47-52 cm; wingspan 120 cm. **1st year** paler than adults;
upperwing surfaces lightly mottled. **Voice** plaintive
descending 'see-err', and whistles 'si-i-i-i-'. **Habitat** open
plains, timbered watercourses, rubbish dumps, abattoirs,
cattle yards. Identify from dark phase of Little Eagle. Birds
soar effortlessly with frequent twistings of forked tail.
Resembles Square-tailed Kite, but in flight wings held flat,
not in a 'V'; wings without pale patches.

Gliding head-on

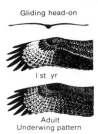

I st yr

Adult
Underwing pattern

RAOU Atlas 229

143 Brahminy Kite *Milvus indus*

Distinctive. Head, neck, breast white; body upper surface
of flight feathers chestnut. **Male** slightly smaller. **Size** F 48-
51, M 45-49 cm; wingspan to 125 cm. **1st year** browner and
mottled, resembling Whistling Kite but tail is shorter. **Voice**
plaintive 'pee-ah-ah-ah'. **Habitat** coastal mud-flats, mangroves,
harbours, offshore islands. Identify imm. from Osprey.

Gliding head-on

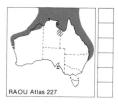

RAOU Atlas 227

144 Whistling Kite *Milvus sphenurus*

Head, underparts light brown with pale streaks. Darker
outer primaries and pale inner primaries; dark
secondaries. Long rounded tail. **Male** slightly smaller.
Size F 52-59, M 51-54 cm; wingspan to 120 cm. **1st
year** brown back spotted with white. **Voice** long
descending 'seeo' followed by an upward staccato 'si-si-si-
si'. **Habitat** soars over open woodlands, plains, streams,
swamps, sea shores. Identify from Little Eagle.

Gliding head-on

146

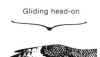

153 Underwing pattern

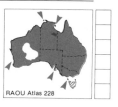

RAOU Atlas 228

145 Square-tailed Kite *Lophoictinia isura*

Slender, very long-winged. Dark brown upperparts. White
crown, face; pale eye. Pale shoulder bar. Underparts
rufous with dark streaks. Underwings have rufous lining,
pale 'bull's-eye' and boldly barred fingers. Tail long,
square-cut. **Female** slightly larger. **Size** F 55-56,
M 50-51 cm; wingspan to 130 cm. **1st year** head,
underparts rich rufous; less streaked. **Voice** hoarse yelp;
weak twitter (chatter). **Habitat** open forests, riverine
woodlands, scrubs, heathlands. Solitary; soars low over or
through tree canopy on raised wings. Identify from Black
Kite, also light morph of Black-breasted Buzzard.

Gliding head-on

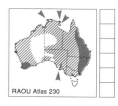

Underwing pattern

RAOU Atlas 230

146 Black-breasted Buzzard
Hamirostra melanosternon

Robust; short-tailed. **Adult** mostly blackish above and
below. Rufous nape, shoulder mottling, thighs and vent.
Prominent white 'bull's-eye' in broad wings. Pale tail.
2-3 year birds paler. Head and underparts light brown;
'bull's-eyes' less distinct. **Female** larger. **Size** F 55-61,
M 51-53 cm; wingspan to 150 cm. **1st year** rich rufous;
dark wingtips, indistinct 'bull's-eyes'; pale tail. **Voice** short
sharp calls; hoarse yelp, thin whistle, harsh sounds.
Habitat arid scrub, riverine and tropical woodlands. Soars
high on raised, back-swept wings. Identify from dark
morph of Little Eagle.

Gliding head-on

2-3 yr.

Adult
Underwing pattern

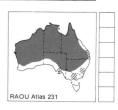

RAOU Atlas 231

142

142
1st yr

142
1st yr

142

145

145
1st yr

145

144
1st yr

144

144
1st yr

144

143
1st yr

143

143

143
1st yr

146

146
1st yr

146
1st yr

146

46

147 Brown Goshawk *Accipiter fasciatus*

Gliding head-on

Foot: toe proportions

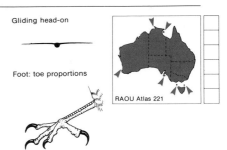

RAOU Atlas 221

Head grey. Eye bright yellow. Body slate-grey or dark brown above; rufous collar across nape. Underparts finely barred rufous and white. Wings rounded; slate-grey or dark brown above; buff and rufous below; wingtips darker. Tail long, rounded; slate-grey or dark brown above; light grey with dark barring below. Legs long, yellow; rufous feathering about thighs. **Male** smaller. **Size** F 45-55, M 38-45 cm. **1st year** head streaked chocolate. Eyes yellow. *No* rufous collar. Body dark brown above; off-white with bold chocolate lower throat and breast streaking below. Belly to undertail coverts strongly barred chestnut-brown. Wings dark brown above; off-white with chocolate barring below. Tail long, rounded; dark brown above; light grey with darker bars below. **2nd year** more like adult; collar not prominent. Breast strongly streaked. Broader chevron belly markings but plumage generally brown, not yet adult underparts or back. Two races: widely distributed *fasciatus*; smaller, paler *didimus*, restricted to far north. (*A.f. didimus* needs investigation; may be a new species.) **Voice** rapid, shrill chatter (female lower-pitch). **Habitat** most timbered types.

148 Collared Sparrowhawk *Accipiter cirrhocephalus*

Gliding head-on

Foot: toe proportions

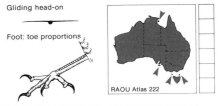

RAOU Atlas 222

Adult/Imm. similar plumage to Brown Goshawk counterparts. **Female** approximates male Brown Goshawk in size. Collared Sparrowhawk distinguished by squarer tail, finer legs and toes. **Male** smaller. **Size** F 35-38, M 29-33 cm. Two races: widely distributed *cirrhocephalus* and smaller, more rufous *quaesitandus*, restricted to far north. **Voice** very rapid, shrill chatter. **Habitat** most terrestrial types.

149 Grey (White) Goshawk *Accipiter novaehollandiae*

Gliding head-on

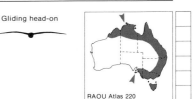

RAOU Atlas 220

Two colour morphs. **Grey morph** head grey; eye dark red. Body grey above; white below, with fine grey chest barrings. Wings rounded; grey above; white below with darker wing-tips. Tail long, rounded; grey above; white below with grey barring. Legs yellow. **1st year** similar but broader chest barring, and often buff-washed areas. **White morph** all plumage pure white in adult and imm. **Male** smaller. **Size** F 50-55, M 38-42 cm. White morph predominates in Kimberley, WA, coastal Vic., and in Tas., where grey morph does not occur. **Voice** rapid, shrill chatter, also repeated rising shrill whistle. **Habitat** various forest types, especially coastal closed forests.

150 Red Goshawk *Erythrotriorchis radiatus*

Gliding head-on

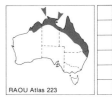

RAOU Atlas 223

Head rufous, streaked black and white; much white on face and throat. Eye yellow. Body rufous above, with bold dark markings; male paler below, with fine black streaking. Wings long, rounded, fingered at tips. Upperwings rufous, streaked with black above; much lighter below, with rufous underwing coverts and darker barring on flight feathers. Tail long, broad; barred grey and rufous-brown above and below. Legs powerful, yellow. **Male** smaller. **Size** F 57-61, M 46-51 cm. **Voice** loud, harsh chatter. **Habitat** coastal, sub-coastal forests, tropical woodlands. Rare, often confused with other rufous raptors. Identify from imm. harriers, Brown Goshawk, Black-breasted Buzzard, Little Eagle.

149
White morph

149
Grey morph

149 ♂
Grey morph

Imm. ♀ **149**
White morph

♂ **149**

149 ♀
Imm.
Grey morph

150

150

ared Honeyeater

148 ♀

148 ♂
Imm.

147 ♀
Imm.

♂ **148**

♀ **148**
Imm.

658
New Holland Honeyeater

147 ♂

♂ **147**
Imm.

♀ **147**

151 White-bellied Sea-Eagle *Haliaeetus leucogaster*

Gliding head-on

White, with grey back, rump, wings and base of tail. Bare whitish legs. **Female** larger. **Size** F 80-85, M 75-77 cm; wingspan 190 cm approx. **1st year** brown with lighter markings; paler on head and rump. Whitish 'bulls-eye' in wings. Tail whitish, shading to light brown at the tip. Tail short; rounded or wedge-shaped. Birds become lighter with age. **Voice** deep goose-like honking or cackling. **Habitat** large rivers, fresh and saline lakes, reservoirs, estuaries, coastal seas, islands. Wings broad and rounded, held stiffly upswept when soaring. Identify imm. from Wedge-tailed Eagle, Black-breasted Buzzard; adult from Australian Pelican

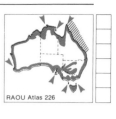

RAOU Atlas 226

Ventral pattern

152 Wedge-tailed Eagle *Aquila audax*

Gliding head-on

Sooty-black with tawny hackles on nape. Pale brown wing coverts and undertail coverts. Feathered legs. Tail long and wedge-shaped. **Female** larger. **Size** F 89-104, M 87-91 cm; wingspan 210 cm approx. **End of 1st year to 4th or 5th year** usually paler than adults. Dark brown with golden-brown nape, uppertail coverts and wing coverts. Whitish undertail coverts. Birds become darker with age. **Voice** feeble yelps and squeals. **Habitat** most types except closed forest. Soars on long, fingered, upswept wings. Identify from Black-breasted Buzzard; imm. White-bellied Sea-Eagle.

Adult at nest

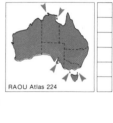

RAOU Atlas 224

153 Little Eagle *Hieraaetus morphnoides*

Gliding head-on

Light morph head buff to pale rufous with blackish streaks on cheeks. Blackish crown feathers extending into a short crest. Upperparts brown, paler on nape and scapulars, with a distinct pale band across the wing. Underparts white with fine black streaks and a buff to rufous wash, especially on breast. Underwing has rufous leading edge and white oblique band contrasting with grey-barred secondaries and black-tipped outer primaries. Tail barred, rather short and square-cut. Legs feathered. **Dark morph** head and underparts light brown with black streaks. Leading edge and oblique band on underwing dark brown. **Female** larger. **Size** F 50-55, M 45-48 cm. **1st year light morph** head and underparts richer rufous, less streaked. **1st year dark morph** more rufous-brown than adults; less streaked. **Voice** loud, excited, high-pitched whistle, usually of two or three notes uttered rapidly. Also a series of mellow or plaintive piping notes. **Habitat** most open forest, woodland and scrub types; open agricultural country. Compact in flight; wings slightly drooped when gliding, held level to slightly raised when soaring. Identify from Whistling Kite, Square-tailed Kite.

153 Dark morph

153 Light morph

146 Underwing pattern

153 Erect 'crest'

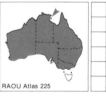

RAOU Atlas 225

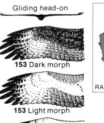

Note An adult Gurney's Eagle *Aquila gurneyi* recorded on Boigu Is., Torres Strait, February 1987 — a new species for Australia. This is an eagle ranging from the Moluccan area to Papua New Guinea, where also a rare bird. Distinguish from Wedge-tailed Eagle (see p. 274).

153
Light morph

153
Light morph: 1st yr

153
Dark morph

153
Light morph: 1st yr

53
ph

153
Dark morph: 1st yr

152

152

152

152
Imm : 1-4 yrs

152

151
Imm : 1st yr

151

151
Juv.

151

151

154 **Spotted Harrier** *Circus assimilis*

Upperparts blue-grey. Wings with prominent black tips.
Face and underparts chestnut with numerous white spots.
Tail prominently barred and slightly wedge-shaped. Long
yellow legs. **Male** much smaller. **Size** F 58-61, M 50-55 cm.
1st year dark brown and buff above; pale buff with brown
streaks below. **Habitat** hunts low over open grassland,
crops and windbreaks. Soars with wings elevated.

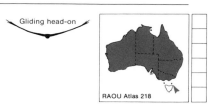

Gliding head-on

RAOU Atlas 218

155 **Swamp (Marsh) Harrier** *Circus approximans*

Adults/Imm. dark brown above; prominent white rump
(uppertail coverts). Tail and wings barred. Long yellow
legs. **Male** slightly smaller. Off-white to buff underparts.
Female rufous underparts. **Size** F 55-61, M 50-57 cm. **1st
year** darker brown; rump brownish; no bars on wings.
Voice high-pitched 'seee-uh' during aerial food transfer
between birds; loud 'kee-a' during courtship flights.
Habitat hunts low over tall grass, reeds, rushes, crops.
Soars with elevated wings; performs courtship dives high
above swamps.

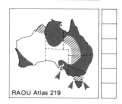

Gliding head-on

RAOU Atlas 219

156 **Papuan Harrier** *Circus spilonotus*

Male black head, nape. Black and silver-grey above. Rump
white. White below, streaked on breast. Trailing wing
edges dark. Colour morphs occur. **Size** F 48-53, M
47-51 cm. This bird is a PNG resident race of the Asian
region's Eastern Marsh Harrier, (presently named as)
C. spilonotus spilonotus. The PNG race is *Circus spilonotus
spilothorax*, formerly given as a distinct New Guinea species.
Vagrant to northern Australia. First Darwin record
withdrawn by its observer. Additional sightings more
recently: Darwin (NT), Torres Strait, and several in N Qld
(Daintree River to Atherton). Confirmation and more
details required (and see MacKay, R. D. (1991), 'Papuan
Harrier ... in North Queensland, with comments on
plumages' *Aust. Bird Watcher* no. 14(4), pp. 144-6).

157 **Black Falcon** *Falco subniger*

Dark brown to sooty-black, with pale chin and face; dark
streak below eye. Heavy-shouldered. Tail usually square-
cut. Legs short. **Male** smaller. **Size** F 52-56, M 45-54 cm. **1st
year** darker than adults, with faint narrow bars under
wings and tail. **Voice** chatters and screeches. **Habitat**
woodland, scrub, shrubland and grassland types in arid
and semi-arid zones. Glides on slightly drooped wings.
Flight swift when hunting, otherwise, leisurely.

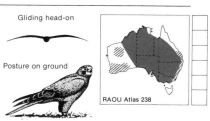

Gliding head-on

Posture on ground

RAOU Atlas 238

158 **Peregrine Falcon** *Falco peregrinus*

Heavily built and compact. Head and cheeks black,
upperparts blue-grey, underparts cream with dark barring
on belly. Race *submelanogenys* of SW of WA is smaller and
darker. **Male** smaller. **Size** F 45-50, M 35-42 cm.
1st year upperparts tinged brown; underparts buff with
heavy dark streaks. **Voice** hoarse chatter and whining
sounds. **Habitat** most land types, especially cliffs and rocky
outcrops, rocky coastal islands. Flight powerful. Wings
held stiffly outstretched when soaring; trailing edge
usually straight. Identify from Australian Hobby.

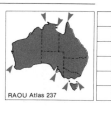

Gliding head-on

Stooping

RAOU Atlas 237

158 ♀

158 1st yr ♂

159 Australian Hobby

158 1st yr ♀

158 ♂

157

157 1st yr

157

157

161 Brown Falcon Dark morph

154 1st yr

155 1st yr

156

154

155

154

155

154 2nd yr

155

155 1st yr

154 1st yr

159 Australian Hobby *Falco longipennis*

Slender and long-winged. Cap and 'mask' black, forehead and half-collar whitish. Upperparts blue-grey; underparts rufous, streaked darker. Race *murchisonianus*, of arid zone, is paler. **Female** larger. **Size** F 34-35.5, M 30-32 cm. **1st year** upperparts tinged brown. **Voice** rapid shrill chatter, also loud chuckling call. **Habitat** most open forest, woodland and scrub types, also urban areas. In flight, silhouette *may* resemble White-throated Needletail, Oriental Cuckoo.

Gliding head-on

Aerial feeding

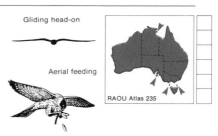

RAOU Atlas 235

160 Grey Falcon *Falco hypoleucos*

Grey above with black streak under eye, black wing-tips. White below with fine dark streaks. Tail grey, faintly barred as are the wings. **Female** larger. **Size** F 41-43, M 33-36 cm. **1st year** darker with heavier streaks on underparts. **Voice** chattering and clucking sounds. **Habitat** woodland and scrub types in arid zone. Heavy-shouldered, Peregrine-like in flight. Rare. Identify from *Elanus* kites; Grey Goshawk.

Gliding head-on

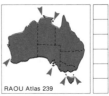

RAOU Atlas 236

161 Brown Falcon *Falco berigora*

Brown above, with dark marks below and behind eye. Underparts either whitish with dark streaks, *or* blotched brown and white, *or* wholly dark brown. Thighs *always* dark brown; may appear as leg-stripe on paler-bellied birds. Underwings barred. Tail rounded. Legs long. Five races: *berigora*, *tasmanica*, *centralia*, *occidentalis* and *melvillensis*. Birds from central Aust. are usually paler, and those from the tropical north are often very dark. **Female** larger. **Size** F 48-51, M 41-45 cm. **1st year** usually darker underparts; broad buff collar; incomplete barring of tail. **Voice** raucous cackles and screeches. **Habitat** most land surface types except closed forest. Glides on raised wings, flight heavy and slow. Hovers 'unsteadily'. Check identity of paler birds from smaller Australian Kestrel when solitary birds observed perched.

Gliding head-on

Hovering

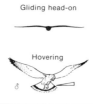

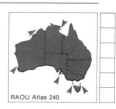

RAOU Atlas 239

162 Australian Kestrel *Falco cenchroides*

Male grey head, pale rufous back and wings. Whitish underparts with fine dark streaks. Grey tail. **Female/1st year** head and tail pale rufous. **Szie** F 33-35.5, M 30-33 cm. **Voice** shrill, excited chatter. **Habitat** most land surface types except forests. Slender, hovers with body horizontal, showing black band near tail-tip.

Gliding head-on

Hovering

δ

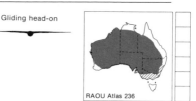

RAOU Atlas 240

158
Peregrine Falcon
1st yr

159

158
Peregrine Falcon

62

159

160

160

159

161
Race *tasmanica*

160

160 ♂
Imm.

♀ 162

162

♀ 160

159

159
Imm.

162
Imm.

♂ 161
Race *berigora*

162 ♂

♂ 161
Race *tasmanica*

♀ 161 Imm.
Race *berigora*

♀ 161
Race *centralia*

N. Day

163 Orange-footed Scrubfowl *Megapodius reinwardt*

Bill reddish-brown. Short, pointed, brown nuchal crest. Dark chestnut-brown above. Neck, underparts slate-grey. Legs orange. **Size** 40-60 cm. **Voice** loud crows, gurgles; often many birds call at once. **Habitat** rainforests, monsoon forests, dense vegetation bordering water.

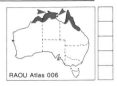

RAOU Atlas 006

164 Malleefowl *Leipoa ocellata*

Bill dark grey. Crown, nape blackish-brown. Head, neck, breast, mantle leaden-grey. Large ear hole. Black streak down central breast. Throat white, streaked black. Upperparts white barred, blotched brown, black and grey. Underparts light fawn. Large feet; legs dark grey. **Size** 60 cm. **Voice** booming (territorial); sharp grunt (alarm); soft lowing call (communication). **Habitat** dry inland scrub, mallee.

Flight

Front view

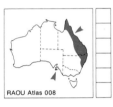

RAOU Atlas 007

165 Australian Brush-turkey *Alectura lathami*

Race *lathami:* **Breeding male** bill black. Bare red skin on head, neck, crown and nape (with sparse black hair-like feathers). Large yellow collar/wattle. Body dull black; underpart feathers edged dull white. Legs brown. **Female** smaller neck band; no wattle. Race *purpureicollis* has purplish-white collar (C. York Pen., Qld). **Size** 70 cm. **Voice** harsh grunts. **Habitat** rainforests and wet open forests; also some dry inland areas.

Perched

Flight

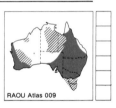

RAOU Atlas 008

166 Stubble Quail *Coturnix pectoralis*

Male bill grey. Eye red. Grey-brown above with obvious cream streaks and dark brown, buff and grey vermiculations. Throat orange. Cream below; strong black and cream streaking on chest and flanks. Legs pale flesh. **Female/Juv.** throat white, tinged brown below **Size** 18 cm. **Voice** high whistle 'titch-u-wip'. **Habitat** grasslands. In flight, a large brown quail with white streaks.

Hatchling

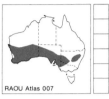

RAOU Atlas 009

167 Swamp Quail *Coturnix ypsilophora*

Confined to Tas.

Now regarded as same species as Brown Quail; larger, darker. Eye pale yellow. **Size** 20 cm. Tasmania.

168 Brown Quail *Coturnix ypsilophora* (formerly *C. australis*)

Male large. Bill black. Eye red to yellow. Chestnut to grey-brown with faint white streaks, black barring. Legs orange-yellow. **Female/Juv.** paler below. **Size** 18 cm. **Voice** 'f-whip' and 'be-quick, be-quick'. **Habitat** dense grassland, often near or in edges of open forest. In flight, rich brown colour seen to advantage; plumage streaks hard to see.

Hatchling

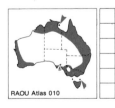

RAOU Atlas 010

169 King Quail *Coturnix chinensis*

Male very small. Bill black. Eye red. Cap, wings brown with faint white streaks and blackish bars. Sides of face, chest and flanks slate-blue. White crescent from eye across upper chest, bordered black. Throat black. Chestnut belly to vent. Legs yellow. **Female/Juv.** dark brown, faintly streaked, with throat white. Eye brown. **Size** 13 cm. **Voice** two to three descending notes. **Habitat** dense grassland, often swampy. In flight a very small, all-dark quail.

Hatchling

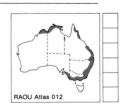

RAOU Atlas 012

163

164

165

169 ♀

169 ♂

♀ 169

167 ♂

168

168

166 ♀

♂ 166

166 ♂

170 Peafowl *Pavo cristatus**

Male blue with fan-shaped crest. Long uppertail coverts ('tail') have green spots with bronze reflections and blue spots surrounded by brown near tips. **Female** body chestnut brown, with a metallic blue sheen. 'Tail' shorter than male. **Size** M 180-200 (including 'tail'), F 90-100 cm. **Voice** 'kee-ow kee-ow'. **Habitat** introduced to Rottnest Island (WA). Also introduced but not established on other islands. Semi-feral populations exist.

Courtship display

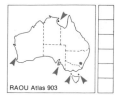
RAOU Atlas 903

171 Feral Chicken *Gallus gallus**

Male many colour variations. Large comb on head. Long, drooping red and green tail. **Female** smaller comb. **Size** 43-75 cm. **Voice** male 'cock a doodle-do'; also clucking. **Habitat** introduced to thick scrub on some Great Barrier Reef islands.

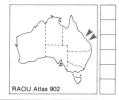
RAOU Atlas 902

172 Common Pheasant *Phasianus colchicus**

Male red facial skin. Blue head. White collar. Body reddish-golden, spotted black below. **Female** brown with buff and blackish mottles. No wattles. Tail shorter. **Size** 76-89 cm. **Voice** 'korrk-koh'. **Habitat** scrub, rank grasslands. Introduced on various islands.

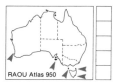
RAOU Atlas 950

173 California Quail *Lophortyx californicus**

Male long black crest. Black and white striped head. Brown nape, upperparts. Black collar finely spotted white. Grey chest. Blackish below, spotted and streaked white. **Female** duller. **Size** 24 cm. **Voice** 'ut-ut'; 'cu-ca-cow'; other calls. **Habitat** introduced on King Island (Bass Strait) in grasslands.

Male perching

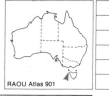
RAOU Atlas 901

— Chukar Partridge *Alectoris chukar**

Plump partridge. Grey-white face, throat surrounded by black line. Bill, eye-ring, legs red. Brown-grey above and on chest. Flanks barred black, white, chestnut. **Size** 33 cm. **Voice** loud wails, drummings. **Habitat** allegedly released for sporting reasons in Gulgong district, NSW. Runs, flies noisily if pressed, then glides. Not on Aust. list yet.

— Common Turkey *Meleagris gallopavo**

Dark brown to blue-black, speckled, slightly iridescent plumage. **Male** naked rear neck purple and white. Fleshy red wattle and throat. **Female** smaller; duller; little head decoration. **Size** M 95-125, F 90-110 cm. **Voice** coarse 'gobbling'; clucks, yelps. **Habitat** feral populations on King and Flinders Islands, Bass Strait. Not on Aust. list yet.

— Helmeted Guinea Fowl *Numida meleagris**

Plump, upright fowl. Grey-black body with fine, white spots. Bluish skin on sides of face, neck. Bony red-brown helmet (casque). **Size** 60 cm. **Voice** squeaking wail. **Habitat** feral populations on Heron and other Great Barrier Reef islands, Qld. Not on Aust. list yet.

* **Introduced**

173 ♀

171 ♂

♂ 173

♀ 171

172 ♂

♀ 172

172 ♂

170 ♂

170 ♀

174 Red-backed Button-quail *Turnix maculosa*

Slender bill. Eye pale. **Female** chestnut on hind neck,
upper back. Wing coverts yellow, spotted black.
Male duller, smaller; little or no chestnut on back.
Size F 16, M 15 cm. **Habitat** moist grasslands.

RAOU Atlas 013

175 Painted Button-quail *Turnix varia*

Hatchling

Female eye red. Crown, face, breast flecked white.
Chestnut shoulder; thin white streaking above.
Male duller, smaller. **Size** F 20, M 19 cm. **Habitat** grassy
forests, woodlands.

RAOU Atlas 014

176 Chestnut-backed Button-quail *Turnix castanota*

Stout bill. Eye yellow. Breast grey-buff with fine whitish
streaks. **Female** larger; back cinnamon, mottled black or
chestnut, also fine white streaks; contrasts with plain
cinnamon rump, tail. **Male** duller. **Size** F 18, M 17 cm.
Habitat grassy woodlands.

RAOU Atlas 015

177 Buff-breasted Button-quail *Turnix olivei*

Similar to Chestnut-backed except bill heavier; breast
plain buff. **Female** larger. **Male** duller. **Size** F 20, M 19 cm.
Habitat grassy woodlands.

RAOU Atlas 016

178 Black-breasted Button-quail *Turnix melanogaster*

Eye white. **Female** larger; black head; breast scalloped
with bold white spots. **Male** paler; less black on head.
Size F 20, M 19 cm. **Habitat** rainforests, lantana thickets.

RAOU Atlas 017

179 Little Button-quail *Turnix velox*

Female heavy grey-blue bill. Eye yellowish or white. Flanks
whitish. Brownish above, faintly streaked white. Rump, tail
reddish-buff, whitish sides. **Male** dark scales on side of neck.
Size F15, M14 cm. **Habitat** dry to arid woodlands, grasslands.

RAOU Atlas 018

180 Red-chested Button-quail *Turnix pyrrhothorax*

Female like Little Button-quail but darker above. Throat,
breast, flanks orange-buff. **Male** duller; black scallops on
side of neck. **Size** F 15, M 14 cm. **Habitat** grasslands.

RAOU Atlas 019

181 Plains-wanderer *Pedionomus torquatus*

Bill long, thin; long, narrow nasal apertures. Iris very
pale yellow. Plumage soft. Wing rounded, soft. Legs, feet
yellow to greenish-yellow; legs longer than button-
quails'. Toes long; hind toes short, prominent.

Dorsal flight

Female larger; usually sandy-red feathers with narrow
black lines. Chestnut patch on breast; collar of black and
white feathers. Breast, upper abdomen with small black
crescents. **Male** paler; buff and white; collar
inconspicuous. **Size** F 17-18, M 15-17 cm. **Juv.** like male.
Voice repetitive 'oom'. **Habitat** native grasslands, old
stubble. Runs crouched, may spread wings; stands erect;
crouches motionless; seldom flies. Rare.

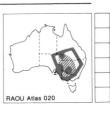
RAOU Atlas 020

Note The Plains-wanderer now known to be a wader, not related to
the Button-quails but probably most closely allied to the Seed-snipes.
(See Family Pedionomidae account on p. 315.)

182 Buff-banded Rail *Gallirallus philippensis*

Race *australis:* Bill brown, shorter than Lewin's. Front of eyebrow white. Chestnut eye-stripe and nape. Throat grey. Upperparts, cap, wings brown; blackish feathers, edged with white spots. Upper chest to underparts black with white bars. Buffy-orange mid-chest band. Legs pink-brown. Race *yorki:* Smaller with narrower darker breast band. **Size** 29-33 cm. **Nestling** sooty-black. **Juv.** duller. **Voice** squeeky 'sswit sswit'; loud throaty croaks; at nest a low clucking. **Habitat** grassy, reedy or thickly vegetated areas usually close to water.

Nestling

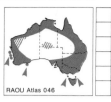

RAOU Atlas 046

183 Lewin's Rail *Dryolimnas pectoralis*

Much smaller than Buff-banded Rail. Bill long, black-tipped, basal two-thirds reddish. Chestnut cap, black streaked. Eyebrow and nape chestnut. Throat, chest olive-grey. Black feathers of upperparts margined olive-brown. Belly to undertail black, barred white. Undertail has two lateral streaks of white. Feet flesh-coloured. **Size** 21-23.5 cm. **Nestling** sooty-black. **Juv.** black head; white bars duller. **Voice** wide variety of soft clicks, crowings, low groanings. **Habitat** like Buff-banded Rail; prefers coastal regions.

Flight

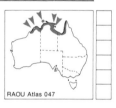

RAOU Atlas 045

184 Chestnut Rail *Eulabeornis castaneoventris*

Swamphen-sized. Bill green but tip horn. Head grey. Throat pink-grey. Neck, all of upperparts olive-chestnut. Glossy pink-chestnut underparts. Grey thighs. Legs olive-yellow. **Male** larger. **Size** 44-52 cm. **Nestling/Juv.** not yet described. **Voice** raucous 'wack, waka, wah-wah' often and rhythmically repeated. Also grunting notes. **Habitat** mangroves.

Calling

RAOU Atlas 047

185 Red-legged Crake *Rallina fasciata*

Smaller than Buff-banded Rail and Red-necked Crake which it resembles. Bill reddish or brown; base red. Head, neck, breast rich rufous. All upperparts olive and chestnut with white barring on wings. Mid-chest to vent black, barred white. Legs red. **Size** 19-24 cm. **Juv.** brown instead of chestnut; duller white barrings. Legs brownish. **Voice** unknown. **Habitat** wet areas in open country, scrub and forest. Asian vagrant.

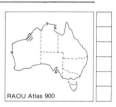

RAOU Atlas 900

186 Red-necked Crake *Rallina tricolor*

Bill green. Head, neck and chest rich chestnut; throat buffy. Upperparts dark slate-grey. Abdomen, lower flanks, vent and undertail sooty-black with dull rufous cross bars. **Size** 27-28 cm. **Juv.** bill duller; duller chestnut and olive upperparts. Duller bars below. **Voice** loud and descending 'raak, rah-rah-rah'; 'kih'; 'toh, toh' or 'plop-plop-plop' often heard in wet season; grunts like piglets. **Habitat** rainforest near water.

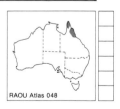

RAOU Atlas 048

183 Nestling

183 Juv.

183

185

182

186

184

187 Corncrake *Crex crex*

Larger than Australian Crake. Bill pale brown, short and stubby. Iris hazel. Eyebrow before and behind eye, and throat grey. Buffy eye-stripe. Cap, hind neck and upperparts black; feathers edged buff-grey. Chest buff-grey; flanks and undertail with brown bars; whitish vent. Wings bright chestnut. Legs pale brown. **Size** 25.5-26.5 cm. **Voice** 'rerp rerp'. **Habitat** meadows, lush vegetation, crops.

Flight

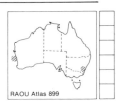

RAOU Atlas 899

188 Baillon's Crake *Porzana pusilla*

Smallest of Aust. crakes. Bill olive-brown. Eye red. Cap, hind neck ochre-brown, streaked black. Eyebrow light blue-grey. Eye-stripe ochre-brown. Upperparts ochre-brown, streaked black; wings have faint white spots on feather edges. Underparts light blue-grey, paler on throat, breast and abdomen. Flanks and undertail coverts barred black and white. Legs olive-brown. **Size** 15-16 cm. **Nestling** greenish-black. **Juv.** browner below, duller bars on underparts. **Voice** 'chutt, krekk' also a trill when alarmed. **Habitat** well vegetated, freshwater to brackish swamps. Often walks over water weed.

Undertail pattern

RAOU Atlas 050

189 Australian (Spotted) Crake *Porzana fluminea*

Largest of Aust. *Porzana* species. Bill olive-green, orange-red at base. Eye red. Cap, neck and upperparts dark olive-brown, streaked black and finely spotted white. Lores black. Face, chest pale slate-grey. Lower flanks black, barred white. Undertail coverts white. Legs olive-green. **Size** 19-21 cm. **Nestling** sooty-black. **Juv.** bill may have a little red at base is dull yellow. Upperparts brownish; buff feather edges. All underparts brown with white tips to feathers; abdomen, flanks have dull brown bars on white. **Voice** many calls; 'doo-ik'; high pitched 'chatter-chatter'; 'kirrik-kirrik-kirrik'; also whine. **Habitat** well-vegetated swamps, estuaries and lagoons.

Undertail pattern

RAOU Atlas 049

190 Spotless Crake *Porzana tabuensis*

Slightly smaller than Australian Crake. Bill black. Iris red. Dark slate-grey head, chin and underparts. Rest of upperparts chocolate-brown. Barred undertail. Legs red. **Size** 18-19 cm. **Juv.** duller brown; iris black. **Voice** a sharp 'kikk, blop-blop-blop' like engine starting; 'krroo'. **Habitat** reedy and grassy freshwater swamps.

Undertail pattern

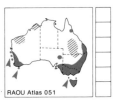

RAOU Atlas 051

191 White-browed Crake *Poliolimnas cinereus*

Small, similar to Spotless Crake. Bill olive-yellow, base red. Cap, lores and eye-stripe blackish. Eyebrow, stripe below dark eye-stripe, and throat, all white. Upperparts black with olive-brown feather margins. Cheeks, upper breast and upper flanks grey. Abdomen white; lower flanks and undertail coverts sandy-buff. Legs olive-green. **Size** 18-19 cm. **Juv.** facial markings duller; cap brown; neck buff. **Voice** various 'nasal' squealing notes. **Habitat** well-vegetated swamps, often walking onto lilypads like a Jacana.

Undertail pattern

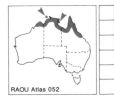

RAOU Atlas 052

187

188 Juv.

188

190 Juv.

190

189 Juv.

189

191 Juv.

191

N. Day

192 Bush-hen *Amaurornis olivacea*

Bill green. Small frontal shield orange. Iris brown. Cap to mantle olive-brown; browner towards tail. Sides of head to abdomen pale slate-grey. Vent dull pink-chestnut. Legs yellow. **Size** 25-26 cm. **Nestling** black; at 5-6 weeks brown with black head. **Juv.** paler; bill all green. **Voice** long, repeated 'nee-u', followed by a shuddering sound. Also clicks and grunts, and a single note repeated. **Habitat** swamps, flooded grasslands, rainforest fringes.

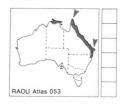

RAOU Atlas 053

193 Tasmanian Native-hen *Gallinula mortierii*

Swamphen-sized. Bill yellow. Iris ruby-red. Upperparts olive-brown, browner on wings. Underparts slate-grey. White patch on flank. Tail, abdomen black. Legs yellow. **Size** 43-45 cm. **Nestling** black down; white spot on flanks. **Juv.** paler. **Voice** frequent 'see-saw'; alarm call; loud scream; low-pitched grunts. **Habitat** grassy regions, usually near water.

Calling

RAOU Atlas 054

194 Black-tailed Native-hen *Gallinula ventralis*

Moorhen-sized. Bill green; base of lower mandible orange. Iris yellow. Upperparts olive-brown. Tail black. Throat to breast blue-grey. Abdomen, undertail coverts black; flanks with pear-shaped white spots. Legs coral-pink. **Size** 32-36 cm. **Nestling** green, black down. **Juv.** paler; spots duller. **Voice** sharp alarm call; very quiet single cackle. **Habitat** close to water, often in open, sheltering in bushes. Runs in groups.

Running tail down

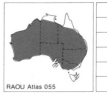

RAOU Atlas 055

195 Dusky Moorhen *Gallinula tenebrosa*

Slightly smaller than Swamphen. Bill, frontal shield red, tip yellow. Iris olive. Body slate-grey. Wings, rump browner. Tail black. White sides to undertail coverts. Legs yellow, scarlet and olive. **Size** 35-38 cm. **Nestling** black with white tips to chin and throat. Skin on cap bluish. Frontal shield red. **Juv.** paler; bill green, horn or black. Legs green. **Voice** many shrill notes. **Habitat** fresh water, usually near reeds.

Flight

Juv.

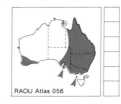

RAOU Atlas 056

196 Purple Swamphen *Porphyrio porphyrio*

Race *melanotus*: Brick-red bill and frontal shield. Red eyes. Head, upperparts black. Underparts, wings deep blue to purple-black. White undertail coverts. Legs red. Race *bellus* of SW Aust. is paler blue on the underparts. **Size** 44-48 cm. **Nestling** black. Bill grey-white, black tip. Legs grey, becoming redder with age. **Juv.** plumage, iris, bill all browner. **Voice** harsh screaming noise 'hee-ow'. **Habitat** swamps, marshy paddocks.

Flight

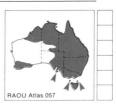

RAOU Atlas 057

197 Eurasian Coot *Fulica atra*

Slightly smaller than Moorhen. Bill, frontal shield white. **Male** frontal shield large; **Female** smaller. Eyes red. Head black. Body dark slate-grey. Legs dark grey; toes lobed. Moulting birds show browner body, wing plumage. **Size** 32-39 cm. **Nestling** black down with yellow hair-like tips; face red; bill cream. **Juv./Imm.** pale throat; smaller, duller than adults. **Voice** various shrill notes. **Habitat** swamps; open, deep lakes; often in large flocks (rafts) on water.

Flight

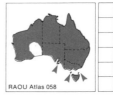

RAOU Atlas 058

198 Kori (Australian) Bustard *Araeotis kori*

Male crown black. White eyebrows. Neck white and finely vermiculated. Black breast band. Back, wings, tail brown, finely marked with buff. Upperwing coverts black and white. Underparts white to grey. Legs, feet pale yellow to grey or olive; has three toes. **Female** narrow brown crown. Neck, breast off-white to grey. Breast band thinner, often not visible. Less black and white on wing. **Size** M stands up to 1 m. F stands up to 0.7 m. **Chick** downy; striped buff and brown. **Voice** males have guttural roar, uttered during display. Harsh barking cry when alarmed; otherwise mainly silent. **Habitat** open grasslands, grassy woodlands, pastoral land, crops. Stately erect posture, head usually tilted upwards. Often stands motionless for extended periods when being observed. Flight slow, powerful; neck, legs extended. Breeding display of males very spectacular: white throat-sac extends to the ground and swings as male steps from side to side, tail raised over back exposing white undertail coverts.

Flight

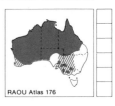

RAOU Atlas 176

Cryptic posture

199 Brolga *Grus rubicundus*

Stately long-legged grey crane with 'bustle' of secondary feathers falling over rump. Head bare; skin on front of crown pale grey. Scarlet on rear of head and nape. Black 'haired' dewlap under chin. Eye yellow. Ear coverts grey. Neck, back silver-grey; back often with brown wash. Wings grey with black primaries. Underparts grey. Legs dark grey-brown to black. **Female** slightly smaller. **Size** stands up to 1.4 m; **Chick** downy; grey with paler markings. **Imm.** skin of face and nape fleshy-pink. **Voice** whooping trumpet uttered in flight and on ground; also harsh croaks. **Habitat** often pairs or parties in shallow swamps, wetlands, pastoral lands. Flies with neck, legs extended; shallow wing beats with upward flick. Dancing displays of leaps, bows, high steps and loud trumpeting calls are performed by both sexes. Brolgas often soar in thermals.

Trumpeting

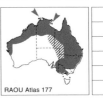

RAOU Atlas 177

200 Sarus Crane *Grus antigone*

Stately long-legged grey crane with 'bustle' of secondary feathers falling over rump. Head, upper neck bare. Scarlet skin on face and upper neck distinguish it from the Brolga. Crown grey. Eye red. *No* dewlap under chin. Back, wings grey. Some white feathers in 'bustle'. Underparts grey. Legs, feet pink. Race in Aust. is *sharpei*. **Size** stands up to 1.5 m. **Imm.** skin on head, upper neck pale rufous. **Voice** whooping trumpet uttered in flight and on ground; also harsh croaks. **Habitat** often pairs or parties in shallow swamps, wetlands, pastoral lands. Mixed flocks of Brolgas and Sarus Cranes have been recorded so observe carefully. Flies with neck and legs extended. Dancing displays of leaps, bows, high steps and loud trumpeting calls are performed by both sexes.

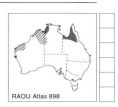

RAOU Atlas 898

200

199

199 Dancing

200

199

199 Imm.

♂ 198

♀ 198

198 Chick

199 Chick

198 Imm.

201 Comb-crested Jacana *Irediparra gallinacea*

Forehead, comb red. Bill green-yellow, tipped brown.
Cheeks golden-yellow. Crown, hind neck, breast band
black. Brown upperparts. Belly, neck white. Long, dull
green legs; extremely long toes. **Size** 23 cm. **Imm.** comb
small; crown brown; breast white. **Voice** squeaky 'pee pee
pee'; shrill alarm call. **Habitat** swamps, lakes, lagoons.
Walks on floating plants.

Hatchling

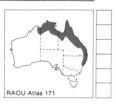
RAOU Atlas 171

202 Pheasant-tailed Jacana *Hydrophasianus chirurgus*

Non-breeding neck pale golden bordered by line of black,
becoming brown. Upperparts dark olive-brown;
underparts white. **Breeding** (unlikely in Aust.). **Size** 31 cm.
Habitat open swamps. First Aust. record in doubt; second
near Kununurra, WA. Not yet confirmed on Aust. list.

Breeding

203 Bush Thick-knee *Burhinus grallarius*

Small black bill. Forehead buff; pale buff eyebrow. Large
yellow eye. Black eye-stripe through neck. Black streaking
on grey-brown upperparts; buff-white underparts. Whitish
shoulder patch. **Size** 55 cm. **Voice** mournful, wailing 'wee
loo' usually at night. **Habitat** open woodlands, sometimes
near beaches. Singly or pairs. Active at night. 'Skulking'
habits; 'rigid' movements. Formerly called Southern Stone
Curlew.

Dorsal flight

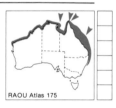
RAOU Atlas 174

204 Beach Thick-knee *Esacus magnirostris*

Large bill with yellow base, black tip. Large yellow eye.
Broad black eye patch; white bands above and below.
Upperparts brown; darker shoulder. White wing patches.
Throat, breast grey; underparts white. Legs olive-yellow.
Size 55 cm. **Voice** repeated, mournful, wailing 'wee loo';
higher, harsher than Bush Thick-knee. **Habitat** reefs, beaches,
coastal mud-flats. Formerly called Beach Stone Curlew.

Flight

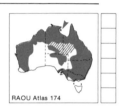
RAOU Atlas 175

205 Painted Snipe *Rostratula benghalensis*

Long, drooped, pinkish bill. **Female** chestnut-black hood.
White eye patch, crown stripe. Curved white collar.
Delicate black, green, grey and buff patterns above.
Male/Imm. smaller, duller; more buff. Eye patch, crown
stripe buff. Wings prominently spotted. **Size** F 25 cm,
M 22 cm. **Voice** booming in display. **Habitat** marsh with
moderate cover. Likely to 'freeze' when approached. Flight
fast; rail-like.

Hatchling

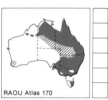
RAOU Atlas 170

206 Pied Oystercatcher *Haematopus ostralegus*

Race *longirostris*: Black with white belly, vent, rump and
half wing-stripe. Bright red eye, eye-ring and bill. Pink
legs. **Size** 48 cm. **Juv.** duller bill, eyes; grey legs.
Voice double 'per-peep'; during display rapid 'pee-pee-pee-
pee'. **Habitat** coastal; prefers beaches, estuaries.

Hatchling

RAOU Atlas 130

207 Sooty Oystercatcher *Haematopus fuliginosus*

Race *fuliginosus*: All black. Red eye, eye-ring and bill.
Pink legs. Race *opthalmicus* (N Aust.) has broader red
eye-ring. **Size** 48 cm. **Voice** like Pied. **Habitat** coastal;
prefers rocky coastline; occasionally estuaries.

Hatchling

RAOU Atlas 131

Note   Recent evolutionary research places the Plains-wanderer (p. 82)
closer to the Painted Snipe than its present position.

201

201
Imm.

202
Non-breeding

205 ♂

205 ♀

205 ♀

203

204

206

206
Juv.

206

207
Race fuliginosus

207
Race opthalmicu

208 Masked Lapwing (Plover) *Vanellus miles*

Brown above; white below. Prominent yellow facial wattles; wing spurs. Black crown, flight feathers. Race *miles* (N Aust.): wattle extends behind eye. Race *novaehollandiae* 'Spur-winged Plover' (SE Aust.): smaller rounded wattle, black hind neck and sides of breast. Hybrids occur. **Size** 35 cm. **Juv.** buff tips to all black and brown dorsal plumage. **Voice** loud 'kerr-kick-ki-ki-ki'; single 'kek'. **Habitat** grasslands, mud-flats, urban parks; calls at night.

Hatchling

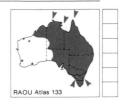
RAOU Atlas 133

209 Banded Lapwing (Plover) *Vanellus tricolor*

Brown above; white below. Red lore wattle. Yellow bill and eye-ring. White line behind eye. Black crown, side of neck, breast band. White wing-stripe. **Size** 25 cm. **Juv.** crown brown, mantle, wing coverts, etc. edged buff. **Voice** crying 'er-chill-cher'. **Habitat** open grasslands, bare plains, fallow/ploughed paddocks. Often heard calling at night.

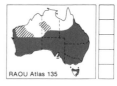
RAOU Atlas 135

210 Grey Plover *Pluvialis squatarola*

Larger, greyer than Lesser Golden Plover. Large head. **Non-breeding** bill black, longer, bulkier than Lesser. Small, pale eyebrow. Mottled grey back. In flight axillaries (armpit) black. Underparts white. White wing bar, rump. White tail, barred black. Legs dark grey. **Breeding** marbled silver and dark grey above. Black belly; white vent. **Size** 28 cm. **Habitat** like Lesser Golden Plover.

Ventral flight

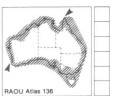
RAOU Atlas 136

211 Lesser (Pacific) Golden Plover *Pluvialis dominica*

Race *fulva*: **Non-breeding** bill black. Eye large. Broad eyebrow, buff to whitish. Golden-buff to cream spots over dark upperparts to tail. Breast golden-brown to cream. Underwing dark grey. Indistinct wing bar. White underparts. Legs dark grey-black. **Breeding** bright gold above, dark mottling. Black from throat to undertail coverts; divided from upperparts by white line from eyebrow to flanks, white bars to sides of undertail coverts. **Size** 25 cm. **Voice** 'too weet'. **Habitat** beaches, mud-flats, sometimes inland.

Ventral flight

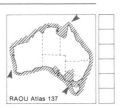
RAOU Atlas 137

212 Eurasian Golden Plover *Pluvialis apricaria*

Like Lesser Golden Plover race *fulva*, except underwing, face white; bit larger. **Size** 27 cm. **Habitat** as Lesser Golden Plover. Suspected vagrant. No claimed Aust. sighting.

Ventral flight

213 Red-kneed Dotterel *Erythrogonys cinctus*

Brown above; white below. Hood, nape, breast band black. White throat. Flanks chestnut, edged white. Trailing wing-edge white. Legs brown-grey; red knees. **Size** 18 cm. **Juv.** brown instead of black; no breast band. **Voice** 'chet chet'. **Habitat** edges of swamps.

Hatchling

RAOU Atlas 132

214 Hooded Plover *Charadrius rubricollis*

Red bill has black tip. Red eye-ring. Black head; white collar. Lower neck, side of breast black; pale grey-brown above. Broad white wing bar. Tail, rump black, edged white. **Size** 19-21 cm. **Juv.** head pale; darker about eye. **Voice** short piping calls. **Habitat** ocean beaches, sometimes coastal lakes. Inland salt lakes in WA.

Hatchling

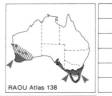
RAOU Atlas 138

208
Race *miles*

208
Race *novaehollandiae*

208
Race *miles*

209

209

210
Non-breeding

211
Breeding

211
-breeding

211
Non-breeding

210
Breeding

210
Non-breeding

212
Non-breeding

213

213 Juv.

213

214

223
Black-fronted
Plover Juv.

214 Juv.

214

N. Ray.

215 Ringed Plover *Charadrius hiaticula*

Breeding grey-brown above; white below. Orange bill has black tip. Orange eye-ring. Black band through eye, with black band above white forehead. Eyebrow black above but white *behind* eye. White collar, black breast band. White wing bar. Legs orange. **Non-breeding** areas of black duller; white eyebrow complete. Breast band incomplete. **Size** 18 cm. **Voice** 'too-li' or 'coo-eep'. **Habitat** shores, marshes. Rare migrant.

Breeding

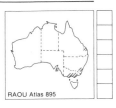

RAOU Atlas 895

216 Little Ringed Plover *Charadrius dubius*

Race *dubius:* Like Ringed Plover but smaller, browner. Bill black. Eye-ring yellow. *Lacks* white wing bar. Legs orange. **Size** 15 cm. **Voice** 'pee-oo'. **Habitat** shores, marshes. Rare migrant.

Breeding

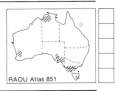

RAOU Atlas 851

217 Mongolian Plover *Charadrius mongolus*

Non-breeding small, black bill. Lores dark brown. Dark eye patch. Dark brown-grey above; white below. Faint grey breast band. **Breeding** chestnut-red nape and breast. Throat white, cut off from breast by a slender black line. Distinctive black eye patch and edge to white forehead. Narrow white wing bar. Legs greyish. **Size** 19-20 cm. **Voice** 'drit drit'. **Habitat** shores, marshes, rarely inland.

RAOU Atlas 139

218 Double-banded Plover *Charadrius bicinctus*

Breeding grey-brown above; white below. Bill short, slender, black. Forehead, eyebrow white. Upper chest-band black; lower band broader, chestnut. White wing bar. Legs yellow-grey or grey-green. **Non-breeding** tinged buff; browner than Mongolian and Large Sand Plovers. **Size** 18-19 cm. **Voice** loud, staccato 'pit-pit'; rapid trill. **Habitat** beaches, mud-flats, grasslands, bare ground.

Head pattern
Juv.

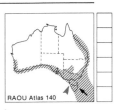

RAOU Atlas 140

219 Large Sand Plover *Charadrius leschenaultii*

Non-breeding like Mongolian. Bill longer, heavier. Face paler; lores often incompletely marked grey-brown. Uniform pale grey-brown above; white below. Broader wing bar. Legs dusky-greenish. **Breeding** narrow chestnut chest band. **Size** 20-23 cm. **Voice** 'chweep-chweep'. **Habitat** like Mongolian.

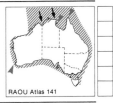

RAOU Atlas 141

220 Caspian Plover *Charadrius asiaticus*

Like Oriental Plover except underwing white; smaller; shorter legs. **Size** 21 cm. **Habitat** like Oriental Plover. Vagrant.

Underwing pattern

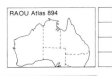

RAOU Atlas 894

221 Oriental Plover *Charadrius veredus*

Slender, long-legged plover. **Non-breeding** fine black bill. Buffy-white eyebrow, throat. Uniform grey-brown upperparts, tail and faint chest band. No wing bar. White below. Legs dusky-olive. **Breeding** white head; faint brown cap, ear coverts. Chestnut breast separated from white belly by black line. **Size** 22-25 cm. **Voice** nasal 'chit-chit'; 'chrreep'. **Habitat** dry inland plains, occasionally coastal.

Underwing pattern

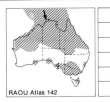

RAOU Atlas 142

216
Non-breeding

215
Non-breeding

215

216

217
Breeding

217
Non-breeding

217
Non-breeding

218
Breeding

218
Non-breeding

218
Non-breeding

219
Non-breeding

219
Breeding

221
Breeding

220
Non-breeding

221
Non-breeding

219
Non-breeding

221
Non-breeding

222 **Red-capped Plover** *Charadrius ruficapillus*

Hatchling

Small. **Male** rufous crown nape, collar; partly edged black. Black eye-stripe, bill, legs. White forehead. Upperparts brown. White wing bar and black rump line in flight. **Female** similar; crown duller; black less distinct. **Non-breeding** upperparts plain grey-brown. **Size** 15 cm. **Juv.** upperparts edged buff. **Voice** sharp 'twink'; piping calls. **Habitat** sandy areas, coastal and inland. Runs in short spurts. (Compare Kentish Plover: vagrant; p. 274.)

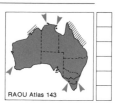

RAOU Atlas 143

223 **Black-fronted Plover** *Charadrius (Elseyornis) melanops*

Hatchling

Small plover with brown upperparts, pale streaks and chestnut shoulder patch. Bill bright red, tip black. Face white; black forehead and black eye-line. Underparts white. Broad black 'V' on chest. **Size** 16 cm. **Juv.** no black on chest. **Voice** metallic 'pink'. **Habitat** margins of freshwater lakes, farm dams; rarely tidal areas. Nomadic. Flight jerky, reveals white wing bars; alights, runs.

RAOU Atlas 144

224 **Inland Dotterel** *Peltohyas australis*

Hatchling

Small. Bill short, black. Upperparts yellowish-buff, streaked dark grey-brown. Forehead, face, upper breast white-buff. Black bar across crown to below large eye. Black mark behind eye joins black collar, extends to a 'V' on chest. Rich chestnut inverted 'V' below black 'V', separates white abdomen from lower breast and dark buff flank. Legs buffy-grey. **Size** 20 cm. **Juv./Non-breeding** may lack black markings. **Voice** mostly silent. **Habitat** ploughed ground, open sparse plains and gibber. Well camouflaged.

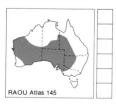

RAOU Atlas 145

225 **Black-winged Stilt** *Himantopus himantopus*

Hatchling

Adult race *leucocephalus*: white; black nape patch, back wings. Long, fine black bill. Red eye. Long coral-pink legs trail in flight. **Size** 36-38 cm. **Imm.** head, nape patch greyish. **Juv.** ashy crown; neck white (no black nape). Back, wings brownish, feathers edged buff. **Voice** yelps. **Habitat** fresh and salt-water marshes. Flooded paddocks.

RAOU Atlas 146

226 **Banded Stilt** *Cladorhynchus leucocephalus*

Hatchling

Breeding white. Prominent red-brown breast band above deep brown mid-belly patch. Long, fine black bill. Eye dark brown. Wings brown-black; white trailing edge in flight, legs flesh-pink; shorter than Black-winged Stilt; trail in flight. **Non-breeding** breast band mottled or absent. **Size** 36-45 cm. **Juv.** underparts white; legs duller. **Voice** single or double 'yook'; 'chogga'. **Habitat** fresh, salt-water marshes, marine mud-flats. Large ephemeral lakes. Often in dense flocks; frequently swims. Nomadic (and migratory?).

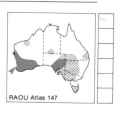

RAOU Atlas 147

227 **Red-necked Avocet** *Recurvirostra novaehollandiae*

Hatchling

Body white. Head, neck chestnut. Long black bill *upcurved* (more steeply in male). Black wing bar, wing-tips, and stripes down side of back are distinctive in flight. Long pale blue-grey legs trail in flight. **Size** 40-46 cm. **Juv.** paler; grey on scapulars. **Voice** yelps, wheezes; musical 'toot toot'. **Habitat** salt lakes, mud-flats, marshes, shallow inland waters. Gregarious, often swims.

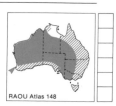

RAOU Atlas 148

227

226 Juv.

225 Imm.

226

225

224

226

225

222

223

Kentish Plover

222 ♂

227

225 Imm.

225 Juv.

226 Juv.

225

222 ♀

222 Juv.

224

223 Juv.

224 Imm.

223

228 Ruddy Turnstone *Arenaria interpres*

Distinctive, thickset, blăck and white wader (especially in flight). Short, wedged-shaped bill. Short orange legs. **Non-breeding** dark brown above and breast band. **Breeding** chestnut upperparts; pied head; black breast band. **Size** 21-25 cm. **Voice** loud rattle. **Habitat** rocky shores.

Juv.

RAOU Atlas 129

229 European Curlew *Numenius arquata*

Like Eastern Curlew but shorter bill. *No* eyebrow or crown stripe. White lower back and rump. Tail barred. **Size** 54-58 cm. Vagrant.

RAOU Atlas 893

230 Eastern Curlew *Numenius madagascariensis*

Large wader. Very long down-curved black bill; pink at base. Pale eyebrow. Streaked dark brown and buff above, including rump. Slightly paler below. **Size** 53-61 cm. **Voice** mournful 'karr-er'; higher 'kerlee-kerlee'. **Habitat** estuaries, mud-flats, mangroves, sandspits.

Bill length

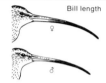

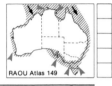
RAOU Atlas 149

231 Whimbrel *Numenius phaeopus*

Race *variegatus:* Like Eastern Curlew but smaller. Bill much shorter. Paler eye-stripe, crown stripe. White lower-back, rump. Race *hudsonicus* (rare) brown rump. **Size** 38-43 cm. **Voice** shrill chattering 'tee-tee-tee'. **Habitat** as Eastern Curlew, occasionally inland.

Race *hudsonicus*

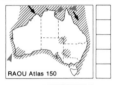
RAOU Atlas 150

232 Little Curlew *Numenius minutus*

Like Lesser Golden Plover; slightly larger. Long down-curved grey bill; lower-base pink. **Size** 31-36 cm. **Voice** flute-like double whistle. **Habitat** open plains, grasslands, sometimes mud-flats.

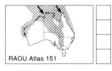
RAOU Atlas 151

233 Upland Sandpiper *Bartramia longicauda*

Generally upright stance; 'plover-like'. Long tail, neck. Buffy coloured, heavily dark-streaked. Bill short, tip slightly down-curved; yellowish base. Small head; dark crown. Large, brown eye; white eye-ring. Rump, tail dark-centred, edged white. Underwing barred. Legs, feet yellowish. **Size** 28-32 cm. One old record.

Underwing pattern

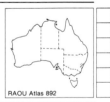
RAOU Atlas 892

234 Wood Sandpiper *Tringa glareola*

Sharp-tailed Sandpiper-sized. Medium, straight, black bill. Longish neck. Back and dark wings spotted white. White rump; tail thinly barred black. Pale, plain underwing. Yellow-greenish legs. **Size** 20-23 cm. **Juv.** wing spots golden. **Voice** loud, rapid, four-note whistle. **Habitat** fresh water; marsh with light cover. Jerky movements. High zigzag flight.

Underwing pattern

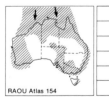
RAOU Atlas 154

235 Green Sandpiper *Tringa ochropus*

Like Common Sandpiper. In flight diagnostic pattern of uniform dark brown upperparts (appearing blackish; no wing bar) contrasts with brilliant white rump. Uppertail broadly barred black. Underwing blackish. **Size** 23 cm. **Habitat** usually fresh water, especially ditches. Vagrant.

Flight

228
Breeding

228
Breeding

228
Non-breeding

229

230

230

231
Race *variegatus*

233

231

232

232

233

234
Juv.

234

234

235

235

236 Grey-tailed Tattler *Tringa brevipes*

Bill straight, grey with nasal groove. White eyebrow.
Light grey above. Grey breast; white below. Legs
yellowish. **Breeding** thinly barred brown-grey below.
Size 26 cm. **Voice** fluty 'troo-eet'; 'weet-eet'.
Habitat estuaries, rocky coasts, reefs.

237 Wandering Tattler *Tringa incana*

Like Grey-tailed. In hand, *deep* section of nasal groove
longer. Eyebrow less distinct. Darker above.
Breeding underparts boldly barred brown-grey. **Size** 27 cm.
Voice trill 6-10 notes 'whee-wee-wee'. **Habitat** reefs, rocks.

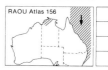

238 Common Sandpiper *Actitis hypoleucos*

White eyebrow, shoulder mark. Brown; finely scaled black
above and on breast sides. White below. **Size** 20 cm.
Habitat banks, rocks near water. Bobs head, tail. Low jerky
flight, shows broad white wing bar; dark centre to rump.

239 Greenshank *Tringa nebularia*

Bill slightly upturned, black, bluish base. Upperparts
grey. Forehead, underparts white; underwing barred.
White on rump extends up back in wedge. Long green
legs trail in flight. **Size** 31-35 cm. **Voice** ringing 'tew-tew'.
Habitat coastal, inland lakes. Nervous. Bobs head.

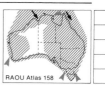

240 Spotted Greenshank *Tringa guttifer*

Like Greenshank. Bill stouter; yellowish base. Underwing
white. Legs short, barely trail in flight. **Breeding** obvious
spotting across breast. **Size** 30 cm. **Voice** loud piercing
'keyew'. **Habitat** as Greenshank.

241 Redshank *Tringa totanus*

Like Greenshank but browner above. Red bill base, legs.
Upperwing with a broad white trailing edge. **Size** 28 cm.
Voice loud 'then-hu-hu'. **Habitat** as Greenshank. Rare
migrant.

242 Lesser Yellowlegs *Tringa flavipes*

Like Wood Sandpiper but larger with long, slender,
straight bill and long neck. Legs bright yellow or orange;
trail in flight. **Size** 27 cm. **Voice** soft, high 'ti-di-ti', 'ti-
dup'. **Habitat** as Greenshank. Vagrant.

243 Marsh Sandpiper *Tringa stagnatilis*

Like a tiny, paler Greenshank. Bill straight, needle-like.
Forehead, underparts white. Legs greenish; trail in flight.
Size 20-23 cm. **Voice** soft 'tee-oo'. **Habitat** as Greenshank,
prefers fresh water.

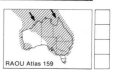

244 Terek Sandpiper *Xenus cinereus*

Grey above; white below. Long slightly upturned bill.
Thin white trailing edge to wings. Yellow to orange legs.
Size 22-23 cm. **Voice** fluty trill 'weeta-weeta-weeta'; rapid
'tee-tee-tee'. **Habitat** coastal mud-flats, occasionally inland.

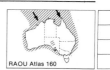

236

238

236
Non-breeding

237
Non-breeding

239

238

239
Non-breeding

240
Non-breeding

241

242

242
Non-breeding

241
Non-breeding

243

244

243
Non-breeding

244
Non-breeding

N. Day

245 Latham's (Japanese) Snipe *Gallinago hardwickii*

Long bill; brown base. Crown dark brown, cream centre.
Dark eye-stripe, cheek stripe. Rest of face pale cream.
Body mottled black, brown, buff; scapulars pale-edged.
Belly white; flanks barred. Tail tip white. **Size** 24-26 cm.
Voice rasping 'shik'. **Habitat** wet grasslands; open, wooded
swamps. Well camouflaged. Erratic flight, often at late dusk.

Tail pattern

16-18 feathers

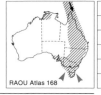

RAOU Atlas 168

246 Pin-tailed Snipe *Gallinago stenura*

Smaller than Latham's. Barring on the back indistinct;
shorter wings. **Size** 23-25 cm. **Voice** abrupt 'charp'.
Habitat as Latham's. Rare migrant to N Aust.

24-28 feathers

RAOU Atlas 852

247 Swinhoe's Snipe *Gallinago megala*

Like Latham's; shorter wings. **Size** 24-26 cm. **Voice** short
'shrek'. **Habitat** as Latham's. Migrant to N Aust.

20-24 feathers

RAOU Atlas 169

248 Asian Dowitcher *Limnodromus semipalmatus*

Great Knot-sized; leg length like godwits. Long, straight
black bill; 'swollen' tip. Plumage like Bar-tailed Godwit.
White tips to secondaries. **Size** 25-35 cm. **Voice** single yelp.
Habitat coastal flats, occasionally inland. Rare migrant.

Breeding

RAOU Atlas 939

249 Black-tailed Godwit *Limosa limosa*

Long, straight bill; pink base. Uniform grey-brown; white
below. White rump, wing bar, underwing. Black flight
feathers, borders to underwing and tail. **Breeding** russet head,
belly. **Size** 36-43 cm. **Habitat** tidal flats, occasionally inland.

Bill length
♀

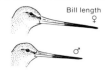

♂

RAOU Atlas 152

250 Bar-tailed Godwit *Limosa lapponica*

Bill long, slightly upturned; pink base. White rump; tail
barred grey-brown. Upperparts, underwing finely barred and
mottled grey-brown. **Breeding male** head, belly rich chestnut-
red. **Size** 38-45 cm. **Habitat** tidal flats, rarely inland.

Bill length
♀

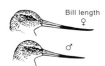

♂

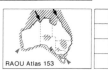

RAOU Atlas 153

251 Hudsonian Godwit *Limosa haemastica*

Like Black-tailed Godwit. Bill slightly upturned.
Underwing almost all black. Wing bar less distinct than
Black-tailed. Less white in rump. **Size** 45 cm. **Habitat** as
other godwits. Vagrant.

♀

Non-breeding

252 Red Knot *Calidris canutus*

Robust, straight, 3 cm bill. Dumpy. **Non-
breeding** upperparts uniform grey; white below.
Breeding rust-red. **Size** 25 cm. **Voice** throaty 'knut' or 'kloot
kloot'. **Habitat** tidal mud-flats, rarely inland.

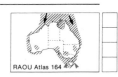

RAOU Atlas 164

253 Great Knot *Calidris tenuirostris*

Like Red Knot but larger, much longer bill (4-5 cm);
heavily streaked above. **Breeding** head, neck striped black.
Black breast spotted white. **Size** 28 cm. **Voice** occasional
'nyut-nyut'. **Habitat** as Red Knot.

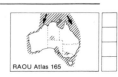

RAOU Atlas 165

246

245

247

245

251
Non-breeding

249
Non-breeding

249
Breeding

249
Non-breeding

250
Non-breeding

250
Juv.

250
Breeding

250
Non-breeding

248
Non-breeding

253
Breeding

253
Non-breeding

250
Breeding

248
Non-breeding

253
Non-breeding

252
Juv.

252
Breeding

252
Non-breeding

252
Non-breeding

254 Sharp-tailed Sandpiper *Calidris acuminata*

Straight black bill; dull olive base. Chestnut crown. Back feathers have black centres, buff edges. Black through rump. Indistinct wing bar. Dark streaked and speckled breast and flanks to undertail sides. White belly. Olive legs. **Voice** 'wit-wit'. **Habitat** inland waters, coastal.

263 Curlew Sandpiper

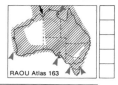

RAOU Atlas 163

255 Pectoral Sandpiper *Calidris melanotos*

Like Sharp-tailed, but smaller head, bill longer; base yellow. Streaked 'V' on breast distinct from white belly. Crown brown, streaked dark, *not* chestnut. Legs yellow. **Voice** reedy, rasping 'krrrt'. **Habitat** prefers inland swamps.

RAOU Atlas 978

256 Cox's Sandpiper *Calidris paramelanotus*

As Pectoral, but bill long, down-curved, black; shorter than Curlew Sandpiper. Small head. Breast *not* strongly marked. Line in white rump thinner. Streaks on undertail coverts. Legs olive; same length or shorter than Pectoral. **Breeding** heavy dark bars below; do not confuse with Dunlin (extremely rare). **Voice** like Pectoral; shriller. **Habitat** marshes, saltworks. Rare; a 'mystery'; perhaps hybrid.

257 Baird's Sandpiper *Calidris bairdii*

Feathers above black, scaled buff. Wings project well past tail at rest. Rump dark. Legs dark olive. **Breeding** deeper buff. **Size** 18 cm. Vagrant.

RAOU Atlas 890

258 White-rumped Sandpiper *Calidris fuscicollis*

Like Baird's; white rump. **Size** 19 cm. Vagrant.

RAOU Atlas 849

259 Western Sandpiper *Calidris mauri*

Like Red-necked Stint. Bill little longer, down-curved. Feet semi-webbed. **Breeding** crown, nape, cheeks rusty; breast, flanks chevroned. **Juv.** rufous scapulars. **Size** 17 cm. Doubtful in Aust.

260 Little Stint *Calidris minuta*

Non-breeding as Red-necked. **Breeding** obvious white throat. Back feathers black centres, chestnut edges. Incomplete orange breast band has dark streaks. Cream 'V' on mantle. **Juv.** streaked black, chestnut above. White 'V' on mantle. **Voice** 'tit'. **Size** 14 cm. **Habitat** as Red-necked. Rare migrant.

RAOU Atlas 857

261 Red-necked Stint *Calidris ruficollis*

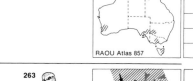

Non-breeding short, black bill. Grey-brown above; white below; thin black line through rump. Obvious white wing bar. **Breeding** back feathers have black centres, chestnut edges. Head, neck, breast pink-chestnut. Legs black. **Size** 15 cm. **Voice** 'chit, chit'; high pitched trill. **Habitat** coastal, inland shores.

263 Curlew Sandpiper

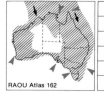

RAOU Atlas 162

262 Long-toed Stint *Calidris subminuta*

Alert posture

Stint-sized 'Sharp-tail'. Long, yellow legs trail in flight. **Breeding** upperparts edged chestnut. **Size** 15 cm. **Voice** rapid 'chre-chre-chre'. **Habitat** inland swamps, rarely coast.

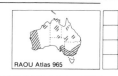

RAOU Atlas 965

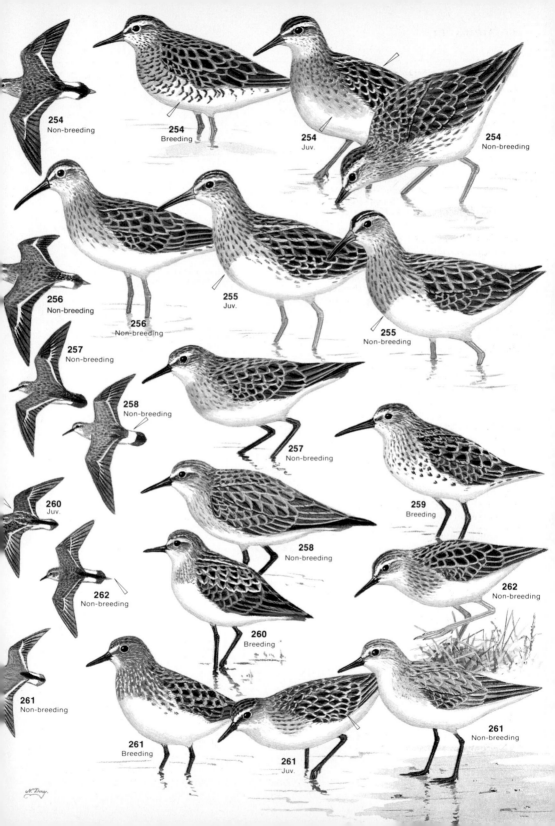

254
Non-breeding

254
Breeding

254
Juv.

254
Non-breeding

256
Non-breeding

256
Non-breeding

255
Juv.

255
Non-breeding

257
Non-breeding

258
Non-breeding

257
Non-breeding

259
Breeding

260
Juv.

258
Non-breeding

262
Non-breeding

262
Non-breeding

261
Non-breeding

260
Breeding

261
Breeding

261
Juv.

261
Non-breeding

N. Day.

263 Curlew Sandpiper *Calidris ferruginea*

Bill long, black, down-curved. **Non-breeding** grey-brown above. Broad white wing bar; white rump. White below. Legs black. **Breeding** copper-red below, barred black. **Size** 21 cm. **Voice** loud 'chirrup'. **Habitat** coastal, inland mud-flats.

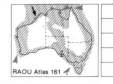

RAOU Atlas 161

264 Dunlin *Calidris alpina*

Like Curlew Sandpiper; smaller. Black centre to rump. **Non-breeding** grey-brown above; white below. Broad white wing bar in flight. **Breeding** chestnut above; black belly. **Size** 20 cm. **Voice** nasal 'tree'. **Habitat** as Curlew Sandpiper. Vagrant.

RAOU Atlas 888

265 Sanderling *Calidris alba*

Larger than Red-necked Stint; longer bill. **Non-breeding** white face, underparts. Silver-grey back. In flight broad white wing bar, blackish forewing. Lacks hind toe. **Breeding** chestnut face, breast. **Size** 20 cm. **Habitat** beaches, rarely inland.

Juv.

RAOU Atlas 166

266 Buff-breasted Sandpiper *Tryngites subruficollis*

Medium-sized sandpiper; 'plover-like' stance. **Non-breeding** small round head. Short straight black bill. All buff-brown above (includes rump, breast) with dark spots. No wing bar. Buff underparts. Underwing white with a dark bar on greater primary coverts. Legs long, yellow-orange. **Size** 21 cm. **Voice** harsh 'krik'; 'tik'. **Habitat** grass near water. Vagrant.

Underwing pattern

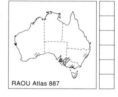

RAOU Atlas 887

267 Broad-billed Sandpiper *Limicola falcinellus*

Slightly larger than stint with long, black bill, heavy at base, drooped at tip. **Non-breeding** crown streaked black; *double* white eyebrow. Dark shoulder patch and line through rump. Slender white wing bar. Legs dark olive. **Breeding** upperpart feathers black centred, buff or rufous edges. **Size** 18 cm. **Voice** trilling. **Habitat** coastal mud-flats, occasionally inland.

Head from above

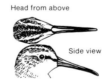

Side view

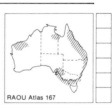

RAOU Atlas 167

268 Ruff (Reeve) *Philomachus pugnax*

Much larger than Sharp-tailed Sandpiper. Small head; long neck; long legs. **Non-breeding** bill straight. Dark brown and buff above (colour variable); scaly look. Head, neck, light grey-brown, streaked darker. Breast light greyish-brown. Whitish below. In flight, white oval patches on sides of dark rump. Legs green, yellow, to red. **Breeding male** develops erectile ruff, ear tufts of various colours. **Breeding female** darker barring above. **Size** M 30, F 23-27 cm. **Voice** 'tu-whit' when flushed. **Habitat** inland wetlands; rarely coast. Rare migrant.

Breeding

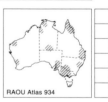

RAOU Atlas 934

269 Stilt Sandpiper *Micropalama himantopus*

Superficially like Curlew Sandpiper but larger. Long yellowish legs; *no* wing bar. **Breeding** blackish upperparts, pale fringes. Chestnut ear coverts and nape. Underparts heavily barred black. **Size** 21 cm. **Voice** 'too too'. **Habitat** swamps. Vagrant.

263
Breeding

263
Non-breeding

263
Non-breeding

263
Juv.

264
Non-breeding

264
Breeding

264
Non-breeding

265
Non-breeding

265
Breeding

265
Non-breeding

267
Non-breeding

267
Breeding

267
Non-breeding

269

266

266

268 ♀
Non-breeding

269

268
Non-breeding

♂ **268**
Non-breeding

270 Red-necked Phalarope *Phalaropus lobatus*

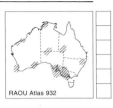

Non-breeding bill black, needle-like. Broad black eye patch. Slender neck. Dusky-grey above, striped white. White below. White wing bars and 'braces' in flight. Black line through rump. Feet lobed. **Breeding female** broad bright rufous neck stripe. Rest of head black. White throat. Blackish above with buff streaks. **Breeding male** much duller. **Size** 17-20 cm. **Voice** 'chek' or 'chik-chik-chik'. **Habitat** oceans, bays, swamps, lakes. Mostly swims for food, bobs head, spins around in circles. Rare migrant.

RAOU Atlas 932

271 Wilson's Phalarope *Phalaropus tricolor*

Bill much longer, even more needle-like than Red-necked Phalarope. **Non-breeding** uniform pale grey above; forehead, eyebrow, underparts white. Grey curving eye-stripe. Tail grey. White rump. Greenish legs. Superficially similar to Marsh Sandpiper; distinguish by shorter, finer bill; shorter legs; lobed feet; lack of white on lower back. **Breeding female** broad black eye-stripe extends down sides of neck to red-brown shoulder, back stripes. Crown, back of neck grey; buffy lower neck. **Breeding male** much duller. White nape spot. **Size** 22-25 cm. **Voice** low-pitched honking. **Habitat** lagoons, lakes, mud-flats, swamps. Feeds by swimming. Occasionally spins. Few Aust. records.

RAOU Atlas 886

272 Grey Phalarope *Phalaropus fulicarius*

Shorter, stouter bill than other phalaropes, tipped black; often yellowish at base (adults). **Non-breeding** grey above; white below. Large black eye patch. Uniform grey upperparts; black line through rump. White wing bar. Feet lobed. **Breeding female** forehead, crown black. Face white. Black above, scaled buff. Entire underparts red-brown. **Breeding male** duller, paler. **Size** 19-22 cm. **Voice** shrill 'twit'. **Habitat** oceans, bays, lakes, swamps. Vagrant.

273 Oriental Pratincole *Glareola maldivarum*

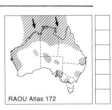

Non-breeding upperparts olive-brown. Bill black; red at gape. Throat buff, edged with broken line of black streaks. Breast dusky grey. White rump. Tail white, dark-tipped, shallow fork. Underparts whitish. In flight swallow-like, showing chestnut underwing coverts and trailing edge black. Legs short, black. **Breeding** bill, gape brighter red. Throat light buff; bordered black. **Size** 23 cm. **Voice** tern-like 'chik chik'; soft 'towheet-towheet'. **Habitat** open plains, bare ground around swamps, claypans. Hawks insects; sometimes in huge flocks.

Dorsal flight

RAOU Atlas 172

274 Australian Pratincole *Stiltia isabella*

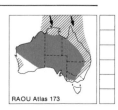

Very slender; long wings. Bill red with black tip. Golden buff above and on upperwing coverts; grey on back. Primaries black. Dark chestnut on flanks to legs. Square tail white, with triangular black sub-terminal mark. Wings project well beyond tail when perched. Legs very long, grey. **Juv.** bill duller. **Size** 22-24 cm. **Habitat** open plains of semi-arid regions; winters on coast in N Aust.

Dorsal flight

RAOU Atlas 173

273 Breeding

273 Breeding

273 Non-breeding

274

274 Juv.

274

273 Breeding

243 Marsh Sandpiper Non-breeding

270 Non-breeding

272 Non-breeding

271 Non-breeding

270 ♀ Breeding

272 Breeding ♀

271 Breeding ♀

270 Non-breeding

243 Marsh Sandpipe Non-breeding

272 Non-breeding

271 Non-breeding

275 Great Skua *Catharacta skua*

Race *lonnbergi*: Large, stocky, gull-like. Bill black. Short tail. Chocolate-brown, flecked buff; boldly streaked buff on back. Dark brown wings with broad white primary bases. Legs black. **Size** 61-66 cm. **Juv.** reddish tinge to upper body. **Habitat** coastal, oceanic. Flight direct, powerful flapping and gliding. All skuas are piratic.

Wing moult

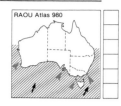

RAOU Atlas 980

276 South Polar Skua *Catharacta maccormicki*

Like Great Skua but smaller. **Light morph** light grey-brown body; pale collar contrasts with dark upperparts. **Dark morph** dark brown to blackish; nape sometimes paler; paler around bill. **Size** 55 cm. **Juv.** bill base, legs blue. Chin, throat paler. **Habitat** oceanic. Few records.

Dark morph

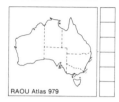

RAOU Atlas 979

277 Arctic Jaeger *Stercorarius parasiticus*

Small skua. Small head. Slender wings. Two long, pointed, central tail streamers. **Light morph breeding** bill, cap black. Collar, throat, upper breast buff. Brown breast band. Belly white. Upperparts, wings brown-grey, little contrast with trailing edge. Underwing dark grey. Bases of primaries white. Tail black, white base. Legs black. **Light morph non-breeding** head paler. Black and white barring on flanks, upper and undertail coverts. Often *lacks* tail streamers. **Light morph Juv.** like non-breeding. Bill base paler. Legs black and blue. Brown above, barred buff and rufous. Underwing coverts barred brown, rufous and white. Short pointed tail streamers. **Dark morph breeding** dark brown: cap black; yellow collar, cheeks. **Dark morph non-breeding** white bars on rump. **Dark morph Juv.** faint buff to rufous bars below. **Size** 40-45 cm. **Habitat** oceanic, coastal, often in bays. All jaegers are piratic.

Juv.

Underwing pattern

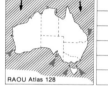

RAOU Atlas 128

278 Pomarine Jaeger *Stercorarius pomarinus*

Like Arctic but larger. Head, bill bigger; body bulkier. All plumages as Arctic Jaeger but wing flashes usually larger. Central streamers short, rounded; twisted when fully grown. Legs black and blue. Non-breeding birds have broader white bars on rump. **Size** 45-50 cm. **Juv.** upperparts brownish; faint to pale barring; *no* rufous bars. Underwing coverts with brown and white bars. **Habitat** more oceanic than Arctic.

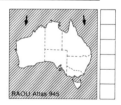

RAOU Atlas 945

279 Long-tailed Jaeger *Stercorarius longicauda*

Like Arctic but body smaller; slender wings; tern-like flight. Long tail with double-length streamers 'pin-like' near tips. Bill sheath blue to horn. Upperparts pale blue-grey, *not* brown; contrasting black secondaries and primaries (usually no white in wing). Legs black to black and blue. **Non-breeding** pale head. Barred flanks, tail coverts. **Juv.** greyish to dark brown above (no rufous), scaled buff-white. Rump, flanks, underwing coverts barred grey and white. White crescents on primary bases. Short central tail feathers *rounded*. **Size** 40-45 cm. **Habitat** oceanic.

Non-breeding
Underwing pattern

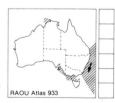

RAOU Atlas 933

277
Light morph
Breeding

277
Dark morph

275

Crested Tern

277
Light morph
Non-breeding

278
Non-breeding

275

276
Light morph

276
Light morph

278
Juv.

278
Dark morph
Breeding

278
Light morph
Breeding

279
Juv.

279
Breeding

58
Wedge-tailed Shearwater

277
Juv.

279
Juv.

280 Silver Gull *Larus novaehollandiae*

Body white. Soft parts red. Iris white. Mantle grey.
Upperwings, inner primaries grey. Outer wing region from
carpal white, with black sub-terminal band through
primaries, white-tipped; three white mirrors (spots).
Size 41 cm. **Juv.** soft parts dark. Faint brown ear patch.
Upperparts mottled brown. Sub-terminal tail band
brownish. **Habitat** coastal, inland waters.

Hatchling

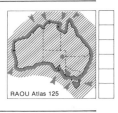

RAOU Atlas 125

281 Pacific Gull *Larus pacificus*

Thick yellow bill; both mandibles tipped red. Eye pale.
Body white. Black mantle and wings with white trailing
edge; black outer primaries. Tail white; thin black sub-
terminal band. Legs yellow. **Size** 63 cm. **Juv.** dark soft parts.
Body dark brown, slightly mottled. Tail black, tip white.
Imm. (1st-3rd year) whiter on body; blacker on back and
wings; matures in four years. **Habitat** coastal.

Imm: 3 yrs
Plumage varies

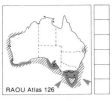

RAOU Atlas 126

282 Kelp Gull *Larus dominicanus*

Like Pacific Gull but finer bill. Red spot on lower bill.
White tips and mirrors (spots) on primaries. Broader
trailing edge. Tail white. Legs olive-yellow. **Size** 57 cm.
Juv. like Pacific juv., but paler, with black band on
secondaries. Ages like Pacific. **Habitat** coastal.

Imm: 2 yrs
Plumage varies

RAOU Atlas 981

283 Lesser Black-backed Gull *Larus fuscus*

Like Kelp Gull. See: Grant, P. J. (1981), *Gulls: A Guide to
Identification*, T. & A. Poyser, Calton, UK. Recent N Aust.
record rejected; species *is* a possible straggler to Aust.

Adult

284 Black-tailed (Japanese) Gull *Larus crassirostris*

Breeding bill lemon, tipped red with a black sub-terminal
band. Eye honey. Body white. Slate-grey back and
upperwings. White trailing edge ends at central primaries;
rest of primaries black. Tail white with black sub-terminal
band. **Non-breeding** grey markings on head. Legs olive-
brown. **Size** 47 cm. **Imm.** greyer head extending to flanks.
Broad tail band. **Juv.** bill flesh-pink, tip black. Vagrant.

Juv.

Breeding adult

RAOU Atlas 856

285 Franklin's Gull *Larus pipixcan*

Breeding black hood. White eyelids. Black bill, tipped red.
Upperwings, back slate-grey; white trailing edge curves
behind black outer band on white-tipped primaries. *New*
underpart feathers have pink tinge. Tail white, with pale
grey centre. Legs red. **Non-breeding** black *hind* crown to
eyes; streaked crown; white frons, throat. Blackish legs.
Size 35 cm. **Imm.** like non-breeding; outer primaries black;
black sub-terminal tail band. Vagrant.

Juv.

Breeding adult

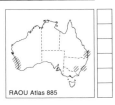

RAOU Atlas 885

286 Sabine's Gull *Xema sabini*

Breeding black hood. Black bill, tipped yellow. *Forked*
white tail. Upperwing has grey shoulder, black outer
primaries with white tips and white triangular trailing
edge. **Non-breeding/Imm.** white head; dark nape. **Juv.** eye
to mantle and shoulders scaly grey-brown. Tail tip black.
Size 34 cm. Vagrant.

Juv.

Breeding adult

RAOU Atlas

Note The Laughing Gull *Larus atricilla* and Black-headed Gull *Larus
ridibundus* are new and confirmed recent records for Australia (see
pp. 274, 275 for descriptions and colour plates).

287 **Whiskered (Marsh) Tern** *Chlidonias hybrida*

Large head on chunky body. Short tail has slight fork.
Long legs. **Breeding** short, thick, crimson bill; cap black;
cheek white. Pearl-grey above. Black belly, white vent.
Non-breeding as breeding; bill dusky red. Forehead, crown
white; some streaking at rear of black cap. Underparts white.
Size 25.5-27 cm. **Juv.** like non-breeding adult but bill
blackish; crown has more black; mantle variegated: dusky
and buff; faint shoulder bars. **Habitat** lakes, estuaries.

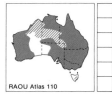

RAOU Atlas 110

288 **White-winged (Black) Tern** *Chlidonias leucoptera*

Small head, body. Short red bill. Short, almost square
tail. **Breeding** head, mantle, breast, belly black.
Upperwing mid-grey; whitish shoulder bars. Underwing
coverts black, primaries grey. **Non-breeding** bill black;
black on crown extends in a lobe to ear coverts behind and
below eye. Central nape black, may be streaked white;
white mask. Upperparts mid-grey. Rump, underparts
white. Dusky shoulder bar. Underwing white, trailing
edge grey. **Size** 22-24 cm. **Juv.** like non-breeding adult but
contrasting blackish mantle, back. **Habitat** lakes, estuaries.

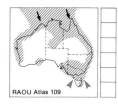

RAOU Atlas 109

289 **Black Tern** *Chlidonias nigra*

Like White-winged Tern but long slender bill; longer
wings and tail (which is obviously forked). **Breeding** bill
black; very like White-winged except mid-grey mantle,
back, tail, wing coverts. **Non-breeding** like White-winged;
look for blackish droop extending from mantle on to
breast sides, and white underwing coverts (beware
moulting White-winged). **Size** 24-25.5 cm. **Juv.** darkest of
Chlidonias at this age; upperwing, mantle, back dark
grey; brownish fringes to latter. **Habitat** lakes, estuaries,
oceans. Very rare in Aust.

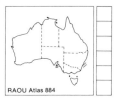

RAOU Atlas 884

290 **Caspian Tern** *Sterna caspia*

The largest tern. Massive red bill. **Breeding** bill has dusky
sub-terminal mark. Cap black. Pale grey above; white
below. Primaries entirely blackish below. **Non-
breeding** black eye, ear coverts. Forehead, crown white;
fine black streaks increasing to nape. **Size** 50-56 cm.
Juv. like non-breeding adult but bill paler; forehead to
nape grey-buff; streaked black. Mantle variegated: dusky
and buff. **Habitat** coastal, inland watercourses.

Hatchling

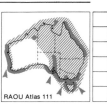

RAOU Atlas 111

291 **Gull-billed Tern** *Sterna nilotica*

Race *macrotarsa:* Very pale, chunky tern; slightly forked
tail. Short, thick, black bill. Long black legs.
Breeding cap black. Upperparts whitish-grey; underparts
white. Underwing white with thick blackish trailing edge
to most of primaries. **Non-breeding** black ear coverts; rest
of head white; usually has faint, dark crown streaks.
Size 35-43 cm. **Juv.** like non-breeding adult but crown
greyish-brown, finely streaked and darker than adult.
Mantle variegated: dusky and pale buff. Race *affinis:*
Smaller; darker above contrasting with whiteness of head
and white underparts; an uncommon non-breeding
summer visitor to N Aust. **Habitat** coastal flats, inland
lakes, ploughed and fallowed fields.

Hatchling

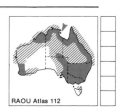

RAOU Atlas 112

287 Non-breeding

289 Breeding

288 Breeding

287 Juv.

288 Juv.

289 Juv.

287 Breeding

287 Non-breeding

289 Non-breeding

288 Non-breeding

289 Non-breeding

288 Non-breeding

287 Breeding

291 Non-breeding

290 Breeding

290 Juv.

290 Non-breeding

291 Breeding

291 Juv.

291 Non-breeding

291 Breeding

290 Breeding

290 Non-breeding

N.DAY

292 Common Tern *Sterna hirundo*

Race *longipennis*: **Breeding** black, mid-length bill. Cap to
bill black. Belly, upperparts mid-grey; rest white. Tail
streamers shorter than folded wings. Underwing *opaque*
against light, with black trailing edge on outer half of
wings. Brown, mid-length legs. Other races vary: black-
tipped, red bill; red legs. **Non-breeding** black bill. Frons
underparts white. Black shoulder bar. Rump, tail pale
greyish, *no* contrast with back. Tail shorter. **Size** 37 cm.
Voice 'ki-ork'; 'kik-kik-kik'. **Habitat** oceans, bays. Race
longipennis common; race *hirundo* rare; race *minussensis* one
specimen, Goolwa, South Australia.

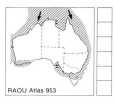

RAOU Atlas 953

293 Arctic Tern *Sterna paradisaea*

Like Common; smaller body. In flight, head projects less
past long slender wings. Contrasting white rump. Shorter
bill. Crown more domed. Shorter legs. **Breeding** bill red.
Tail streamers project past primaries (longer in Roseate).
Legs red. In flight, under primaries strongly *translucent*
against light, with a strongly defined black trailing edge
of constant width. **Non-breeding** bill blackish. Top of
crown, frons white; head black at rear. Legs darker.
Size 36 cm. **Habitat** oceans, coastal. Rare.

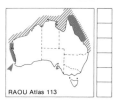

RAOU Atlas 952

294 Roseate Tern *Sterna dougallii*

Much smaller body than other Aust. 'commic' terns. Wings,
long legs red. **Breeding** bill very long, slender, slightly
drooped; varies from red with black tip, to black with red
base. Cap black. Upperparts, tail pale grey. When
developed, tail streamers longer than other 'commic' terns.
White below; new plumage has soft pink tinge.
Underwing white. **Non-breeding/Imm.** black bill.
Forehead like Common. Underparts white. Upperwing
slender, black wing bar; outer primaries black due to
suspended moult. Legs blackish. **Size** 32 cm. **Juv.** crown
feathers edged silver. Scapulars banded black, white edges.
Tail short; feathers blotched black sub-terminally.
Voice 'chew-ich'; grating 'aach'. **Habitat** oceanic.

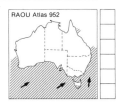

RAOU Atlas 113

295 White-fronted Tern *Sterna striata*

Largest 'commic' tern. **Breeding** bill, cap black; separated
by white frons. Upperparts pale grey; *no* rump contrast.
Underwing white. Folded primaries show a white line
along upper edge. Underparts white. Tail white, a little
longer than primaries. Legs dusky-red. **Non-breeding**
forehead like non-breeding Common Tern. **Size** 39 cm.
Juv. upperparts, central tail feathers boldly barred blackish.
Upperwing has broad black triangle on shoulder. Dark outer
primaries; the rest whitish. **Voice** 'kech kech'; 'kee-ech-
kee-ech'. **Habitat** oceanic.

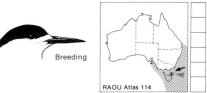

Breeding

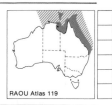

RAOU Atlas 114

296 Black-naped Tern *Sterna sumatrana*

Bill black. Head, underparts, tail white. Thin black line
from eye front on to nape. Upperparts pale grey. Tail
deeply forked. Legs black. **Size** 31 cm. **Juv.** bill base dusky
yellow. Distinguish from juv. Roseate by grey nape and
whitish-grey bases to dark-fringed upperpart feathers;
bulkier body, shorter legs. **Habitat** coastal, oceanic.

294 Juv.

296 Juv.

Head pattern

RAOU Atlas 119

Note The Antarctic Tern *Sterna vittata* is a recent and confirmed
record for Australia (see p. 275 for description and colour plate).

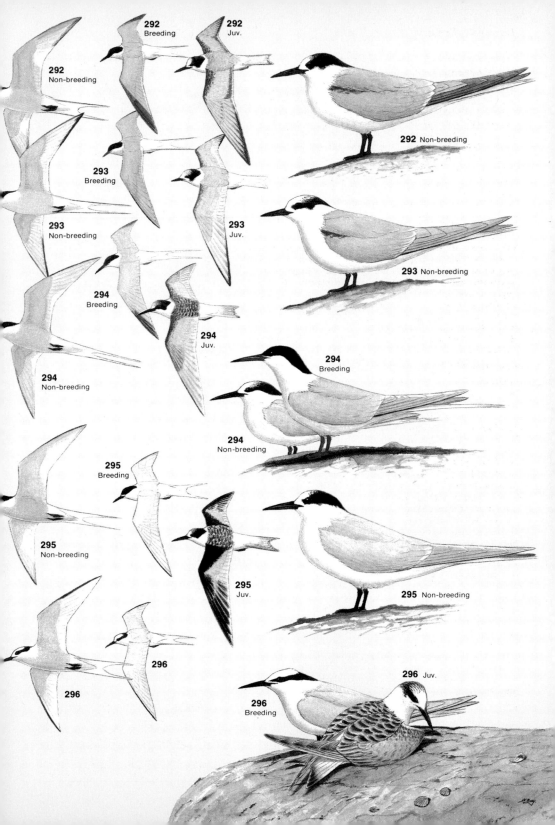

292 Non-breeding

292 Breeding

292 Juv.

292 Non-breeding

293 Breeding

293 Non-breeding

293 Juv.

293 Non-breeding

294 Breeding

294 Juv.

294 Non-breeding

294 Breeding

294 Non-breeding

295 Breeding

295 Non-breeding

295 Juv.

295 Non-breeding

296

296

296 Juv.

296 Breeding

297 Sooty Tern *Sterna fuscata*

Broad, triangular, white forehead patch. Upperparts black. Tail deeply forked, outer tail feathers white. Underparts white; faint grey on belly when breeding. Underwing white; primaries, secondaries black. **Size** 40-46 cm. **Juv.** dark brown upperparts; feathers tipped pale buffish to white. Underwing coverts pale grey; vent white. Tail short. **Habitat** oceans, islands.

Breeding

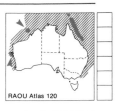

RAOU Atlas 120

298 Bridled Tern *Sterna anaethetus*

Like Sooty Tern but has less white on forecrown. White extends as an eyebrow past the eye. Back dark grey-brown. Underparts slightly darker grey when breeding. Underwing like Sooty but primary bases slightly silvery-grey. **Size** 36-42 cm. **Juv.** cap strongly streaked white. Lores white with a black mark in front of eye. Upperparts grey-brown, buffy-tipped. Underparts white; underwing same as adult. Tail shorter, less deeply forked. **Habitat** oceans, coasts, islands.

Breeding

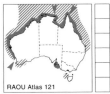

RAOU Atlas 121

299 Little Tern *Sterna albifrons*

Race *sinensis:* Very small grey and white tern with long, narrow wings; rapid wing beats. Smaller head, flatter crown, noticeably longer legs and body more slender than Fairy Tern. **Breeding** bill mid-yellow, *usually* black tip. Triangular white forehead from bill to above eye. Black line through lores. Rest of cap black. Pale grey upperparts contrast with forked white tail. Upperwing pale grey, contrasting with blackish outer three or four primaries. **Non-breeding** bill black. Lores to rear of crown white; black band remains from eye to nape. Upperwing has a dusty-greyish shoulder bar. Outer primaries slightly darker than remaining wing; these wear (abrade) to black. Legs blackish-brown. **Size** 20-23 cm. **Juv.** bill black, brownish base. Cap streaked dusky and buff; dark ear patch. Upperparts grey with dark sub-terminal feather bands and buffish fringes. Darker, broader shoulder bar than non-breeding birds. Secondaries grey, tipped white. **Habitat** coasts, sometimes inland watercourses.

Breeding

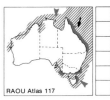

RAOU Atlas 117

300 Fairy Tern *Sterna nereis*

Like Little Tern but larger head with more rounded profile. Also has noticeably bulkier body, giving round-bellied appearance, and shorter, thicker legs. **Breeding** like Little Tern but bill all bright orange. Larger white forehead area. Lores white with black patch in front of eye. Pearl-grey upperparts give *less* contrast with whitish tail. Legs bright orange. **Non-breeding** bill dusky orange-brown, blackish at tip and often at base of upper bill. White *only* on forehead. Upperwing as breeding adult but outer primaries *less* contrasting; *no* dark shoulder bar. **Size** 22-24 cm. **Juv.** like juv. Little Tern but generally darker and *no* dark wing bar. Outer wing dark greyish, grading to pale grey inner wing, secondaries whitish (grey in Little Tern). **Habitat** coasts, occasionally inland watercourses.

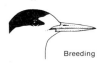

Breeding

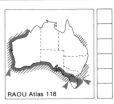

RAOU Atlas 118

298

297

297
Juv.

298
Juv.

298

297

297

298

300
Breeding

300
Non-breeding

299
Non-breeding

299
Breeding

299
Breeding

292
Common Tern
Non-breeding

300
Juv.

299
Juv.

299
Non-breeding

300
Breeding

300
Non-breeding

N. Day.

301 Crested Tern *Sterna bergii*

Breeding bill lemon-yellow; sometimes orange-yellow. Frons white. Cap black; short, shaggy crest on nape. **Non-breeding** forecrown black, scalloped white; rest of cap black. **Size** 43-48 cm. **Juv.** bill greenish-yellow; as non-breeding but cap black, extends as collar to throat sides. Upperparts variegated: dark grey and white. Black shoulder.

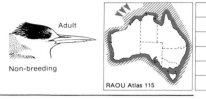

302 Lesser Crested Tern *Sterna bengalensis*

Breeding like Crested Tern but smaller. Smaller bright orange bill; paler grey upperparts. Front black to bill. **Non-breeding** upper crown white. **Juv.** bill dull orange. Variegated and paler than Crested. Shoulder bar paler grey; forehead, crown whiter. Feet, legs *often* dull orange. **Voice** like Crested, shriller. **Habitat** estuaries, seas, islands.

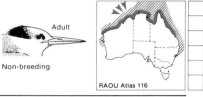

303 Common Noddy *Anous stolidus*

Largest noddy. Bill shorter, thicker than other noddies. Indistinct white crown. Black line through lores. Rest of bird brown. Tail long, wedged, with shallow central notch. Underwing grey-brown, edges blacker. **Size** 37-41 cm. **Juv.** like adult; upperparts have fine pale fringing; duller, poorly defined greyish-brown cap. **Voice** purring and 'kraa, kraa'. **Habitat** seas, islands. Glides low to sea, wings forward, slow wing beats.

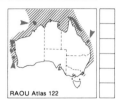

304 Lesser Noddy *Anous tenuirostris*

Like Black Noddy but shorter bill; head greyer, contrasts less with white cap. Frons grey. **Juv.** cap may be whiter. **Size** 30-34 cm. **Voice** rattling alarm; purring call. **Habitat** oceans, coastal islands.

305 Black (White-capped) Noddy *Anous minutus*

Smaller than Common Noddy. Longer, finer bill. Frons black. Distinguish in flight from Common Noddy by white cap, blackish body, black underwing, short tail with wider fork. **Juv.** like adult. **Size** 35-38 cm. **Voice** 'kirr'; cackling 'krik-krik-krik'. **Habitat** oceans, coastal.

306 Grey Ternlet *Procelsterna albivittata*

Small. Shape similar to Black Noddy. **Pale phase** pale grey; head, underparts whitish. Upperwing pale grey; dark grey trailing edge. Underwing white, trailing edge darker. **Dark phase** dark grey overall. Face, cap white; underwing grey. Long legs, black with yellow webs. **Size** 25-30 cm. **Juv.** brownish wash on upperparts. **Habitat** oceans. Feeds by bouncing on the water like storm-petrel.

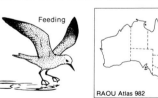

307 White Tern *Gygis alba*

White with black eye, primary shafts and upturned bill. Almost transparent wings. Tail short. Legs blue. **Size** 28-33 cm. **Juv.** dusky ear coverts, nape and mantle. **Habitat** oceans.

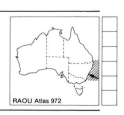

297 Sooty Tern Juv.

307

305

303

304

288 White-winged Tern Non-breeding

306

303

304 Juv.

304

307 Juv.

306

305

302 Juv.

302 Breeding

301 Non-breeding

301 Juv.

302 Non-breeding

301 Breeding

308 Banded Fruit-Dove *Ptilinopus cinctus*

Head, neck white. Breast band, upperparts black. Rump, belly mid-grey. Tail black; broad grey tip. **Size** 33-35.5 cm. **Juv.** pale grey head, tail. **Voice** strong, low, repeated cooing. **Habitat** forested gullies of rocky escarpments, woodlands.

Adult   Juv.

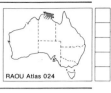

RAOU Atlas 024

309 Superb Fruit-Dove *Ptilinopus superbus*

Male crown purple. Cheeks pale green. Throat, breast blue-grey. Hind neck, collar orange. Upperparts green, spotted black; tail tip white. Black breast band; belly white. Green barred flanks. **Female** dull blue crown; *lacks* black breast band and orange on neck. **Size** 22-24 cm. **Juv.** as female, *lacks* crown patch. **Voice** five to six clear, deep whoops. **Habitat** rainforests, adjacent mangroves; eucalypt forests, scrublands with native fruits.

RAOU Atlas 023

310 Rose-crowned Fruit-Dove *Ptilinopus regina*

Male crown rose, edged yellow. Rest of head and breast blue, spotted white. Upperparts green-grey. Tail tip yellow. Abdomen orange. **Female** duller. Race *ewingii:* Crown paler, rose-pink; throat yellower. **Size** 22-24.5 cm. **Juv.** mostly green, *lacks* rose crown. **Voice** 'woo-hoo' repeated, becoming faster, ending in rapid 'hoo-hoo-hoo'. **Habitat** rainforests, monsoon and paperbark forests, eucalypt woodlands, vine groves, fruit trees.

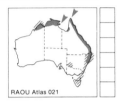

RAOU Atlas 021

311 Wompoo Fruit-Dove *Ptilinopus magnificus*

Dorsal view

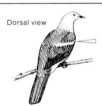

Head, neck light blue-grey. Eye red. Back, upperparts green; wing bar golden. Breast plum-purple; abdomen yellow. Races *keri* (Cairns-Atherton area) and *assimilis* (C. York Pen.) smaller than *magnificus* (south of Rockhampton). **Size** 35-55 cm. **Juv.** purple breast blotched green. **Voice** deep, carrying 'wallock-a-woo'; softer 'book-a-roo, book'. **Habitat** rainforests.

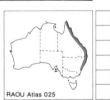

RAOU Atlas 025

312 Torresian Imperial-Pigeon *Ducula bicolor*

White; black eye. Primaries, end of tail, blackish. Belly scaled black. **Size** 38-44 cm. **Voice** deep 'coo woo'. **Habitat** coastal rainforests, mangroves, islands.

Ventral flight

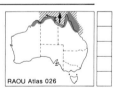

RAOU Atlas 026

313 Black-collared Fruit-Pigeon *Ducula mullerii*

Crown pink. Broad black collar. Mantle, sides of chest glossy claret. Silver-grey throat band between black collar and dark mauve-pink underparts. Wings, back, tail dark grey. Broad silver-grey mid-tail band. **Size** 43 cm. **Voice** little known. **Habitat** tree-lined creeks, low-lying woodlands.

Ventral view

314 Topknot Pigeon *Lopholaimus antarcticus*

Grey; black primaries. Long swept-back crest; grey in front; rusty behind. Black tail with pale grey central band. **Size** 40-46 cm. **Voice** occasional sharp screech. **Habitat** rainforests, adjacent woodlands or forests; palms; groves; fruit trees.

Ventral flight

RAOU Atlas 027

311

308

312

313

314

309
Juv.

310
Juv.

♀ 309

310 ♂

♂ 309

315 White-headed Pigeon *Columba leucomela*

Head, breast white; often with buff or grey wash. Back, wings, tail black with glossy margins to the feathers. Lower breast, abdomen, undertail grey. **Female** generally has some grey mottling to head and breast. Crown darker. **Size** 38-42 cm. **Juv.** crown, sides of head grey to brown; underparts mottled grey-brown. **Voice** low, mournful, repeated and ventriloquial 'oom coo'. **Habitat** rainforests and scrubs, occasionally in regrowth forest or isolated trees.

RAOU Atlas 028

316 Feral Pigeon *Columba livia**

Plumage immensely variable but with the basic pattern of blue-grey with glossy sheen on neck; wings black with a chequered pattern, or two black wing bars. **Size** 33 cm. **Voice** deep moaning 'cooo'; display call 'racketty-coo' or 'co-coo-coo-coo'. **Habitat** mainly urban areas, city buildings, crop margins along roads, railways. Flocks of racing pigeons may be seen.

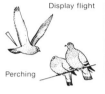

Display flight

Perching

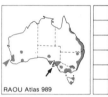

RAOU Atlas 957

317 Spotted Turtle-Dove *Streptopelia chinensis**

Head grey, tinged pink. Nape and back of neck black, spotted white. Wing, back and tail mottled dark and light brown. Underparts pinkish-fawn. Tail long. Undertail grey; outer feathers tipped white. Race *tigrina* differs from *chinensis* by having wing coverts streaked black, undertail coverts white, and feathers on front of wings lighter grey. **Size** 31.5 cm. **Juv.** lacks nape pattern. **Voice** mellow, musical 'coo', 'coocoo, croo' 'coo-coo-croo-coor'. **Habitat** cities; suburban gardens, parks; established grain-growing areas of coastal, eastern Australia. Raises and lowers tail on alighting.

Display flight

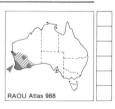

RAOU Atlas 989

318 Laughing Turtle-Dove *Streptopelia senegalensis**

Head, neck mauve-pink. Back brown with mauve-pink tinge. Broad black-spotted buffish band on lower throat. Breast mauve-pink, shading to white on abdomen. Shoulder, wings, lower back, and uppertail coverts slaty blue-grey. Outer tail tipped white. **Size** 25.5 cm. **Juv.** duller; without blue-grey on wings. **Voice** musical, laughing or bubbling 'coo coo coo'; 'coo oo coo'. **Habitat** city and suburban areas of Perth and surrounding region; Kalgoorlie and Esperence, WA.

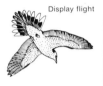

Display flight

RAOU Atlas 988

319 Brown Cuckoo-Dove *Macropygia amboinensis*

Dark copper-brown upperparts; iridescent on neck. Lighter cinnamon-brown underparts. **Female** chestnut on crown, dark mottling on throat and breast. Tail long. **Size** 38-43 cm. **Juv.** crown chestnut. Neck and upper breast finely barred black. Wings mottled brown and chestnut. **Voice** 'whoop-a-whoop', last note rising in tone and longer. **Habitat** rainforests, forest margins, regrowth thickets.

Feeding

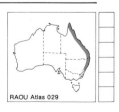

RAOU Atlas 029

* Introduced

319 ♀

319 ♂

315 ♂

Juv. 315

316

316

316

316

316

316

316

692 ♂
House Sparrow

693
Tree Sparrow

317
Juv.

318
Juv.

318

317

317

320 Peaceful Dove *Geopelia placida*

Race *tranquilla:* Forehead, throat blue-grey. Crown grey-brown, fine black streaks. Back, wings, grey-brown, buff-toned; breast blue-grey; *all* are barred black. Races *placida* darker, smaller; *clelandi* paler. **Size** 21-23 cm.
Juv. browner. **Voice** carrying 'woodle-woo', and 'woo-luk'; softer cooing. **Habitat** lightly timbered country near water.

Tail pattern

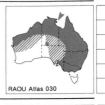
RAOU Atlas 030

321 Diamond Dove *Geopelia cuneata*

Red eye-ring. Blue-grey; smoky-brown back, wings. Fine white wing spots. **Female** browner. **Size** 19-20 cm.
Juv. browner with buff marks, appears banded. **Voice** soft, mournful; cooing. **Habitat** watercourses in woodlands, hills.

Tail pattern

RAOU Atlas 031

322 Bar-shouldered Dove *Geopelia humeralis*

Race *humeralis:* Hind neck, mantle bronze, scalloped black. Throat, upper breast blue-grey. Upperparts dark grey-brown, scalloped black. Wings in flight chestnut. Clinal colour changes occur. **Size** 26.5-30 cm. **Juv.** duller.
Voice 'cukoo-woop'; coos. **Habitat** scrubby bush, mangroves, eucalypt woodlands.

Tail pattern

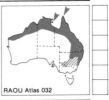
RAOU Atlas 032

323 Emerald Ground-Dove *Chalcophaps indica*

Race *chrysochlora:* Bill, legs reddish. Dull purple-brown head, neck and underparts, tinged wine-red. Wings emerald. White shoulder patch. **Female** shoulder grey. Race *longirostris:* Larger, less wine-red; female has white shoulder. Race *melvillensis* (Melville Is., NT): Paler. **Size** 23-25.5 cm. **Juv.** head, wings, underparts marked black. **Voice** low, repeated cooing. **Habitat** rainforests and wet eucalypt forests, mangroves.

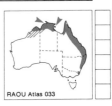
RAOU Atlas 033

324 Common Bronzewing *Phaps chalcoptera*

Male forehead cream; crown, sides of nape purple-brown. White line under eye. Back brown, feathers pale-edged. Metallic sheen on wings, back. Breast pink-brown. **Female** forehead grey; breast grey-buff. Races are clinal: *chalcoptera, murchisoni* and *consobrina*. **Size** 28-35 cm. **Imm.** duller. **Voice** resonant, deep, repeated 'oom'. **Habitat** dry forest, woodlands, mallee, heath, coastal scrub.

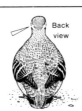
Back view

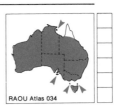
RAOU Atlas 034

325 Brush Bronzewing *Phaps elegans*

Eye-stripe, throat, back of neck, shoulder, rich chestnut. Crown buff. Back, wings, chestnut to brown with metallic feathers, tipped white. Breast blue-grey; darker below. **Female** dark grey-brown upperparts, *not* chestnut. **Size** 25-33 cm. **Imm.** like female, duller. **Voice** repeated, muffled 'oom'. **Habitat** woodlands, heathlands; some mallee areas.

Back view ♂

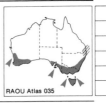
RAOU Atlas 035

326 Flock Bronzewing *Phaps histrionica*

Male head black. Frons, chin, ear-mark white. Back, wings rich sandy-brown. White upper-chest bar. Grey underparts. **Female** duller; head brown; white areas less distinct. **Juv.** as female; scalloped light brown. **Size** 27-30 cm. **Voice** usually silent. **Habitat** grassy plains, near water.

Flight

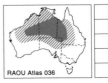
RAOU Atlas 036

320

321

322

323 Juv.

321
Juv.

323

♀ 326

325 ♀

♂ 326

325 ♂

324 ♀

324 ♂

327 Crested Pigeon *Geophaps lophotes*

Eye, eye-ring red. Grey body. Black crest upright, long, slender. Brown wings have conspicuous black bars, metallic green to purple patch. Abdomen brown. Tail tip white. Race *whitlocki* (central and northern WA): narrower black wing bars; less white on tail tip. **Size** 31-35 cm. **Juv.** duller. **Voice** explosive 'whoop'; low 'coo'. **Habitat** lightly wooded grasslands near water; roadsides; stubble; rail yards, towns in grain-crop areas.

Tail flick on alighting

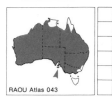

RAOU Atlas 043

328 Squatter Pigeon *Geophaps scripta*

Sexes alike. Crown, upperparts brown. Face black, white marks at eye, neck, chin, throat. Wings brown; pale feather margins give mottled effect. Breast blue-grey, deep white 'V' below. N Queensland morph: red eye-ring. **Size** 26-32 cm. **Juv.** duller; upperparts flecked chestnut. **Voice** low 'coo'. **Habitat** grassy plains; woodlands.

Crest erect

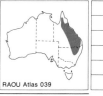

RAOU Atlas 039

329 Partridge Pigeon *Geophaps smithii*

Heavy black bill. Crown, neck, back, wings, tail brown. Bare facial skin red (race *smithii*, NT) or yellow (*blaauwi*, NW of WA), edged white. Throat white. Breast pink-brown. Black scallops on purple-grey breast patch. Deep white 'V' below. **Size** 25-28 cm. **Juv.** upperparts fine-flecked chestnut. **Voice** low 'coo'. **Habitat** grassy woodlands; open areas by water.

Crest erect

RAOU Atlas 040

Y = Yellow morph = Race *blaauwi*
R = Red morph = Race *smithii*

330A White-quilled Rock-Pigeon *Petrophassa albipennis*

Dark brown with light scalloping. Throat black, white spots. Outer primary bases show white (variable) in flight. Two races include: reddish morph *albipennis*; *boothi*, almost no white wing mark (Stokes Range area, NT). **Size** 28-32 cm. **Voice** loud 'coo-corook'; low 'coo'. **Habitat** sandstone gorges.

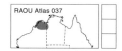

RAOU Atlas 037

330B Chestnut-quilled Rock-Pigeon *Petrophassa rufipennis*

Dark brown, light scalloping. Head, face, neck spotted grey. Throat white. Chestnut wing patch in flight. **Size** 28-32 cm. **Voice** like 330A. **Habitat** cliffs (W Arnhem Land).

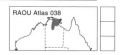

RAOU Atlas 038

331 Spinifex Pigeon *Geophaps plumifera*

Thin erect crest. Bare eye skin red. Chin, face stripe white. Frons, cheek blue-grey. Throat black. Back, uppertail, tail, wings rich red-brown; wing coverts barred black, grey; wing patch bronze-green. Breast red-brown, narrow black and grey bar. 'Race' *ferruginea* abdomen red-brown. 'Race' *leucogaster* lower breast, abdomen white; flanks brown, back darker. **Size** 20.5-22.5 cm. **Juv.** no wing bars, head marks. **Voice** soft, high 'ooar'; deep 'coo-rrr'. **Habitat** spinifex grasslands; rocky hills; by water.

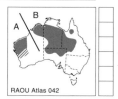

RAOU Atlas 042

A = Race *ferruginea*
B = Race *leucogaster*

332 Wonga Pigeon *Leucosarcia melanoleuca*

Ventral pattern

Generally grey. White frons. Upper breast has broad white 'V'. Lower breast, abdomen, flanks, undertail white, bold black marks. **Size** 36-38.5 cm. **Juv.** upperparts browner; 'V' duller. **Voice** resonant; repeated high 'coo-coo'. **Habitat** coastal, dense forests, scrubs; rainforests.

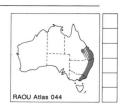

RAOU Atlas 044

331
White-bellied morph

330B

330A

330A

331
Red-bellied morph

330B

327

329
Red-faced morph
Race *smithii*

329
Race *blaauwi*

332

328
Nth Qld morph

328

N. Day.

333 Palm Cockatoo *Probosciger aterrimus*

Distinctive. *Only* wholly dark cockatoo. Prominent crest. Massive pointed bill, female's smaller. **Size** 60 cm. **Imm.** bill tip white. **Voice** disyllabic when perched; wailing flight call; alarm harsh screech. **Habitat** closed tropical forest; adjacent savannah woodlands. Broad wings, deep slow beat.

Ventral flight

RAOU Atlas 263

334 Red-tailed Black-Cockatoo *Calyptorhynchus banksii*

Rounded helmet-like crest and massive bill are diagnostic. **Male** sooty-black; red panels in tail. **Female** duller, spotted and barred yellow. Bill whitish. Tail orange-yellow, barred black. **Size** 63 cm. **Imm.** resembles female but duller. **Voice** metallic, rolling, far-carrying 'creee creee'. **Habitat** coastal forest and woodlands in N Aust.; inland woodlands and open shrubland near water, open forest in SE Aust. Noisy flocks, often large. Buoyant flight.

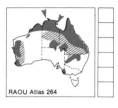

RAOU Atlas 264

335 Glossy Black-Cockatoo *Calyptorhynchus lathami*

Smallest black-cockatoo. **Male** similar to Red-tailed Black-Cockatoo but brownish-black, less red in tail, shorter crest, more bulbous bill. **Female** irregular yellow blotches on head, neck. Bill paler. Red tail panels have black bars, yellow edges on inner webs. **Size** 48 cm. **Imm.** like female; brownish head. **Voice** soft, wailing 'tarr-red'. **Habitat** open forest, especially in she-oaks, where feed quietly.

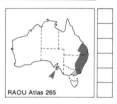

RAOU Atlas 265

336A Yellow-tailed Black-Cockatoo *Calyptorhynchus funereus*

Yellow tail panels, cheek patches. Most body feathers edged pale yellow. **Male** pink eye-ring; small cheek patch. **Female** grey eye-ring; larger patch. **Size** 56-66 cm. **Imm.** as female. **Voice** wailing 'kee-ow'. **Habitat** open forest, farms, pines. Flocks. Buoyant flight, slow wing beat; tail very long.

RAOU Atlas 267

336B White-tailed Black-Cockatoo *Calyptorhynchus latirostris*

White tail panels, cheek patches. **Male** pink eye-ring. **Female** grey eye-ring. Identify from Long-billed Black-Cockatoo by bill, contact calls. **Size** 55-62 cm. **Imm.** as female. **Habitat** sandplain woodlands, mallee. Former race of 336A.

RAOU Atlas 267

337 Long-billed Black-Cockatoo
Calyptorhynchus baudinii

Bill longer than White-tailed Black-Cockatoo. Otherwise smaller, browner. **Male** red eye-ring. **Female** grey eye-ring. **Size** 56 cm. **Habitat** largely confined to karri and marri open forests, surrounding farmland, wandoo woodlands.

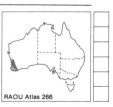

RAOU Atlas 266

338 Gang-Gang Cockatoo *Callocephalon fimbriatum*

Male slate-grey, scarlet head, wispy crest. **Female/Imm.** grey head, crest; feathers of underparts edged salmon-pink. **Size** 34 cm. **Voice** unmistakable 'creaky-door' screech. **Habitat** open forests; move in autumn/winter to woodland, farms, suburbs. Quiet when feeding. Flight erratic.

Feeding

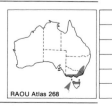

RAOU Atlas 268

334 ♂

335 ♂

333

37

336A

♂ 335

335 ♀

334 ♂

♀ 334

38

337 ♂

338 ♂

♀ 338

♂ 338

♂ 336A

339 Galah *Cacatua roseicapilla*

Distinctive grey and pink cockatoo. **Male** brown iris. **Female** red iris. **Imm.** duller; grey about face, breast; iris brown. Race *assimilis* grey eye-ring. Race *roseicapilla* pink eye-ring. **Size** 36 cm. **Voice** shrill 'chi-chi'. **Habitat** woodlands, open shrublands, grasslands, parks.

Erect crest

A = Race *roseicapilla*
B = Race *assimilis*

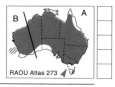

RAOU Atlas 273

340 Long-billed (Slender-billed) Corella *Cacatua tenuirostris*

White. Distinctive long upper mandible. Bluish bare skin around eye. Orange-red lores, cere, forehead, splashes at throat, breast. Pale yellow wash underwings, tail. **Size** 38-41 cm. **Voice** high-pitched, quavering three-note call (in flight). **Habitat** River Red Gum woodlands, farmlands. Feeds on ground in large flocks.

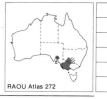

RAOU Atlas 272

341 Little Corella *Cacatua pastinator*

White. Short crest; small whitish bill. Bluish bare skin around eye. Salmon-pink lores. Underwing, undertail sulphur-yellow. *No* red on breast or cere. Race *gymnopis* short-billed. Race *pastinator* (SW Aust.) elongated upper mandible; may be new species. **Size** 36-39 cm. **Voice** like Long-billed; lower pitch, shorter, two notes. **Habitat** semi-arid, monsoonal woodlands, shrublands; farmlands, trees by watercourses, tanks. Often vast, noisy flocks.

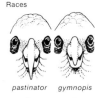

Races

pastinator   *gymnopis*
B   A

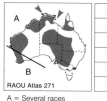

RAOU Atlas 271

A = Several races
B = Race *pastinator*

342 Pink Cockatoo *Cacatua leadbeateri*

Upperparts white. Face, neck, underwings, underparts pink. Long crest, bright red and yellow bands. **Male** iris brown. **Female** iris red. Broader yellow band in crest. **Size** 35 cm. **Voice** distinctive; quavering, falsetto, two-note cry. **Habitat** mallee, mulga, Murray Pine and sheoke associations. Usually small flocks; buoyant flight.

Crest pattern

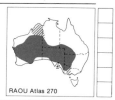

RAOU Atlas 270

343 Sulphur-crested Cockatoo *Cacatua galerita*

White. Sulphur-yellow forward-curving crest. Underwing, undertail washed yellow. **Size** 45 cm. **Voice** extremely loud, raucous screech. **Habitat** wide-ranging in temperate to tropical areas. Flight distinctive; uneven wing beat (flap, flap, glide) on stiff, broad, rounded wings.

Erect crest

RAOU Atlas 269

344 Eclectus Parrot *Eclectus roratus*

Plump, unmistakable. Sexual dimorphism extreme. **Male** bright green. Scarlet underwing coverts and sides of abdomen. Upper bill orange; lower bill black. **Female** scarlet. Bill black. Broad blue band across lower breast, mantle. **Size** 40 cm. **Imm.** brownish bill. **Voice** harsh screech. **Habitat** rainforests S to Cooktown, adjacent savannah woodlands. In flight wings very broad, dark; tail short. Slow shallow wing beat but fast flight.

Ventral flight

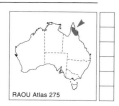

RAOU Atlas 275

345 Red-cheeked Parrot *Geoffroyus geoffroyi*

Male bright green. Bright red face, forehead; blue-violet crown. Blue underwing coverts. Upper bill red, lower bill grey. **Female** head brownish; all of bill grey. **Size** 23 cm. **Imm.** head greenish. **Voice** metallic 'honk honk', repeated rapidly. **Habitat** tropical rainforests. Noisy, active. Flight swift, direct, like Common Starling.

Flight

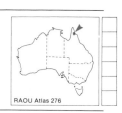

RAOU Atlas 276

Note In SW Western Australia, a probable third species of Corella exists. The Long-billed, present nominate race *C. pastinator pastinator* may be separated as new species, 'Western Long-billed Corella'.

341 Race *pastinator*

340

345 ♀

345 Imm.

345 ♂

344 ♀

149 Grey Goshawk white morph

343

343

344 ♂

340

342

341

339

339

342 ♂

343

341

341

339

340

339 ♀ Race *assimilis*

342 ♀

339 ♂ Race *roseicapilla*

346 Rainbow Lorikeet *Trichoglossus haematodus*

Dark blue head. Bill bright red. Yellow-green collar. Abdomen deep violet-blue. Underwing coverts orange. **Imm.** duller; bill brown. **Size** 28 cm. **Voice** continuous screeching, chattering. **Habitat** rainforests, open forests, woodlands, heaths, gardens.

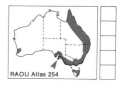

RAOU Atlas 254

347 Red-collared Lorikeet *Trichoglossus rubritorquis*

Often regarded as race of Rainbow Lorikeet. Orange-red collar extending down side of breast. Abdomen blackish-blue. **Size** 28 cm. **Imm.** as Rainbow. Voice as Rainbow. **Habitat** tropical open forests.

RAOU Atlas 255

348 Scaly-breasted Lorikeet *Trichoglossus chlorolepidotus*

Only lorikeet with completely green head. Bill red. Yellow crescents on breast, flanks, thighs. Orange-red underwing. **Size** 23 cm. **Imm.** bill brown. **Habitat** coastal open forests, and modified habitat. Behaviour and calls resemble Rainbow Lorikeet's.

RAOU Atlas 256

349 Varied Lorikeet *Psitteuteles versicolor*

Male bill bright orange-red. Bluish nape; yellow streaks on back, nape, shoulders. Crown, forehead, lores bright red. White naked skin around eye. Cheeks lime-yellow. Breast pale pink, yellow streaks. Green underwings. **Female** duller; olive-green crown. **Size** 19 cm. **Imm.** like female but green crown, brown bill. **Voice** less strident, higher-pitched than Rainbow. **Habitat** monsoonal woodlands, melaleuca swamps, streamsides, open forests.

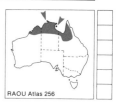

RAOU Atlas 256

350 Musk Lorikeet *Glossopsitta concinna*

Bright green. Bill black, tipped red. Scarlet forehead, lores, ear patches. Blue crown. **Size** 22 cm. **Imm.** bill all dark. **Voice** metallic screech. **Habitat** open forests, woodlands; agricultural, suburban lands. Avoids tall open forest.

RAOU Atlas 258

351 Purple-crowned Lorikeet *Glossopsitta porphyrocephala*

Bill black. Upperparts bright green. Crown purple. Forehead, lores, ear patch yellow-orange. Throat, breast, abdomen pale blue-green. Crimson underwing. **Size** 16 cm. **Imm.** *no* purple on crown. **Voice** short sharp 'zit-zit-zit'. **Habitat** drier open forests, woodlands, mallee.

Juv.

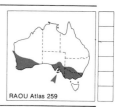

RAOU Atlas 259

352 Little Lorikeet *Glossopsitta pusilla*

Bright green. Bill black. Red face, forehead, throat. Green underwing. **Size** 16 cm. **Voice** a shrill 'zit' (in flight) repeated often. **Habitat** tall open forests, woodlands, orchards, parks, street trees.

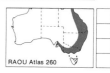

RAOU Atlas 260

353 Double-eyed Fig-Parrot *Cyclopsitta diophthalma*

Smallest Aust. parrot. Bright green. Yellow sides to breast. Complex facial pattern varies with sex, race. **Female** *coxeni* (not illustrated) like its male; less red in cheek. Other races are *macleayana, marshalli*. **Size** 14 cm. **Voice** thin 'zeet-zeet' in flight. **Habitat** rainforests, gardens with soft-fruit trees.

A = Race *marshalli*
B = Race *macleayana*
C = Race *coxeni*

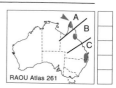

RAOU Atlas 261

Note The Red-collared Lorikeet remains as a race (sub-species) of the Rainbow Lorikeet at present and is thus *Trichoglossus haematodus rubritorquis*.

353 ♂ Race *marshalli*

353 ♀ Race *marshalli*

♀ **353** Race *marshalli*

♂ **353** Race *macleayana*

♀ **353** Race *macleayana*

♂ **353** Race *coxeni*

351

352

349

350

348

347

351

352

346

349

350

363

348

346

347

N. DAY.

354 Australian King Parrot *Alisterus scapularis*

Distinctive. **Male** head, neck, underparts brilliant scarlet. Back green; rump blue; tail blackish-blue. Green crescents on abdomen and undertail coverts. Light green shoulder stripes. **Female/Imm.** head and neck light green, usually no light shoulder stripe; otherwise like male. **Size** 42 cm. **Voice** loud 'carrak-carrak' in flight; male gives far-carrying, piping whistle. **Habitat** moist, tall forest and adjacent farmland. Orchards, parks and gardens in autumn and winter. Small flocks. Strong but erratic flight. Raids fruit trees.

Ventral flight

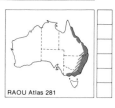
RAOU Atlas 281

355 Red-winged Parrot *Aprosmictus erythropterus*

Male brilliant light green head, neck, underparts. Bottle green back, wings, tail. Deep blue lower back and rump. Large scarlet shoulder patch. **Female/Imm.** uniform mid-green with smaller shoulder patch. **Size** 32 cm. **Voice** brassy 'crillik-crillik' in flight. **Habitat** subtropical and semi-arid eucalypt and casuarina woodlands and mulga shrublands. Strong, erratic, rocking flight with deep wing beat; noisy, wary.

Ventral flight

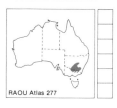
RAOU Atlas 280

356 Superb Parrot *Polytelis swainsonii*

Slender, long-tailed parrot. **Male** brilliant green. Canary-yellow forehead, throat, cheeks. Broad scarlet border to throat. **Female/Imm.** all green; blue on throat and cheeks. **Size** 38 cm. **Voice** rolling 'currak-currak' in flight. Not as harsh as Regent Parrot. **Habitat** riverine and flood-plain open forest and woodland, particularly River Red Gum; also stubble and roadsides. Small flocks.

Ventral flight

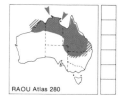
RAOU Atlas 277

357 Regent Parrot *Polytelis anthopeplus*

Lovely, slender, yellow and dark green parrot. **Male** golden-yellow head, neck, underparts, shoulder patch. Dark green back. Blue-black flight feathers and tail. Red band across wing. **Female/Imm.** similar; greener, particularly about head and neck. **Size** 39 cm. **Voice** loud, harsh 'currak-currak' in flight. **Habitat** River Red Gum, Black Box and casuarina woodlands, mallee and acacia shrublands, adjacent farmlands. Pairs or small groups. Flight graceful, swift, erratic; wings swept back.

Ventral flight

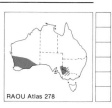
RAOU Atlas 278

358 Alexandra's Parrot *Polytelis alexandrae*

Male crown and sides of head pastel blue. Upperparts and flight feathers light olive except for violet rump, light green shoulder and purple greater coverts. Cheek, throat rose-pink. Breast yellow-grey. Abdomen pinkish-mauve. **Female/Imm.** duller. **Size** F 35, M 46 cm. **Voice** prolonged clackering; 'queet-queet' alarm call. **Habitat** arid shrublands, particularly mulga, Desert Oak and spinifex country. Trees along watercourses. Pairs or small parties. Flight undulating; very long tail conspicuous.

Ventral flight

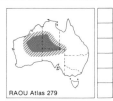
RAOU Atlas 279

358 ♀

358 ♂

♀ 356

♂ 356

354 ♀

♂ 354

355 ♀

355 ♂

♂ 357

357 ♀

N. Day

359 Cockatiel *Leptolophus (Nymphicus) hollandicus*

Distinctive crest. **Male** grey-brown. Large white shoulder patch. Lemon forehead, crest, face, throat, cheeks; orange ear patch. **Female/Imm.** paler yellow face; dull ear patch. Grey crest. Rump, upper tail barred pale yellow. **Size** 32 cm. **Voice** loud, rolling 'weero-weero'. **Habitat** semi-arid to arid country; usually near water; cereal crops. Flocks. Graceful flight; pointed wings, long tail, flashing white shoulders. Escaped domestic varieties: yellow, white most common.

Flight patterns

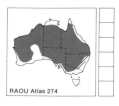

RAOU Atlas 274

360 Ground Parrot *Pezoporus wallicus*

Race *wallicus*: E Aust.; bright green, barred and spotted yellow, black. Black streaks on forehead, crown. Frons red. Legs, toes long. Outer tail feathers yellow-barred. Race *flaviventris*: SW Aust.; plainer yellow belly. **Size** 30 cm. **Imm.** frons green. **Voice** distinctive, bell-like; at dawn, dusk. **Habitat** coastal, tableland heaths, sedgelands; 'button-grass plains' (Tas.). Terrestrial; emerges dusk. Flies swiftly if flushed — yellow bars on long tail diagnostic. Flight 'snipe-like'; plunges into thickets, then runs.

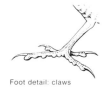

Foot detail: claws

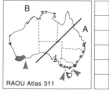

RAOU Atlas 311

A = Race *wallicus*
B = Race *flaviventris*

361 Night Parrot *Pezoporus (Geopsittacus) occidentalis*

Thick-set; short-tailed. Upperparts dull yellowish-green, mottled, barred black, dark brown. Underparts yellowish; primaries brown. *No* red frons. **Size** 23 cm. **Imm.** browner; more so head, neck. **Voice** peculiar croaking alarm; drawn-out mournful whistle. **Habitat** inland plains, breakaways, samphire about salt lakes. By day hides in dense saltbush or spinifex; emerges dusk. Shy. Flight 'quail-like', drops after short distance; runs to cover. Recent specimen 1990 — dead beside road near Boulia, W. Qld.

Foot detail: claws

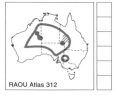

RAOU Atlas 312

362 Budgerigar *Melopsittacus undulatus*

Slender, bright green; yellow throat, forehead. **Size** 18 cm. **Imm.** iris brown; black barring on frons, cheeks. **Voice** continuous 'chirrup'; 'zitting' alarm call. **Habitat** arid and semi-arid woodlands, grasslands. Farms, grassy woodlands in summer. Densely packed, wheeling flocks. Escaped domestic varieties also.

Juv.

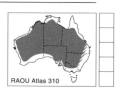

RAOU Atlas 310

363 Swift Parrot *Lathamus discolor*

Slender, narrow-tailed, lorikeet-like. **Adult** pale iris. Bright green; red *around* bill base, throat, forehead. Lores, edges of red throat patch, yellow. Crown bluish-purple. Shoulders bright red. Greater coverts blue; red underwing coverts obvious in flight (*c.f.* lorikeets). Undertail coverts variably red. **Size** 24 cm. **Imm.** duller; less red on face, undertail; brown iris. **Voice** high 'clink clink'. **Habitat** drier open forests, woodlands, gardens. Swift erratic flight.

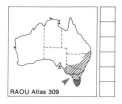

RAOU Atlas 309

364 Red-capped Parrot *Purpureicephalus spurius*

Male forehead, crown dark red. Bill pale grey; upper bill elongated. Face, throat, rump lime-green. Upperparts dark green. Breast, upper abdomen purple. Lower abdomen, undertail coverts red. Undertail light blue. **Female** similar; duller. **Size** 36 cm. **Imm.** crown green, red frons. Violet-grey breast, abdomen. **Voice** harsh 'shrek shrek'. **Habitat** open forests, woodlands, orchards, gardens. Undulating flight.

Feeding

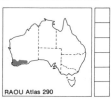

RAOU Atlas 290

363 Imm.

363

363

359 ♂

359 ♀

364 Imm.

364 ♂

364 ♂

359 ♂

359 Domestic variety

362

359 ♀

360

362

Domestic varieties

360

360 Imm.

361

362

361

N.DAY.

365 Green Rosella *Platycercus caledonicus*

Red band over bill. Dark green upperparts; bright yellow head, underparts. Variable red wash on throat, breast, undertail coverts. Blue cheeks, throat. **Size** 37 cm. **Imm.** duller; greener. **Voice** loud 'cussick cussick' (in flight); bell-like (perched). **Habitat** dense mountain forests, farmlands, gardens.

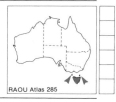

RAOU Atlas 285

366 Crimson Rosella *Platycercus elegans*

Race *elegans*: Rich crimson and blue. **Imm.** crimson and green. Race *flaveolus* 'Yellow Rosella': Crimson replaced by yellow except for red frontal band. Race *adelaidae* 'Adelaide Rosella': Varying amounts of orange replace yellow of *flaveolus* on head, neck, underparts. **Size** 35 cm. **Voice** brassy 'kweek-kweek' (in flight); mellow piping whistle (perched). **Habitat** Crimson: moist forests, farmlands, parks. 'Yellow': floodplain open forest, woodland adjacent farmland. 'Adelaide': watercourses, adjacent timbered farmland. Seven races exist.

Race *flaveolus*

Ventral flight

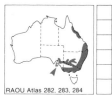

RAOU Atlas 282, 283, 284

White-cheeked Rosella complex:
367 Eastern Rosella *Platycercus eximius*

Male red head, upper breast, undertail coverts; white cheeks. Scapulars black. Back black, each feather broadly edged green or yellowish, giving strongly striated effect. Back may be yellower in northern population. Belly yellow. Rump, lower abdomen, inner tail feathers dark/leaf green; rump, outer tail feathers blue. **Female** slightly duller overall. **Size** 30 cm. **Juv./Imm.** like female. **Voice** high 'clink-clink' (in flight); piping 'pee pit-ee' or slow 'kwink-kwink' (perched). **Habitat** woodlands, farms with eucalypt copses; gardens. Hybridises with Pale-headed Rosella.

Ventral flight

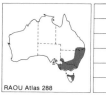

RAOU Atlas 288

368 Pale-headed Rosella *Platycercus adscitus*

White or pale yellow head and nape, diagnostic. White and violet-blue cheeks. Lower back greenish; yellow rump. Upper breast yellowish; lower breast pale blue. Race *palliceps*: All white head; pale blue underparts. **Size** 30 cm. **Voice** like Eastern Rosella. **Habitat** lowland open forests, woodlands, semi-arid shrublands, farmlands.

Race *palliceps*

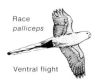

Ventral flight

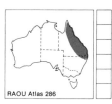

RAOU Atlas 286

369 Northern Rosella *Platycercus venustus*

Distinguished by black cap, white and violet cheeks. Uppertail bluish-black. Rump, underparts yellow with variable black scalloping. **Size** 29 cm. **Imm.** duller; red specks on head. **Voice** like Eastern Rosella. **Habitat** monsoonal eucalypt and melaleuca open forests, woodlands. Usually in hills near water.

Ventral flight

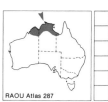

RAOU Atlas 287

370 Western Rosella *Platycercus icterotis*

Red head and underparts, and yellow cheeks, diagnostic. Wings, rump, uppertail greenish-black, except deep blue bend of wing. **Female** green head; breast, flanks have red flecks; underwing stripe always present. **Size** 26 cm. **Imm.** as female; lacks cheek patches. **Voice** soft 'clink-clink'. **Habitat** open forests, woodlands, farmlands.

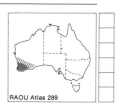

RAOU Atlas 289

Note It is considered that Eastern Rosella, Pale-headed Rosella, and Northern Rosella are races of one species *Platycercus eximius*, which *could* now be called the 'White-cheeked Rosella'.

365
Imm.

365

366 Imm.
Race *elegans*

366
Race *elegans*

366
Race *adelaidae*

366
Imm.
Race *adelaidae*

366 Imm.
Race *flaveolus*

366
Race *flaveolus*

369

368

'0
m.

367

367 ♂

370 ♂

368

367 ♀

Ringneck complex:
371 Mallee Ringneck *Barnardius barnardi*
Blue and green head. Red frontal band. Hind neck, mantle blue-black. Collar yellow; some have yellow breast band. Upperwing coverts, rump green, turquoise. Primaries blue. Race *macgillivrayi* 'Cloncurry Parrot': smaller, paler; *no* frontal band; yellow below. **Size** 35 cm. **Imm.** duller. **Voice** ringing. **Habitat** semi-arid woodlands, flood plains, farms.

Dorsal flight

RAOU Atlas 291

A = Race *barnardi*
B = Race *macgillivrayi*

372 Ringneck (Port Lincoln) *Barnardius zonarius*
Probably race of Mallee Ringneck. Race *zonarius*: Like Mallee Ringneck but black head, blue cheeks. *No* frontal band. Darker green above; yellow belly. Race *semitorquatus* 'Twenty-eight Parrot': Green below; red frontal band. **Size** 37 cm. **Voice** strident. Race *semitorquatus* calls 'twentee-eight'. **Habitat** tall, wet forest (SW Aust.) to mallee, mulga.

Dorsal flight

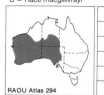
RAOU Atlas 294

373 Red-rumped Parrot *Psephotus haematonotus*
Male green. Rump red. Shoulder patch, abdomen yellow. **Female** dull olive-green; green rump. **Imm.** duller. **Size** 27 cm. **Voice** two-syllable whistle. **Habitat** open woodlands, Red Gums, grasslands, farms.

Ventral flight

RAOU Atlas 295

374 Mulga Parrot *Psephotus varius*
Male emerald green. Yellow frontal band, shoulder patch. Russet crown, abdomen, thighs, rump spot. **Female/Imm.** pale brown-olive, dull orange frontal band, nape, shoulder patch. **Size** 28 cm. **Voice** 3-4 flute-like notes. **Habitat** arid shrublands.

Dorsal flight

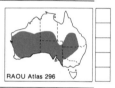
RAOU Atlas 296

375 Golden-shouldered Parrot *Psephotus chrysopterygius*
Male turquoise. Black crown. Yellow frons. Brown above; golden shoulder. Reddish vent. **Female/Imm.** light yellow-green. Pale blue-green cheeks. Lower underparts pale blue; some red on vent. **Size** 26 cm. **Voice** double whistle. **Habitat** savannah woodlands with termite mounds.

RAOU Atlas 300

376 Hooded Parrot *Psephotus dissimilis*
Like Golden-shouldered Parrot. Black hood to lower bill; shoulder patch larger, brighter.

Dorsal flight

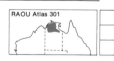
RAOU Atlas 301

377 Paradise Parrot *Psephotus pulcherrimus*
Extinct? **Male** brown above. Turquoise rump, underparts. Red frontal band, shoulder, abdomen, undertail coverts. **Female/Imm.** much duller. **Size** 27 cm. **Voice** unknown. **Habitat** grassy eucalypt woodlands with termite mounds.

RAOU Atlas 299

378 Blue Bonnet *Northiella haematogaster*
Brown, blue-faced parrot. Race *haematogaster*: wing band blue; upperwing coverts olive-yellow; belly red; vent yellow. Race *haematorrhous*: wing band green; upperwing coverts red; vent red. Race *narethae*: smaller; blue face, frons turquoise; belly yellow, vent red. **Female/Imm.** duller. **Size** 26-30 cm. **Voice** harsh 'chack chack'; piping whistle. **Habitat** semi-arid woodlands.

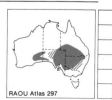
RAOU Atlas 297

Note It is considered the Ringneck and Mallee Ringneck are members of a superspecies, which could be called the Ringneck complex.

144

371
Race *macgillivrayi*

378
Race *narethae*

378
Race *haematorrhous*

378
Race *haematogaster*

372

372
Race *semitorquatus*

1

♀ **373**

373
♂

♀ **374**

373

♂ **373**

374

373 ♀

♂ **374**

375 ♂

♀ **375**

377 ♂

376 ♀

♂ **376**

377 ♀

379 Bourke's Parrot *Neophema bourkii*

Distinctive pinkish-brown. **Male** whitish about eye, face.
Variable blue frontal band. Upperparts brown; wing
feathers edged yellowish-white. Salmon-pink below;
undertail pale blue. **Female/Imm.** dull; *lacks* frontal band.
Size 19 cm. **Voice** soft twitter. **Habitat** arid to semi-arid
scrublands, mainly mulga.

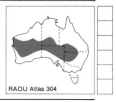

RAOU Atlas 304

380 Blue-winged Parrot *Neophema chrysostoma*

Male olive-green above. Yellow lores. Deep blue frontal
band but *not* over eye. Shoulder brilliant deep blue.
Green cheeks, underparts, merging to yellow abdomen,
which may be orange-centred. **Female/Imm.** dull;
indistinct frontal band. **Size** 21 cm. **Voice** tinkling (in
flight); sharp 'sit-sit' (alarm). **Habitat** open forests,
woodlands, grasslands, coastal heath, saltmarshes.

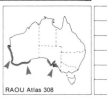

Flight

RAOU Atlas 306

381 Elegant Parrot *Neophema elegans*

Male like Blue-winged, but olive-yellow above; brighter
yellow rump, uppertail coverts, outer tail. Less of *two-
toned* blue in wing. Blues of frontal band extend *above,
behind* eye. **Female/Imm.** dull; *lacks* frontal band.
Size 22 cm. **Voice** sharp (in flight); soft (feeding).
Habitat open country; semi-arid scrublands.

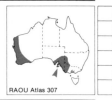

RAOU Atlas 307

382 Rock Parrot *Neophema petrophila*

Dullest *Neophema*. **Male** dark olive above; yellowish-olive
below. Frontal band deep blue, pale-edged; some blue
about eye. Bright yellow undertail coverts.
Female/Imm. dull. **Imm.** *lacks* frontal band. **Size** 22 cm.
Voice double 'sit-tee' (in flight). **Habitat** coastal dunes,
saltmarsh, rocky islands.

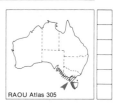

RAOU Atlas 308

383 Orange-bellied Parrot *Neophema chrysogaster*

Male rich grass-green above. Broad blue frontal band to
eye. Deep violet-blue in wing. Face, throat, breast
greenish-yellow; yellow abdomen with variable orange
centre. **Female/Imm.** duller. **Imm.** olive head, neck, breast.
Size 21 cm. **Voice** diagnostic 'buzz-buzz' (alarm).
Habitat breeds in open-forest copses in heath. Winters in
coastal saltmarsh, dunes, damp grasslands.

Feeding

RAOU Atlas 305

384 Turquoise Parrot *Neophema pulchella*

Male distinctive. Bright green above. Turquoise blue
crown, face. *Two-tone* blue on shoulder. Deep blue flight
feathers. Upperwing patch chestnut-red. Upper breast has
orange tint. Yellow abdomen *may* have orange centre.
Female/Imm. duller; whitish lores; *no* red on shoulder.
Size 20 cm. **Voice** like Blue-winged. **Habitat** open forests.

♂
at nest

RAOU Atlas 302

385 Scarlet-chested Parrot *Neophema splendida*

Male brilliant. Green above. Yellow outer tail. Bright blue
face; darker on chin. Light blue shoulder. Breast scarlet;
bright yellow below. **Female/Imm.** breast greenish.
Crown, face *less* blue. Distinguish from female/imm.
Turquoise by blue lores; pale blue in wing. **Size** 20 cm.
Voice quiet twittering. **Habitat** mulga, mallee.

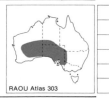

RAOU Atlas 303

♂ 379

385 ♀

385 ♂

384 ♀

♂ 384

383
Imm.

383

381

380

382

382
Imm.

386 Oriental Cuckoo *Cuculus saturatus*

Large cuckoo. Grey above; paler grey breast. Whitish belly, barred black. Eye-ring, bill base, legs bright yellow. Long, dark grey tail, spotted on edges, tipped white. Primaries grey, barred black. Underwing white, barred black; leading edge white. **Red morph female** upperparts chestnut; body barred black. **Size** 30-34 cm. **Voice** allegedly silent in Aust. **Habitat** forests. Summer migrant to N Aust.

386

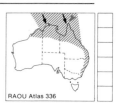
RAOU Atlas 336

159 Australian Hobby

387 Pallid Cuckoo *Cuculus pallidus*

Black bill. Yellow eye-ring. Dark grey eye-stripe; pale eyebrow, nape. Tail dark grey, notched white. Grey above; white below. **Size** 33 cm. **Juv.** boldly streaked dark brown and white all over. **Imm.** upperparts heavily mottled brown and chestnut. Underparts grey; buff breast, barred brown. **Voice** an ascending and accelerating series of hoarse, whistles 'too-too-too...'. **Habitat** open areas with trees.

Ventral flight

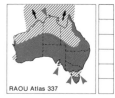
RAOU Atlas 337

388 Brush Cuckoo *Cuculus variolosus*

Grey-brown above. Grey eye-ring. Pale grey below, tinged buff. Tail square, tipped white, no notches above; shorter than Fan-tailed Cuckoo. Undertail broadly barred brown, thin whitish notching on inner web. **Size** 22-23 cm. **Juv./Imm.** rufous, barred dark brown above (including tail); paler below. **Voice** six or seven descending notes; mournful 'ther-er-wee' repeated. **Habitat** wet forests, brush.

Ventral flight

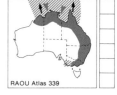
RAOU Atlas 339

389 Chestnut-breasted Cuckoo
Cuculus castaneiventris

Like Fan-tailed Cuckoo, but smaller. Darker above; brighter chestnut below. Undertail bands broader. **Size** 24 cm. **Juv./Imm.** like Fan-tailed juv. but pale cinnamon below. **Voice** like Fan-tailed. **Habitat** rainforest and its borders.

390 Juv.

389 Juv

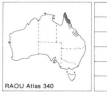
RAOU Atlas 340

390 Fan-tailed Cuckoo *Cuculus flabelliformis*

Dark grey above. Yellow eye-ring. Tail strongly notched white, wedge-shaped. Dull fawn-chestnut below. Undertail barred black and white. Distinguish from Brush Cuckoo by notched, wedge-shaped tail, larger size, often brighter underparts. NE Aust. birds brighter chestnut below and smaller. **Size** 24.5-28.5 cm. **Juv.** dark brown above, barred reddish-brown. Head streaked dark brown. Finely barred grey and brown below. Distinguish from juv. Brush by yellow eye-ring, tail shape. **Voice** mournful descending trill, repeated; other calls. **Habitat** forests, woodlands.

Ventral flight

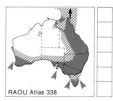
RAOU Atlas 338

391 Black-eared Cuckoo *Chrysococcyx osculans*

Greyish above, with slight metallic sheen. Black eye-stripe, broadest behind eye. Whitish eyebrow, throat. Pale rump. Cream below. Tail grey, tipped white. Undertail barred black and cream. Distinguish from juv. Horsfield's Bronze-Cuckoo by *lack* of rufous on tail, *broader* black eye-stripe. **Size** 19-20 cm. **Juv./Imm.** duller brown eye-stripe. **Voice** descending 'feeeuw' singly or repeated; is lower, longer and more mournful than Horsfield's. **Habitat** inland low bushes to dry forest.

Juv.

Ventral flight

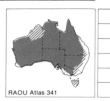
RAOU Atlas 341

386
Red morph ♀

386

387
Imm.

387

387
Juv.

388

389

390

390
Juv.

391

388
Juv.

392 Horsfield's Bronze-Cuckoo *Chrysococcyx basalis*

Bronze-sheen above; cap duller. Brown eye-stripe; pale eyebrow. Tail edged rufous. Cream below with *incomplete* bronze bars. Undertail black and white, rusty centre. **Size** 17 cm. **Juv./Imm.** duller; sometimes *lacks* bars. Distinguish from Black-eared Cuckoo by rufous tail, size, less obvious eye-stripe. **Voice** descending whistle 'fee-ew'; shorter, higher than Black-eared. **Habitat** open country.

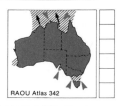

RAOU Atlas 342

393 Shining Bronze-Cuckoo *Chrysococcyx lucidus*

Race *plagosus* 'Golden Bronze-Cuckoo': Copper cap. Metallic green upperparts. Sometimes pale spots on crown. Face, underparts white with complete bronze bars. *No rufous in tail.* Undertail black and white. **Juv.** duller; bars on flanks only. Race *lucidus* 'Shining Bronze-Cuckoo': Metallic green above; no head contrast; white flecks on forehead prominent; bars green. Bill broader than 'Golden Bronze'. **Size** 17-18 cm. **Voice** reverse of Horsfield's call: repeated 'few-ee'. **Habitat** forest.

Underwing bar
Bronze-Cuckoos
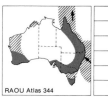

RAOU Atlas 344

394 Little Bronze-Cuckoo *Chrysococcyx malayanus*

NW Aust. race *minutillus*. **Male** metallic green above. Red eye-ring, eyes. White eyebrow. White below; *complete* green bars. 3-4 black bars on white outer tail feathers; inners rusty, black sub-terminally, white tips. **Female** duller. Cream eye-ring; brown eyes. **Size** 16 cm. **Juv./Imm.** as female but duller; flank bars only. Race *barnardi* migratory in NE Aust. **Voice** high, short, accelerating and descending 'see-see'. **Habitat** forests, mangroves. Hybridises with Gould's.

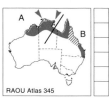

RAOU Atlas 345

A = Race *minutillus*
B = Race *barnardi*

395 Gould's Bronze-Cuckoo *Chrysococcyx m. russatus*

Male like Little Bronze-Cuckoo but upperparts edged bronze. Side of chest pale to bright rust; bars bronze. Eyebrow buff. Rusty outer webs to tail. **Female** as female Little, but rusty breast and tail. **Juv./Imm.** like female, duller; bars only on flanks. **Voice** and **Habitat** as Little. Now considered a race of the Little Bronze-Cuckoo.

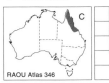

RAOU Atlas 346

C = Race *russatus*

396 Common Koel *Eudynamys scolopacea*

Male black; red eye; long tail. **Female** black cap. Brown spotted above, barred white. Throat buff. White below, barred brown. Eye red. **Size** 39-46 cm. **Juv./Imm.** like female; head mottled brown; eye brown. **Voice** 'koo-well' and 'wurra wurra'. **Habitat** forests, tall trees.

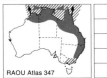

RAOU Atlas 347

397 Channel-billed Cuckoo *Scythrops novaehollandiae*

Very large. Huge pale bill. Grey above with a long tail. White below, faintly barred black. **Size** 60 cm. **Juv.** head, neck pale buff. **Voice** bubbling trumpet. **Habitat** tall trees. Breeds in Aust.; winters in New Guinea, Indonesia.

RAOU Atlas 348

398 Pheasant Coucal *Centropus phasianinus*

Breeding black head, underparts. Barred rufous, black and cream above. Long, pheasant-like tail. Short bill. **Non breeding** and **Juv./Imm.** duller; body all brown. **Size** 60-80 cm. **Voice** low bass 'coo-coo-coo-coo-coo-coo-coocal'. **Habitat** thick undergrowth, canefields.

Adult
Non-breeding
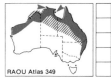

RAOU Atlas 349

150

392

392

394 ♀

394 ♂

393
ce *plagosus*

393
Race *lucidus*

♂ **395**

395 ♀

396 ♀

397

396 ♂

398

399 Rufous Owl *Ninox rufa*

Race *rufa:* Rufous colouration. Flat crown. Greenish-yellow eyes in indistinct facial mask. Upperparts very closely barred dark rufous-brown and buff. Underparts closely barred brownish-rufous and whitish. Race *meesi* (C. York Pen.): Smaller. Race *queenslandica* (Mackay area): Darker. **Size** 51 cm. **Juv.** head, underparts pure white, except distinct dark facial discs. **Voice** deep double-hoot, second note shorter. **Habitat** closed forests.

Juv.

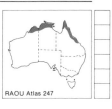

RAOU Atlas 247

400 Powerful Owl *Ninox strenua*

Smallish, dark yellow eyes. Short, broad head. Upperparts, tail, dark greyish-brown with indistinct off-white bars. Underparts whitish with dark greyish-brown chevrons. **Male** larger. **Size** 55 cm. **Juv.** white underparts and crown contrast with small dark streaks and dark eye patches. **Voice** slow, deep, resonant double-hoot; occasionally single. **Habitat** tall open forests. Slow deliberate flight on huge wings.

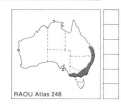

RAOU Atlas 248

401 Southern Boobook *Ninox novaeseelandiae*

Distinct, dark facial discs contrast sharply with surrounding pale borders. Eyes green-yellow. Upperparts dark chocolate-brown; upperwing coverts, scapulars spotted off-white. Underparts reddish-brown. Upper breast mottled buff becoming reddish-brown. White-streaked belly. **Size** 30 cm. **Juv.** crown whitish, streaked darker centrally; facial discs very distinct. Upperparts dark chocolate-brown, profusely spotted white and buff. Underparts downy white; tawny wash on upper breast. Great variation within and between races. Tas. birds smaller, darker; mantle spotted. Western, northern and central birds paler, more reddish; less clearly marked. NE rainforest birds smaller, darker, less spotted. **Voice** falsetto double-hoot; continuous hooting. **Habitat** woodlands, forests, scrublands. Delicate flight; rarely glides.

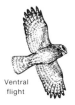

Ventral flight

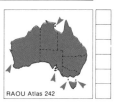

RAOU Atlas 242

402 Barking Owl *Ninox connivens*

Large, bright yellow eyes. Almost no facial mask. Upperparts brownish-grey, coarsely spotted white. Flight feathers, tail, barred lighter. Underparts white, streaked brownish-grey. **Male** larger. **Size** 40 cm. **Juv.** incomplete collar; flanks and breast have pattern like adults. Northern birds browner, darker, smaller. **Voice** explosive, dog-like, double-bark; wavering human-like scream; grating trill; various growls. **Habitat** forests, woodlands.

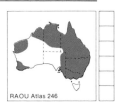

RAOU Atlas 246

403 Brown Hawk-Owl *Ninox scutulata*

Eyes yellow. Indistinct facial mask; whitish forehead, lores. Upperparts uniform dark brown. Underparts off-white, streaked brown. Pointed wings. Tail longish, dark brown, lighter bars. **Size** 29 cm. **Voice** musical double-hoot, second note brief, higher-pitched. **Habitat** forests, woodlands. One Aust. record, race *japonica*.

404 Barn Owl *Tyto alba*

Slim; upright posture. Small black eyes. Rounded heart-shaped mask: brown border, white disc, dark tear marks. Upperparts soft grey, patchily washed golden-fawn and marked with fine black, white-tipped spots. Underparts white, sparsely dark-flecked. Long, unfeathered lower legs protrude *just beyond tail* in flight. **Size** F 35, M 34 cm. **Voice** rasping screech. **Habitat** grasslands, farmlands, woodlands. May roost on ground; in caves.

Roosting

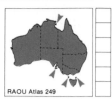

RAOU Atlas 249

405 Masked Owl *Tyto novaehollandiae*

Robust; crouched posture. Black eyes. Round, dark bordered mask. Dark chestnut near eyes. **Dark phase** chestnut disc; upperparts blackish-brown, washed rufous and speckled white; underparts pale rufous, coarsely dark-spotted. **Intermediate phase** off-white disc; upperparts blackish-brown, washed yellow and densely speckled white; underparts off-white, coarsely dark-spotted. **Light phase** white disc; upperparts pale grey, washed yellow, dark and white speckled; underparts white, sparsely grey-flecked. In S Aust., 'dark' females and 'intermediate' males predominate. In N Aust. smaller 'intermediate' females and 'light' males predominate. Legs heavy. Feet heavy. **Female** larger. **Size** F 47, M 37 cm. **Voice** deep, rasping screech; various twitterings. **Habitat** forests, woodlands, caves. Active in middle storey.

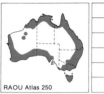

RAOU Atlas 250

406 Eastern Grass Owl *Tyto capensis*

Slim; upright posture. Very small, black eyes. Heart-shaped mask: brown and white border, white disc, dark tear marks. Upperparts dark brown, washed orange, white spotted. Underparts white, finely dark spotted; breast washed orange. Very long unfeathered lower legs protrude *well beyond tail* in flight. **Size** F 37, M 34 cm. **Voice** deep, soft screech; high-pitched trills. **Habitat** swampy heaths, grasslands. Usually roosts and always breeds on ground. In flight back appears bluish-grey.

Body feathers

404

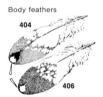

406

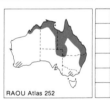

RAOU Atlas 252

407 Sooty Owl *Tyto tenebricosa*

Robust; crouched posture. Large, black eyes. Round mask: dark-grey border, grey disc, darkest near eyes. Upperparts and underparts dark brownish-grey, densely whitish-flecked. Belly paler grey, mottled whitish. Tail stumpy. Feathered legs. Heavy feet. **Female** larger. **Size** F 48, M 40 cm. **Voice** descending whistle; chirruping trills. **Habitat** closed and tall open forests, especially gullies. Active in canopy.

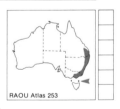

RAOU Atlas 253

408 Lesser Sooty Owl *Tyto multipunctata*

Much smaller than Sooty Owl. Robust; crouched posture. Large, black eyes. Disc whitish near border. Upperparts coarsely and densely spotted. Breast washed dark grey. Underparts greyish-white, barred blackish-grey. **Size** F 37, M 33 cm. **Voice** higher-pitched than Sooty Owl. **Habitat** similar to Sooty Owl.

408

405 Light morph

404

404

406

407 Light morph

♂ **405**
Race *kimberlyi*

406

405 ♀
Race *castanops*

409 Tawny Frogmouth *Podargus strigoides*

Broad, grey bill, edged by grey plumes. Gape, eye yellow. Flat crown. Pale grey eyebrow. Grey to reddish-brown above with grey patches, streaked black. Underparts paler. Tail short, ungraduated. Five races: northern birds smaller; grey and red morphs exist. **Size** 34-46 cm. **Nestling** head, back speckled grey down; underparts paler. **Juv.** sides of breast streaked. **Voice** a constant 'oo-oom . . .'. **Habitat** woodlands.

 Ventral flight

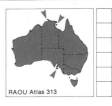 RAOU Atlas 313

410 Papuan Frogmouth *Podargus papuensis*

Like Tawny Frogmouth but larger; bigger head. Cream eyebrow. Red eye. Grey to rufous with black-edged white or grey marbling; paler below. Graduated long tail. **Size** 45-54 cm. **Nestling** downy fawn. **Voice** ooms; clacks by snapping of bill. **Habitat** forests.

 RAOU Atlas 316

411 Marbled Frogmouth *Podargus ocellatus*

Race *plumiferus* 'Plumed Frogmouth': Tawny Frogmouth-sized. Rounded crown (in profile). Long, banded facial plumes. Bright orange eye. Buff to white eyebrow prominent. Deep rufous-brown to greyish above, delicately marbled cream, black-bordered. Underparts have black streaks and white spots on feather tips. Long graduated tail. Race *marmoratus* 'Marbled Frogmouth': Longer tail. **Size** 40-48 cm. **Juv.** downy rufous-brown above; downy fawn below. **Voice** high 'coo-lew'; low 'coo-lew'; loud tocking, then laughing 'cor-cor-' followed by six gobbles. **Habitat** rainforests with palms.

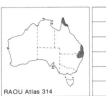 RAOU Atlas 314

412 Australian Owlet-nightjar *Aegotheles cristatus*

Bill black. Large brown eye; non-reflective to lights. Head has wide black eye-stripes meeting behind and extending to crown. Black collar. Upperparts, tail grey, finely barred blackish. Paler underparts. Feet pink. Northern, central birds lighter; rufous-washed. **Size** 21-24 cm. **Voice** grating, strident churring. **Habitat** woodlands with tree hollows.

 Dorsal flight

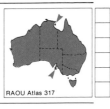 RAOU Atlas 317

413 White-throated Nightjar *Eurostopodus mysticalis*

Bill black. Eye brown; most highly reflective to lights of our nightjars. Small white spots on primaries. Pointed wings. Dark grey above with black, sandy and whitish spots, patches, bars. Black throat; white patches at sides. Underparts grade to cinnamon belly; dark-barred. **Size** 33 cm. **Imm.** duller, redder. **Voice** accelerating 'kook-kook . . .'. **Habitat** forests, woodlands.

 Ventral flight

 RAOU Atlas 330

414 Spotted Nightjar *Eurostopodus argus*

Like White-throated; smaller. All-white throat. Large white wing spot. Rounded wings. **Size** 30 cm. **Juv./Imm.** paler, duller. **Voice** few 'kook-kook', then repeated faster. **Habitat** forests, woodlands, scrubs, deserts. May flock.

 Ventral flight

 RAOU Atlas 331

415 Large-tailed Nightjar *Caprimulgus macrurus*

Smaller, greyer nightjar with large white wing and tail-tip spots. Throat as White-throated. Rounded wings. **Size** 27 cm. **Voice** monotonous chopping. **Habitat** tropical woodland margins.

 Ventral flight

 RAOU Atlas 332

Note The genus *Eurostopodus* is now in use for the Spotted and White-throated Nightjars. Changes in use of generic names indicate continuing research in the fields of molecular biology and taxonomy.

411
Pale morph

410
Red morph

411

409
Red morph

409
Nestling

409

412

412
Red morph

410

415

414

416 Glossy Swiftlet *Collocalia esculenta*

Small. Shiny black-blue above, including rump; sometimes looks black. Chest black; belly white; intermediate area spotted. Underwing black. Tail rounded with a shallow notch. Upperparts *and* underparts must be seen to distinguish from White-rumped Swiftlet with pale belly. **Size** 9-11.5 cm. **Voice** soft twittering. **Habitat** over coastal ranges and islands. Vagrant.

Ventral flight

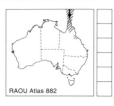

RAOU Atlas 882

417 White-rumped Swiftlet *Aerodramus spodiopygia*

Small. Dark grey above; slightly glossy on wings. Rump pale grey. Tail black. Chest grey; belly, vent slightly paler. In strong light can look whitish. Tail rounded with a shallow notch. A form breeding at Chillago (NE Qld) darker above; paler belly. **Size** 11 cm. **Voice** chips and twitters. Uses clicks in caves for echo location. **Habitat** aerial, over coastal ranges and islands. Breeds in caves.

449 Tree Martin
Dorsal flight

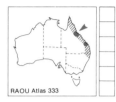

RAOU Atlas 333

418 Uniform Swiftlet *Aerodramus vanikorensis*

All grey-brown; upperparts darker with faint metallic sheen; rump slightly paler. Throat, undertail paler than belly. Tail shape like other swiftlets. In the field *inseparable* from similar New Guinea and Asian swifts. **Size** 12 cm. **Voice** soft twittering. **Habitat** over coastal ranges and islands. One specimen recorded in Aust. Unidentified completely dark swiftlets have been seen occasionally. Note: if completely dark swiftlets are seen, then notes on subtle body colour changes, shape, flight actions and calls should be taken for *future* reference.

Ventral flight

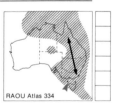

RAOU Atlas 881

419 White-throated Needletail *Hirundapus caudacutus*

Race *caudacutus:* Largest Aust. swift. Body all dark with white throat, vent, flanks. Frons pale grey. Edges of tertiary feathers white. Back, rump, brown. Rest of upperparts have a glossy green sheen. Wings swept back (curved, anchor-shaped). Tail black, rounded. **Size** 20 cm. **Voice** twittering, chattering. **Habitat** aerial, mainly in E Aust., often associated with coastal and mountain regions. Flight long-winged, raking glides, slow turns. N Asian migrant. Previously called Spine-tailed Swift.

Perched

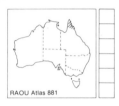

RAOU Atlas 334

420 Little Swift *Apus affinis*

Dark grey. Similar to Fork-tailed Swift with white rump and throat, but tail shorter, very shallowly forked, becoming square when fanned. Smaller, stockier, proportionately broader-winged than Fork-tailed. **Size** 15 cm. **Voice** shrill rattling trill. **Habitat** aerial, over open areas. Vagrant. Could prove to be more regular than single specimen suggests.

Ventral flight

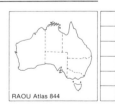

RAOU Atlas 844

421 Fork-tailed Swift *Apus pacificus*

All blackish. Pale throat. White rump. Body slimmer than White-throated Needletail. Tail is long and thin; deeply forked when fanned; fork invisible when tail closed. **Size** 17.5 cm. **Voice** twittering, buzzing. **Habitat** aerial, over a variety of habitats. N Asian migrant. Flight bat-like.

Ventral flight

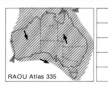

RAOU Atlas 335

422 Azure Kingfisher *Alcedo azurea*

Long black bill. Rufous spot before eye. Buff-white mark on side of neck. Upperparts violet-blue. Pale throat. Underparts rufous (variable). Legs bright orange. **Size** 18 cm. **Imm.** dull blue upperparts; pale underparts. **Voice** high-pitched whistle. **Habitat** rivers, creeks mangroves. Flight swift, low over water.

Diving sequence

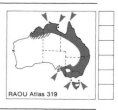

RAOU Atlas 319

423 Little Kingfisher *Alcedo pusilla*

Long black bill. White spot before eye and on side of neck. Upperparts blue. Underparts white. Legs black. **Size** 12 cm. **Imm.** duller; crown scalloped. **Voice** shrill whistle, higher than Azure Kingfisher. **Habitat** mangroves rivers, creeks.

422   423

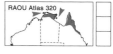

RAOU Atlas 320

424 Laughing Kookaburra *Dacelo novaeguineae*

Largest kingfisher. Massive bill, black above, horn below. Large cream-white head; brown marks on crown. Brown eye-stripe. Back, wings brown; mottled blue on wings. **Male** often has blue patch on rump. Tail barred rufous-brown and black, margined white. **Female** brown rump; head more buff. Race *novaeguineae* larger than race *minor* of C. York Pen. **Size** 45 cm. **Imm.** duller, like female. **Voice** raucous 'laughter'. **Habitat** open forests, woodlands. Flight heavy, direct; raises tail on alighting.

Watching for prey

Dorsal pattern

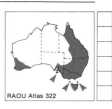

RAOU Atlas 322

425 Blue-winged Kookaburra *Dacelo leachii*

Large bill, dark above, horn below. Large cream-white head, variably streaked brown. Pale eye. *No* eye stripe. Back brown; wings mostly blue. Rump blue. **Male** tail deep blue. **Female** tail rufous, barred dark blue. Formerly four races; now two. Large, white-headed *cliftoni* in Pilbara, WA; *leachii* smaller, dark streaks on head, from Kimberley, WA to SE Qld. **Size** 40-45 cm. **Juv./Imm.** duller; head paler; underparts scalloped brown. **Voice** harsh, cackling scream. **Habitat** woods, open forests, paperbark swamps.

Eastern

Western

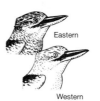

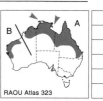

RAOU Atlas 323

A = Race *leachii*
B = Race *cliftoni*

426 Forest Kingfisher *Todirhamphus (Halcyon) macleayii*

Head deep blue. White spot before eye. Bill black, pale lower base. Broad black stripe from bill to ear coverts. Back, rump blue. Wings, tail rich blue. White wing spot on wing. **Female** blue back of neck. Race *incincta*: greener on back; white wing spot smaller. Race *macleayii*: more blue on back; wing spot larger. **Size** 20 cm. **Imm.** duller; forehead, shoulders scalloped white. Head spot, wing spot, underparts all buff. **Voice** harsh trill, high whistle. **Habitat** coastal open forests, wooded swamps, mangroves, woodlands.

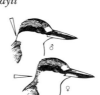

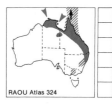

RAOU Atlas 324

427 Red-backed Kingfisher *Todirhamphus (Halcyon) pyrrhopygia*

Bill black, with pale lower base. Crown streaked grey-green and white. Black eye-stripe, ear coverts, nape of neck. Collar white. Wings, tail blue-green. Lower back, rump, undertail coverts rufous-red. **Female** duller. **Size** 20 cm. **Imm.** speckled breast. **Voice** mournful; harsh alarm near nest. **Habitat** dry woodlands.

Nest burrow

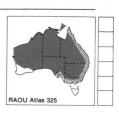

RAOU Atlas 325

Note The generic name *Todirhamphus* has now replaced the generic name *Halcyon*; this has affected four species.

424

425 ♀

425 ♂

427

426

426

422

423

423
Imm.

N. Day.

428 Sacred Kingfisher *Todirhampus (Halcyon) sancta*

Head, back green. Black band through eye and ear coverts to back of neck. Buff spot before eye. White collar with buff tinge. Wings, rump, tail blue. Underparts white to buff. **Female** duller. **Size** 19-23.5 cm. **Imm.** speckled brown. **Voice** loud four-note call. Harsh alarm call near nest. **Habitat** eucalypt, paperbark forests; woodlands; mangroves.

426 Forest Kingfisher

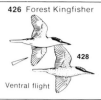

428

Ventral flight

RAOU Atlas 326

429 Collared Kingfisher *Todirhampus (Halcyon) chloris*

Bill longer than Sacred Kingfisher. Green-blue on wings and tail. Head, back green. Black band through eye and ear coverts to back of neck. White spot before eye. White collar. Wings, tail blue. White underparts. **Female** duller. Aust. race *sordida*. **Size** 25-29 cm. **Imm.** speckled brown. **Voice** two-note call. **Habitat** mangroves, coastal areas.

Nesting in termite colony

RAOU Atlas 327

430 Yellow-billed Kingfisher *Syma torotoro*

Bill yellow. Black ring around eye. **Male** rusty head. Back, wings green. Rump, tail rufous. Underparts rufous. Black mark on side of neck. Legs yellow. **Female** large patch of black on rusty crown; larger black mark on neck; paler underparts. **Size** 18-21 cm. **Voice** loud, mournful trill. **Habitat** rainforest edges.

RAOU Atlas 321

431 Buff-breasted Paradise-Kingfisher *Tanysiptera sylvia*

Bill orange-red. Crown, shoulders blue. Black band through eye, nape to upper back. Back, rump white. Tail blue with long white central feathers. Underparts rich rufous. Legs orange-red. **Size** 29-35 cm (includes all tail). **Imm.** dark bill; crown, wings dull blue; tail short, grey. **Juv.** dark bill; body brown, blackish striations on breast; face mask not very distinct. **Voice** trilling call. **Habitat** lowland rainforests Breeds in terrestrial termitaria.

Tail flick

RAOU Atlas 328

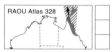

432 Common Paradise-Kingfisher *Tanysiptera galatea*

Bill red. Blue and black upperparts. White underparts. Blue and white tail with long blue central feathers, white racquets. **Size** 40 cm (includes all of tail). One Aust. record (Darnley Is., Torres Strait. Qld) now in doubt.

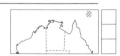

433 Rainbow Bee-eater *Merops ornatus*

Bill black. Rufous crown Black eye-stripe, edged blue. Black band on yellow throat. Back light green. Tail black with extended central feathers, longer in male. **Size** 23-28 cm (includes all of tail). **Imm.** *no black throat band*. **Voice** high-pitched chitter. **Habitat** open country.

Leaving burrow

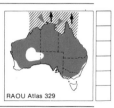

RAOU Atlas 329

434 Dollarbird *Eurystomus orientalis*

Sexes similar. Bill, legs red. Upperparts brown. Blue throat. Wings green-blue. Tail blue. Pale blue wing spots in flight. Red legs, feet. Aust. race *pacificus*. **Size** 27-31 cm. **Juv.** dark bill, legs, feet; brown-grey body. **Voice** harsh. **Habitat** woodlands. N-S summer migrant, breeds Aust. Perches prominently; characteristic silhouette. Hawks aerial insects; tumbling flight.

434 Perches prominently

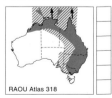

RAOU Atlas 318

434

433

433
Imm.

♂ 433

434

431

432

429 Imm.

429

♀ 430

♂ 430

428

428
Imm.

N. Day.

435 Red-bellied Pitta *Pitta erythrogaster*

Forehead, crown dark brown. Brown-red nape. Chest, rump, shoulders bright blue. Black line divides chest from red belly. Back, wings, tail blue-green. Note: pittas have dark underwings with white patch conspicuous in swift, direct flight. Legs dark grey. **Size** 16-19 cm. **Imm.** duller red below. **Voice** harsh 'kraa-kraa'. **Habitat** tropical closed forests, scrubs.

Flight

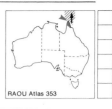

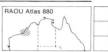
Bobbing   RAOU Atlas 353

436 Blue-winged Pitta *Pitta moluccensis*

Like Noisy Pitta but white throat; rufous-buff underparts. **Size** 17-19 cm. Vagrant from SE Asia.

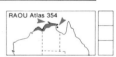
RAOU Atlas 880

437 Noisy Pitta *Pitta versicolor*

Head, throat black. Crown chestnut, black central stripe. Rich green above; shoulders, rump iridescent turquoise. Buff below; black central stripe extends to red vent. Short green tail. Long flesh-pink legs. **Size** 20 cm. **Imm.** similar, duller. **Voice** loud whistle 'walk-to-work'; a single high 'keow' alarm. **Habitat** rainforests, tropical and subtropical scrubs.

Flight

Perched   RAOU Atlas 352

438 Rainbow Pitta *Pitta iris*

Like Noisy Pitta but buffy underparts replaced by black. **Size** 18 cm. **Voice** like Noisy but softer. **Habitat** closed forests, thick scrub, occasionally mangrove edges.

Flight

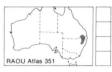
RAOU Atlas 354

439 Albert's Lyrebird *Menura alberti*

Like Superb Lyrebird; smaller. Rufous-brown above; buff-grey below. **Male** blackish-brown; broad grey outer tail. **Size** M 80-90, F 65-75 cm. **Voice** not unlike Superb. **Habitat** rainforests. Displays on platform of vine-stems.

Displaying

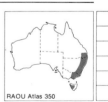
RAOU Atlas 351

440 Superb Lyrebird *Menura novaehollandiae*

Male dark brown above; grey-brown below. Long filamentous tail feathers, solid outer feathers patterned chestnut, white and black. Long legs; powerful feet dark grey. **Female/Imm.** smaller; shorter plain grey tail. **Size** M 80-98, F 74-84 cm. **Voice** loud, protracted and complex song with expert mimicry and loud alarm whistles. **Habitat** wet forests, temperate and subtropical rainforests. Male performs spectacular courtship display on earthern 'dancing' mounds.

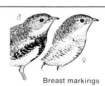
Flight

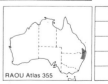
RAOU Atlas 350

441 Rufous Scrub-bird *Atrichornis rufescens*

Appears soft-plumaged. Rufous-brown with fine black bars. Throat whitish. **Male** chest blackish to abdomen sides. **Female** *no* black markings. **Size** 16 cm. **Juv.** unknown. **Voice** loud territorial song; softer notes; mimicry. **Habitat** dense, often secondary undergrowth in forests. Rare.

Breast markings   RAOU Atlas 355

442 Noisy Scrub-bird *Atrichornis clamosus*

Male dark brown above with fine black bars. Upper chest blackish, paler below. White throat extends down sides of breast. **Female** *no* black chest. **Size** 21 cm. **Juv.** no barring. **Habitat** low, thick, coastal vegetation. Very rare.

Breast markings   RAOU Atlas 356

435

♂ 441

442
Juv.

436

437

♂ 442

438

♀ 439

♂ 439

440 ♀   ♂ 440

N.Day

443 Singing Bushlark *Mirafra javanica*

Colour variable. Distinct pale eyebrow. Brown body, dark brown streaks above. Breast speckled black. Rufous wing patch distinctive in flight. White-edged tail. Aust. race *horsfieldi*. **Size** 12-15 cm. **Imm.** paler. **Voice** melodious songs, including mimicry. **Habitat** grassland, crops.

Dorsal flight
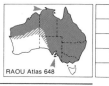
RAOU Atlas 648

444 Skylark *Alauda arvensis**

Buff eyebrow. Small crest. Larger, paler than Singing Bushlark. Darker above; lighter below; streaked breast and flanks. *No* rufous wing patch. White-edged tail. **Size** 17-19 cm. **Imm.** paler. **Juv.** no crest, shorter tail. **Voice** chirrup; musical warbling. **Habitat** grassland. Hovering aerial flight and dive.

Dorsal flight

RAOU Atlas 993

445 White-backed Swallow *Cheramoeca leucosternum*

White crown, throat and back. Nape, body dull black. Deeply forked tail. **Size** 15 cm. **Imm.** similar. **Voice** single note in flight. **Habitat** prefers dry, sandy country. Flight more fluttering than *Hirundo* swallows.

Perched
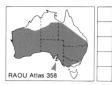
RAOU Atlas 358

446 Barn Swallow *Hirundo rustica*

Chestnut-red throat and forehead. Deeply forked tail. Glossy blue-black above; white below; blue-black breast band. Race *gutturalis* reaches Aust. **Size** 15 cm. **Imm.** duller; paler, narrower breast band; tail shorter. **Voice** twitter; pleasant warbling. **Habitat** open country, cultivated land, urban areas.

Perched
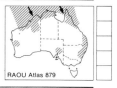
RAOU Atlas 879

447 Welcome Swallow *Hirundo neoxena*

Rufous-red throat and forehead. Forked tail. Blue-black above; dull white below; *no* black on breast. **Size** 15 cm. **Imm.** duller. **Juv.** smaller; cream gape prominent. **Voice** twittering chatter. **Habitat** all kinds, especially near water.

447
Perched
Pacific Swallow

RAOU Atlas 357

448 Red-rumped Swallow *Hirundo daurica*

Conspicuous rufous to chestnut rump. White to pale chestnut underparts, streaked. Browner, broader-winged than Barn Swallow; *no* dark chest bar. Deeply forked tail; longer tail streamers than Aust. swallows. **Size** 16-18 cm. **Habitat** open areas; woodlands. Asian vagrant.

Perched

449 Tree Martin *Hirundo nigricans*

Appears black-headed. Glossy blue-black above. Square tail; 'dirty' white rump. **Size** 13 cm. **Imm.** browner; breast streaked brown. **Voice** pleasant twitter. **Habitat** open woodland.

450
449
Perched
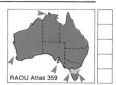
RAOU Atlas 359

450 Fairy Martin *Hirundo ariel*

Appears rufous-headed. Blue-black above; white streaks on back. Gleaming white rump. Square tail. Faint breast streaks. **Size** 12 cm. **Imm.** similar; duller. **Voice** distinct chirrup and sweet twittering. **Habitat** open country near water.

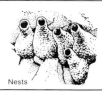
Nests
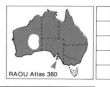
RAOU Atlas 360

* **Introduced** **Note** Pacific Swallow *Hirundo tahitica* not yet officially identified in Australia.

451 Richard's Pipit *Anthus novaeseelandiae*

Brown bird with darker brown streaks above. Pale buff
eyebrow stripe and below cheek. Slender bill. Underparts
buff with brown spots and streaks on whitish breast.
Unstreaked flanks. Long legs. Long white-edged tail.
Size 17-18 cm. **Imm.** like adults. **Voice** chirrups; trilling
calls in flight. **Habitat** open country. Wags tail up and
down.

Tail wag

Dorsal flight
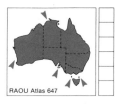
RAOU Atlas 647

452 Yellow Wagtail *Motacilla flava*

Three races recorded in Aust. but hardly distinguishable in
non-breeding plumage. Eyebrow runs to base of bill, where
appears pointed (sharp). Back olive-green; greenish-yellow
rump. Long black tail edged white; black legs. *No prominent*
white wing. **Breeding** race *simillina* grey crown, ear coverts;
underparts yellow; eyebrow white, broad and 'sharp'. Race
taivana olive crown; yellow eyebrow. Race *tschutschensis* grey
crown, white eyebrow and throat. **Non-breeding** (all races)
brown-grey upperparts; paler eyebrow; buffish
underparts. **Size** 15-17 cm. **Juv.** white underparts. **Voice**
shrill, trilling. **Habitat** salt works, paddocks, marshes.

Dorsal flight

Tail wag
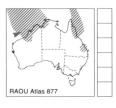
RAOU Atlas 877

453 Yellow-headed (Citrine) Wagtail *Motacilla citreola*

Sexes different in breeding plumage. **Breeding male**
bright yellow head; neck with black nape. **Breeding
female/Non-breeding male and female** plumage similar,
like non-breeding Yellow Wagtail, race *taivana*, but paler
yellow on sides of head, more grey on back; white, double
wing bars on dark wings; dark grey rump. **Size** 16-17 cm.
Juv. soft grey upperparts; white underparts; *no* olive and
often *no* yellow in plumage. **Voice** louder, shriller than
Yellow Wagtail. **Habitat** wet grasslands.

Dorsal flight ♀
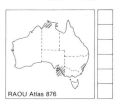
RAOU Atlas 876

454 Grey Wagtail *Motacilla cinerea*

Sexes different in breeding plumage. **Breeding male** black
throat. **Breeding female/Non-breeding male and female**
similar; grey upperparts; yellow underparts, brightest
under tail. White eyebrow. Yellowish-green rump,
uppertail coverts. Narrow, white wing band conspicuous
in flight. Tail very long, black, edged white. Pale legs.
Size 17-18 cm. **Juv.** buffish below; brown tinge above;
speckled breast. Yellow only on tail coverts. **Voice** sharp
'tit' or 'chichit'. **Habitat** prefers higher altitudes near water
but may be found anywhere.

Dorsal flight ♂
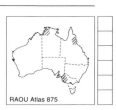
RAOU Atlas 875

455 White Wagtail *Motacilla alba*

Black and white bird with long black tail, edged white.
White underparts; conspicuous white wing bars. **Size**
18 cm. Several sightings in WA. Specimen collected near
Geraldton identified as race *ocularis*. One bird at Gippsland
Lakes, Vic., 1985 (race unknown). Most Aust. sightings in
coastal areas (see p. 275 for comparison with Black-backed
Wagtail *M. lugens*).

Non-br. ♂   Non-br. ♀
Br ♀   Juv.
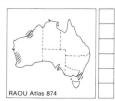
RAOU Atlas 874

451

455
Breeding

♂ **454**
Breeding

454
Non-breeding

454
Non-breeding

452
Race *simillina*
Breeding

452
Juv.

452
Non-breeding

452
Race *taivana*
Breeding

453
Non-breeding

453 ♂
Breeding

453
Juv.

N. Day.

456 Black-faced Cuckoo-shrike *Coracina novaehollandiae*

Race *novaehollandiae:* Black face. Grey upperparts; paler below. Tail tipped white. Race *subpallidus* (coastal WA): Paler. **Size** 33 cm. **Juv./Imm.** broad black eye-stripe from bill to *behind* eye. Breast finely barred. **Voice** creaky 'kreeark'. **Habitat** open woodlands, forests. Undulating flight. Shuffles wings when lands. Check for White-bellied Cuckoo-shrike.

Wing shuffle

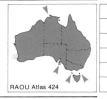

RAOU Atlas 424

457 Yellow-eyed Cuckoo-shrike *Coracina lineata*

Face dark; lores black; eye yellow. Dark grey above; wings darker. Breast to abdomen white, strongly barred black. **Size** 26-28 cm. **Juv.** whitish below. **Imm.** lighter barring below. **Habitat** rainforests, open forests. Pairs or large groups. Check for Oriental Cuckoo.

Ventral flight

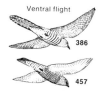

386

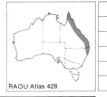

457

RAOU Atlas 428

458 White-bellied Cuckoo-shrike *Coracina papuensis*

Race *hypoleuca:* Black lores *to* eye. White below. Tail black, tipped white. Race *robusta* (E Aust.): Larger; sometimes has black face; sometimes has black head. Breasts vary from white to grey. **Size** 26-28 cm. **Imm.** underparts mottled grey-brown. **Voice** shrill 'kseak'. **Habitat** woodlands. Check for imm. Black-faced Cuckoo-shrike.

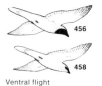

456

458

Ventral flight

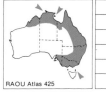

RAOU Atlas 425

459 Cicadabird *Coracina tenuirostris*

Small cuckoo-shrike. **Male** blue grey. Flight, tail feathers black, edged grey. **Female** pale eyebrow. Browner above; buff below. Underparts finely barred. Like Varied Triller. Races *tenuirostris* widespread; *melvillensis* (NT). **Size** 24-26 cm. **Imm.** like female; more heavily barred. **Voice** cicada-like trill. **Habitat** forests, woodlands.

Juv.

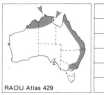

RAOU Atlas 429

460 Ground Cuckoo-shrike *Coracina maxima*

Largest cuckoo-shrike. Face dark grey; eye yellow. Silvery body. Wings, forked tail black. Rump, uppertail coverts, belly, flanks distinctively barred black. **Size** 33-37 cm. **Imm.** upperparts finely barred black. **Voice** distinctive, metallic. **Habitat** drier inland, open woodlands. A ground-feeder. Often in small family groups.

Ventral flight

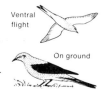

On ground

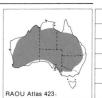

RAOU Atlas 423

461 White-winged Triller *Lalage tricolor*

Male breeding shoulder, edges of wing-feathers marked white. Light grey rump. Upperparts black; underparts white. **Male non-breeding** crown, back brown. **Female/Imm.** like non-breeding male except for buff wing, head markings. **Size** 18 cm. **Voice** trilling call. **Habitat** open country, woodlands.

Singing in flight ♂

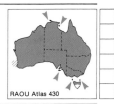

RAOU Atlas 430

462 Varied Triller *Lalage leucomela*

Male white eyebrow. Upperparts black; dark grey rump; white markings through wing. Underparts white, fine dark barring. Light cinnamon vent. **Female/Imm.** like male, browner above. Underparts grey-buff with barring; vent cinnamon. **Size** 19 cm. Three races: *leucomela* (east coast Aust.); *yorki* (C. York Pen.) cinnamon belly; *rufiventris* (NW Aust.) cinnamon breast. **Voice** distinctive trill. **Habitat** rainforests, woodlands.

Imm.

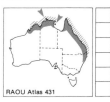

RAOU Atlas 431

456

457
Imm.

457

458
Race *robusta*
Dark form

458
Juv.

459 ♂

460
Imm.

460

458
Race *hypoleuca*

♀
459

♀
461

461 ♂
Breeding

462
♂

462
♀

461 ♂
Non-breeding

463 Red-whiskered Bulbul *Pycnonotus jocosus**

Head black. Tall pointed black crest. Black cheek line with red patch above. White throat. Olive to grey-brown above; greyish below. Undertail coverts red. Outer tail feathers with broad white tips. **Size** 20 cm. **Juv.** *no* red cheek; undertail coverts pink. **Voice** melodic whistles, chirps. **Habitat** introduced to urban areas, scrub fringes. Note: Red-vented Bulbul *Pycnonotus cafer* (introduced) now extinct in Melbourne, Vic. Black head, throat; scaled chest.

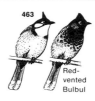
463

Red-vented Bulbul

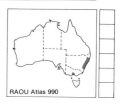
RAOU Atlas 990

464A Bassian (White's or Ground) Thrush *Zoothera lunulata*

Race *lunulata:* tan above; white below. Black scaly edges to body feathers except abdomen. Pale wing bar in flight. Pale eye-ring; dark eye. Dark bill. Grey-flesh legs. **Size** 26 cm. Race *cuneata* (Atherton Tablelands, Qld): larger-billed; buff chest. **Voice** high contact/alarm calls; pleasant soft complex Blackbird-like warble. **Habitat** wettish forest; dryer areas in winter. Seen on ground; flies if pressed.

Underwing pattern

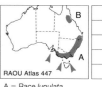
RAOU Atlas 447

A = Race *lunulata*
B = Race *cuneata*

464B Russet-tailed Thrush *Zoothera heinei*

Similar to Bassian Thrush, less prominent scaling; hardly visible on rump. Richer rufous plumage on rump, tail. Tail tip whiter. **Size** 25 cm. **Voice** strong, pleasant, two-note 'theea thooa'. **Habitat** lowlands of mid-central Qld.

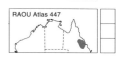
RAOU Atlas 447

465 Blackbird *Turdus merula**

Male black. Bill, eye-ring orange-yellow. **Female** dark brown above; rufous-brown below. Pale chin. Faintly streaked breast. **Size** 25 cm. **Juv.** dark bill. Underparts more rufous than female, upperparts streaked. **Voice** complicated, pleasant song; sharp clucking alarm calls. **Habitat** urban gardens, orchards, blackberries, farmland, native forest. Often perches in tree, on fence, etc., to sing.

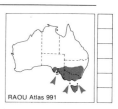
Dorsal flight

RAOU Atlas 991

466 Song Thrush *Turdus philomelos**

Sexes alike. Grey-brown above. Cream cheeks, upper breast. Dark brown cheek streaks. Dark upper, yellow lower bill. Chevrons on chest. White lower belly, undertail coverts. Legs yellow-brown. **Size** 23 cm. **Juv.** faint mottles on back. **Voice** superb, complicated song; high contact call. **Habitat** urban parks, gardens. Perches in tree to sing.

Singing

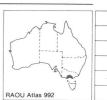
RAOU Atlas 992

467 Northern Scrub-robin *Drymodes superciliaris*

Olive-brown above. Face, underparts cream. Flanks buff. Black vertical eye-stripe. Wings black, two white wing bars. Rump rufous-brown. Tail tipped white. Legs pink. **Size** 22 cm. **Imm.** similar; softer colours. **Voice** four high descending notes; scolding call. **Habitat** rainforest floors. Northern Territory population possibly now extinct.

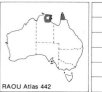
RAOU Atlas 442

468 Southern Scrub-robin *Drymodes brunneopygia*

Grey. White eye-ring; faint dark vertical eye-line. Wing feathers tipped white. Rump chestnut-brown. Tail dark grey, tipped white. **Size** 23 cm. **Juv.** browner above; paler, mottled underparts. **Voice** pleasant, loud whistles, typically 'clock-o-pee-er' but variable. **Habitat** mallee, scrubland.

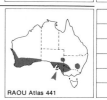
RAOU Atlas 441

---

* Introduced   **Note** The isolated race *cuneata* of Bassian Thrush from the Atherton Tablelands, N Qld, may ultimately prove to be a third species.

463

465
Juv.

♀ 465

♂ 465

464
Race *lunulata*

466

466

467

468

469 Rose Robin *Petroica rosea*

Male breast rose-red. Deep grey throat, back. White frons, abdomen, under and outer tail. *No* wing bars.
Female/Imm. greyish-brown upperparts; throat, breast greyish-white with occasional pale rose wash. Wing bars whitish. Dark brown tail, outer-tail shafts white.
Size 11 cm. **Voice** male has characteristic calls; both sexes 'tick'. **Habitat** breeds in deep gullies of tall open forests and rainforests. An autumn-winter dispersal to more open forest. Singly or pairs; most acrobatic of *Petroica* genus. Often feeds in high canopy.

Tail pattern

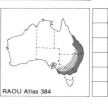

RAOU Atlas 384

470 Pink Robin *Petroica rodinogaster*

Male breast, abdomen rose-pink. Throat, upper breast sooty-black. White frons. *No* white on wings or tail.
Female/Imm. darker brown upperparts; brownish-buff underparts. Two buff wing bars. *No* white in tail.
Size 12 cm. **Voice** rarely calls. **Habitat** breeds in dense gullies of tall open forest. An autumn-winter dispersal to more open forest. Singly or pairs; often perches low down in cover, motionless and silent, before darting down upon food.

Tail pattern

RAOU Atlas 383

471 Flame Robin *Petroica phoenicea*

Male throat, breast, abdomen flame-red. Dark grey upperparts. White frons, wing bar, outer-tail shafts.
Female/Imm. upperparts brown; buff to white wing bars. Brown tail; outer-tail shafts white. Underparts lighter.
Size 14 cm. **Habitat** forages along the ground in series of short hops, runs and flights, preferring close-cropped pastoral land adjacent to woodland. Roosts in dense scrubs, citrus orchards. Nests in low open forest (coastal to alpine). Small flocks in autumn-winter dispersal. Upright stance; gives occasional flicks of wings and tail.

Tail pattern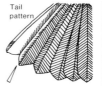

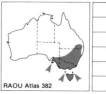

RAOU Atlas 382

472 Scarlet Robin *Petroica multicolor*

Male scarlet breast; back, throat black. White on forehead, prominent wing bar, outer-tail shafts. **Female** pale red wash on breast. **Size** 13 cm. **Imm.** resembles duller female but initially lacks red. **Voice** male territorial song repeated. **Habitat** breeds in closed and tall open forest; an autumn-winter altitudinal dispersal to more open localities. Single or pairs.

Tail pattern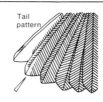

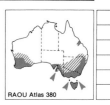

RAOU Atlas 380

473 Red-capped Robin *Petroica goodenovii*

Male scarlet cap, breast. Back, throat dull black. Bold white wing bar, outer-tail shafts. **Female** forehead red-brown; grey-brown upperparts; darker brown wings, tail. Some individuals have slight red wash on breast. Pale buff wing patch. Outer-tail shafts white. **Size** 12 cm. **Juv.** brownish streaks and blotches. **Imm.** no red on frons; males may have slightly red-washed breast. **Voice** male has characteristic calls; both sexes 'tick'. **Habitat** dryer scrub, woodlands. Autumn-winter dispersal. Single or pairs. Restless; flicks wings and tail while perched watchfully on stump or low branch; feeds mainly on ground. Identify females from Scarlet Robin and Flame Robin females.

Tail pattern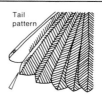

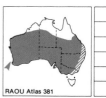

RAOU Atlas 381

469 ♂

♀ 470

♀ 469

470 ♂

473 ♂

♂ 471

♀ 473

♀ 471

♀ 472

472 ♂

474 Hooded Robin *Melanodryas cucullata*

Male black hood. Bill black. Eye dark brown. Black above with white wing bars and bottom half of outer tail feathers white. Underparts white. Legs black. **Female/Imm.** head, back grey-brown; throat pale grey. Tail, wings darker with same markings as male. **Size** 16 cm. **Voice** piping whistles, trilling; usually quiet. **Habitat** dry forests, woodlands, mallee, scrublands.

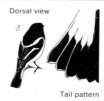
Dorsal view

Tail pattern

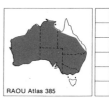
RAOU Atlas 385

475 Dusky Robin *Melanodryas vittata*

Head, upperparts brown, darker on wings, tail. Eyes brown. Bill dark brown. Underparts pale brown. Pale edging below bend of wing, wing patch and tail. Legs dark brown. **Juv.** paler streaking above; darker mottling below. Race *kingi* (King Is., Tas.): Olive wash above; browner below. **Size** 16.5 cm. **Voice** low, penetrating 'choo-wee'. **Habitat** open forest woodlands, scrublands, usually close to cleared land.

Young at nest

RAOU Atlas 386

476 Mangrove Robin *Eopsaltria pulverulenta*

Slaty-grey above; darker around eye and lores. Eyes dark brown. Bill black. Underparts white; grey wash to upper sides of breast. Tail blackish; bottom half of outer feathers white. Legs black. **Juv.** upperparts brown, streaked paler. Mottled buff breast. Three races: *cinereiceps, alligator* and *leucura* upperparts darkening from west to east respectively. **Size** 16 cm. **Voice** plaintive double whistle; melodious song; harsh 'chuk'. **Habitat** mangroves.

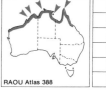
Tail pattern

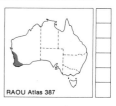
RAOU Atlas 388

477 White-breasted Robin *Eopsaltria georgiana*

Upperparts blue-grey. Paler eyebrow; darker on lores, wings, tail. Eyes dark brown. Bill black. Breast grey-washed; white below. Tips of outer tail white. Legs black. Smaller northern birds sooty-grey above. **Juv.** spotted brown above. **Size** 14.5 cm. **Voice** piping whistles 'wee-oh'; harsh chattering 'chit-chit'. **Habitat** southern birds: open forests, usually near streams. Northern birds: coastal scrubs or thickets.

Trunk perching:Typical of genus *Eopsaltria*

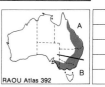
RAOU Atlas 387

478 Eastern Yellow Robin *Eopsaltria australis*

Up to five races described; two accepted. Head, back grey. Bill dark grey to black. Eye dark brown. Rump, uppertail coverts olive (southern birds) to bright yellow (northern birds). Upper throat whitish. Underparts yellow. Wings, tail brown-grey. Legs brownish-black. **Size** 15 cm. **Juv.** brown; mottled. **Voice** monotone piping; harsh 'chit'. **Habitat** wet open forests, woodlands, coastal thickets.

Juv.

RAOU Atlas 392

A = Race *chrysorrhoa*
B = Race *australis*

479 Western Yellow Robin *Eopsaltria griseogularis*

Like Eastern Yellow Robin but breast pale grey. Race *griseogularis* (SW of WA): Rump yellow. Race *rosinae* (Eyre Pen., SA): Rump olive-yellow. **Size** 15 cm. **Juv.** brown; mottled. **Voice** like Eastern Yellow Robin. **Habitat** open forests, woodlands, mallee, coastal scrubs.

478, 479
Wing bars in flight

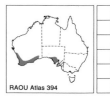
RAOU Atlas 394

475

474 ♂

474 ♀

477

478
Race *chrysorrhoa*

478
Race *australis*

479
Race *rosinae*

476

480 Yellow-legged Flycatcher *Microeca griseoceps*

Head, nape grey; pale brown wash on face, ear coverts. Pale lores and thin eye-ring. Broad bill dark above, cream below. Back, upperwing coverts yellowish-olive. Throat dull white. Rest of underparts lemon-yellow with buff wash on breast. Wings, tail brown, edged lemon-yellow. Legs orange-yellow. **Juv.** dully spotted white. **Size** 12 cm. **Voice** 'zzt-zzt-zzt'; also fine trilling song 'I-don't-ever-want-to-see-you-again, again'. **Habitat** rainforests, adjacent forests. Identify from Lemon-bellied Flycatcher, 'yellow robin' group and Grey Whistler (race *griseiceps*).

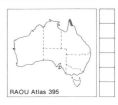

RAOU Atlas 395

481 Lemon-bellied Flycatcher *Microeca flavigaster*

Upperparts olive-brown, darker on wings and tail, yellow wash on rump. Pale streak on lores. Broad bill dark above, paler below. Throat white; rest of underparts yellow; olive wash on breast. Minor race *terraereginae* (Cape York Pen.) allegedly yellower. **Size** 12 cm. **Juv.** *lacks* yellow below. Cream spotted above. **Voice** varied melodious songs; 'choo-choo-suri-so-we-choo'. **Habitat** woodlands, streamside vegetation, mangroves. Identify from Grey Whistler (race *griseiceps*), Yellow-legged Flycatcher and 'yellow robin' group.

Juv. moulting

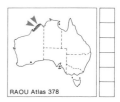

RAOU Atlas 379

482 Kimberley Flycatcher *Microeca flavigaster tormenti*

Like Lemon-bellied Flycatcher, but underparts pale grey, washed buff on breast. Broad, short bill wholly dark-brown. Legs black. **Size** 12.5 cm. **Juv.** contrasting mottles, spots. **Voice** like Lemon-bellied Flycatcher. **Habitat** mangroves, river thickets. Identify from Jacky Winter, Grey Whistler (race *simplex*) and juvenile Lemon-bellied Flycatcher. The Kimberley Flycatcher is now considered a race of the Lemon-bellied Flycatcher.

RAOU Atlas 378

483 Jacky Winter *Microeca leucophaea*

Black bill. Narrow black line through eye; narrow whitish eyebrow. Head, back grey-brown; darker on wings which are edged white. Pale grey breast; underparts whitish. Tail blackish-brown with white outer tail feathers. Legs black. Races *leucophaea* (SE Aust.) darkest race; *assimilis* (southern mallee, south and west area) black basal half to outer tail feathers, *not* white; *barcoo* (central Aust.) palest race; *pallida* (N Aust.) upperparts paler than *leucophaea*. **Size** 13 cm. **Juv.** spotted white above. **Voice** sweet, continuous, rapid 'jacky-jacky-winter-winter-winter'. **Habitat** dry forests, woodlands, mallee, farmlands. Identify from Kimberley Flycatcher. Perches on trees and vigorously waves tail from side to side, emphasising its white edges.

Tail wag

RAOU Atlas 377

494
Grey Whistler
Race *griseiceps*

494
Grey Whistler
Race *simplex*

480

483
Juv.

481

483

483

482

484 Pale-yellow Robin *Tregellasia capito*

Head olive-grey, darker on forehead; paler on ear coverts, nape. White lores and throat. Back, shoulder, rump olive. Wings, tail dark olive-brown, edged olive. Underparts pale yellow, washed olive on flanks. Legs pinkish. Race *nana* (Cooktown to Townsville, Qld) lores buff. **Size** 13 cm. **Juv.** browner above; feathers tipped cinnamon. **Voice** 'cheep'; monotonous whistles. **Habitat** rainforests.

Adult in nest

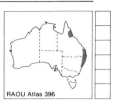
RAOU Atlas 396

485 White-faced Robin *Tregellasia leucops*

Distinctive white face, including sides of forehead, lores, eye-ring, upper throat. Rest of head olive-black. Back, shoulders, rump olive-green. Wings, tail olive-brown, edged olive. Underparts bright yellow; olive wash on breast. Legs pale yellow. **Size** 13 cm. **Juv.** browner above; duller below. **Voice** harsh 'chee-chee', like Pale-yellow Robin. **Habitat** rainforests. Aust. race is *albigularis*.

Face pattern

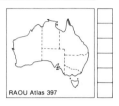
RAOU Atlas 397

486 White-browed Robin *Poecilodryas superciliosa*

Race *superciliosa* (Cape York Pen.): Upperparts uniformly dark brown. White eyebrow and patch below eye. Underparts white, washed light grey on breast. White wing patch; tail tipped white. Race *cerviniventris* 'Buff-sided Robin' (N and NW Aust.): Head darker; less white below eye. Buff flanks, undertail coverts. Flight feathers tipped white. **Size** 15 cm. **Voice** loud piping whistle; quieter whistles, harsh 'botta-chew'. **Habitat** race *superciliosa*: stream vegetation, rainforests, woodlands, vine scrub. Race *cerviniventris*: mangroves, swampy thickets, jungles, streamside vegetation.

Nest

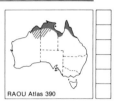
RAOU Atlas 390

487 Grey-headed Robin *Poecilodryas albispecularis*

Forehead, crown grey to nape; paler eyebrow. Bill black with yellow tip. Lores black. White line behind eye and white crescent below eye, lower face and throat. Blackish immediately behind eye-line, becoming brown on cheeks. Wings blackish-brown with two white wing bars. Rump to base of tail chestnut; rest of tail dark brown, tipped paler on outer tail feathers. Breast pale grey. Abdomen whitish; buff flanks. Legs flesh. **Juv.** brown above; head, underparts blotched rust. Bill pale brown. **Size** 17 cm. **Voice** piping whistle, often four notes long. **Habitat** rainforests, usually above 300 m.

Dorsal pattern

Chick in nest

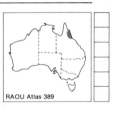
RAOU Atlas 389

488 Crested Shrike-tit *Falcunculus frontatus*

Three races. **Male** race *frontatus* 'Eastern Shrike-tit' (SE Aust.): Distinctive crested head, black with two broad white bands and patch at base of robust bill. Back, rump olive-green. Throat black. Rest of underparts yellow. Wings, tail darker grey. Race *leucogaster* 'Western Shrike-tit' (SW of WA): Abdomen white; undertail coverts yellow. Yellower above. Race *whitei* 'Northern Shrike-tit' (N Aust.): Smaller; yellower overall. **Female** throat olive-green in each race. **Juv.** pale throat; back brown in each race. **Size** 15-19 cm. **Voice** 'knock-at-the-door'; repeated plaintive whistle. **Habitat** open forests, woodlands, mallee. Observer's attention may be drawn by tearing of bark.

Juv.

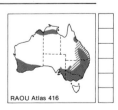
RAOU Atlas 416

488 ♂
Race *leucogaster*

488 ♂
Race *whitei*

488 ♀
Race *frontatus*

487

485

♂ **488**
Race *frontatus*

484
Race *nana*

486

486
Race *cerviniventris*

484

489 Olive Whistler *Pachycephala olivacea*

Male head dark grey. Rest of upperparts dark olive-brown. Bill blackish-brown. Throat white with broken grey barrings. Underparts buff-brown with grey wash on breast. **Female** similar but generally duller. Head more olive-brown. Throat without barrings. Race *macphersoniana* (Macpherson Ranges, Qld): lighter body colouration. **Size** 20.5 cm. **Juv.** upperparts rufous-brown. **Voice** various two- and three-syllabic whistles; also territorial call 'jo-jo-jo'. Whipcrack rather like Eastern Whipbird. **Habitat** tall wet forest and rainforest, woodland, alpine heaths. Northern populations in beech forest.

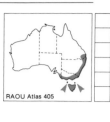

RAOU Atlas 405

490 Red-lored Whistler *Pachycephala rufogularis*

Slightly larger than Gilbert's Whistler. **Male** upperparts brownish-grey. Orange lores and throat. Eye red. Breast grey. Abdomen orange-buff. **Female** similar, except paler overall. **Size** 20.5 cm. **Juv.** upperparts, flanks rufous-brown. Underparts white, streaked dusky. **Voice** typically whistle followed by sound like indrawn breath 'see-saw'. **Habitat** mallee, low shrubland.

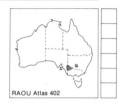

RAOU Atlas 402

491 Gilbert's Whistler *Pachycephala inornata*

Male upperparts brownish-grey with black lores. Eye red. Throat and upper breast deep orange. Rest of breast and abdomen pale grey. Undertail coverts buff-white. **Female** uniform grey above; lighter grey below, with darker breast. Eye red-brown. Race *gilberti* (SW Aust. to Nullarbor Plain): generally darker. **Size** 19.5 cm. **Juv.** upperparts, breast rufous-brown. **Voice** whistle 'pooo-ee' rising at the end. Also repeated 'jock'. **Habitat** shrubby woodland, mallee.

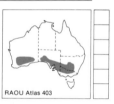

RAOU Atlas 403

492 Golden Whistler *Pachycephala pectoralis*

Male head black to nape and extending around upper breast in a band. Throat white. Nape yellow extending around to breast and abdomen. Back olive-green; wings black, edged yellow-green. Tail black, or grey and black. **Female** upperparts brownish-grey, sometimes with an olive wash. Pale grey stripe on wings. Underparts grey-buff to dull white. Some northern birds with lemon wash on undertail coverts. **Size** 17 cm. **Imm.** as female; wing feathers edged rufous. **Juv.** rich rufous; wings grey, edged rufous. **Voice** rich, melodious, sometimes with whip-cracking ending 'wi-wi-wi-whit!'. **Habitat** rainforests, open forests, woodlands, mallee, coastal vegetation.

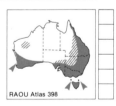

RAOU Atlas 398

493 Mangrove Golden Whistler *Pachycephala melanura*

Male similar to, but slightly smaller than male Golden Whistler. Yellow band of nape is broader, wings black, edged yellow-grey and tail base sometimes yellow-green. **Female** upperparts buff-grey with olive wash on back and wings. Throat dull white. Rest of underparts yellow. Race *robusta* (W Kimberley, WA, to E Qld): female tail black. **Size** 15.5 cm. **Imm.** as female; wing feathers edged rufous. **Juv.** rich rufous; wings grey, edged rufous. **Voice** generally like Golden Whistler. **Habitat** mangroves, riversides, coastal forests.

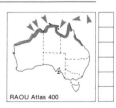

RAOU Atlas 400

Note Juvenile whistlers begin moulting out of their first plumage within a few weeks of fledging. Detailed information is required on these plumages for all species, and from all over the continent.

493 ♂

493 ♀

493 ♀
Race *robusta*

492 ♂

492
Imm.

♀ **492**

491 ♂

491 ♀

♂ **490**

490 ♀

489

494 Grey Whistler *Pachycephala simplex*

Two races. In the past regarded as two separate species but now treated as a species complex. Sexes generally similar. Race *simplex* (Arnhem Land, NT) 'Brown Whistler': upperparts grey-brown. Pale buff eyebrow. Pale grey-buff band across faintly streaked upper breast. Underparts white, buff-white. Race *griseiceps* 'Grey Whistler' (N Qld): head grey. Back olive. Throat buff-white; upper breast olive-buff merging with pale yellow lower breast, abdomen. Wings olive-brown, small white 'flash' near bend of wing. Tail olive-brown. **Size** 14.5 cm. **Juv.** upperparts rufous-brown. Wings edged rufous. **Voice** *simplex*: single note repeated several times, also melodious song; *griseiceps*: a whistle 'dum dum dee daa dum'. **Habitat** *simplex*: mangroves, wet forest; *griseiceps:* coastal rainforest and mangroves.

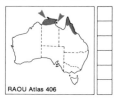

RAOU Atlas 406

495 Rufous Whistler *Pachycephala rufiventris*

Male head and back grey. Black from bill through eye and extending down around upper breast in a band. Throat white. Lower breast and abdomen deep buff. Wings and tail blackish-brown. **Female** upperparts olive-grey, darker on wings and tail. Throat white, merging into pale buff breast and abdomen, with dark streaking on throat and breast, fainter on abdomen. Six races recognised with two major patterns of variation (clines): one of decreasing size from south to north, and one of increasingly darker colouration from continental interior to coastal periphery. Race *falcata* (Melville Is. and Arnhem Land, NT) richly coloured but smaller than southern birds; *colletti* (NW Aust./interior of NT) intermediate between *falcata* and *pallida*; *pallida* (Normanton, Qld) palest race; *dulcior* (Townsville to Cape York Penin.) paler below than *rufiventris*; *rufiventris* (southern Aust.) large and dark; *maudae* (central Aust.) paler than *rufiventris*. **Size** 17 cm. **Juv.** underparts white, heavily streaked. **Voice** ringing, whipcrack-like 'ee-chong!'; also 'joey-joey-joey' repeated many times. **Habitat** mostly open forest, woodland, mallee and scrub of arid interior; less common in wetter tall forests. Nomadic or migratory in parts of Australia.

♂
Singing

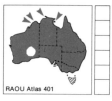

RAOU Atlas 401

♀

496 White-breasted Whistler *Pachycephala lanioides*

Male bill black. Head black to nape and extending around upper breast in a band. Nape rufous, with narrower rufous band extending around below black band. Throat, rest of breast and abdomen white. Back grey to grey-black. Wings black, edged grey (variable). Upper tail black. **Female** bill brownish. Dark streaking on throat, breast. Upperparts grey-brown, darker on wings, tail. Underparts buff, paler on throat. Pale grey wash on breast. Three races recognised: *carnarvoni* (Carnarvon to Eighty Mile Beach, WA) females brownish above, buff below; *lanioides* (Broome to King Sound, WA) females grey or olive above, paler below than *carnarvoni*; *fretorum* (NE Kimberley, WA to Karumba, Qld) smaller than *lanioides*. **Size** 19.5 cm. **Juv.** similar to female. Upperparts washed pale rufous; underparts more strongly streaked. **Voice** melodious song, also whistles. **Habitat** mangroves; less common in adjacent coastal rainforest. Forages on mud at low tide. Often quiet, inconspicuous, but responds to 'calling up'.

Feeding on crab

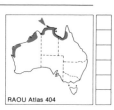

RAOU Atlas 404

494
Race *griseiceps*

480
Yellow-legged Flycatcher

494
Race *simplex*

495 ♂
Race *pallida*

495 ♂
Râce *rufiventris*

495 ♀
Race *rufiventris*

496 ♂
Race *lanioides*

♀ **496**
lanioides

497 Little Shrike-thrush *Colluricincla megarhyncha*

Many races described in Aust.; two recognised here. Race *rufigaster* (E Aust.) olive-brown above; paler on face. Bill pinkish-brown. Underparts cinnamon, slightly streaked on upper breast and paler throat. Race *parvula* (NW Aust.) light brown above. Bill blackish-brown. White lores and throat. Underparts cinnamon-buff. Faint streaking on throat, upper breast. **Size** 19 cm. **Voice** 'tu-ee, wot-wot-wot'; also harsh wheeze. **Habitat** race *rufigaster* rainforest, coastal woodland, swamps, mangroves. Race *parvula* mangroves, swamp thickets.

RAOU Atlas 413

A = Race *rufigaster*
B = Race *parvula*

498 Bower's Shrike-thrush *Colluricincla boweri*

Blue-grey head and back. Pale lores and throat. Cinnamon breast; paler on abdomen. Throat and breast darkly streaked. Wings and tail grey-brown. **Size** 20.5 cm. **Imm.** browner, duller; more heavily streaked. **Voice** melodious; quieter than other shrike-thrushes. **Habitat** rainforest above 300 m.

RAOU Atlas 414

499 Sandstone Shrike-thrush
Colluricincla woodwardi

Buff streak from bill to eye and on throat. Head dull grey. Back olive-brown. Breast, abdomen cinnamon. Grey wash on breast. Finely streaked throat and breast. Wings, tail olive-brown. Race *assimilis* (Kimberley region, WA) larger; throat whiter; underparts darker. **Size** 24 cm. **Juv.** underparts paler, slightly streaked. Wing feathers edged rufous. **Voice** rich, variable song. **Habitat** sandstone cliffy areas. Occurs almost entirely on the ground.

Singing

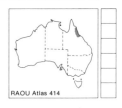

RAOU Atlas 411

500 Grey Shrike-thrush *Colluricincla harmonica*

Race *harmonica* (SE Aust.): **Male** head grey; white stripe from bill to eye. Back brown. Underparts light grey. Wings, tail grey. In NSW Aust. upperparts plain grey-brown; underparts paler. **Female** white eye-ring and eye-stripe less distinct. Underside of bill paler, fine streaking on throat. Race *rufiventris* ('Western Shrike-thrush' of central and W Aust.): back and wings darker grey; undertail coverts cinnamon-buff. **Size** 24 cm. **Juv./Imm.** light brown eye-ring extends midway to bill. Eyebrow tan to buff; varies in extent. Strongly streaked throat, breast. **Voice** liquid melodious 'pip-pip-pip-ho-ee!'; harsh 'yorrick'. **Habitat** forest, woodland, scrub, mallee, gardens.

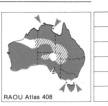

RAOU Atlas 408

501 Crested Bellbird *Oreoica gutturalis*

Male crown feathers can be raised into a crest. White forehead and throat encircled by a black band extending from crest through eye and down around breast. Eye orange. Back of head to nape grey. Back grey-brown. Underparts buff, richer colour on undertail coverts. Wings and tail grey-brown. **Female** lacks crest. Head grey with black crown. Eye red-brown. Throat, breast, back and wings grey, paling to white abdomen. **Size** 21.5 cm. **Voice** distinctive, ventriloquial. **Habitat** dry inland and sub-inland woodland and scrub.

Erect crest

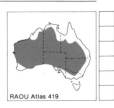

RAOU Atlas 419

497
Race *megarhyncha*

497
Race *parvula*

498
Juv.

498

499

501

♂ **501**

500
North-west form

500 ♂

500
Imm.

501

500
Race *rufiventris*

502 Yellow-breasted Boatbill
Machaerirhynchus flaviventer

Head: ventral view

Male bill large, black; 'boat-shaped' from below. Yellow eyebrow. Upperparts black; white shoulder bars, tail tips. Throat white; underparts bright yellow. **Female** like male; olive grey-brown above, underparts paler. **Size** 11-12 cm. **Juv.** like female, duller yellow; flanks barred (may persist in adult females). **Voice** soft, like Brown Thornbill, 'pee-dee-dee-dee-wit'. **Habitat** rainforests; hovers before foliage; cocks tail.

RAOU Atlas 368
Wren-like posture

503 Black-faced Monarch *Monarcha melanopsis*

Bill, legs blue. Black forehead joins black throat. Eye black; pale grey eye-ring. Upperparts, chest blue-grey. Wings, tail dark grey. Underparts rusty-rufous, **Size** 15-20 cm **Juv.** *no* black in face. **Voice** whistling 'why-you-wichye-oo'; also creaks, chatters. **Habitat** forests.

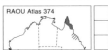
RAOU Atlas 373

504 Black-winged Monarch *Monarcha frater*

Like Black-faced Monarch but slightly pearly-grey above; conspicuous black wings, tail. **Size** 18-19 cm. **Juv.** *less* black in face. **Voice** like Black-faced. **Habitat** rainforests, adjacent forests.

RAOU Atlas 374

505 Spectacled Monarch *Monarcha trivirgatus*

Bill, legs blue. Bill to ear coverts, throat black. Slaty-grey above. Tail black, white tip. Cheeks, chest, flanks variably rusty-orange. Race *albiventris* (C. York) flanks, belly, vent white. **Size** 14-16 cm. **Juv.** mottled. **Imm.** paler grey above; dark grey face, chin, white facial marks vary. Underparts duller. **Voice** harsh buzz. **Habitat** wet forests, mangroves.

Incubating

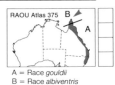
RAOU Atlas 375 B
A
A = Race *gouldii*
B = Race *albiventris*

506 White-eared Monarch *Monarcha leucotis*

Bill, legs blue. Head, upperparts all black except for white on eyebrow, spot before bill, cheek, wing bars, rump, tail tips. Underparts pale grey. **Size** 13 cm. **Juv.** upperparts sooty grey-brown; buffy wash below. Head white; black crown, forehead streaks, ear coverts. **Voice** like bronze-cuckoo 'thee-ou'; also buzzings. **Habitat** rainforests.

738
Juv.
506
Adult
Drawn to scale

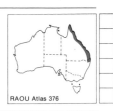
RAOU Atlas 376

507 Frilled Monarch *Arses telescopthalmus*

Foraging

Male bill blue. Eye-ring sky-blue, 'vertically oval'. Cap, chin black. Erectile white neck frill. Upperparts black. Scapulars, back, underparts white. **Female** chin white, lores light grey. Buff on sides of chest (varies). Aust. race *lorealis*. **Size** 14-17 cm. **Juv.** upperparts tinged brown. **Voice** scolding trills; 'frog-like' squawk. **Habitat** rainforest areas.

RAOU Atlas 371

508 Pied Monarch *Arses kaupi*

Male like Frilled Monarch, but broad black chest band; white chin. Eye-ring blue-grey, rounded. **Female** head black. White nape tufts, throat, faintly scaled black. Chest band broader. **Size** 14-15 cm. **Juv.** brown-grey, *not* black; white head areas scaled dark. **Voice** ten or more soft, high, whistles; a continuous buzzing; a flycatcher 'creak'. **Habitat** rainforests, adjacent forests.

Foraging

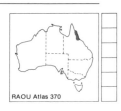
RAOU Atlas 370

Note   Recent DNA hybridisation studies suggest that the Spangled Drongo is closely related to the monarchs, and that Magpie-larks are also large monarchs, closely related to the White-eared Monarch.

503

503
Juv.

504
Juv.

504

506

505
Juv.

505

♀ 502

♂ 502

508 ♀

♂ 508

507 ♀

♂ 507

509 Broad-billed Flycatcher *Myiagra ruficollis*

Head: dorsal view

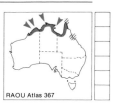

RAOU Atlas 367

Bill blue-black; boat-shaped. Small erectile crest. **Male** crown, lores, cheeks, upperparts glossy blue-grey. Eye-ring pale. Eye brown. Chin, throat, upper breast rufous-orange (brighter than female Leaden). Underparts white. Wings, tail grey-brown, edged pale grey. Undertail darker than plate. Feet grey-black. **Female** paler. Lores light grey. Back greyer; whiter under tail. **Size** 14-17 cm. **Juv.** like juv. Leaden; pale eyebrow. **Voice** harsh 'shwek'; may be harsher than Leaden, Satin; also repeated loud 'thee-ooo-uu', whirrings. **Habitat** tropical mangroves, monsoon forests, adjacent woods.

510 Leaden Flycatcher *Myiagra rubecula*

Head: dorsal view

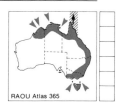

RAOU Atlas 365

Sexes strongly dimorphic. Bill blue, tip black; broad, not boat-shaped as Broad-billed. Small erectile crest. **Male** lores black. Eyes dark brown. Upperparts and upper chest blue-grey. Underparts white. Legs black. Undertail grey. **Female** upperparts duller. Pale eye-ring; grey lores. Chin, throat, upper breast rufous-orange. Underparts white. Wings, tail feathers pale-edged. **Size** 14-17 cm. **Juv.** upperparts brown-grey. Pale streaks, buff edges to wings. Underparts whitish, throat, upper breast mottled brown, washed rufous. **Voice** harsh rattles, buzzes; deep 'burping'; whistling 'zoo-wee'. **Habitat** tall, medium open forests.

511 Satin Flycatcher *Myiagra cyanoleuca*

Incubating

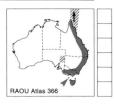

RAOU Atlas 366

Sexes strongly dimorphic. **Male** like Leaden male. Glossy blue-black above, on chest. Undertail darker. **Female** like female Leaden. Throat *may be* brighter. Upperparts darker grey. Wings, tail grey-brown, paler edged. **Size** 15-18 cm. **Juv.** like juvenile Leaden; upperparts darker, pale streaked and buff-edged. Throat feathers darker edged. **Voice** louder than Leaden; churrings; strong, carrying, repeated whistles. **Habitat** tall and medium open forests.

512 Shining Flycatcher *Myiagra alecto*

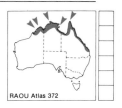

RAOU Atlas 372

Sexes strongly dimorphic. Bill slender, blue, tipped black. Small erectile crest. **Male** body entirely glossy black with intense blue sheen. **Female** lores black. Crown, sides of face, nape, glossy blue-black. Upperparts rich rufous-chestnut. Underparts white. Race *wardelli* (N Qld) undertail coverts white, washed rufous. **Size** 15-18 cm. **Juv.** like female but duller; crown greyer. **Voice** a considerable variety of clear whistles; harsh grating calls. **Habitat** tropical mangroves; forest streamside vegetation.

513 Restless Flycatcher *Myiagra inquieta*

Hawking

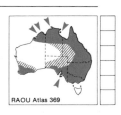

RAOU Atlas 369

Largest *Myiagra*. Sexes similar. Small erectile crest. Bill blue-black. Iris dark brown. **Male** lores black; crown, sides of face, upperparts glossy blue-black. Wings browner. Chin, throat to undertail coverts white. Pale buff wash on breast variable. Legs black. **Female** lores grey. Race *nana* smaller with slightly broader bill. **Size** 16.5-21 cm. **Juv.** like adult; upperparts grey-black. Wing feathers edged buff. Throat, upper breast washed buff. **Voice** continuous whirring hisses as hovering ('scissor's grinder' call). **Habitat** open forests, farmland. Identify from Willie Wagtail.

Note *Myiagra nana* 'Paperbark Flycatcher' of northern Aust. not included on plate, but is probable, not yet confirmed, new species. Previously considered race of Restless Flycatcher of tropical *Melaleuca* forests.

509 Juv.

509

510 ♀

510 ♂

511 ♀

511 ♂

510 Juv.

512 ♀

511 Juv.

512 ♂

513 Juv.

513 ♂

N.DAY.

514 Rufous Fantail *Rhipidura rufifrons*

Eye, bill, legs dark brown. Eyebrow rufous. Rest of head, mantle, wings grey-brown. Throat white, black band on upper chest. Rest of chest feathers black, scaled white. Underparts white. Lower back, tail base orange-rufous. Tail blackish, white tip. **Size** 15-16 cm. **Juv.** duller, brown; markings less distinct. **Voice** thin, ascending, high whistles; also a 'chip'. **Habitat** wet forests, occasionally more open forests. Very active; fans, waves long tail up and down, or side to side. Often in deep shade close to the ground.

Ventral view

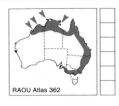

RAOU Atlas 362

515A Grey Fantail *Rhipidura fuliginosa*

Race *albicauda*

Five races. Race *alisteri*: eye, bill, legs black. Mid-grey above with white eyebrow, ear mark, throat, two narrow wing bars. White tail shafts, tips, except central feathers; pale grey inner webs; outer feather white. Upper breast sooty. Rest of underparts cream, some sooty chest spots. **Juv.** broader buffy wing bars, head markings. Race *preissi*: as *alisteri* but breast grey. Race *albiscapa*: as *alisteri* but broader breast band; tail less white; upperparts darker. Race *keasti*: very dark above; pale buff below; wing bars, tail edges reduced. Race *albicauda*: tail distinctive, white except central feathers; broader wing bars; paler grey breast. **Size** 15-17 cm. **Voice** *alisteri* variety of rich, loud, rising whistles, also chatters; *albicauda* softer; faster 'trilling'. **Habitat** forests, woods; *albicauda* mulga only. Very active; erratic flight, fans tail constantly; perches sideways.

Ventral view

RAOU Atlas 361

'Wineglass' Fantail nest

515B Mangrove Fantail *Rhipidura phasiana*

Small; pallid; light grey above; pale buff below. Narrow darkish chest band. Bill large. Wings, tail short. Wider white wing bars. **Size** 14.5-16 cm. **Juv.** duller, browner; markings less distinct. **Voice** soft; series of short twittering whistles. **Habitat** confined to mangroves.

Mangrove Fantail ventral view

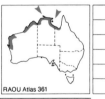

RAOU Atlas 361

516 Northern Fantail *Rhipidura rufiventris*

Large black bill. Eye brown. Legs black. Upperparts pale grey; brown wash on wings. White eyebrow; no ear mark. Throat white. Upper breast grey, streaked white; otherwise white below. Tail all grey, a third of the three outer-tail feathers broadly tipped white; outer feathers all white. **Size** 16-18.5 cm. **Juv.** throat, tail tips buff. **Voice** six-note song like gerygones. Also various 'chips', 'chunks'. **Habitat** open forests, edges of rainforests, mangroves. Only occasionally fans tail; tends to perch vertically; appears less active. Identify from Grey Fantail, Jacky Winter.

Ventral view

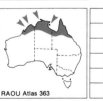

RAOU Atlas 363

517 Willie Wagtail *Rhipidura leucophrys*

Eyebrow expanded

Eye, bill, legs black. White eyebrow. Lower cheek stripe spotted white. Head, upperparts, upper chest and (long) tail glossy black; brown tinge to wings. Underparts otherwise white. **Size** 19-21.5 cm. **Juv.** upperparts have buff spotting on tips of black feathers. **Voice** scolding 'chick-a-chick-a-chick'. A chattering, musical 'sweet, pretty creature' song. **Habitat** everywhere except very wet forests. Runs on ground; wags tail around in a fan. Perches on livestock. Identify from Restless Flycatcher.

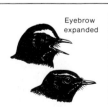

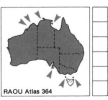

RAOU Atlas 364

516

516 Juv.

515

515 Juv.

514

514 Juv.

517

517 Juv.

518 Logrunner *Orthonyx temminckii*

Male crown rufous. Face grey. Upperparts rufous, mottled black. Rump rufous. Throat white with broad black edge. Shafts of tail feathers project, forming spine tips. **Female** throat orange. **Size** 17-20 cm. **Juv.** mottled brown. **Voice** rapid, excited 'weet weet'. **Habitat** floors of subtropical rainforests.

Juv.

RAOU Atlas 434

519 Chowchilla *Orthonyx spaldingii*

Male head black. Eye-ring pale. Upperparts dark brown. Throat and breast white. Tail feathers tipped with spines. **Female** throat, upper breast orange. **Size** 26-28 cm. **Juv.** browner, cinnamon mottling. **Voice** very vocal — parties may dominate dawn chorus with loud repeated 'chow-chilla' — 'chowry chook chook'. **Habitat** floors of tropical rainforests.

Juv.

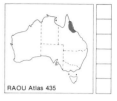
RAOU Atlas 435

520 Eastern Whipbird *Psophodes olivaceus*

A dark, crested bird with long, broad tail. Head and crest black. Bold white cheek stripes on sides of black throat. Upperparts and tail dark olive-green. Breast black. Tail tipped white. Race *lateralis* (NE Qld): smaller, browner; tail shorter, brown at tip. **Size** 25-30 cm. **Juv.** olive-brown, lacks white cheek stripes and dark throat. **Imm.** duller; throat mottled. **Voice** ringing 'whipcrack' (male); sharp 'choo choo' (female response). Other harsh scolding notes. **Habitat** dense understories of rainforests, coastal scrubs, wet sclerophyll forests, riparian (stream-side) forest.

Juv.

Imm.

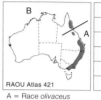
RAOU Atlas 421
A = Race *olivaceus*
B = Race *lateralis*

521 Western Whipbird *Psophodes nigrogularis*

An elusive, olive-green bird with small crest and long, broad tail. Head and crest grey. Upperparts pale olive. Race *nigrogularis* (SW Aust.): throat black; white cheek stripes fully edged with black; underparts plain olive-cream or grey. Race *leucogaster* (SE Aust.): white on belly; cheek stripes only partly edged black; outer tail feathers tipped white. **Size** 21-25 cm. **Juv./Imm.** throat greyish, not black; no cheek stripe. **Voice** antiphonal — male first, female responds. A variety of harsh, grating calls; chattering alarm call; other calls. **Habitat** dense thickets of coastal heath; dense mallee scrub.

Eastern race
Western race

A
B
RAOU Atlas 422
A = Race *nigrogularis*
B = Race *leucogaster*

522 Chirruping Wedgebill *Psophodes cristatus*

Distinctive. Crest and upperparts light brown. Underparts light grey; faint streaking on breast. Black, wedge-shaped bill. Long, white-tipped tail. **Size** 19-21 cm. **Juv.** pale bill; buff markings on wings. **Voice** 'tootsie cheer' (male); 'ee cheer' (female response) repeated monotonously with sparrow-like quality. **Habitat** semi-arid areas with low scrub, acacia woodlands, savannah.

Often in groups

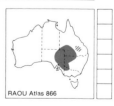
RAOU Atlas 866

523 Chiming Wedgebill *Psophodes occidentalis*

Almost identical, except for voice and distribution, to Chirruping Wedgebill. **Size** 19-22 cm. **Voice** descending chime 'why did you get drunk?' repeated monotonously with haunting quality. **Habitat** dense acacia, melaleuca, tea-tree scrub in arid areas.

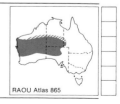
RAOU Atlas 865

♂ 518

518 ♀

♀ 519

519

520

521

522

523

M. Day.

524 Spotted Quail-thrush *Cinclosoma punctatum*

Juv.

Flight

Male white eyebrow. Face black. White patch on sides of black throat. Neck, breast grey. Broad black spots on back, flanks. Shoulder black, spotted white. Tail tipped white. **Female** paler; dull orange patch on side of buff-white throat. **Size** 25-28 cm. **Imm.** resembles female. **Voice** thin high-pitched contact calls (the typical quail-thrush is very difficult to tune the human ear to); also loud double-whistle; occasional richer whistlings. **Habitat** dry and wet sclerophyll forests but ideally on leaf-littered rocky ridges with short tussock grass. Occasionally perches in trees.

RAOU Atlas 436

525 Chestnut Quail-thrush *Cinclosoma castanotum*

Juv.

Male throat, face, upper breast black. White eyebrow. Broad white streak on sides of throat. Upper back grey-brown, becoming chestnut on lower back. Tail tipped white. **Female** paler; face brown; upper breast grey. **Size** M 22-26, F 17-23 cm. **Imm.** like female. **Voice** thin, high-pitched. Also rosella-like piping whistle. **Habitat** mallee and mulga scrub; inland desert heaths, woodlands.

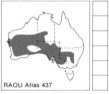

RAOU Atlas 437

526 Chestnut-breasted Quail-thrush
Cinclosoma castaneothorax

♀
A

Race
castaneothorax

♀
B

Race
marginatum

Race *castaneothorax:* **Male** upperparts warm cinnamon-brown; breast rich cinnamon-yellow *(not* chestnut as name suggests). **Female** like female *cinnamomeum* but has rufous wash on grey breast. Race *marginatum* 'Western Quail-thrush': **Male** larger than nominate race. Upperparts rich chestnut. Breast reddish-brown. **Female** resembles female *castaneothorax*. **Size** 18-24 cm. **Imm.** all races generally like female. **Voice** thin, high-pitched ventriloquial notes; far-carrying whistles. **Habitat** *castaneothorax* and *marginatum* favour low acacia-covered ridges.

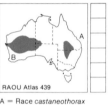

RAOU Atlas 439

A = Race *castaneothorax*
B = Race *marginatum*

527 Cinnamon Quail-thrush *Cinclosoma cinnamomeum*

♀
A

Race
cinnamomeum

Two races recognised. Nominate race is *cinnamomeum:* **Male** white eyebrow; black face. Broad white streak down sides of black throat. Upperparts plain cinnamon-rufous. Buff-white patch on upper breast; broad black band below. Outer tail feathers black, tipped white. **Female** duller; buff throat and eyebrow. Upper breast pale grey, *no* black below. **Imm.** males of race *cinnamomeum* may have indistinct breast band. Race *alisteri* 'Nullarbor Quail-thrush': **Male** face, throat, upper breast black. White eyebrow. Irregular white streak on sides of throat. Upperparts reddish-cinnamon. Outer tail feathers black, tipped white. **Female** duller; face grey-brown; throat, upper breast grey. **Size** 18-20 cm. **Imm.** resembles female but less clearly marked. **Voice** not well known. **Habitat** *cinnamomeum* on gibber plains, sparse vegetation along usually dry watercourses. Race *alisteri* low vegetation associated with the Nullarbor Plain limestone outcroppings.

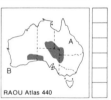

RAOU Atlas 440

A = Race *cinnamomeum*
B = Race *alisteri*

♀ 524

524 ♂

♀ 525

525 ♂

♀ 527
Race alisteri

527 ♂ Race alisteri

♀ 527
Race cinnamomeum

526 ♂
Race castaneothorax

♂ 527
cinnamomeum

526 ♂
Race marginatum

528 Grey-crowned Babbler
Pomatostomus temporalis

Largest and only babbler *without* dark crown. Head has narrow grey crown, bordered by broad white eyebrow. Dark brown eye-stripe. Eye pale yellow. Bill black, long and down-curved. Upperparts greyish-brown; rump darker. Throat, upper breast white, merging into grey breast and rufous-brown belly. Wings dark brown; chestnut patch in flight. Tail long, blackish-brown, broad white tip. Legs black. Race *rubeculus* has reddish-brown breast, darker brown underparts. **Size** 25-29 cm. **Juv.** duller, rufous wash on eyebrow and wing bars buff. Bill shorter; eyes dark. **Voice** loud 'yahoo'; chirring notes; cat-like meowing. **Habitat** dryer, more open forests, scrubby woodlands, trees by roads, farmland with isolated trees. In *all* babblers a dark ('masked face') eye-stripe, bordered by white eyebrows, and white throat, gives a 'band of thieves' appearance to any group of these birds.

Dorsal pattern

RAOU Atlas 443

529 White-browed Babbler
Pomatostomus superciliosus

The plainest babbler. Crown dark brown; prominent white eyebrow. Bill black, down-curved. Eye-stripe brown. Upper back, wings greyish-brown; rump dark brown. Throat, breast white, merging into grey-brown flanks and belly. Tail blackish-brown, tipped white. Legs dark grey. **Size** 18-22 cm. **Juv.** duller, brow, throat washed buff. Bill shorter. **Voice** high-pitched chatter; variety of chirring, scolding notes. **Habitat** dryer, more open forests with shrubby understorey, mallee, mulga scrubs. A very active, noisy and seemingly 'quarrelsome' bird.

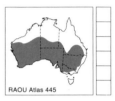

Dorsal flight

RAOU Atlas 445

530 Hall's Babbler *Pomatostomus halli*

Similar to White-browed Babbler but darker and more definitely marked. Narrow, dark brown crown; broad white eyebrow. Eye dark. Bill black, down-curved. Eye-stripe dark, appears black. White throat, upper breast well demarcated from dark brown underparts. Tail sooty-brown, tipped white. Legs black. **Size** 23-25 cm. **Juv.** duller; brow, throat washed buff. **Voice** excited high-pitched chatter; other typical babbler calls. **Habitat** mainly ridges of dry acacia shrubs; dry eucalypt woodlands.

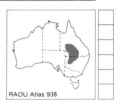

RAOU Atlas 938

531 Chestnut-crowned Babbler
Pomatostomus ruficeps

Rather 'dapper' appearance. Crown rich chestnut, highlighted by narrow white eyebrow. Eye brown. Bill dark, down-curved. Eye-stripe brown. Back mottled greyish-brown. Two white wing bars diagnostic, identifying this from all other babblers. Throat, breast white, grading into grey-brown belly. Flanks dark brown. Tail blackish-brown, tipped white. Legs dark grey. **Size** 20.5-23 cm. **Juv.** duller; crown browner. Brow and wing bars washed rufous. **Voice** harsh chatter; other whistling calls. **Habitat** dry inland mulga, mallee scrubs, more open arid woodlands; she-oaks; acacia trees near edges of salt lakes.

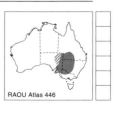

531 Communal roosting nest

RAOU Atlas 446

528
Race *rubeculus*

528

528
Juv.

529

529

530

531

N.Day.

532 Clamorous Reed-warbler *Acrocephalus stentoreus*

Race *australis:* Bill slender; dark above, pale below.
Upperparts warm brown. Eyebrow, throat cream. Buffy-
cream below. **Size** 17 cm. **Voice** clear, sweet 'crut-crut-crut,
deet-deet-deet, crotchy-crotchy-crotchy' with variations
and various scolding calls. **Habitat** dense vegetation near
water.

Incubating

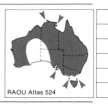

RAOU Atlas 524

533 Great Reed-warbler *Acrocephalus arundinaceus*

Race *orientalis:* Like Clamorous; bill deeper. **Non-breeding**
fine streaks on throat and upper breast. **Size** 19 cm. **Voice**
like Clamorous but much harsher, faster and lower.
Habitat like Clamorous. Rare migrant.

Bill profile

532

533

RAOU Atlas 872

534 Tawny Grassbird *Megalurus timoriensis*

Race *alisteri:* Rufous crown unstreaked. Brown upperparts
dark streaked. Whitish unstreaked underparts. Long
brown tail. **Size** 19 cm. **Voice** descending wren-like reels;
scolding calls. **Habitat** like Little Grassbird, also open
grasslands.

RAOU Atlas 523

535 Little Grassbird *Megalurus gramineus*

Crown, throat and brown upperparts distinctly streaked
dark. Long graduated wing feathers, edged white.
Underparts grey-brown. **Size** 14 cm. **Voice** distinct 't-thee-
thee'. **Habitat** reeds, tussocks on swamps.

RAOU Atlas 522

536 Spinifexbird *Eremiornis carteri*

Rufous crown and nape. Upperparts rufous-brown,
unstreaked. Whitish underparts. Long, graduated, dark
tail, tipped buff. **Size** 15 cm. **Voice** pleasant warble.
Habitat spinifex, dense grasses.

Tail cocked

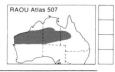

RAOU Atlas 507

537 Zitting Cisticola *Cisticola juncidus*

Race *leanyeri:* **Breeding male** head buff-brown, spotted
black. Nape *unstreaked.* Upperparts like Golden-headed.
Undertail pale grey, sub-terminal black spots. Tail always
tipped white. **Female/Non-breeding male** like Golden-
headed in same plumage. Other races exist. **Size** 10 cm.
Voice monotonous insect-like 'tik-tik' and 'see-sick, see-
sick'. **Habitat** rank grasslands.

Breeding

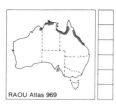

RAOU Atlas 969

538 Golden-headed Cisticola *Cisticola exilis*

Breeding male uniform golden crown, nape. Upperparts
cinnamon-brown to rufous, streaked black. Underparts
cream to golden buff. Dark undertail, tipped cinnamon.
Breeding female crown streaked black. **Non-breeding
male/female** crown streaked black; tail longer. **Juv.** duller.
Size 10 cm. **Voice** 'churr, lik-lik'. **Habitat** long grasses.

Display flight

RAOU Atlas 525

539 Arctic Warbler *Phylloscopus borealis*

Dark olive upperparts. Yellowish-white, long, straight
eyebrow. Whitish below. **Size** 12 cm. **Voice** distinctive loud
'twzee-et'. **Habitat** wooded areas, mangroves. One Aust.
record, Scott Reef off NW Aust.

RAOU Atlas 831

539

532

533

536

537 ♂
Breeding
Race *leanyeri*

♂ 538
Non-breeding

534

♂ 538
Breeding

535

N. Ray.

540 Rufous Songlark *Cinclorhamphus mathewsi*

Pale, white eyebrow. Streaky brown upperparts. Rufous rump, uppertail coverts. Whitish underparts. Dark brown tail. **Male** bill black; breast may have fine spots. **Female** bill pale brown. **Size** 16-19 cm. **Juv.** paler; dark spots on breast, throat. **Voice** melodious song (in flight or perched); singing males very apparent in breeding season. **Habitat** woodland, parklands, hedges, lightly timbered grasslands.

RAOU Atlas 509

541 Brown Songlark *Cinclorhamphus cruralis*

Singing in flight

Male pale eyebrow; black bill. Streaked brown upperparts; brownish-black underparts. Longish, pointed tail. **Female/ Juv.** *much* smaller; paler. Pinkish-brown bill. Pale throat. Breast light buff, faintly streaked. Black-brown belly. **Size** M 23-35, F 18-23 cm. **Voice** loud, creaky. **Habitat** grasslands, crops. Males often perch with crown, tail raised. Conspicuous climbing, then gliding song flight. Note different sex sizes. Males often appear very dark. Identify females from Rufous Songlark, female White-winged Triller, Skylark and Richard's Pipit.

RAOU Atlas 508

542 Purple-crowned Fairy-wren *Malurus coronatus*

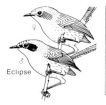

Eclipse

Male breeding frons and most of crown purple. Black, central crown patch. Face, nape, lores black. Back sandy-brown. Tail blue. Underparts buff-white. **Male eclipse** brown head, black eye patch. **Female** mainly buff. Chestnut face and ear coverts are diagnostic. Tail blue. Race *macgillivrayi* (Gulf of Carpentaria): **Male** darker above; white below. **Female/Imm.** crown, nape blue-grey; chestnut ear coverts. **Size** 16.5 cm. **Voice** high-pitched. **Habitat** mangroves, cane grass, pandanus near water.

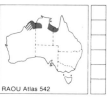

RAOU Atlas 542

543 Superb Fairy-wren *Malurus cyaneus*

Eclipse

Male bill black. Crown, upper back, ear coverts bright blue. Breast, nape, lower back black. Tail dark blue. Underparts buffy-white. **Male eclipse** like female; tail shorter, blue. **Female** brown. Bill, lores, eyebrow reddish-brown. Tail brownish. **Size** 14 cm. **Voice** musical trill. **Habitat** open forests, swamps, coastal areas, rainforests; gardens.

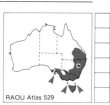

RAOU Atlas 529

544 Splendid Fairy-wren *Malurus splendens*

A = Race *splendens*
B = Race *callainus*
C = Race *melanotus*

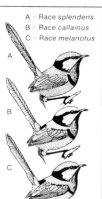

Male bill black. Forehead, ear coverts light blue. Rump blue. Tail broad, short. **Male eclipse** like female; bill black; tail dark blue. **Female** brown like Superb Fairy-wren female but slightly bluish tail. Race *callainus* 'Turquoise Fairy-wren': **Male** like race *splendens*: much lighter blue upperparts, belly; black rump. **Male eclipse** wings coverts, tail blue. **Female/Imm. male** like *splendens* female. Race *melanotus* 'Black-backed Fairy-wren': **Male** light blue ear coverts. Breast band narrower. Black rump. Tail blue. **Male eclipse** like female; wings, tail blue. **Female** brown like Superb Fairy-wren female; tail faintly dull blue. **Size** 14 cm. **Voice** resembles Superb Fairy-wren. **Habitat** race *splendens*: forest margins, dryer inland areas; often feeds higher in trees, shrubs than other wrens. Race *callainus*: dense mulga, mallee, saltbush. Race *melanotus*: mallee, porcupine grass.

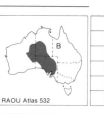

RAOU Atlas 532

RAOU Atlas 532

540

♂ 541

541 ♀

♀ 542

542 ♂
Breeding

♀ 543

♂ 543
Breeding

♂ 544
Breeding

544 ♀

544 ♂
Non-breeding

545A Variegated Fairy-wren *Malurus lamberti*

A = Race *lamberti*
B = Race *assimilis*
C = Race *dulcis*
D = Race *rogersi*

Four races. Race *lamberti* (nominate): **Male** bill black; iris dark brown. Mid-blue crown and mantle. Paler blue ear coverts. Frons, chest and neck black. Sides of chest dark blue. Wings brownish; shoulders chestnut. Rump black. Tail blue with white tips. Underparts whitish. Legs dark brown. **Male eclipse** grey upperparts; white underparts. Black bill and white eye-ring. Tail blue. **Female/Imm.** grey with red bill, lores and eye-ring. Tail dull blue. Legs reddish. Race *assimilis* 'Purple-backed Fairy-wren': like *lamberti* but **Male** has darker blue cap and mantle. Race *dulcis* 'Lavender-flanked Fairy-wren': **Male** like *assimilis* but has purplish flanks. **Female** grey-blue with white eye-ring. Race *rogersi* also called 'Lavender-flanked Fairy-wren': like *dulcis* but **Female** has red eye-ring, lores and bill. **Size** 14-15 cm. **Voice** like Superb Fairy-wren but faster, far more metallic. **Habitat** race *lamberti* heathlands, open forests of coastal ranges in E Aust. Race *assimilis* across inland Australia. Race *dulcis* rocky escarpments, Arnhem Land, NT. Race *rogersi* rocky escarpments, Kimberley region WA.

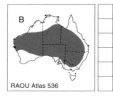

RAOU Atlas 536

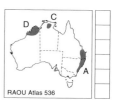

RAOU Atlas 536

545B Lovely Fairy-wren *Malurus amabilis*

Male like *lamberti* but blue areas are lighter blue. Ear coverts broader. Wings dark with brown edges. Tail dark blue, shorter, with broad white tips. **Female** bright blue upperparts. White eye-ring. Lores white. White underparts. Tail hazy-blue, also tipped white. **Size** 12-13 cm. **Voice** a variety of single and whistling, trilling calls. **Habitat** rainforest edges of NE Qld. Frequently in trees, above ground level. Former race *amabilis*, now considered a full species.

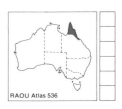

RAOU Atlas 536

546 Blue-breasted Fairy-wren
Malurus pulcherrimus

Like Variegated Fairy-wren, race *assimilis*, in every respect except: **Male** crown, mantle dark blue with a purplish sheen; ear coverts slightly paler. Breast dark slaty, with a blue to navy blue sheen; no contrast between blue sides of breast and black centre as in 'Purple-backed Fairy-wren'. **Size** 15 cm. **Voice** like Variegated Fairy-wren. **Habitat** sand plains, heath, mallee, mulga-eucalypt and jarrah forests.

Eclipse

RAOU Atlas 540

547 Red-winged Fairy-wren *Malurus elegans*

Like Blue-breasted Fairy-wren except crown and mantle are pale blue; ear coverts even paler. **Female** dull black bill. **Voice** like Variegated Fairy-wren. **Size** 15 cm. **Habitat** near water; swamps in Darling and Stirling Ranges, SW of WA.

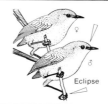

Eclipse

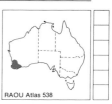

RAOU Atlas 538

543 Superb Fairy-wren

544 Splendid Fairy-wren

545 Variegated Fairy-wren

545A ♀
Race *rogersi*

♀ **545B**

♂ **545B**
Breeding

545A ♀
Race *lamberti*

545A ♂
Race *lamberti*
Non-breeding

545A ♂
Race *lamberti*
Breeding

547 ♀

547 ♂
Breeding

546 ♀

♂ **546**
Breeding

N. Day.

548 White-winged Fairy-wren *Malurus leucopterus*

Race *leucopterus* 'Black and White Fairy-wren'; **Male breeding** velvety black plumage with white wings; tail deep blue. Note: some have blue in the body plumage. **Male eclipse** patchy black or brown above; tail brown. **Female/Imm.** dull grey-brown above; whitish below; lacks red eye-ring. Race *leuconotus* 'White-winged Fairy-wren': **Male breeding** distinctive bright to deep blue; wings white; tail deep blue. **Male eclipse** like female; bill dark horn. **Female/Imm.** as *leucopterus*. **Size** 11.5-14.5 cm. **Voice** distinctive 'thin' musical trilling, higher than Superb Fairy-wren. **Habitat** race *leucopterus* confined to Dirk Hartog and Barrow Islands, off WA coast; heathlands, saltbush. Race *leuconotus* arid to semi-arid saltbush, spinifex and cane-grass areas.

RAOU Atlas 535

A = Race *leucopterus*
B = Race *leuconotus*

♂ Dorsal pattern
Race *leuconotus*

549 Red-backed Fairy-wren *Malurus melanocephalus*

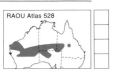

Male breeding black with a crimson to bright orange-red lower back and rump; these feathers are puffed out in display. Short blackish tail. **Male eclipse** like female; traces of red may appear on back. Legs pale pink to fawny-brown. **Female** grey-brown upperparts; *no* red eye-ring; fawnish-white below; tail brown. **Size** 12-13.5 cm. **Voice** drawn out, reedy or chattering songs and notes, similar to White-winged. **Habitat** spinifex, tropical swamps, samphire tidal flats and dense undergrowth. In family parties 'brown birds' predominate. Check female Variegated Fairy-wren.

♂ Dorsal pattern

RAOU Atlas 541

550A Rufous-crowned Emu-wren *Stipiturus ruficeps*

Juv.

Male bright rufous, unstreaked crown. Face, throat blue. Grey-brown to rufous-brown above, feathers streaked black. Six dark filamentous tail feathers. **Female** face, throat grey (no blue colouration). **Size** 14-15.2 cm. **Voice** high, trilling, rapid; often softer than fairy-wrens. **Habitat** spinifex; sometimes in adjacent or associated mallee scrub.

RAOU Atlas 528

550B Mallee Emu-wren *Stipiturus mallee*

Male chestnut forehead; crown dull brown with slight streaking. Eyebrow, cheek, upper breast light grey-blue. Upperparts darker. **Female** lacks blue-grey colouration of face, throat. Tail filamentous, shorter than Rufous-crowned and Southern Emu-wrens. **Size** 16.5 cm. **Voice** high, trilling, rapid; often softer than fairy-wrens. **Habitat** spinifex; sometimes in adjacent or associated mallee scrub.

RAOU Atlas 528

551 Southern Emu-wren *Stipiturus malachurus*

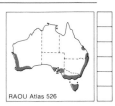

Male crown dark rufous, streaked black. Grey-brown to grey above. Grey-blue eyebrow, throat, upper breast. Orange-brown underparts. Six feathers of tail very long (10 cm). **Female** similar; *lacks* grey-blue and rufous colouring. **Size** 17.5-20 cm. **Imm.** like female; markings less distinct. **Voice** like fairy-wrens, thin, trilling, descending; also soft chirps; short harsh alarm calls. **Habitat** coastal heathlands, tea-tree swamps and dense vegetation. Flight feeble.

Flight

RAOU Atlas 526

548 ♀

♂ 548
Race *leucopterus*

548 ♂
Race *leuconotus*

♀ 549

♂ 549

551 ♀

551 ♂

♂ 550B
Mallee Emu-wren

♀ 550A
Race *ruficeps*

♂ 550A Race *ruficeps*

552 Black Grasswren *Amytornis housei*

Male mostly black; bold white streaks on head, back, breast. **Female** *not* black; light chestnut below; dark undertail coverts. **Size** 21 cm. **Juv.** darker; whitish streaks. **Voice** wren-like; ticking, grating. **Habitat** spinifex in gullies.

Juv.

RAOU Atlas 518

553 White-throated Grasswren *Amytornis woodwardi*

Male black; white streaks above. Black whisker-mark. White throat, rusty below. **Female** brighter; white lores. Diagnostic rusty underparts. **Size** 22 cm. **Voice** rising and falling trills. **Habitat** spinifex on escarpments.

RAOU Atlas 516

554 Carpentarian Grasswren *Amytornis dorotheae*

Male face, frons black, streaked white. Black whisker-mark. Chestnut lores, lower back. Throat, breast white. Primaries edged reddish-brown. **Female** chestnut flanks, lower belly. **Size** 16-17 cm. **Juv.** duller. **Voice** cricket-like buzz. **Habitat** on spinifex escarpments.

Juv.

RAOU Atlas 517

555 Striated Grasswren *Amytornis striatus*

Race *striatus*: **Male** bold chestnut above (inland WA); brownish above (SE Aust.). All birds are streaked white. Black whisker-mark. Orange-buff eyebrow. White throat. Buff-white below. **Female** chestnut flanks. Other races: *whitei* (NW of WA); *merrotsyi* (Flinders Ranges, SA). **Size** 14.5-17.5 cm. **Juv.** duller; markings indistinct. **Voice** thin squeak. **Habitat** porcupine grass, mallee.

Race *merrotsyi*
Juv.
Race *striatus*

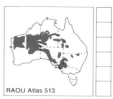
RAOU Atlas 513

556 Eyrean Grasswren *Amytornis goyderi*

Male faint whisker-mark. Crown, nape greyish-brown. Upper back, tail coverts rufous-brown, streaked white. Throat white; greyish below. Flanks pale buff. **Female** faint whisker-mark; richer rufous flanks. **Size** 15 cm. **Voice** faint two-note whistle. **Habitat** cane grass on high dunes.

RAOU Atlas 515

557 Grey Grasswren *Amytornis barbatus*

Male ginger-brown, streaked white; white below. Black crown streaked white. White facial area. Black eye-stripe. Thin black throat band. Flanks pale buff. **Female** breast streaked. **Size** 18-20 cm. **Voice** high, twittering; two notes. **Habitat** cane grass; lignum clumps. Two races.

Juv.

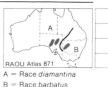
RAOU Atlas 871
A = Race *diamantina*
B = Race *barbatus*

558 Thick-billed Grasswren *Amytornis textilis*

Male stout bill. Head streaks; whisker-mark. Dark amber-brown above; pale brown below. Throat, breast streaked white. **Female** rufous flanks. Race *modestus*: **Male** pale fawn. **Female** chestnut flanks. **Juv.** duller. **Size** 15-20 cm. **Voice** high squeak. **Habitat** saltbush, cane grass.

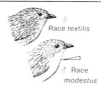
Race *textilis*
♂ Race *modestus*

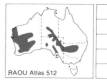
RAOU Atlas 512

559 Dusky Grasswren *Amytornis purnelli*

Race *purnelli*: **Male** reddish-brown; streaked. Slender bill. *No* black whisker-mark. Rich buff below; flanks grey-brown. **Female** rufous flanks. Race *ballarae* (W Qld): **Male** pale below; flanks pale grey. **Female** flanks also rufous. **Size** 16.5-17 cm. **Voice** shrill alarm. **Habitat** tussock grasslands.

♂ Race *purnelli*
♂ Race *ballarae*

RAOU Atlas 511

♂ 552

552 ♀

♀ 553

♂ 553

♂ 554

♀ 554

♂ 556

556 ♀

♂ 555
Race *whitei*

♀ 555
Race *striatus*

555 ♂
Race *striatus*

♂ 557

559 ♂

♀ 558

558 ♂

♀ 559

J.C.Day.

560 Eastern Bristlebird *Dasyornis brachypterus*

Pale eyebrow, throat, Upperparts and underparts rich to
soft browns and grey-browns, tinted olive. Light scaly
pattern on breast. **Size** 20-22 cm. **Juv./Imm.** no reliable
data. **Voice** loud, penetrating four-part call; harsh, short
notes. **Habitat** dense coastal and mountain heaths; taller
swamps, stream thickets.

RAOU Atlas 519

561 Western Bristlebird *Dasyornis longirostris*

Bill longer and tail shorter than other bristlebirds. Crown,
nape brownish-black, dappled grey. Pale eyebrow.
Upperparts and underparts subtle browns and greys tinted
olive and rufous. Faint scaly pattern on breast. **Size** 17-
20 cm. **Juv./Imm.** no reliable data. **Voice** five-part call,
probably male only; three-part call, probably female only.
Also 'tink'. Also short, harsh notes. **Habitat** dense coastal
heaths; taller swamp and stream thickets.

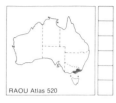

RAOU Atlas 520

562 Rufous Bristlebird *Dasyornis broadbenti*

Pale eyebrow, lores. Rich rufous crown, nape, ear coverts (less
rich from western to eastern areas of range.) Throat, breast
pale grey, with dark scaly pattern. Back greyish or darker
brown, tinted olive. Centre wing, rump cinnamon-brown.
Tail dark-brown. **Female** slightly smaller. Race *littoralis*
(WA): Smaller, may be extinct. **Size** 23-27 cm. **Juv./Imm.** no
reliable data. **Voice** penetrating, repetitive call and squeaking
variations; also short, sharp 'tik'. **Habitat** dense coastal
heaths, taller thickets; wet forest (Otway Ranges, Vic.).

RAOU Atlas 521

563 Pilotbird *Pycnoptilus floccosus*

Sturdy; terrestrial. Eye red. Rich reddish-buff from frons
to throat, darker, scaly pattern. Upperparts dark-brown;
rufous-washed rump. Underparts rufous-brown; centre
belly whitish. Chestnut-pink undertail coverts. **Size** 16.5-
17 cm. **Voice** sweet, penetrating 'a-guinea-a-week' (male);
less distinct call (female). **Habitat** dense, wet forest gullies,
all altitudes. Identify from Origma in NSW by rather
broad, semi-erect tail flicked up and down.

Associates with
440 Superb Lyrebird

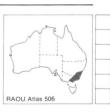

RAOU Atlas 506

564 Origma (Rock Warbler) *Origma solitaria*

Frons, front cinnamon-brown. Upperparts dark-brown.
Rich rufous underparts, contrast with greyish-white throat.
Rump washed rufous. Tail blackish. **Size** 14 cm. **Voice**
shrill, melancholy, repeated ' goodbye'; staccato, softer and
rasping notes. **Habitat** floors of rocky gullies; caves in
sandstone, limestone. Tail flicked sideways.

563

Tail flick

564

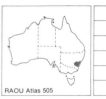

RAOU Atlas 505

565 Australian Fernwren *Crateroscelis gutturalis*

Male white eyebrow and throat. Fairly long bill.
Upperparts dark olive-brown, crown darker. Underparts
paler. **Female** duller. **Size** 12-14 cm. **Juv.** dark brown
without facial markings. **Voice** a scolding note; high-
pitched squeaks; strong whistling; chattering.
Habitat rainforest floors above 650 m. Bows head; flicks
short tail.

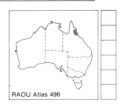

RAOU Atlas 496

560

561

562

563

564

565
Juv.

565 ♂

566 Atherton Scrubwren *Sericornis keri*

Dark olive-brown; face slightly paler; chin, throat lighter
still. Bill black. Slightly larger, longer-legged, shorter-
winged, more terrestrial than Large-billed Scrubwren.
Size 13.5 cm. **Voice** scolding call. **Habitat** rainforests above
650 m.

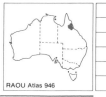
RAOU Atlas 946

567 Large-billed Scrubwren *Sericornis magnirostris*

Dark eye; longish black bill. Face, lores sandy-buff.
Upperparts olive-brown; underparts paler. **Size** 12-13 cm.
Voice soft twitterings, scolding notes and repeated
's-cheer'. **Habitat** dense, wet forests. Rarely on ground;
active to above middle storey.

RAOU Atlas 494

568 Yellow-throated Scrubwren
Sericornis citreogularis

Male black face, forehead, ear coverts. White and yellow
eyebrow; bright yellow throat. Outer primary edges
yellowish. Legs longish; cream or pinkish-brown.
Female facial area brownish. **Size** 12.5-15 cm. **Voice** clear,
melodious and mimicry; harsh chatter. **Habitat** dense,
wet forest gullies. Largely terrestrial.

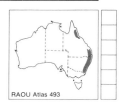
RAOU Atlas 493

569 Tropical Scrubwren *Sericornis beccarii*

Male eye reddish; discontinuous white eye-ring. Forehead,
lores blackish. White mark above lores. Double white
wing bar on dark shoulders. **Female** olive-brown forehead
and lores. Race *dubius* (SE part of range): Plainer markings
less distinct. **Size** 11-11.5 cm. **Voice** soft, musical warble;
harsher notes. **Habitat** rainforests, monsoon forests, dense
riverine scrubs. Active to middle storey.

Race *dubius*

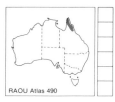
RAOU Atlas 490

570 White-browed Scrubwren *Sericornis frontalis*

Male pale eye; blackish lores; grey ear coverts. White
eyebrow and white stripe well below eye. Throat white
with faint dark streaks. Small white marks on dark
shoulders. Upperparts dark olive-brown; rump rufous.
Underparts dirty yellow, darker at sides. **Female** greyer.
Race *maculatus* 'Spotted Scrubwren' (west of Spencer
Gulf, SA): Spotted black throat, breast. Race *laevigaster*
(Qld): Black ear coverts; tail tipped white; underparts
brighter. Race *humilis* (Tas. and Bass Strait islands):
Plainer face and wing markings; larger and darker.
Size 11-14 cm. **Juv.** duller; browner. **Voice** repeated
'ts-cheer'; harsh scolding notes. **Habitat** dense undergrowth
all altitudes, including urban areas, salt marshes, heaths.

Juv.

Race *frontalis*

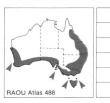
RAOU Atlas 488

571 Scrubtit *Sericornis magnus*

Eye brown. Whitish eye-ring, eyebrow, lores and throat.
Ear coverts grey. White spots near shoulder. White edges
to wing-tips. **Size** 11-11.5 cm. **Voice** 'too-whe-too', like
White-browed Scrubwren (race *humilis*) and Brown
Thornbill. Also whistling. **Habitat** dense, ferny, wet forest
undergrowth. May move higher into trees.

RAOU Atlas 487

567

571

♂ **570**
Race *humilis*

570

♂ **570**
Race *frontalis*

♂ **570**
Race *maculatus*

♂ **570**
Race *laevigaster*

566

♂ **568**

569 ♀

569 ♂

572 Chestnut-rumped Hylacola *Sericornis pyrrhopygius*

Male dull white eyebrow. Upperparts olive-brown; crown greyer. Greyish-white throat and breast, streaked dark brown. Chestnut rump. Erect tail; dark band before white tip. Belly buff; flanks washed yellow. **Female** underparts duller. **Size** 13-14 cm. **Voice** varied, lengthy, canary-like song interwoven with mimicry; also a harsh 'chip'. **Habitat** heaths of coastal, mountain and hinterland areas; dense undergrowth of forests and woodlands.

Tail cocked

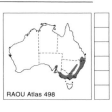

RAOU Atlas 498

573 Shy Hylacola *Sericornis cautus*

Male conspicuous white eyebrow. Upperparts olive-brown; crown greyer. White shoulder spot. White throat and breast boldly streaked black. Rich rufous rump. Erect dark tail with white tip. Flanks grey-brown; undertail coverts rich rufous. **Female** slightly duller. **Size** 12-14 cm. **Voice** strong song but less mimicry and vocal range than Chestnut-rumped Hylacola. Also sharp, harsh notes. **Habitat** coastal thickets and sandplain country in SW Aust., elsewhere in low undergrowth of mallee.

Dorsal pattern

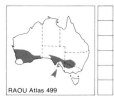

RAOU Atlas 499

574 Redthroat *Sericornis brunneus*

Male pale eyebrow and lores. Throat has chestnut-red centre. Upperparts grey-brown washed olive on back and rump. Tail darker; white outer tail feathers and tip. Underparts greyish. **Female** throat grey; chin white. **Size** 11.5-12 cm. **Voice** rich and varied like Clamorous Reed-Warbler but softer. An accomplished mimic; female less so. **Habitat** mallee, mulga, saltbush, bluebush, lignum and spinifex country; coastal areas in western part of range.

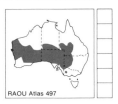

RAOU Atlas 497

575A Striated Calamanthus *Sericornis fuliginosus*

Dull white eyebrow. Dark upperparts, heavily streaked black. Underparts buff-yellow, also streaked. Tail often erect. **Size** 12-14 cm. **Voice** sharp, musical, lengthy, twittering song. **Habitat** damp coastal and mountain heaths; sparse low ground cover. Perches on bushes to sing. Identify from Little Grassbird.

Singing

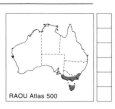

RAOU Atlas 500

575B Rufous Calamanthus *Sericornis campestris*

Dull whitish eyebrow. Upperparts variable, heavily streaked; darker in SW of Aust.; inland birds more rufous. Underparts white, streaked black. Tail often erect; has dark band before white tip. Three races. **Size** 12-13 cm. **Voice** lengthy, musical. **Habitat** patchy distribution across arid plains, WA, SA, Vic. Perches on bushes to sing.

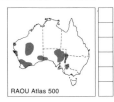

RAOU Atlas 500

576 Speckled Warbler *Sericornis sagittatus*

Eyebrow, lores and behind ear coverts whitish. A black line along side of head. Crown brownish, finely streaked white. Back and wings grey-brown, broadly streaked darker. Cream underparts, boldly streaked blackish. Tail has broad dark band before white tip. **Size** 11.5-12.5 cm. **Voice** soft, musical, variable song; a harsh grating twitter; mimicry. **Habitat** open woodlands. Usually on or near ground litter; often with thornbills.

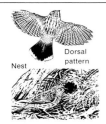

Dorsal pattern

Nest

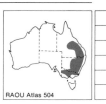

RAOU Atlas 504

572

573

575B

535
Little Grassbird

575A

574 ♂

♀ 574

♂ 576

576 ♀

577 Weebill *Smicrornis brevirostris*

Pale eyebrow. Bill short, pale. Face pale; ear streaked. Back olive; abdomen yellow. Race *flavescens:* Brighter. **Size** 8-9 cm. **Voice** clear, high, sharp, repeated 'tiz'. **Habitat** dry forests, woodlands, mallee. Identify from pardalotes and Yellow Thornbill.

596

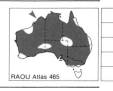
RAOU Atlas 465

578 Brown Gerygone *Gerygone mouki*

Long white eyebrow. Face violet-grey. Eye red-brown. Olive-brown above. Dark tail band; tail tips white. Race *richmondi:* Buff-brown above. **Size** 9.5-10 cm. **Voice** weak, repetitious. **Habitat** rainforests, open forests.

Undertail pattern

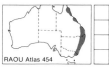
RAOU Atlas 454

579 Large-billed Gerygone *Gerygone magnirostris*

No eyebrow mark. Dark. Thin white eye-ring. Pale buff flanks. *No* white tail tips. **Size** 10.5-11.5 cm. **Voice** downward song. **Habitat** about mangroves, streams.

Undertail pattern
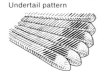

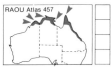
RAOU Atlas 457

580 Dusky Gerygone *Gerygone tenebrosa*

Pale frons, eyebrow; white eye. Plain brown above; dusky below. *No* tail marks. **Size** 11.5 cm. **Voice** plaintive, downward. **Habitat** mangroves, creeks, gorges.

Undertail pattern
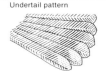

RAOU Atlas 461

581 Mangrove Gerygone *Gerygone laevigaster*

Bold white eyebrow; reddish eye. Face, upperparts ashy-brown. Dark tail, tipped white. Race *cantator:* Darker. **Imm.** yellowish below. **Size** 11 cm. **Voice** sustained warble. **Habitat** mangroves, nearby forests.

Undertail pattern

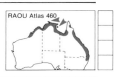
RAOU Atlas 460

582 Western Gerygone *Gerygone fusca*

Dull white eyebrow; red eye. Greyish-brown above. Tail bold black and white. **Size** 11-11.5 cm. **Imm.** yellowish. **Voice** clear rising, falling. **Habitat** open woodlands, mallee.

Undertail pattern

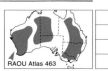
RAOU Atlas 463

583 Green-backed Gerygone *Gerygone chloronota*

Eye red. Dull green above. Light grey below. Grey head. Tail brown. **Size** 10 cm. **Voice** similar to but lighter than Western Gerygone. **Habitat** dense edges of paperbark swamps, estuaries; nearby open forests.

Undertail pattern
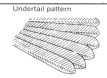

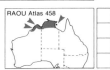
RAOU Atlas 458

584 Fairy Gerygone *Gerygone palpebrosa*

Race *personata:* **Male** blackish throat; white cheek stripe. Brownish-green above; lemon below. Race *flavida:* **Male** throat pale lemon; blackish on chin. White tail marks. **Female** (both races) whitish throat. **Size** 10-11.5 cm. **Imm.** (both races) pale yellow throat. **Voice** long warble. **Habitat** rainforests, mangroves.

Race *flavida*   ♂

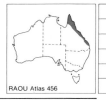
RAOU Atlas 456

585 White-throated Gerygone *Gerygone olivacea*

Eye red. Throat white. White forehead spot. Upperparts grey-brown. Tail dark, white tips. Bright yellow below. **Size** 10 cm. **Imm.** all yellow below. **Voice** downward. **Habitat** open forests, woodlands.

RAOU Atlas 453

Note Earlier publications often refer to the gerygones as 'warblers' or 'fairy-warblers'.

577
vescens

577
Race *brevirostris*

585

585
Imm.

♀ **584**

584
Juv.

♂ **584**
Race *personata*

583

578

581
Imm.

582

581

579

580

586 Mountain Thornbill *Acanthiza katherina*

Forehead buff-olive with pale crescents. Eye whitish. Greenish-brown upperparts. Dull rufous rump. Pale to greenish-yellow underparts. **Size** 10 cm. **Voice** not recorded. **Habitat** restricted range in rainforests of NE Aust.

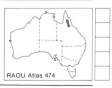

RAOU Atlas 474

587 Brown Thornbill *Acanthiza pusilla*

Juv.

Forehead rufous with pale crescents. Dark red eye. Throat, chest light grey, streaked black. Olive-brown upperparts. Cinnamon-brown rump. **Size** 10 cm. **Voice** short, pleasant warble; harsh alarm call. **Habitat** most forested areas where sufficient undergrowth. Often in lower vegetation. Identify from Striated Thornbill, Weebill, White-browed Scrubwren, Brown Gerygone.

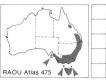

RAOU Atlas 475

588 Inland Thornbill *Acanthiza pusilla apicalis*

Tail cocked

Forehead greyish-brown with white crescents. Eye red. Dark striations on throat, chest. Upperparts pale olive-brown. Reddish rump. Underparts pale. Races *hamiltoni* and *albiventris* rump rich red; *whitlocki* rump paler; *leeuwinensis*, SW of WA. Minor race is *tanami*, western NT. **Size** 10 cm. **Voice** like Brown Thornbill. **Habitat** dry scrub to coastal heaths. Carries tail cocked. The Brown Thornbill and Inland Thornbill are now considered to be one species, Brown Thornbill.

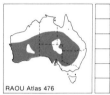

RAOU Atlas 476

589 Tasmanian Thornbill *Acanthiza ewingii*

Faintly marked tawny forehead. Eye red. Throat, breast grey, dappled light and dark. White flanks. Rufous-brown wing patch; darker edge to wing feathers. **Size** 10 cm. **Voice** like Brown Thornbill, except in breeding season. **Habitat** Tas. woodlands and scrub. Identify from Brown Thornbill, Scrubtit and White-browed Scrubwren (race *humilis*).

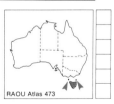

RAOU Atlas 473

590 Chestnut-rumped Thornbill
Acanthiza uropygialis

Hollow nest

Forehead light brown, speckled white. Eye white. Face pale, freckled. Upperparts dull brown. Rump chestnut. Tail black, tipped white. Underparts white. **Size** 10 cm. **Voice** short, melodious song; also penetrating 'seee-tit-tit-seee'. **Habitat** dry woodlands, mallee, mulga.

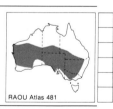

RAOU Atlas 481

591 Slaty-backed Thornbill *Acanthiza robustirostris*

Forehead, crown grey with dark streaks. Eye red-brown. Slaty-grey upperparts. Pale cinnamon rump. Black tail, tipped dull white. Underparts greyish-white. **Size** 9-9.5 cm. **Voice** 'seep-seec'; also harsh 'treeit'. **Habitat** inland scrub-covered plains and mulga.

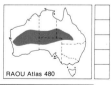

RAOU Atlas 480

592 Western Thornbill *Acanthiza inornata*

Forehead light, freckled brown. Whitish eye. Upperparts grey-brown. Pale olive rump. Tail brown. Underparts pale buff, *no* streaks. **Size** 10 cm. **Voice** soft twittering; good mimic. **Habitat** open woodlands, karri and jarrah forests.

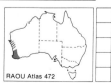

RAOU Atlas 472

586

591

591

587

588

70
White-browed Scrubwren

589

588

590

592

587

589

592

590

593 Buff-rumped Thornbill *Acanthiza reguloides*

Forehead, face buff; white feather tips. *No* eyebrow; white eye. Pale buff rump. Underparts pale yellowish; throat speckled grey. Broad black tail band, tipped white. Race *squamata*: Brighter yellow. **Size** 11 cm. **Voice** metallic warble. **Habitat** open forests, lightly timbered ranges.

RAOU Atlas 484

594 Slender-billed Thornbill *Acanthiza iredalei*

Pale speckled forehead, face. Pale eye. Greyish-olive above; pale buff rump. Creamy underparts. Tail dark brown, tipped white. Race *hedleyi*: Darker. **Size** 9 cm. **Voice** musical twitter in flight. **Habitat** samphire near salt pans; semi-desert. Race *hedleyi*: mallee.

Rump variations

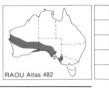

RAOU Atlas 482

595 Yellow-rumped Thornbill
Acanthiza chrysorrhoa

Forehead black, spotted white; crown light brown. White eyebrow. Grey and white cheek spots. Back olive-grey. Rump bright yellow. Underparts pale yellowish. Dark tail, tipped white. **Size** 10-12 cm. **Voice** tinkling. **Habitat** open woods, parklands; often on ground.

Bulky nest

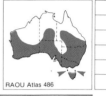

RAOU Atlas 486

596 Yellow (Little) Thornbill *Acanthiza nana*

Crown brown, unmarked. Eye dark; *no* eyebrow. Streaked ear coverts. Dull olive-green upperparts. Underparts yellow. Tail brown; black sub-terminal band. **Size** 10 cm. **Voice** persistent 'tizz tizz'. **Habitat** dry forests; often in acacias.

577

RAOU Atlas 471

597 Striated Thornbill *Acanthiza lineata*

Brown crown, streaked white. Face, ear coverts, throat, breast light with dark striations. Eye grey-brown. Back olive-brown. Abdomen light-yellowish brown. **Size** 10 cm. **Voice** like Yellow Thornbill, but softer. **Habitat** dry forest.

Front view

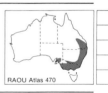

RAOU Atlas 470

598 Southern Whiteface *Aphelocephala leucopsis*

Face white, bordered black on forehead. Eye white. Upperparts grey-brown. Underparts off-white, with buff flanks. Brown tail, tipped white. Race *castaneiventris*, (WA): Chestnut flanks. **Size** 10 cm. **Voice** tinkling, wistful. **Habitat** open arid country, especially near dead trees.

RAOU Atlas 466

599 Chestnut-breasted Whiteface
Aphelocephala pectoralis

Face white, bordered black before grey crown. Eye white. Back rusty-brown. Chestnut band across chest. Rufous flank marks. **Size** 10 cm. **Voice** plaintive bell-like tinkle. **Habitat** gibber plains, semi-desert.

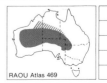

RAOU Atlas 468

600 Banded Whiteface *Aphelocephala nigricincta*

White face, bordered black on forehead. Eye white. Chestnut-brown above. Narrow black breast band. Rufous flank marks. **Size** 10 cm. **Voice** musical, but weaker than Southern Whiteface. **Habitat** stony plains; sandhills with scattered plants.

RAOU Atlas 469

596

597

594

594

595

595

593

593

593
Race squamata

598
Race castaneiventris

599

600

598

601 **Varied Sittella** *Daphoenositta chrysoptera*

Head white, grey, black or a mixture. Back whitish, grey
or brown, streaked black in northern and eastern races.
Wing black with broad white bar (northern races) or
cinnamon bar (southern). Underparts white, streaked dark
in eastern races. **Size** 10-11 cm. **Juv.** white marks on crown
and back. Buff wing covert margins. **Voice** incessant 'chip';
upward inflected whistles. **Habitat** sclerophyll forests
and woodlands. Very active; in groups up to 20.

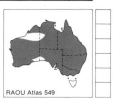

602 **White-throated Treecreeper** *Cormobates leucophaea*

White throat, breast; striped flanks. **Female** orange spot on
cheek. Race *minor:* Smaller, darker; mottled belly; grey breast.
Size 13-15 cm. **Juv.** indistinct white streaks on scapulars;
females have orange-chestnut rump. **Voice** repeated piping
note; tremulous calls. **Habitat** rainforests (all races);
sclerophyll forests and woodlands (*leucophaea* only).

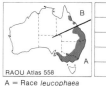

A = Race *leucophaea*
B = Race *minor*

603 **Red-browed Treecreeper** *Climacteris erythrops*

Reddish face, eyebrow. Boldly striped belly. **Male** face
brownish-orange. **Female** chestnut face and stripes on
chest. **Size** 15 cm. **Juv.** grey face; buffish-grey underparts.
Voice descending chatter, often answered with two sharp
notes. **Habitat** eucalypt forests and sub-alpine woodlands.

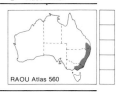

604 **White-browed Treecreeper** *Climacteris affinis*

White eyebrow. Bold black and white striped belly.
Female chestnut line over brow and faint stripes on chest.
Size 14 cm. **Juv.** brow indistinct. **Voice** weak, insect-like
notes and song. **Habitat** acacia woodlands, belar, *Callitris*.

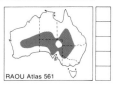

605 **Brown Treecreeper** *Climacteris picumnus*

Broad pale-buff eyebrow, fine buff and black streaked
belly. Upperparts brown (race *picumnus*) to almost black
(*melanota*). **Male** black marks on chest. **Female** rufous
marks on chest (often hidden). **Size** 16-18 cm. **Juv.** darker,
more colourful. **Voice** staccato notes, harsh rattle;
chuckling songs. **Habitat** open woodlands, forest clearings
and edges; eucalypts along watercourses. Often on
ground; bobs tail when resting.

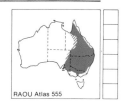

606 **Rufous Treecreeper** *Climacteris rufa*

Cinnamon-rufous face, belly. **Male** black and white
streaks on chest. **Female** rufous and white chest streaks.
Size 15-17 cm. **Voice** like Brown Treecreeper but higher-
pitched. **Habitat** eucalypt forests, woodlands. Habits
similar to Brown.

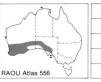

607 **Black-tailed Treecreeper** *Climacteris melanura*

Brownish-black head, upperparts. No eyebrow. Dull
rufous belly. **Male** white-streaked black throat.
Female white throat; chestnut and white chest stripes.
Size 17-19 cm. **Voice** piping notes like White-throated
Treecreeper; song like Brown Treecreeper. **Habitat** similar
to Brown. Habits similar to Brown.

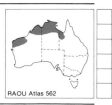

601
Race *chrysoptera* ♀ ♂

601 ♂
Race *striata*

601 ♀
Race *striata*

601
Race *pileata*
♂

601 ♀
Race *pileata*

601 ♀
ucoptera

601 ♂
ucoptera

601
Race *chrysoptera*

607 ♀

603 ♂

601
Race *leucocephala*

603
Juv.

603 ♀

♀ 604

604

♂ 602

♀ 602
Juv.

♀ 605
Race *picumnus*

♂ 605
Race
picumnus

♀ 606

608 Red Wattlebird *Anthochaera carunculata*

Grey-brown bird, white streaks. Crown blackish; silvery-white face. Dark pink pendulous wattle at ear. Dark red iris. Belly yellow. Legs pink. **Female** smaller. Western race *woodwardi* more streaked than eastern *carunculata*. **Size** 31-39 cm. **Juv.** browner, especially crown; smaller wattles. Iris red-brown. **Voice** raucous 'tobacco box', 'chokk'. **Habitat** forests, woods, suburbs.

Dorsal flight
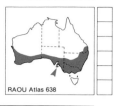
RAOU Atlas 638

609 Yellow Wattlebird *Anthochaera paradoxa*

Grey-brown bird, white streaks. Crown blackish, boldly streaked white. Face, chin, eyebrow white. Long, pendulous, yellow-orange wattle at ear. Yellow patch on belly. **Female** smaller. **Size** 38-48 cm. **Juv.** paler; smaller wattles; less yellow on abdomen. **Voice** raucous 'kuk', 'kukuk'. **Habitat** restricted to Tas.; widespread in coastal heaths with emergent eucalypts, forests, suburban gardens.

Imm.

RAOU Atlas 639

610A Little Wattlebird *Anthochaera lunulata*

Dark olive-brown, finely streaked and spotted with white. Iris red-brown. Face and cheek whitish. Wattle inconspicuous. Belly grey-white. Rufous wing patch conspicuous in flight. **Female** smaller. **Size** 26-33 cm. **Voice** drawn-out complex song; rapid twitterings. **Habitat** woodlands, coastal heaths and scrubs; gardens.

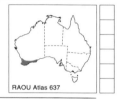
RAOU Atlas 637

610B Brush Wattlebird *Anthochaera chrysoptera*

Dark olive-brown, finely streaked and spotted with white. Iris khaki. Face and cheek grey-white; less white than *A. lunulata*. Belly grey-white. Rufous wing patch conspicuous in flight. Wattle inconspicuous. **Female** smaller. Race *tasmanica* (Tas.) larger, darker. **Size** 26-33 cm. **Voice** harsh cackles, 'cockay cock', 'quok'. **Habitat** coastal woodlands, heaths, scrubs, especially in *Banksia*; suburban gardens. This bird recently separated taxonomically from *A. lunulata* of SW of WA.

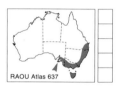
RAOU Atlas 637

611 Spiny-cheeked Honeyeater *Acanthagenys rufogularis*

Bill pink with dark tip. Crown grey-brown, lightly scalloped with darker brown. Iris pale blue. White 'spiny' feathers from bill to cheek. Bare pink skin under eye and around gape. Throat and breast cinnamon. Back grey-brown, mottled darker brown. Conspicuous whitish rump. Abdomen creamy-white with brownish spots. Tail tipped white. **Female** smaller. **Size** 22-27 cm. **Juv.** duller; spiny cheek feathers yellow. **Voice** strong melodious warble, not unlike butcherbird; also short 'tock'. **Habitat** desert scrubs, mallee, woodlands, orchards.

Dorsal flight

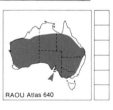
RAOU Atlas 640

612 Striped Honeyeater *Plectorhyncha lanceolata*

Bill grey-blue. Head, nape streaked black, white. Throat white. Throat, upper breast feathers long and thin (lanceolate) with white centre. Back dark grey, mottled black. Abdomen whitish or buff, scattered fine brown streaks. Legs grey-blue. **Size** 20-23 cm. **Juv.** not boldly streaked. **Voice** melodious 'cherr-cherr-cherry-cherry'. **Habitat** woods, forests, mainly inland, rarely mangroves.

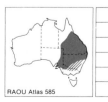
RAOU Atlas 585

608

608
Juv.

609

610B
Brush Wattlebird

611

612

613 Helmeted Friarbird *Philemon buceroides*

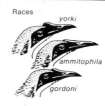
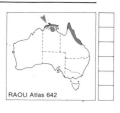

Races

yorki

ammitophila

gordoni

RAOU Atlas 642

Race *yorki*: Silver crown has a frilled whitish nape. Large, gently sloping knob (casque) at forehead. Facial skin bare, dark leaden-grey. Iris red-brown. Back, rump, tail dull grey-brown. Underparts paler, silvery-brown and lightly streaked. **Female** smaller. Race *gordoni* 'Melville Island Friarbird': Smaller; inhabits mangroves. Race *ammitophila* 'Sandstone Friarbird': Large; no knob; inhabits sandstone areas. **Size** 30-37 cm. **Juv.** throat, breast less streaked; smaller knob. **Voice** harsh, metallic whistles or cackles; 'poor devil, poor devil'; 'wach-a-wehre'; 'watch-out'; 'sergeant major'. **Habitat** forests, woodlands, mangroves. Pugnacious, noisy bird.

614 Silver-crowned Friarbird *Philemon argenticeps*

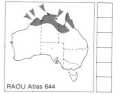

Head: dorsal view

RAOU Atlas 644

Like Helmeted Friarbird but smaller. Forehead, crown, nape silvery-white. Bare facial skin dark leaden-grey. Small, erect knob at forehead is very conspicuous. Iris red-brown. Back, rump, tail dull grey-brown. Underparts paler, silvery-grey. **Female** smaller. **Size** 27-32 cm. **Juv.** duller, smaller knob. **Voice** like Helmeted but softer; also 'more tobacco, uh-more tobacco-uh'. **Habitat** open forests, woodlands, mangroves.

615 Noisy Friarbird *Philemon corniculatus*

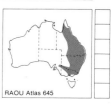

Calling

RAOU Atlas 645

Head with bare black skin; buffy eyebrow and silvery chin feathers. Small erect, conspicuous knob on bill at forehead. Long silvery feathers with dark shafts on throat, breast, slightly hackled or tufted. Back, rump, tail dull grey. Underparts pale grey. **Female** smaller. **Size** 31-36 cm. **Juv.** neck, back of head feathered. Small knob. Throat, breast *lack* lanceolated feathers. **Voice** loud, raucous 'four-o-clock', 'chokk chokk'; other squawks. **Habitat** open forests, woodlands.

616 Little Friarbird *Philemon citreogularis*

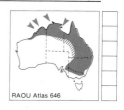

RAOU Atlas 646

Head grey-brown. Darker feathers above and below the bare, bluish-black facial skin. *No* knob on bill. Whitish nape. Fine silky-white feathers on chin. Silvery-white streaks on breast. Back dark grey-brown. Underparts pale grey. **Female** smaller. **Size** 25-29 cm. **Juv.** paler; facial skin lighter; yellowish wash over chin, throat. Yellow spots on side of breast. **Voice** raucous; 'arr-koo', 'rockety krook-shank'. **Habitat** open forests, woodlands.

617 Regent Honeyeater *Xanthomyza phrygia*

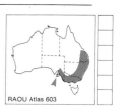

Dorsal pattern

RAOU Atlas 603

Sexes similar. **Male** bill black, larger. Head, neck, throat, upper breast black; bare facial skin yellowish, warty; extends over eye. Back, breast pale lemon, scaled black. Wings mainly black, conspicuous yellow patches. Belly feathers pale lemon, black margins; white undertail coverts. Yellow outer-web to black tail feathers. **Female** smaller; bare skin beneath eye only; less black on throat. **Size** 20-23 cm. **Juv./1st year** duller; browner; like female. Paler bill. **Voice** quiet, melodious, flute-like or chiming. May mimic larger honeyeaters. Bobs head when calling. **Habitat** open forests, woodlands; particularly in blossoming eucalypts, mistletoe. Identify from White-fronted Honeyeater.

615

613

615
Juv.

614

613
Juv.

617 ♂

616
Juv.

616

N. Day.

618 Blue-faced Honeyeater *Entomyzon cyanotis*

Head black. Large patch of light blue bare skin around
eye. White line on nape. Chin and throat dark grey. Back
olive-yellow; underparts white. Three races: *harteri* smaller
with larger face patch than *cyanotis*; *albipennis* white in
wing and with discontinuous line on nape. **Size** 25-32 cm.
Juv. dark brown on head. Facial skin yellow or green.
Voice loud 'ki-owt'. **Habitat** open forests.

Race
albipennis

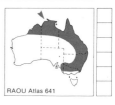
RAOU Atlas 641

619 Bell Miner *Manorina melanophrys*

Head and back olive-green. Bill orange. Forehead and
edge of throat black; lores bright yellow; bare skin behind
eye bright orange. Legs orange. Underparts olive-green.
Female smaller. **Size** 17-20 cm. **Juv.** skin around eye paler.
Voice bell-like 'tink-tink'. **Habitat** forests, woodlands.
Colonial species.

RAOU Atlas 633

620 Noisy Miner *Manorina melanocephala*

Crown, most of face and ear black; rest of head grey. Bare
skin behind eye yellow. Bill yellow. Back and rump grey.
Underparts pale grey with darker scallops on breast.
Female smaller. **Size** 24-28 cm. **Juv.** similar. **Voice** harsh
calls and piping 'pwee-pwee-pwee'. **Habitat** woodlands,
suburbs. Colonial species.

Flight

RAOU Atlas 634

621 Yellow-throated Miner *Manorina flavigula*

Two yellow streaks of bare skin from bill. Like Noisy Miner
but rump white, crown grey, forehead and side of neck
washed with yellow. **Female** smaller. Several races: *obscura*
(SW Aust.) duskier; *lutea* (NW Aust.) smaller and whiter
than *flavigula* (central Aust.). **Size** 23-28 cm. **Voice** similar
to Noisy Miner. **Habitat** dry woodlands, especially mallee.
Usually in flocks.

Flight

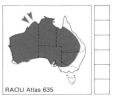
RAOU Atlas 635

622 Black-eared Miner *Manorina melanotis*

Like Yellow-throated Miner but darker-bodied; black ear
patch and *less* yellow forehead, cheeks, neck. Crown,
throat, breast, back, rump, dark grey. Tail tips dark.
Female smaller. **Size** 24-27 cm. **Voice** similar to Noisy
Miner. **Habitat** *dense* mallee. Bird rare; endangered. The
Black-eared Miner is now considered a race of Yellow-
throated Miner.

Flight

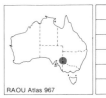
RAOU Atlas 967

623 Macleay's Honeyeater *Xanthotis macleayana*

Head and neck brown-black; nape speckled white. Naked
skin below eye yellowish. Yellow-orange ear tufts. Back
brown, heavily mottled buff-yellow and white. Chin grey.
Breast darker, streaked olive-brown and white. **Size**
18-21 cm. **Juv.** duller. **Voice** musical 'to wit, too weeee twit'.
Habitat rainforests, mangroves, gardens.

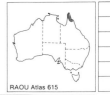
RAOU Atlas 615

624 Tawny-breasted Honeyeater *Xanthotis flaviventer*

Upperparts olive-brown with nape faintly speckled grey.
White streak under eye from gape to nape. Small yellow
ear tuft. Throat, sides of neck and ear coverts grey. Breast
tawny-brown, faintly streaked. **Size** 18-22 cm. **Juv.** similar.
Voice noisy whistles. **Habitat** mangroves, rainforests,
forests.

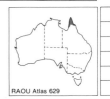
RAOU Atlas 629

625 Lewin's Honeyeater *Meliphaga lewinii*

Dark olive-green, slightly streaked. Darker head, squarish yellow ear tufts. Eye blue. Cream gape extends under eye. **Size** 18-22 cm. **Juv.** less streaked. Base of bill yellow. **Voice** loud staccato chatter. **Habitat** wet forests.

Bill: from above

Bill: from side

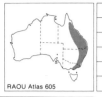

RAOU Atlas 605

626 Yellow-spotted Honeyeater *Meliphaga notata*

Like Lewin's Honeyeater but paler, with yellow gape and rounder ear patch. Eye brown. **Size** 16-19 cm. **Voice** piercing 'ee yeu', 'tchu-chua'. **Habitat** wet forests.

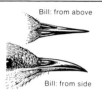

Bill: from above

Bill: from side

RAOU Atlas 606

627 Graceful Honeyeater *Meliphaga gracilis*

Like Yellow-spotted Honeyeater but smaller, with a longer, thinner bill. Eye brown. **Size** 14-17 cm. **Voice** 'plik'. **Habitat** wet forests.

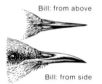

Bill: from above

Bill: from side

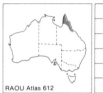

RAOU Atlas 612

628 White-lined Honeyeater *Meliphaga albilineata*

Grey-brown. Whitish line from gape passing under eye to small whitish ear tuft. **Female** smaller. **Size** 17-20 cm. **Voice** loud 'tu-wheer, tuwhit'. **Habitat** wooded gorges.

RAOU Atlas 607

629 Eungella Honeyeater *Lichenostomus hindwoodi*

Smaller than Bridled Honeyeater. Short black bill. Stripe below eye whitish. Greyer with white streaks on breast; lacks patch on side of neck. **Size** 16-18 cm. **Voice** laughing whistle; a recorded call is 'pee pee pip-pip-pip-pip-pip-pip', slower at end. **Habitat** Eungella rainforests, Qld. A recently described species.

Facial pattern

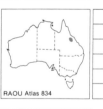

RAOU Atlas 834

630 Yellow-faced Honeyeater *Lichenostomus chrysops*

Grey-brown. Broad yellow stripe under eye which is bordered by black. **Size** 15-18 cm. **Voice** 'chick-up'. **Habitat** forests.

630

632
Singing Honeyeater

RAOU Atlas 614

631 Bridled Honeyeater *Lichenostomus frenatus*

Dark brown with blackish head. Iris blue. Yellowish streak from gape to nape. Bill black with yellow base. Small whitish area behind eye; thin yellow ear tuft. Silver-buff patch on side of neck. **Size** 18-22 cm. **Juv.** similar. **Voice** loud 'we-arr', 'wachita'. **Habitat** rainforests.

631

630

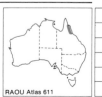

RAOU Atlas 611

632 Singing Honeyeater *Lichenostomus virescens*

Grey-brown. Broad black band from bill through eye on to neck. Yellow streak below eye. Ear tuft yellow, tip white. Breast pale grey, streaked dark grey. **Size** 17-22 cm. **Habitat** arid and coastal shrublands, woodlands, suburbs (WA).

Feeding on fruit

RAOU Atlas 608

633 Varied Honeyeater *Lichenostomus versicolor*

Like Singing Honeyeater but yellower. Underparts yellow, streaked brown. **Size** 18-21 cm. **Habitat** mangroves.

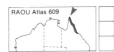

RAOU Atlas 609

634 Mangrove Honeyeater *Lichenostomus fasciogularis*

Like Singing Honeyeater but darker, especially on breast. Throat yellowish, scalloped brown. Hybridisation occurs between Varied and Mangrove Honeyeaters. **Size** 18-21 cm. **Habitat** mangroves. The Mangrove Honeyeater is now considered a race of Varied Honeyeater.

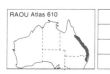

RAOU Atlas 610

635 White-gaped Honeyeater *Lichenostomus unicolor*

Dark olive-grey upperparts; greenish wash on wings. Conspicuous white gape. Underparts mid-grey. **Size** 18-22 cm. **Juv.** similar, yellow gape. **Voice** variable loud 'whit-o-weee'. **Habitat** mangroves, riverine forests.

RAOU Atlas 628

636 Yellow Honeyeater *Lichenostomus flavus*

Bright yellow-green. Thin dark line through eye. **Size** 16-19 cm. **Juv.** duller. **Voice** varied loud whistles 'wheee-a'. **Habitat** coastal and riverine forests, mangroves, gardens.

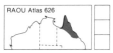

RAOU Atlas 626

637 White-eared Honeyeater *Lichenostomus leucotis*

Crown grey with fine black striations. Face, chin, throat black. Conspicuous white ear patch. Olive-green back and tail. Yellowish green abdomen. **Female** smaller. Two races: *leucotis* (E Aust.) is larger and brighter than *novaenorciae* (WA). **Size** 18-22 cm. **Juv.** duller with olive-green crown; cream ear patch. **Voice** loud 'chock up, chock up' and other softer calls. **Habitat** forests, woodlands, mallee.

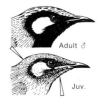

Adult ♂

Juv.

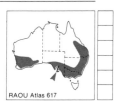

RAOU Atlas 617

638 Yellow-throated Honeyeater *Lichenostomus flavicollis*

Dark grey crown, face, upper breast. Bright yellow chin and throat. Small silvery-grey ear patch, tipped yellowish. Back olive-green. Abdomen grey-yellow. **Female** smaller. **Size** 18-22 cm. **Juv.** paler, particularly on throat. **Voice** loud 'tonk, tonk' often repeated; also 'pick-em-up'. **Habitat** most habitats on Tas. and Bass Strait islands.

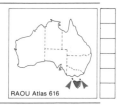

RAOU Atlas 616

639 Yellow-tufted Honeyeater *Lichenostomus melanops*

Forehead, crown, chin, throat yellow. Centre of throat blackish, streaked yellow. Forehead feathers tufted. Black feathers from bill through eye expanding on ear coverts; bright golden ear tuft. Back olive-green; abdomen olive-yellow. **Female** smaller. Four races in SE Aust. that vary in size and darkness of plumage, including *cassidix* ('Helmeted Honeyeater'). **Size** 17-23 cm. **Juv.** similar; duller. **Habitat** eucalypt forests and woodlands with shrub layer, particularly along watercourses.

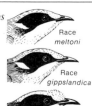

Race *meltoni*

Race *gippslandica*

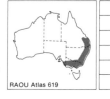

RAOU Atlas 619

Race *cassidix*

634

633

632

636

635

638

637

639
Race *cassidix*

639

N. Day.

640 Purple-gaped Honeyeater *Lichenostomus cratitius*

Head grey. Blackish mask through eye. Grey ear coverts; small yellow ear tuft. Line of purple skin from gape to cheek. Side of throat yellow. Back olive-green; abdomen yellow-grey. **Size** 16-20 cm. **Juv.** duller with yellow gape. **Voice** harsh chattering. **Habitat** mallee, woodlands.

632
Singing Honeyeater

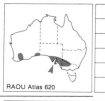

RAOU Atlas 620

641 Grey-headed Honeyeater *Lichenostomus keartlandi*

Pale grey head. Blackish face; dark grey ear coverts. Crescent-shaped yellow ear tuft. Breast pale yellow, faintly streaked darker. Buff-olive back. **Size** 15-17 cm. **Juv.** duller. **Voice** loud 'chee toyt' repeated. **Habitat** mulga, woodlands, rocky hillsides and gorges.

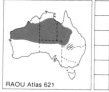

RAOU Atlas 621

642 Yellow-plumed Honeyeater *Lichenostomus ornatus*

Bill black. Greenish-olive crown; darker face. Faint yellow line under eye. Ear coverts tipped dark brown. Yellow neck plume. Olive-brown back. Underparts fawn, heavily streaked olive-brown. **Female** smaller. **Size** 15-18 cm. **Juv.** duller; base of bill and gape orange-yellow. **Voice** loud 'chick-owee', 'chikwididee'. **Habitat** mallee, semi-arid eucalypt woodlands.

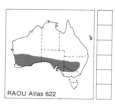

RAOU Atlas 622

643 Grey-fronted Honeyeater *Lichenostomus plumulus*

Bill black. Head yellowish; face darker. Fine black line from bill to below ear. Thin black plume in front of large yellow neck plume. Back olive-green. Underparts buffish-grey, lightly streaked dark brown. **Size** 15-17 cm. **Juv.** base of bill and gape yellowish. **Habitat** open woodlands, mulga, mallee.

Juv.

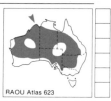

RAOU Atlas 623

644 Fuscous Honeyeater *Lichenostomus fuscus*

Bill black. Dull olive-brown, paler below. Face darker. Dusky ear coverts, tipped yellow. Gape, base of bill and eye-ring yellow or black (breeding). **Size** 14-17 cm. **Juv.** similar, bill brownish. **Voice** loud 'arig rig-a-taw-taw'. **Habitat** open forests, woodlands. Fuscous Honeyeater now considered a race of Yellow-tinted Honeyeater.

Breeding

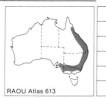

RAOU Atlas 613

645 Yellow-tinted Honeyeater *Lichenostomus flavescens*

Bill black. Forehead and face yellow. Black, crescent-shaped mark at ear. Thin, bright yellow (but inconspicuous) plume. Olive-buff back. Underparts yellow, faintly streaked. **Size** 14-17 cm. **Juv.** similar; brownish bill. **Voice** 'chee-uk-ooo-wee'; 'porra-chu-porra-cheu-cheu-cheu'. **Habitat** woodlands.

Juv.

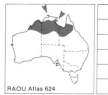

RAOU Atlas 624

646 White-plumed Honeyeater *Lichenostomus penicillatus*

Bill black. Olive-grey bird with yellower head. Faint black line before white neck plume. **Female** smaller. Several races; *carteri* (WA) is yellower and *penicillatus* (southern Aust.) is greener than *leilavalensis* (central Aust.). **Size** 15-19 cm. **Juv.** similar; base of bill orange. **Voice** 'chick-owee'; 'chick-abiddy'. **Habitat** open forests, woodlands, particularly *Eucalyptus camaldulensis* along watercourses.

Display flight

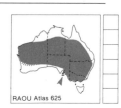

RAOU Atlas 625

640

641

645

643

644
Non-breeding

642 Juv.

642

646

646
Juv.

647 Black-chinned Honeyeater *Melithreptus gularis*

Race *gularis* (S & E Aust.): Bill black. Head black; white line across nape. Eye-skin pale blue. Centre of chin and throat black; sides of throat whitish. Back olive-grey. Underparts pale grey. Race *laetior* (N & W Aust.): Golden back; green-yellow eye-skin; buffish underparts. **Size** 15-17 cm. **Juv.** similar; crown brown; eye-skin, bill yellow-orange. **Voice** loud churring. **Habitat** woodlands.

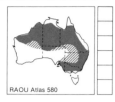

RAOU Atlas 580

648 Strong-billed Honeyeater *Melithreptus validirostris*

Like Black-chinned Honeyeater but back olive-brown; abdomen grey. Two races: *kingi* (King Is.) underparts darker than *validirostris*. **Female** smaller. **Size** 15-17 cm. **Juv.** crown dark brown; eye-skin, base of bill orange. **Voice** loud 'cheep'. **Habitat** forests on Tas. and Bass Strait islands.

Juv.

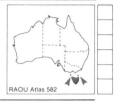

RAOU Atlas 582

649 Brown-headed Honeyeater *Melithreptus brevirostris*

Upperparts olive-brown. Head grey-brown with pale buffish line across nape. Eye-skin dull yellow-orange. Underparts pale grey-buff. Several races: *brevirostris* (E Aust.), *augustus* (SA), and *leucogenus* (W Aust.) with progressively darker heads; *magnirostris* (Kangaroo Is.) has larger bill. **Size** 13-15 cm. **Juv.** similar; eye-skin bluish; gape yellow-orange. **Voice** 'chick'; 'breeet, breeet'. **Habitat** woodlands, mallee.

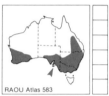

RAOU Atlas 583

650 White-throated Honeyeater *Melithreptus albogularis*

Bill black. Head black, but only above upper bill. Chin white. White line across nape extends to eye. Eye-skin bluish-white. Black shoulder crescent. Back olive-yellow; underparts white. **Size** 13-15 cm. **Juv.** similar; brownish head; gape and bill yellow-orange. **Voice** 'tserp-tserp'; 'pi-pi-pi...'. **Habitat** woodlands.

Head pattern

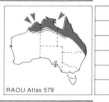

RAOU Atlas 579

651 White-naped Honeyeater *Melithreptus lunatus*

Like White-throated Honeyeater but black on face continues below bill and just on to chin; white nape-line does *not* reach eye. Eye-skin red (race *lunatus*, E Aust.), or whitish (race *chloropsis*, W. Aust.). **Female** smaller. **Size** 13-15 cm. **Juv.** crown brown; base of bill orange. **Voice** 'mjerp, mjerp'. **Habitat** forests.

Head pattern

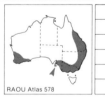

RAOU Atlas 578

652 Black-headed Honeyeater *Melithreptus affinis*

Like White-throated Honeyeater, but chin, throat entirely black; *no* white on nape. **Size** 13-15 cm **Juv.** head dark brown; bill brown. **Voice** sharp whistle. **Habitat** forests, gardens of Tas. and Bass Strait islands.

Juv.

RAOU Atlas 584

653 Green-backed Honeyeater *Glycichaera fallax*

Bill dark grey. Upperparts dull greenish-grey. Faint, narrow eye-ring of whitish feathers. Throat whitish; breast, abdomen yellowish. **Size** 11-12 cm. **Juv.** unknown. **Habitat** rainforests of northern C. York Pen. Identify from *Gerygone* species.

RAOU Atlas 604

647

647
Juv.

647
Race *laetior*

648

649

649
Juv.

651

651
Race *chloropsis*

651
Juv.

650
Juv.

650

653

652

654 Brown Honeyeater *Lichmera indistincta*

Dull olive-brown with darker face. Wedge of yellow or white behind eye. Western race *indistincta* larger than eastern race *osculans*. **Size** 12-16 cm. **Juv.** yellower; face paler. **Voice** loud penetrating call. **Habitat** mangroves, forests, suburbs, heaths with emergent trees.

Breeding

RAOU Atlas 597

655 White-streaked Honeyeater *Trichodere cockerelli*

Head and back dark brown; yellow ear spot. White specks on shoulder. Golden wash over wings and tail. Underparts grey; breast lightly streaked. **Size** 15-19 cm. **Juv.** duller with yellow chin. **Voice** like Brown. **Habitat** swamps, woodlands.

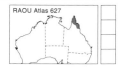

RAOU Atlas 627

656 Tawny-crowned Honeyeater *Phylidonyris melanops*

Crown tawny. Eyebrow, chin white. Dark grey-brown face, ear coverts and crescent on shoulder. Black grey-brown with darker streaks. Underparts dull white; brown specks on flanks. Cinnamon underwing. **Female** smaller. **Size** 15-18 cm. **Juv.** crown grey; crown and back with pale streaks; chin pale yellow. **Voice** musical, flute-like. **Habitat** heaths. Birds often run on the ground.

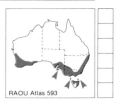

RAOU Atlas 593

657 Crescent Honeyeater *Phylidonyris pyrrhoptera*

Male dark grey with yellow patch in wing. Red-brown eye. Underside paler; broad dark crescent across shoulder and side of breast with whitish line immediately under it. **Female** similar but dull olive-brown; smaller. **Size** 14-17 cm. **Juv.** like adult. **Voice** loud 'egypt' and melodic song. **Habitat** coastal heaths to forests.

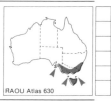

RAOU Atlas 630

658 New Holland Honeyeater *Phylidonyris novaehollandiae*

Streaked black and white with yellow wing patch. White iris. Eyebrow commences at eye; small white ear patch; white 'beard'. White tip to tail. Race *longirostris* (SW Aust.) has longer bill than *novaehollandiae* (SE Aust.). **Female** smaller. **Size** 16-19 cm. **Juv.** yellowish instead of white; rump brown. Iris dark; gape yellow. Yellow edge to alula. **Imm.** eye grey; browner body. **Habitat** coastal heaths to woodlands.

Juv.

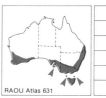

RAOU Atlas 631

659 White-cheeked Honeyeater *Phylidonyris nigra*

Like New Holland but iris is dark brown; eyebrow commences at bill. *No* 'beard' but large white cheek patch. *No* white tip to tail. Western race *gouldii* has longer bill than eastern race *nigra*. **Female** smaller. **Size** 16-19 cm. **Juv.** duller with yellow gape. **Imm.** like adult. **Habitat** coastal heaths to woodlands.

Juv.

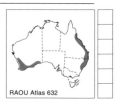

RAOU Atlas 632

660 White-fronted Honeyeater *Phylidonyris albifrons*

Forehead (except centre), lores, eye-ring and moustache white; grey cheek patch. Red spot behind eye. Throat black with specks of white. Back brownish-black; abdomen white. **Female** smaller. **Size** 16-18 cm. **Juv.** browner on head, back and throat. **Voice** melodic eerie song. **Habitat** arid shrublands to woodlands.

Juv.

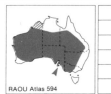

RAOU Atlas 594

655

657 ♂

657 ♀

659

658

660

656

656
Juv.

654

N. Day.

661 Painted Honeyeater *Grantiella picta*

Male pink bill. Black head and back. Yellow wash over wings and tail. Underparts white; black streaks on flank. **Females/Juv.** browner; *no* streaks on flank. **Size** 15-17 cm. **Habitat** open forests, woodlands, particularly where trees are infested with mistletoe.

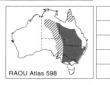
RAOU Atlas 598

662 Brown-backed Honeyeater *Ramsayornis modestus*

Thin whitish line under eye. Drab brown above; dull white below. Breast scalloped pale brown. **Size** 11-12 cm. **Juv.** similar; breast streaked. **Voice** chattering song. **Habitat** near swamps, mangroves.

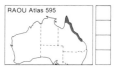
RAOU Atlas 595

663 Bar-breasted Honeyeater *Ramsayornis fasciatus*

Crown dark brown, scalloped white. Face, chin white. Black line on jaw. Back drab brown with whitish streaks. Breast whitish with bold black bars. **Size** 12-15 cm. **Juv.** streaked breast. **Voice** chattering song. **Habitat** melaleuca swamps, woodlands.

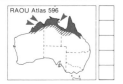
RAOU Atlas 596

664 Rufous-banded Honeyeater *Conopophila albogularis*

Head grey. Chin, throat white. Back brown, lemon-yellow wing patch. Broad rufous breast band. Flanks grey-brown; abdomen white. **Size** 11-13 cm. **Juv.** lacks breast band. **Voice** musical twitter. **Habitat** near swamps, mangroves.

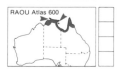
RAOU Atlas 600

665 Rufous-throated Honeyeater *Conopophila rufogularis*

Head, back grey-brown. Chin, throat rufous. Lemon-yellow wing patch. Underparts pale grey-buff. **Size** 11-15 cm. **Juv.** browner; white throat. **Voice** rasping chatter. **Habitat** riverine forests, woodlands.

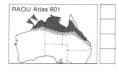
RAOU Atlas 601

666 Grey Honeyeater *Conopophila whitei*

Dull grey-brown above; yellowish-green wash over wings. Underparts dull white; darker throat, breast. **Size** 10-12 cm. **Juv.** similar; pale eye-ring. **Habitat** arid scrub.

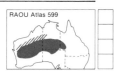
RAOU Atlas 599

667 Eastern Spinebill *Acanthorhynchus tenuirostris*

Male long thin bill. Head glossy black. Red eye. Chin, throat white with rufous centre. Black crescent over shoulder. Back grey-brown; rufous nape. Outer tail tipped white. Underparts cinnamon-brown. **Female** smaller, duller; crown olive-grey. Several races differ in size and colour shades. **Size** 13-16 cm. **Juv.** chin, throat cinnamon. Base of bill orange. Iris brown-red. **Voice** rapid piping. **Habitat** heaths, forests with heath.

Tail pattern
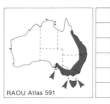
RAOU Atlas 591

668 Western Spinebill *Acanthorhynchus superciliosus*

Dark olive-grey above. Broad chestnut collar over nape extending to chestnut throat and breast. White, then black bands across breast. Abdomen buff. **Female** smaller, duller; lacks breast bands; no chestnut on throat. **Size** 13-16 cm. **Juv.** like female; yellowish base to bill. **Voice** shrill 'kleet-kleet'. **Habitat** heaths, woodlands.

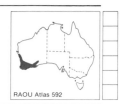
RAOU Atlas 592

669 Banded Honeyeater *Certhionyx pectoralis*

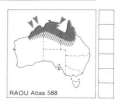

Bill black. Face (including eye), crown and back black; nape freckled grey. Lower back grey; rump white. Underparts white. Black band across breast. **Size** 11-14 cm. **Juv.** a yellow patch behind eye. Crown, underparts creamy-white with dusky breast band. **Voice** tinkling twitter. **Habitat** forests, woodlands.

Speckles on back
Imm.

RAOU Atlas 588

670 Black Honeyeater *Certhionyx niger*

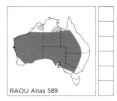

Male long, decurved black bill. Head, throat, back, wings, tail, and stripe down centre of belly are all sooty-black; rest white. Legs black. **Female** breast grey-brown speckled; whitish abdomen. Faint, pale buff stripe above eye. **Size** 10-12 cm. **Juv.** like female. **Voice** feeble 'peeee'. **Habitat** arid shrublands.

Ventral view

RAOU Atlas 589

671 Pied Honeyeater *Certhionyx variegatus*

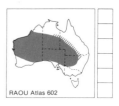

Male black head and throat. Small blue wattle below eye. Bill grey-blue. Breast, rump, abdomen white. Broad white streak on black wings. Tail white except for two black central feathers and broad black tip. **Female** mottled grey-brown above; throat, breast slightly streaked grey-brown. Mottled wing-stripe. Abdomen whitish. **Size** 15-18 cm. **Voice** 'tee-titee-tee-tee'. **Habitat** arid savannah.

Display flight

RAOU Atlas 602

672 Dusky Honeyeater *Myzomela obscura*

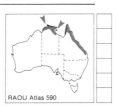

Uniform dark grey-brown, slightly darker on head; paler on belly. No distinctive markings. Bill black. **Female** smaller. **Size** 12-14 cm. **Juv.** similar; duller with orange-grey lower bill. **Voice** 'chirp chirp chirp'; trills and 'tip-tip-eeee-chip'. **Habitat** rainforests, mangroves, woodlands, near swamps.

Juv.

RAOU Atlas 590

673 Red-headed Honeyeater *Myzomela erythrocephala*

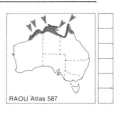

Male head, neck, chin, throat and rump scarlet. Lores black. Back, wings, lower breast sooty-brown; abdomen grey-brown. **Female** forehead, throat tinged crimson; crown, back, wings and rump brown. Throat, breast smoky-grey. Abdomen whitish. **Size** 11-13 cm. **Juv.** like female. **Voice** harsh whistles. **Habitat** in and near mangroves.

Ventral view

RAOU Atlas 587

674 Scarlet Honeyeater *Myzomela sanguinolenta*

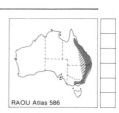

Male like male Red-headed Honeyeater but scarlet on breast, head and rump. Wings black with white edges to feathers. Back black and scarlet. Abdomen light creamy-grey. **Female** very like female Red-headed but more olive-brown. **Size** 10-11 cm. **Juv.** like female. **Voice** tinkling bell-like 'clink-clink-clink'. **Habitat** mangroves, coastal forests and woodlands.

Singing

RAOU Atlas 586

672

669
Juv.

673 ♂

669

♀ 673

674 ♂

671 ♂

♀ 674

♀ 671

670 ♂

670 ♀

675 **Crimson Chat** *Ephthianura tricolor*

Male brilliant crimson forehead, crown, breast, flanks, rump. White throat, centre belly, undertail coverts. Eyes creamy-white. Nape, ear coverts, lores blackish-brown. Back dark brown. Note: *all* chats have black or dark bills and legs; short blackish-brown tails, tipped white. **Female** upperparts, head light brown. Throat, belly white. pale red and buff patches on breast, flanks, rump. **Size** 10-12 cm. **Juv.** like female; *lacks* red on breast. **Voice** high 'see-ee-ee'; melodious whistle; short harsh metallic notes. **Habitat** salty areas of inland plains, rocky hills, mallee heath. Flocks of mixed chat species may occur.

Flock in flight

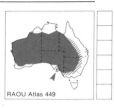

RAOU Atlas 449

676 **Orange Chat** *Ephthianura aurifrons*

Male head, rump, underparts pale orange-yellow, becoming luminous orange on forehead, breast. Eyes reddish-brown. Throat, lores black. Back fawny-yellow, mottled darker. **Female/Juv.** grey to yellowish-brown above. Whitish eyebrow. Rump yellowish. Pale yellow below; breast washed grey-brown; belly washed lemon. **Size** 10-12 cm. **Voice** metallic 'tang'; 'cheep-cheep' in flight. **Habitat** low shrubs in salty areas, gibber plains where shrubs; coastal swamps in WA.

♂ at nest

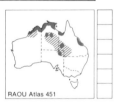

RAOU Atlas 450

677 **Yellow Chat** *Ephthianura crocea*

Male forehead, face, rump, underparts bright yellow. Narrow blackish breast band. Eyes creamy. Thin dark eye line to bill. Crown, back grey-brown, washed yellow. **Female** paler, *lacks* breast band. **Size** 10.5-12 cm. **Juv.** like female; greyer. **Voice** metallic 'tang'; cricket-like note; musical 'pee-eep'. **Habitat** coastal and inland swamps, including vegetated bore-drains. Also shrubby saltbush flats. A little-known species.

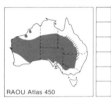

RAOU Atlas 451

678 **White-fronted Chat** *Ephthianura albifrons*

Male white forehead, face, throat and belly. Black band from back of crown and nape across breast. Eyes pinky-white. Bill black. Back grey. Legs black. **Female** upperparts, including forehead, grey-brown. Pale eyebrow. Underparts white or pale grey; narrow blackish-brown breast band. **Size** 11-12.5 cm. **Juv.** like very pale female; breast band absent or indistinct. **Voice** repeated, soft, finch-like 'tang'. **Habitat** low vegetation in salty coastal and inland areas; crops. High, jerky flight; perches prominently.

Juv.

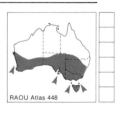

RAOU Atlas 448

679 **Gibberbird** *Ashbyia lovensis*

Male crown grey-fawn. Yellow eyebrow, lores, face, underparts. Eyes white to yellow. Back, rump grey-brown to buffy-brown. Yellow breast, flanks, washed grey-brown. **Female** browner above; paler below; breast band buffy-brown. **Size** 12-13 cm. **Juv.** bill horn; like female, but brown. **Voice** 'wheet-wheet-wheet' in flight; musical chatter; alarm of 5-6 piercing notes. **Habitat** stony, open inland plains. Upright posture. Resembles chats but 'pipit-like'. Stands on rocks; runs; wags tail like Richard's Pipit.

Tail wag

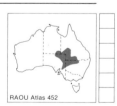

RAOU Atlas 452

680 Yellow-bellied Sunbird *Nectarinia jugularis*

Long, slender, curved black bill. **Male** olive-yellow above; deep yellow below. Chin to upper breast dark metallic purplish-blue. Tail tipped white. **Female** *no* metallic blue bib. **Size** 10-12 cm. **Voice** high-pitched 'dzit-dzit'; hissing whistle; trill. **Habitat** rainforest edges, mangroves, gardens. Also called Olive-backed Sunbird.

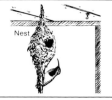

Nest

RAOU Atlas 572

681 Mistletoebird *Dicaeum hirundinaceum*

Male head, upperparts glossy blue-black. Throat, breast, undertail coverts scarlet. Bill dark, short. Underparts grey-white; dark streak on breast. **Female** brownish-grey above; undertail coverts pale scarlet. **Size** 10-11 cm. **Juv.** as female; bill pink. **Voice** high double note; warble; soft mimicry of other birds. **Habitat** wherever mistletoe grows.

Incubating

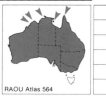

RAOU Atlas 564

682 Spotted Pardalote *Pardalotus punctatus*

Black crown with rows of white spots. Wings, tail black, spotted white. Eyebrow white. Rump chestnut. **Male** throat, undertail coverts bright yellow. Back fawn with buff spots; pale underside. **Female** throat cream; crown spots yellow. **Size** 8-9.5 cm. **Juv.** like female; crown paler, not spotted. **Voice** double or triple notes. **Habitat** eucalypt forests.

Flight

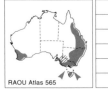

RAOU Atlas 565

683 Yellow-rumped Pardalote
Pardalotus xanthopygus

Like Spotted Pardalote but rump bright yellow. Back greyer, spotted light grey. **Size** 9-10 cm. **Voice** same as Spotted Pardalote. **Habitat** dry eucalypt woodlands, especially mallee. Yellow-rumped Pardalote is now considered a race of Spotted Pardalote.

Flight

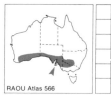

RAOU Atlas 566

684 Forty-spotted Pardalote *Pardalotus quadragintus*

Ear coverts lemon-yellow. Body dull olive-green; pale below. Small white spots on dark wings. Tail dark with white spots. **Size** 9-12 cm. **Voice** soft double note; also repeated single note (hollow and faint). **Habitat** Tas. coastal forest.

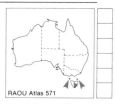

RAOU Atlas 571

685 Red-browed Pardalote *Pardalotus rubricatus*

Body pale fawn-grey. Dark crown spotted white. Eyebrow spot orange to red. Orange-buff wing patch. Some yellow on breast. **Size** 10-12 cm. **Voice** five notes, increasing in pitch and speed. **Habitat** inland woodlands.

Red on brow often absent

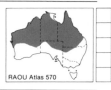

RAOU Atlas 570

686 Striated Pardalote *Pardalotus striatus*

Variable across Aust. in no. of primaries edged white, crown-streaking, wing spot, rump colour. Sexes similar. Mostly grey. Yellow throat, eyebrow. Crown black, white streaks. White edging, red/yellow spot on dark wings. Back brown; rump paler. Tail black, white tip. Underparts pale; flanks yellow. **Male** brighter. **Size** 9-11.5 cm. **Juv.** dull, *no* crown streaks. **Voice** loud, repetitive, double, triple notes. **Habitat** eucalypt forests, woodlands; in tree crowns. Winter flocks.

Pardalotes are acrobatic foragers

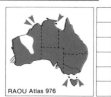

RAOU Atlas 976

♂ 680

680 ♀

681
Imm.

♀ 681

♂ 681

682 ♀

682
Juv.

684

685
Juv.

♂ 682

685

♂ 683

♀ 683

686
Race *melanocephalus*

686
Race *ornatus*

686
Juv.

686
Race *striatus*

686
Race *substriatus*

N^ Day.

687 Pale White-eye *Zosterops citrinella*

Conspicuous white eye-ring. Eye brown. Bill dark brown.
Olive-yellow above; darker on wings. Throat lemon-
yellow. Breast, abdomen off-white. Undertail coverts
lemon-yellow. Legs brown. Aust. race is *albiventris*.
Size 12 cm. **Voice** not recorded. **Habitat** woodlands and
forests on islands off NE Qld.

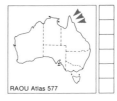

RAOU Atlas 577

688 Yellow White-eye *Zosterops lutea*

Three races recognised. Race *lutea* (east of Wyndham,
WA): Conspicuous white eye-ring. Olive-yellow above.
Forehead and underparts lemon-yellow. Bill dark brown.
Eye brown. Legs brown. Race *balstoni* (west of
Wyndham, WA): Colours duller, upperparts slightly
greyer. Race *hecla* (intermediate zone). **Size** 10.5 cm.
Voice rapid, loud warbling song. **Habitat** coastal
mangroves and adjacent thickets.

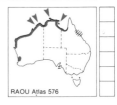

RAOU Atlas 576

689 Silvereye *Zosterops lateralis*

Bill black. Flanks of males darker than in females; all
with conspicuous white eye-ring. Seven races in Aust.
Race *gouldii* (SW of WA): Whole of upperparts olive-
green. Throat greenish-yellow; breast, abdomen pale grey.
Flanks pale buff. Undertail coverts yellow. Six races
(S to E Aust.) are all grey-backed. Race *halmaturina* (SA
and W Vic.): Basically like *lateralis*, but with buff
flanks and variable throat colouration from wholly yellow
to almost totally lacking yellow. Race *lateralis* (Tas.;
large numbers cross Bass Strait to spend winter in SE
Aust.): Rufous flanks. Throat grey or white, sometimes
yellow near chin. Undertail coverts whitish. Race
familiaris (E Aust. to Rockhampton, Qld): Yellow-green
head, wings and rump. Throat yellow or pale green,
breast and abdomen grey. North of Sydney, NSW,
undertail coverts are lemon-yellow. Race *ramsayi* (Mackay
to Iron Range, N Qld): Similar to, but brighter than
familiaris; undertail coverts richer yellow. Race
chlorocephala: Distinct Great Barrier Reef island form.
Yellower above, whiter below than mainland birds;
similar to Pale White-eye in many respects. **Size** 12 cm.
Voice repeated high-pitched 'tee-oow'; pleasant warbling
song. **Habitat** most natural vegetation types within their
range; orchards, gardens. Identify from Large-billed and
Green-backed Gerygones. Also called Grey-backed Silvereye.
Race *chlorocephala* sometimes called Capricorn Silvereye.

Ventral flight

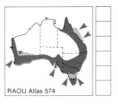

RAOU Atlas 574

Facial pattern

687

689
Race *chlorocephala*

688

689
Race *gouldii*

689
Race *lateralis*

583
Green-backed Gerygone

689
Race *familiaris*

653
Green-backed Honeyeater

690 European Goldfinch *Carduelis carduelis**

Red-faced; white and brown finch with large yellow wing bars conspicuous in flight. Pinkish-white bill. **Male** bright red face; black lores, crown and shoulders. Tail and trailing edge of wing tipped white. Back and flanks tawny-brown. Side of head, rump, abdomen white. **Female** less red on face. **Size** 13 cm. **Juv.** brownish head, streaked plumage. **Voice** liquid 'tu-leep', 'tsi-i-it'; liquid twittering song. **Habitat** settlements and agricultural areas. Undulating flight.

Dorsal flight

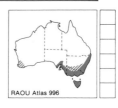
RAOU Atlas 996

691 European Greenfinch *Carduelis chloris**

Stoutly built, dull-green finch with green-yellow streaked wings and side of tail; tail black and forked. **Male** heavy ivory bill; large head. **Female** duller, yellow less obvious. **Size** 15 cm. **Juv.** duller bill and plumage. **Voice** 'chip-chip-chip'; nasal 'twe-e-ee'; song is trill followed by ascending 'zeep'. **Habitat** gardens and parks. In pairs or flocks; flight undulating.

Dorsal flight

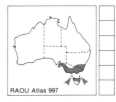
RAOU Atlas 997

692 House Sparrow *Passer domesticus**

Male bill black; grey crown. Large black bib and breast. Chestnut nape. Whitish-grey ear coverts, underparts and rump. White bar on shoulder. Tail brownish-grey. **Non-breeding male** bill horn-brown; breast smudged black. **Female** horn-brown bill, no black on face. Pale stripe extends back from eye. Whitish-grey underparts. **Size** 15 cm. **Juv.** paler, yellowish-ivory bill with yellow gape flanges. **Voice** harsh 'cheer-up', and chattering song. **Habitat** human habitation.

Dorsal flight

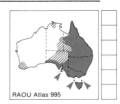
RAOU Atlas 995

693 Tree Sparrow *Passer montanus**

Bill black; chestnut crown. Small crescent-shaped black spot on cheek; black throat. Upperparts streaked brown and black; grey below. **Non-breeding** bill blackish-brown to yellow at base. **Size** 14 cm. **Juv.** paler bill; pale brown plumage. **Voice** soft 'tek', and twittering song. **Habitat** human habitation.

Dorsal flight

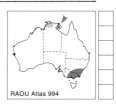
RAOU Atlas 994

694 White-winged Wydah *Euplectes albonotatus**

Male black finch; very long black tail. Blue-grey bill. Upperparts of wings white; shoulder brownish yellow to yellow. **Female** brown bill; upperparts streaked brown and black. Underparts buff, streaked with brown below. **Non-breeding male** as female but white on wings, yellow on shoulder. **Size** 15-18 cm. **Voice** 'cheee-eee'. **Habitat** reed-beds, grassland near rivers. May now be extinct in NSW.

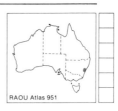
RAOU Atlas 951

695 Red Bishop *Euplectes orix**

Solid black and scarlet finch. **Male** upperparts and undertail coverts scarlet. Bill, front half of head and underparts black. Short dark brown tail. **Female/Non-breeding male** buff eyebrow; upperparts streaked brown, buff and black. Underparts buff. Distinguished from female House Sparrow by brown-streaked breast and flanks. **Size** 11 cm. **Voice** 'zik zik zik', and others. **Habitat** reed beds. Not recorded recently; believed extinct.

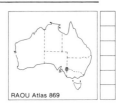
RAOU Atlas 869

* **Introduced**

693

♂ 692
Non-breeding

692 ♀

♂ 692
Breeding

691

691
Juv.

695 ♀

694 ♀

♂ 694

690

690
Juv.

♂ 695

N. Day.

696 Diamond Firetail *Stagonopleura guttata*

Male solid 'upright' finch. Maroon bill; lores black. Grey above, white below; black chest band. Flanks spotted white. Crimson rump. **Female** bill coral-pink; lores brownish. **Size** 12 cm. **Juv.** blackish bill; dull, indistinct chest bar. **Voice** two-syllable plaintive whistle descends, then ascends. **Habitat** grassy woodland. Hops vigorously.

Chest band

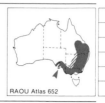

RAOU Atlas 652

697 Beautiful Firetail *Emblema bellum*

Olive-brown. Red bill; black mask. Crimson rump, uppertail coverts. Barred chest, bold barring on flanks. **Male** centre abdomen black. **Size** 11-12 cm. **Juv.** duller; bill black. **Voice** mournful 'floating' whistle; song unknown. **Habitat** thick forest and scrub; often near she-oak and tea-tree thickets.

RAOU Atlas 650

698 Red-eared Firetail *Emblema oculata*

Olive-brown, finely barred in black. Red bill; crimson rump and uppertail coverts. Small crimson ear patch. Bold white spots on black flanks. **Breeding female** paler ear patch, bill. **Size** 11.5-12 cm. **Juv.** duller; bill black. **Voice** piercing, 'floating', single note 'oooee'. **Habitat** dense coastal forest and scrub.

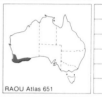

RAOU Atlas 651

699 Painted Firetail *Emblema pictum*

Male slim, brown-backed. Scarlet face, rump and mid-belly. Bill long, tapered to fine red-tipped point. Large white flank spots. **Female** face duller; red bill, lores and rump; white flanks spots larger. **Size** 10-12 cm. **Juv.** duller than female; red rump only. **Voice** loud, harsh 'trut'. **Habitat** stony hills on spinifex plains.

Flight

RAOU Atlas 654

700 Star Finch *Neochmia ruficauda*

Male red face. Dark olive above, yellow-olive below. Chest, flanks, rump and tail spotted white. **Female** duller; red only on lores and forehead. **Size** 10-12 cm. **Juv.** brownish-olive; bill black. **Voice** loud penetrating 'sseet'. **Habitat** tall grass beside swamps and rivers.

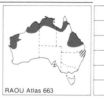

RAOU Atlas 663

701 Crimson Finch *Neochmia phaeton*

Male slender 'upright' crimson finch with long tapered tail. Nape and crown grey. Upperparts washed grey. Belly and undertail coverts black (white on C. York Pen. morph). Fine white flank spots. **Female** crimson, washed brownish-olive; centre belly pale creamish-fawn. **Size** 12-14 cm. **Juv.** duller than female; bill black. **Voice** piercing 'che-che-che'. **Habitat** watercourses with tall grass, pandanus; cane fields. Flicks tail.

Tail flick

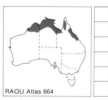

RAOU Atlas 664

702 Red-browed Firetail *Neochmia temporalis*

Olive-green and grey. Scarlet rump, eyebrow, sides of bill. **Size** 11-12 cm. **Juv.** duller; bill black; eyebrow shorter. **Voice** high-pitched, almost inaudible, piercing 'seee'. **Habitat** varied; usually dense shrubs interspersed with open grass areas; near watercourses, small lakes.

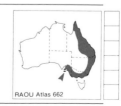

RAOU Atlas 662

701 ♀

701 ♂

701 ♂
Cape York Pen. morph

702
Juv.

702

698

697

♀ 699

699 ♂

700
Juv.

♂ 700

696

696
Juv.

703 **Plum-headed Finch** *Neochmia modesta*

Male olive-brown above; spotted white on wings. White below, barred brown. Forehead, crown, chin deep claret. Bill, lores and tail black. **Female** *no* claret chin spot. Thin white line above and to rear of eye. **Size** 11-12.5 cm. **Juv.** *no* claret head markings; faint barring on abdomen. **Voice** long, drawn-out 'ting'. **Habitat** open woodland bordering watercourses.

Courtship behaviour

RAOU Atlas 661

704 **Zebra Finch** *Taeniopygia guttata*

Grey body. Wax-red bill; black and white tear stripes. White rump and zebra-barred tail conspicuous on fleeing. **Male** chestnut ear patch, black chest bar; fine black and white barring on throat. Flanks chestnut, spotted white. White abdomen. **Female** abdomen buff. **Size** 10 cm. **Juv.** as female but bill black. **Voice** nasal twang 'tiaah'; soft rhythmic song. **Habitat** most open country; not Cape York Peninsula.

Rump

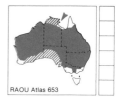
RAOU Atlas 653

705 **Double-barred Finch** *Taeniopygia bichenovii*

Neat 'owl-faced', brownish-grey finch. Bill greyish-blue. Face white, bordered black. White underparts with two narrow black bands above and below chest. Black wings spotted white. Black tail; rump white (black rump is race *annulosa*, W of Gulf of Carpentaria). **Size** 10-11 cm. **Juv.** duller; chest bars indistinct. **Voice** high-pitched 'floating' nasal 'tiaah'. **Habitat** varied; open forests, grasslands, beside creeks.

Tail flick

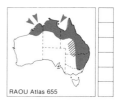
RAOU Atlas 655

706 **Masked Finch** *Poephila personata*

Slender body; red-brown above; buff below. Bill heavy, waxy-yellow. Black mask and chin. White rump; long black pointed tail. **Female** smaller mask; less black on chin. Race *leucotis* (C. York Pen.): pale on cheeks and lower flanks. **Size** 12-13.5 cm. **Juv.** duller; bill black. **Voice** long nasal 'tiat'; soft 'tet'; soft mechanical song. **Habitat** open woodland. Flicks tail frequently.

Tail flick

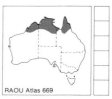
RAOU Atlas 669

707 **Long-tailed Finch** *Poephila acuticauda*

Male fawnish-tan. Blue-grey head; black lores. Large black bib. Bill varies from waxy yellow (W Aust.) to orange-red (W Qld). Long, sharply tapered black tail; white rump; orange legs. **Female** smaller bib. **Size** 15-16.5 cm. **Juv.** duller; bill black. **Voice** soft 'tet', and loud, long pure whistle; soft musical song. **Habitat** open woodland near creeks. Jerks head on landing.

Rump

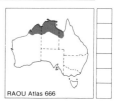
RAOU Atlas 666

708 **Black-throated Finch** *Poephila cincta*

Male stocky pinkish-fawn. Blue-grey head; black bill. Large black bib; short black tail. Black rump on C. York Pen. birds — race *atropygialis*. White rump to the south — race *cincta*. **Female** smaller; rounder bib. **Size** 10 cm. **Juv.** duller. **Voice** hoarse 'floating' whistle; soft 'tet'; very soft musical song. **Habitat** open forest, woodland. Jerks head up and down on landing.

Head jerks

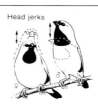

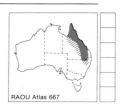
RAOU Atlas 667

705

705
Race *annulosa*

704
Juv.

♀ **704**

704 ♂

707
W Aust. morph

707
W Qld morph

706

706
Race *leucotis*

707
Juv.

♀ **703**

703 ♂

708
Race *cincta*

708
Race *atropygialis*

709 Pictorella Mannikin *Heteromunia pectoralis*

Male black-faced grey finch with white breast mottled black. Cinnamon crescent over eye and ear to side of neck. Fine white spots on wings. **Female** face brownish-black, more black on breast. **Size** 11 cm. **Juv.** bill dark; plumage grey-brown. **Voice** loud 'teet'. **Habitat** open grassland.

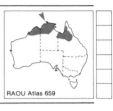

RAOU Atlas 659

710 Chestnut-breasted Mannikin
Lonchura castaneothorax

Male solid brownish finch with black face, grey crown and heavy grey bill. Chestnut breast divided from white abdomen by heavy black bar. Golden-brown rump and tail. **Female** paler. **Size** 10 cm. **Juv.** dark bill; olive-brown above, buff below. **Voice** bell-like 'teet'. **Habitat** reed beds, rank grass.

Ventral pattern

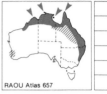

RAOU Atlas 657

711 Yellow-rumped Mannikin *Lonchura flaviprymna*

Solid finch. Pale grey head. Back and wings cinnamon-brown; cream-buff underparts. Straw-brown rump and tail. **Size** 10 cm. **Voice** bell-like 'teet'. **Habitat** reeds and rank grass.

Juv.

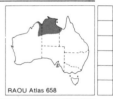

RAOU Atlas 658

712 Black-headed Mannikin *Lonchura malacca**

Stout body; heavy grey bill. Head, nape, throat, undertail coverts and belly black. Remainder underparts white. Upperparts and wings light chestnut with deep chestnut rump. **Size** 11 cm. **Juv.** grey head; paler above, buff below. **Voice** shrill 'peep-peep'. **Habitat** reed beds.

Lonchura singing posture

RAOU Atlas 870

713 Nutmeg Mannikin *Lonchura punctulata**

Bill grey; head and throat chocolate-brown. Upperparts grey-brown. Underparts dull-white, scalloped dark brown. **Size** 11 cm. **Juv.** brownish-yellow below. **Voice** 'ki-ki-te-te'. **Habitat** reeds, rank grass. Flicks tail constantly.

Tail flick

RAOU Atlas 983

714 Blue-faced Finch *Erythrura trichroa*

Male grass-green finch with cobalt-blue face and throat. Black bill. Dull scarlet rump and uppertail coverts. **Female** duller, with less blue. **Size** 12 cm. **Juv.** dull, with pale grey bill. **Voice** high-pitched 'tseet-tseet'. **Habitat** edges of rainforest.

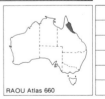

RAOU Atlas 660

715 Gouldian Finch *Erythrura gouldiae*

Male elegant, colourful finch with lilac chest and yellow abdomen. Ivory bill, red tip. Face black in most but crimson in some and yellow-ochre in rare individuals. Grass-green above with cobalt-blue rump. Black tail drawn into fine, thin wisps. **Female** duller. **Size** 14 cm. **Juv.** upper bill blackish, lower bill white; plumage ashy-grey and olive. **Voice** 'ssitt'. **Habitat** open woodland and grassland.

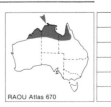

RAOU Atlas 670

* Introduced

256

♂ 709

♂ 714

712

713

710
Juv.

♂ 715
Yellow-faced morph

711

710

♂ 715
Red-faced morph

715 ♂

715
Juv.

♀ 715

716 Metallic Starling *Aplonis metallica*

Lustrous black body. Bright red eye. Bill, legs, black.
Size 21-24 cm. **Imm.** eye dark. Brown above; striated below.
Voice harsh, chattering, wheezing. **Habitat** tropical forests,
woodlands, gardens. Conspicuous nest colonies high in
trees. Flocks.

Juv./Imm.

Nest colony

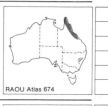
RAOU Atlas 674

717 Common Starling *Sturnus vulgaris**

Glossy black. Bill straw-yellow. After post-breeding moult
body speckled; bill black. **Size** 20-22 cm. **Fledgling/
Juv.** mouse-grey/brown, bill dark. **Voice** chattering
twitters, whistles; mimicry. **Habitat** urban and country
areas. Flocks feed on ground. Roosts colonially.

Flock in flight

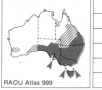
RAOU Atlas 999

718 Common Mynah *Acridotheres tristis**

Cocoa body. Black head, throat. Yellow bill, facial skin,
legs, feet. White wing patches obvious in flight. **Size** 23-
25 cm. **Fledgling/Juv.** like adult; brownish head.
Voice varied, noisy. **Habitat** about urban areas. Mainly on
ground; 'bouncing' walk; 'arrogant'. Roosts colonially.

Dorsal flight

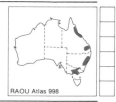
RAOU Atlas 998

719 Yellow Oriole *Oriolus flavocinctus*

Khaki-yellow/green above; lightly streaked below. Bill
orange. Eye red. Wing dark, edged cream. Tail dark,
tipped cream. **Female** paler. **Size** 25-30 cm. **Imm.** duller;
streaked yellow; bill dark. **Voice** melodious roll of repeated
notes; ventriloquial. **Habitat** tropical forested areas;
mangroves.

Imm.

RAOU Atlas 672

720 Olive-backed Oriole *Oriolus sagittatus*

Bill reddish; eye red. Back finely streaked; heavy streaking
below. **Male** greener; wing-feathers edged grey.
Female greyer, wing-feathers edged cinnamon. **Size** 25-
28 cm. **Imm.** duller; rufous on head, upperwing covert edges;
bill dark. Eyebrow conspicuous, creamy. **Voice** rolling
'orry-orry-ole'; ventriloquial. Peaceful Dove call similar.
Habitat wooded areas.

Imm.

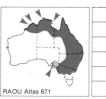
RAOU Atlas 671

721 Figbird *Sphecotheres viridis*

Male facial skin pinkish, red or orange. Back olive-green.
Northern males brilliant yellow below (race *flaviventris*
'Yellow Figbird'). Southern males duller grey-bluish; green
below (race *vieilloti* 'Green Figbird'). **Female** (both races)
upperparts brownish. Face skin bluish. Throat and breast
cream, heavily streaked. **Size** 27-29.5 cm. **Voice** soft musical;
short sharp yelps. **Habitat** tropical rainforest edges, parks.

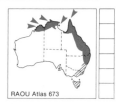
RAOU Atlas 673

722 Spangled Drongo *Dicrurus bracteatus*

Bill heavy, black; bristles at base. Eye red. Body black; breast,
wings, tail glossy black. Flaring tail fork. **Size** M 30-32,
F 28-30 cm. **Imm.** dusky black, speckled below. Eye brown.
Voice varied: rasping, hissing, crackling. Very vocal.
Habitat open forests (wet), urban areas, woodlands. Swift,
erratic flight. Singly; small flocks.

Hawking

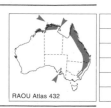
RAOU Atlas 432

Notes Spangled Drongo is now considered closely allied to the
monarchs (see pp. 354-6). Spelling of 'Mynah', as in Common Mynah,
increasingly appearing in print without the 'h', viz. Common Myna.

719

716

722

720

♀
721

♂
721
Race *flaviventris*

717
Juv.

♂
721
Race *vieilloti*

718

717
Breeding

717
Post-moult

723 Golden Bowerbird *Prionodura newtoniana*

Male underparts, central crown, nape yellow. Upperparts, central tail feathers golden-olive brown. **Female** olive-brown, ash-grey below. **Size** 23-25 cm. **Imm.** belly, flanks washed yellow, increasing until some yellow feathers clearly apparent before moult to adult. **Voice** rattles, croaks, mimicry. **Habitat** tropical rainforest above approx. 900 m. Solitary, or imm. male associations of two to six.

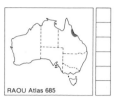

RAOU Atlas 685

724 Satin Bowerbird *Ptilonorhynchus violaceus*

Male glossy blue-black. Bill and legs whitish. Eye blue. **Female** dull green; rufous wings, tail. Underparts off-white, washed greenish, scalloped brown-grey; throat dull. Bill, legs dark. **Size** 27-33 cm. **Imm.** as female to fourth year when throat greener, bill paler, then odd blue-black feathers until seventh-year moult. **Voice** two-note whistle, hissing, buzzing, mimicry. **Habitat** rainforests, nearby areas.

Mixed flock

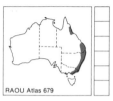

RAOU Atlas 679

725 Regent Bowerbird *Sericulus chrysocephalus*

Male black and gold; pale bill. **Female** bill, throat patch, rear crown black. Wings, tail brown-olive; rest greyish or fawn, mottled and scalloped brown. **Size** 24-28 cm. **Imm.** as female; gradual male plumage after two years. **Voice** infrequent; scolds, chatterings, mimicry. **Habitat** rainforests and nearby areas; forests, scrubs, orchards.

Imm. ♂

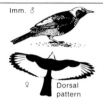

♀ Dorsal pattern

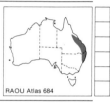

RAOU Atlas 684

726A Spotted Bowerbird *Chlamydera maculata*

Dusky brown to black-brown above, head paler. Body heavily spotted buff to rufous. Pink nape (nuchal) crest. Ash-grey hind neck. Throat, breast finely spotted black. Underparts paler buff-grey than Western Bowerbird (plate a little too dark). **Size** 27-31 cm. **Voice** grating hissings; mechanical sounds, mimicry. **Habitat** dry open woodland.

Courtship behaviour: crest presentation ♂

RAOU Atlas 680

726B Western Bowerbird *Chlamydera guttata*

Smaller, darker. No ash-grey hind neck. Boldly spotted orange-brown; tail tip same colour. Underparts richer colour than Spotted. **Size** 25-28 cm. **Voice** generally similar to Spotted. **Habitat** arid open woodland. Former western race *guttata* of Spotted Bowerbird, now considered a full species.

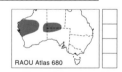

RAOU Atlas 680

727 Great Bowerbird *Chlamydera nuchalis*

Grey with brownish-grey back; wings and tail heavily spotted pale grey. Stout decurved bill. Lilac nape crest which females and imm. frequently lack. **Size** 32-37.5 cm. **Imm.** slight abdomen and flank barring. **Voice** like Spotted Bowerbird. **Habitat** dryer woodlands, low open forest, particularly watercourses.

Courtship behaviour: parade posture ♂

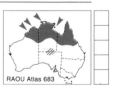

RAOU Atlas 683

728 Fawn-breasted Bowerbird *Chlamydera cerviniventris*

Grey-brown with back, wings and tail feathers finely tipped whitish; contrasting fawn lower breast, abdomen and flanks. Decurved black bill. More white about face. **Size** 25-30.5 cm. **Voice** like other *Chlamydera*. **Habitat** coastal vegetation, often near rainforest; mangroves, watercourses, vine forests, eucalypt-melaleuca woodlands.

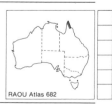

RAOU Atlas 682

♂ 723

723 ♀

724 ♂

♀ 724

♂ 725

725 ♀

726B

726A

727

728

729 Tooth-billed Bowerbird *Scenopoeetes dentirostris*

Singing over court

Stocky. Pale buff cheeks. Stout black bill. Upperparts dark olive-brown. Dirty white underparts. Legs much shorter than Green Catbird. **Size** 24-27 cm. **Voice** over display court: strong varied, predominantly bird mimicry and 'chuck', otherwise silent save harsh flight alarm. **Habitat** tropical rainforest approx. 600 to 1400 m.

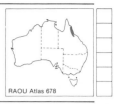
RAOU Atlas 678

730 Spotted Catbird *Ailuroedus melanotis*

Stout. Bright green; paler below; heavy whitish spotting. Bill whitish; eye red. Head whitish and buff with contrasting black markings. Greater coverts, secondaries, tail finely tipped white. **Size** 26-30 cm. **Voice** cat-like wailings; single or double high-pitched 'chip' or 'tick'. **Habitat** tropical rainforest, more common on highlands.·

RAOU Atlas 677

731 Green Catbird *Ailuroedus crassirostris*

Like Spotted Catbird but more uniform green; no black markings. White patch each side of lower throat. **Size** 28-33 cm. **Voice** like Spotted Catbird. **Habitat** temperate rainforest.

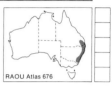
RAOU Atlas 676

732 Paradise Riflebird *Ptiloris paradiseus*

Male velvet black. Long decurved bill. Iridescent blue-green crown, throat-breast 'shield' and central tail. Lower breast and abdomen black, broadly scalloped oil-green. Rustling flight. **Female** dark olive-brown. White eyebrow. Chestnut wings and tail. Underparts buff-white with brown chevrons and barring. **Size** 25-30 cm. **Imm. male** like females until black feathers and flight-rustle develop. **Voice** double, sometimes single explosive 'yaas'. **Habitat** temperate rainforest. Riflebirds climb and tear rotten wood.

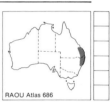
RAOU Atlas 686

733 Victoria's Riflebird *Ptiloris victoriae*

Male as Paradise Riflebird, but broader, more greyish-velvet black between throat-breast 'shield' and oil-green abdomen. Central tail feathers iridescent blue-green. **Female** as Paradise but rich cinnamon-buff below. **Size** 23-25 cm. **Imm.** as Paradise. **Voice** single or explosive 'yaas'. **Habitat** tropical rainforest.

♂ Displaying

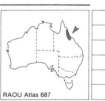
RAOU Atlas 687

734 Magnificent Riflebird *Ptiloris magnificus*

Imm. ♂ moulting

Male velvet black. Iridescent crown. Broad blue-green throat-breast 'shield'. Central tail feathers iridescent blue-green. Remaining underparts and filamentous flank plumes black, suffused purple-red. **Female** like other riflebirds. More cinnamon above, dull white below, barred blackish-brown. **Size** M 28-33, F 26-28 cm. **Voice** clear loud whistle 'wheew-whit'. **Habitat** tropical rainforest.

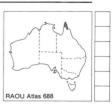
RAOU Atlas 688

735 Trumpet Manucode *Manucodia keraudrenii*

Starling-like. Short bill; red eye; elongated nape plumes. Glossy black with iridescent sheen; long rounded tail. **Size** 27-32 cm. **Voice** powerful, long, trumpet-like blast. **Habitat** tropical rainforest.

RAOU Atlas 689

Note Some authors consider Spotted Catbird is a race of Green Catbird.

736 White-winged Chough *Corcorax melanorhamphos*

Black, open wings show large white area. Eye red. Long down-curved bill. Long tail. **Imm.** eye brown. **Size** 45 cm. **Voice** descending whistles; harsh gratings. **Habitat** dry woodland. In parties; identify from currawongs, corvids.

Nest

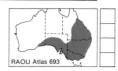

RAOU Atlas 693

737 Apostlebird *Struthidea cinerea*

Grey, pale streaks. Stout bill. Brown wings. **Size** 29-32 cm. **Voice** harsh chattering. **Habitat** open forests, woodlands and scrub. In parties.

RAOU Atlas 675

738 Australian Magpie-lark *Grallina cyanoleuca*

Black and white. White bill, eye. **Male** white eyebrow; black throat. **Female** white face *and* throat. **Imm.** dark bill and eye, white *eyebrow* and *throat*. Slender black legs. **Size** 27 cm. **Voice** 'pee-wee'; also 'pee-o-wit'. **Habitat** open areas, often near water. 'Plover-like' walk.

Imm.

RAOU Atlas 415

739 White-breasted Woodswallow *Artamus leucorhynchus*

White rump, breast and belly, cut-off from uniform dark grey-brown throat, upperparts and all-dark tail. **Size** 17 cm. **Juv.** dark areas mottled. **Voice** 'pert, pert'; chattering. **Habitat** trees near water, including mangroves.

Clumping

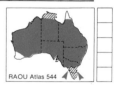

RAOU Atlas 543

740 Masked Woodswallow *Artamus personatus*

Male clear-cut black face and throat, edged white. Pale grey below. Mid-bluish grey above. Tail thinly tipped white. **Female** washed dusky. **Size** 19 cm. **Juv.** mottled. **Voice** 'chap, chap'; chattering. **Habitat** open forests to gibber, often with White-browed Woodswallow.

RAOU Atlas 544

741 White-browed Woodswallow *Artamus superciliosus*

Male broad white eyebrow. Upperparts, throat deep blue-grey. Breast, belly rich chestnut. Undertail coverts, tail thinly tipped white. **Female** duller eyebrow; more pastel overall. **Size** 19 cm. **Juv.** mottled. **Voice** and **Habitat** like Masked Woodswallow.

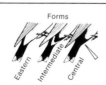

Foliage feeding

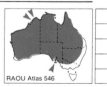

RAOU Atlas 545

742 Black-faced Woodswallow *Artamus cinereus*

Smoky-grey overall except black face, rump, vent and broad white tail tip. Underparts paler. Race *albiventris* (NE Qld): White undertail coverts; whitish underparts. **Size** 18 cm. **Juv.** mottled. **Voice** 'chep, chep'; chattering. **Habitat** open forests, gibber.

Forms

Eastern Intermediate Central

RAOU Atlas 546

743 Dusky Woodswallow *Artamus cyanopterus*

White leading edge to blue-grey wing; body smoky-brown. Black tail with broad white tip. **Size** 18 cm. **Juv.** mottled. **Voice** 'vut, vut'; chattering. **Habitat** open forests, woodlands.

Artamus Tail wag

RAOU Atlas 547

744 Little Woodswallow *Artamus minor*

Dark chocolate-brown body. Greyish-blue wings, tail. Broad white tail tip. **Size** 12 cm. **Juv.** speckled cream. **Voice** 'peat-peat'; chattering. **Habitat** open forests, grasslands, gorges.

Juv.

RAOU Atlas 548

Note The Australian Magpie-lark is now considered a monarch (see pp. 354-6).

736

738

741

739

742

736

740

744

737

♀ 738

743

741 ♀

739
Juv.

1

742

739

♀ 740

740
Juv.

744

40

743

743
Juv.

745 Black Butcherbird *Cracticus quoyi*

Whole body bluish-black. Sexes similar in appearance. **Male** larger. **Size** Arnhem Land and C. York Pen. birds larger, 42-44 cm; Endeavour to Herbert Rivers smaller, 33-38 cm. Two or three races named; not detailed here. **Juv./Imm.** two morphs: one entirely dull blue-black; other (NE Qld) dark brown, streaked rufous above, light cinnamon below (some birds reported to have bred in this plumage). **Voice** musical, yodelling call. **Habitat** tropical rainforest, mangroves, and adjacent fringes. Shy.

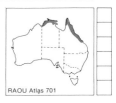

RAOU Atlas 701

746 Grey Butcherbird *Cracticus torquatus*

Black head; prominent white collar; grey back. Black wing has narrow white streak. Underparts white, washed grey. White rump. Tail black, tipped white. Female browner. **Size** 24-30 cm. **Imm.** brown above, crown streaked lighter. Collar, underparts, rump, tail tip are buff. Bill darker. Race *argenteus* 'Silver-backed Butcherbird' (northern NT): Smaller; lighter grey on back; white underparts; more white on tail, wing. Race *latens* (northern WA): Like *argenteus* but partly developed black bib on breast; small black chin patch. **Voice** rich melodious piping. **Habitat** open forest, woodland and mallee; agricultural land. Direct flight.

Calling in flight

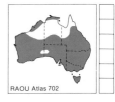

RAOU Atlas 702

747 Black-backed Butcherbird *Cracticus mentalis*

Strikingly black and white, with grey rump. White on shoulder extends down middle of black wing. Underparts white. Terminal white band on black tail. **Size** 25-28 cm. **Imm.** brown *not* black; back greyer. **Voice** melodic song but weaker than Grey. **Habitat** open forest, woodland, agricultural land. May become race of Grey Butcherbird.

Ventral flight

RAOU Atlas 704

748 Pied Butcherbird *Cracticus nigrogularis*

Strikingly black and white, with white rump. Wide white collar separates black head from back. Black bib. White bar on black wing. Tip of black tail has white corners. **Size** 32 cm. **Imm.** grey-brown *not* black; indistinct collar is lighter brown. **Juv.** bib buff (or absent in very young birds); underparts dirty white. **Voice** beautiful flute-like song. **Habitat** open woodland, scrubland, rangeland.

748

738 ♂

738
Australian Magpie-lark

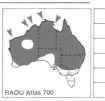

RAOU Atlas 700

749 Australian Magpie *Gymnorhina tibicen*

A variable species; glossy black and white. Race *tibicen* 'Black-backed Magpie': **Male** black head separated from black back by wide white collar. White shoulder, wing band, rump and undertail coverts. White tail has black terminal band. Underparts and wing black. **Female** collar and lower back light grey. **Imm.** like female but grey-brown *not* black. Race *hypoleuca* 'White-backed Magpie': **Male** back entirely white. **Female** back mottled grey. **Imm.** like female; black areas mottled brown-black. Race *dorsalis* 'Western Magpie': **Male** like *hypoleuca*. **Female** central back feathers black, white-edged, giving mottled appearance. **Imm.** back, underparts grey-brown; generally duller bird. **Size** 36-44 cm. **Voice** familiar flute-like carolling. **Habitat** open forest, woodland, agricultural and urban land. Strong direct flight.

Race
hypoleuca

Race
tibicen

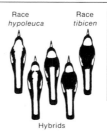

Hybrids

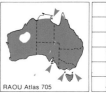

RAOU Atlas 705

746
Race *argenteus*

745
Juv. dark brown morph
NE Qld

745

747
Imm.

748
Juv.

747

748

746

746
Juv.

749

♂ **749**
Race *hypoleuca*

749 ♀
Race *dorsalis*

749

749 ♀
Race *hypoleuca*

749 ♂
Race *tibicen*

749 ♀ Race *tibicen*

749 Juv
Race *tibicen*

750 Pied Currawong *Strepera graculina*

Bill robust with well-defined hook. Black body; large and prominent white crescent-shaped patch on wing. Undertail coverts, base of tail and tip, white. Less white in birds at SW of their range; can be confused with Grey Currawong. **Size** 41-51 cm. **Imm.** markings as for adult, but generally greyer and brownish around throat. **Voice** noisy, distinctive and ringing, double-call 'curra-wong'. **Habitat** open and low open forest, woodland, scrub, agricultural and urban lands.

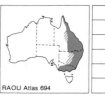

Dorsal flight

RAOU Atlas 694

751 Black Currawong *Strepera fuliginosa*

Tas. only. Bill more robust than Pied, with well-defined hook. Black body; white tip to tail and primaries. Tail significantly shorter than Pied and Grey. Small white patch on wing. **Size** 46-48 cm. **Imm.** duller. **Voice** usual call described as musical 'Kar-week week-kar'. **Habitat** open forest, woodland, scrub, heathland and agricultural lands. To be identified from Forest Raven.

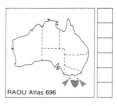

Dorsal flight

RAOU Atlas 696

752 Grey Currawong *Strepera versicolor*

Variable species; grey with white markings. Bill slender without well-defined hook. Race *versicolor:* Grey with darker crown and shading around eye. Large and prominent white window in wing. Flight and tail feathers tipped white; white undertail coverts. **Female** smaller. **Imm.** duller, brownish. Note that west of Melbourne (Vic.) plumage becomes progressively darker, and white of wing patch is reduced; can be confused with Pied. Race *arguta* 'Clinking Currawong' (Tas.): Darkest race, almost black. Race *intermedia* 'Brown Currawong' (Yorke and Eyre Peninsulas, SA): Darker and browner than *versicolor*. Race *melanoptera* 'Black-winged Currawong' (mallee regions): Darkest mainland form; very dark grey and lacking white wing patch. (Darker forms of nominate race *versicolor*, *plumbea* of WA, and *centralia* of central Aust., are *not* considered to be distinct races.) **Sizes** 45-53 cm. **Voice** ringing, clinking call. **Habitat** open and low open forest; woodland generally, mallee heath, scrub and agricultural lands. May resemble Laughing Kookaburra when flying through forest away from observer.

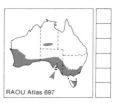

Race *versicolor*

Dorsal flight

RAOU Atlas 697

Race *arguta*

Dorsal flight

Dorsal flight

Race *melanoptera*

753

751

752 Race *versicolor*

750

750

736

752
Race *versicolor*

752
Race *arguta*

52
termedia

752
Race *melanoptera*

751

N. Day.

753 Australian Raven *Corvus coronoides*

Black. Plumage glistens in sunlight. Long, floppy throat hackles. White eye. In hand, feather bases grey; sides of chin unfeathered. **Size** 52 cm. **1st year** extensive bare pink skin on sides of chin. Brown eye. **Voice** high, child-like wailing; series of slow notes, with strangled, dying finish. **Habitat** most types except closed forests. When calling, throat hackles fanned to form long 'beard'.

Throat hackle

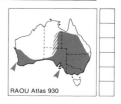

RAOU Atlas 930

754A Forest Raven *Corvus tasmanicus*

Black. White eye. Feather bases grey (in hand). Very prominent bill. Short tail. **Size** 52 cm. **1st year** brown eye. **Voice** very deep; harsh; 'rolls its Rs'. Notes uttered slowly, last one fades away. **Habitat** most in its range. The only Tas. corvid. Looks large, heavily built, ponderous in flight.

Throat hackle

RAOU Atlas 868

754B Relict Raven *Corvus boreus*

Black. Longer tail, larger wings than Forest Raven. Isolated population recently recognised as new species.

RAOU Atlas 868

755 Little Raven *Corvus mellori*

Black. White eye. In hand, feather bases grey. Slightly smaller than other ravens. **Size** 50 cm. **1st year** brown eye. **Voice** a series of rapid-fire, rather deep, guttural barks, notes abruptly cut off. **Habitat** most types, except closed forests. When perched, each note accompanied by flick of both wings above back. Flight quicker than other ravens.

Throat hackle

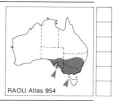

RAOU Atlas 954

756 Little Crow *Corvus bennetti*

Black. White eye. Slender bill. In hand, feather bases white. Small (Australian Magpie-sized) crow in comparison to other Aust. corvids. **Male** slightly larger. **Size** 48 cm. **1st year** brown eye. **Voice** flat, hoarse, very nasal, rather deep; a monotonous series of notes uttered rather rapidly but with each note prolonged. **Habitat** most types in arid and semi-arid zones, outback towns. Flight more rapid, agile than Torresian Crow.

Throat hackle

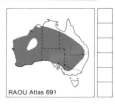

RAOU Atlas 691

757 Torresian Crow *Corvus orru*

Black. White eye. In hand, feather bases white. Slightly smaller than the two large ravens. **Size** 50 cm. **1st year** brown eye. **Voice** high-pitched series of staccato honkings, usually rapid but can finish with one or more longer notes; also a series of harsh, snarling notes, the last note dying away. In the arid zone, also a loud falsetto stutter. **Habitat** most types. After perching, often lifts and settles the wings several times. More heavily built, tail broader, squarer than Little Crow.

Throat hackle

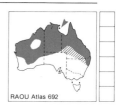

RAOU Atlas 692

758 House Crow *Corvus splendens**

Mostly black; broad pale to grey-brown nape, collar, mantle and breast. Brown eye. **Size** 43 cm. **Voice** repeated cawing sounds. **Habitat** urban areas. Ship-assisted potential colonist from southern Asia (Iran to India and W China). Records from Fremantle, WA and Melbourne, Vic.; a bird, paler on mantle than our plate, near Melbourne Zoo, 1991.

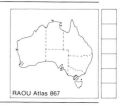

RAOU Atlas 867

*Introduced

755

755

753

754A

753
1st yr

756

753

757

756

757

757
1st yr

758

N. Lig.

Rare bird bulletin

The Rare Birds' Appraisal Committee is drawn widely from lay and professional ornithological circles. It referees new bird records to establish their authenticity, accepting or rejecting them in relation to the Australian species list.

We wish you to report your observations of true rarities or range extensions in Australia or its territories. You may have the great satisfaction of adding a 'new bird' to the national or state lists! Make the effort to marshal all your facts of the sighting, including date, precise locality, time of day, *very detailed* written field descriptions, drawings, photographs or specimen (if any), plus the names of collaborating observers. Submit your evidence to the Rare Birds' Appraisal Committee, 21 Gladstone St, Moonee Ponds, Victoria 3039, Australia; telephone (03) 370 1422; fax (03) 370 9194.

Only by *you* taking the initiative will new bird species formally be confirmed and added to the Australian list, and new geographic areas for local birds (distribution or range extensions) be accepted. The committee will not seek you out!

Species presented below are recently accepted records, plus a couple which have been reliably observed and reported very recently — we are confident they will be accepted.

The status of rare Australian birds is comprehensively covered in Garnett, Stephen (1992), *Threatened and Extinct Birds of Australia*, Royal Australasian Ornithologists Union, Moonee Ponds, Victoria.

Laysan Albatross *Diomedea immutabilis*

Bill pink, tipped black. Lores black extending through eye, grading to grey smudge on face. Head, neck, underparts, rump white. Upperparts, upper wings blackish. Tail dark grey. Underwings white, broadly edged black and coverts extensively marked black (variable). **Size** 80 cm; wingspan 190-200 cm. **Habitat** tropical, northern Pacific Ocean; pelagic. Breeds northern Hawaiian island chain. One bird recently at Norfolk Is.; also seen at sea off Wollongong, NSW.

Juan Fernandez Petrel *Pterodroma externa*

Dark above; pale below. Grey-brown crown; shows little white neck. Broad black 'M' across wings. Shorter diagonal black mark in underwing than White-necked Petrel *P. cervicalis* (see p. 32). Tail darker than *cervicalis*. **Size** 40-43 cm. Former nominate race of *Pterodroma externa*, breeds at the Juan Fernandez islands off W coast of Chile. Recently recognised at sea off the E. Aust. coast. Identify also from Cook's, Gould's Petrels; Buller's and Great Shearwaters.

Barau's Petrel *Pterodroma baraui*

Grey above with broad black 'M' on wings. Diagonal black line in white underwing. **Size** 38 cm. Identify from approx. similarly sized White-necked, Juan Fernandez Petrels, Buller's, Great and Streaked Shearwaters, and smaller Gould's and Black-winged Petrels. Records W Vic.; off WA.

Reading

Carter, M., Reid, T. & Lansley, P. (1989), 'Barau's Petrel *Pterodroma baraui*, a new species for Australia', *Australian Bird Watcher* **13**, 39-43.

Stahl, J. C. & Bartle, J. A. (1991), 'Distribution, abundance and aspects of the pelagic ecology of Barau's Petrel *Pterodroma baraui*, in the south-west Indian Ocean', *Notornis* **38**, 211-25.

Bulwer's Petrel *Bulweria bulwerii*

Very small petrel; similar size to prions but entire plumage dark sooty-brown. Sexes look alike. **Male** larger-bodied. Bill black; large nail at tip. Tail long, wedge-shaped. Feet variable in colour, grey to pink; may be bicoloured. **Size** 26-27 cm. **Habitat** tropical, subtropical seas of all oceans. Distinct genus; allied to *Pterodroma* petrels; identify from largest all-dark storm-petrels; may accompany Wedge-tailed Shearwaters; erratic, buoyant flight. Vagrant in southern Australia.

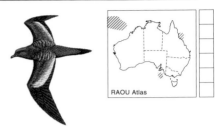

Reading
Carter, M. & Reid, T. (1989), 'A Bulwer's Petrel *Bulweria bulwerii* in Victoria', *Aust. Bird Watcher* **13** (4), 114-17.
Cheshire, N. G. (1989), 'A Bulwer's Petrel *Bulweria bulwerii* off north-eastern Australia', *Aust. Bird Watcher* **13** (2), 61-2.
Warham, J. (1990), *The Petrels, Their Ecology and Breeding Systems*, Academic Press Ltd, London & San Diego, pp. 131-40.

Pink-footed Shearwater *Puffinus creatopus*

Dark-tipped pink bill. Dark grey-brown above, scaled paler. Variable amount of grey-brown on head, throat, flanks, underwing and undertail coverts. Underparts mainly white. Legs, feet pink. **Size** 48 cm. Identify from Streaked Shearwater and light morph of Wedge-tailed Shearwater by heavier build and shorter tail. **Habitat** coastal, oceanic. An E Pacific Ocean species. One accepted Aust. sighting off Wollongong, NSW, March 1986.

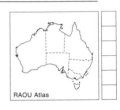

Great Shearwater *Puffinus gravis*

Slender dark bill. Distinctive dark cap and white collar. Upperparts dark grey-brown, scaled paler. Underwings white with dark streaks forming diagonal marks on inner wing; broad black trailing edge. Underparts white; sooty smudge on belly. **Size** 43-51 cm. **Habitat** oceans. Identify from White-necked Petrel. Mostly an Atlantic Ocean species. Single sightings at sea off Robe, South Aust., Jan.-Feb. 1989.

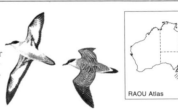

Northern Pintail *Anas acuta*

Male distinctive, slender-necked. Bill pale grey, marked black. Head dark brown. Neck black with white stripe to breast. Flanks, upperparts pale grey-brown. Scapulars striped black. Green speculum in wing. Underparts white. Undertail black. Legs grey. Eclipse similar to female. **Female** bill grey. Head, neck brown, finely streaked pale buff. Upperparts and underparts brown with edges and chevrons variously buff and white. Speculum brown. Legs grey. **Size** 66 cm. **Habitat** coastal wetlands, farmlands, reservoirs. Identify female from female Mallard, shovellers and teal. One adult male, breeding plumage, Chandala Swamp, NE of Perth, WA, July 1985.

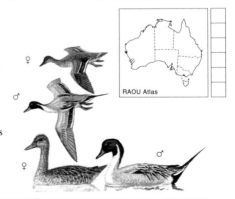

Reading
Agar, G., Jaensch, R. & Vervest, R. (1988), 'A Northern Pintail *Anas acuta* in Australia', *Aust. Bird Watcher* **12** (6), 204-5.

Gurney's Eagle *Aquila gurneyi*

Adult Identify from Wedge-tailed Eagle by uniform dark plumage (lacks golden neck, shoulder), rounded tail, flat glide. Smaller than Wedge-tailed. **Size** F 70-76 cm; M 66-72 cm. **Imm.** head, underparts buff; browner on crown, breast. Upperparts brown, mottled grey-buff. Some barring on underwings, upper and under tail. Darker head, longer tail and more 'trousered' legs than imm. White-bellied Sea-Eagle. **Habitat** lowland forest, coastal areas, offshore islands. Rare in PNG. Vagrant to Torres Strait (Boigu Is.), Feb. 1987.

Reading
Garnett, S. (1987), 'An Australian record of Gurney's Eagle *Aquila gurneyi*', *Aust. Bird Watcher* **12** (4), 134-5.

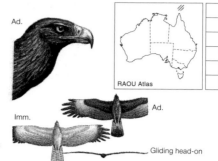

RAOU Atlas

Gliding head-on

Kentish Plover *Charadrius alexandrinus*

Male like smaller but closely related Red-capped Plover. Bill thicker, longer. White eyebrow extends further behind eye. White frons wider. Crown browner. Complete white collar. Blackish patches at side of breast larger; do *not* extend across upper edge of mantle. Longer legs paler. **Non-breeding/Female** dark markings on head, sides of breast browner and contrast *less* with upperparts. **Size** 15-17.5 cm. **Juv.** like female. More buffy. pale-tinged upperparts. **Habitat** beaches, tidal flats, salt lakes. Vagrant. Identify from Red-capped Plover; also non-breeding Ringed, Little-ringed, Mongolian, Double-banded and Large Sand Plovers. One adult male, Darwin, NT, late 1988.

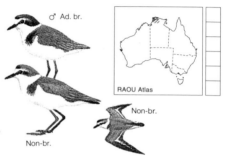

RAOU Atlas

Spotted Redshank *Tringa erythropus*

Non-breeding bill long, slender. Lower bill base, legs orange-red. Eyebrow white; line through eye black. Upperparts grey. Mantle, wing feathers edged, notched white; no white trailing edge to wing. Underparts white, greyish breast; barring on flank, undertail coverts. **Breeding** entirely black. Back, upper wings spotted white. Underwings white. **Size** 29-32 cm. **Juv.** underparts finely barred grey. **Voice** 'chew-it' whistle in flight. **Habitat** marshes, mudflats. Solitary or in groups. Swims. Several unconfirmed sightings; one in winter plumage Carrum Downs Mar.-Aug. 1992; photos; many observers.

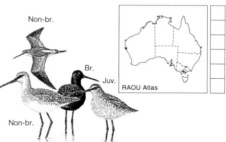

RAOU Atlas

Laughing Gull *Larus atricilla*

Identify in Aust. from Franklin's Gull by wing pattern. Smaller, darker than Silver Gull. Appears long-winged in flight. (A) **Breeding adult** (America) black hood. White eyelids. Upperparts slate grey. Wings tipped black; trailing edge white. (B) **Non-breeding** like Franklin's: less hood. Smaller wing mirrors. (C) **1st year/Imm. winter** like Franklin's: less hood. Dusky breast and flanks. Broader tail band. (D) **adult winter** in flight. **Size** 38 cm approx. (E) **1st year/Imm. winter** in flight (partly based on photos of Cairns birds). **Juv.** like Franklin's; darker-winged. Vagrant from E tropical Americas. Two birds at Cairns, N Qld, autumn 1988, adult and 1st year, both winter plumage.

Reading
Fisher, K. & Fisher, L. (1989), 'Laughing Gull *Larus atricilla*: a new record for Australia', *Aust. Bird Watcher* **13** (1), 34-5.

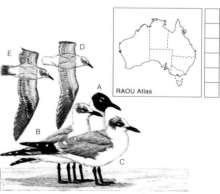

RAOU Atlas

Black-headed Gull *Larus ridibundus*

Identify from Laughing, Franklin's Gulls in Aust. by wing pattern. (A) **Breeding adult** (Europe) brown hood. Incomplete eye-ring. Bill dark red-brown. Back, upper wings pale grey. Nape, neck, underparts to tail white. Primaries broad white leading edge; thin black trailing edge. Legs red-brown. (B) **Adult non-breeding** like breeding. Bill tipped black; head white, dark ear spot. (C) **Second** (northern) **summer** bill orange, tipped black. Hood incomplete. Brown marks on wing. **Size** 38-40 cm. (D) **Imm.** like juv. Head whiter. Back pale grey. (E) **Juv.** bill pink, tipped black. Incomplete buff-brown hood. Back, wings scaled brown. Underparts white; sides of breast marked brown. Legs flesh. Vagrant. Broome Sewage Ponds, NW of WA, from 19 Oct. 1991; many observers.

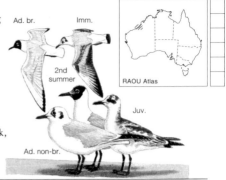

Antarctic Tern *Sterna vittata*

Identify from Arctic, Common, White-fronted Terns by 'bulkier' size; heavier, brighter bill. **Adult breeding** like Arctic. Bill red. White facial stripe separates black cap from grey throat. Upperparts grey. Dark leading edge of wing fainter than Common. Underwing like Arctic. Rest of underparts grey paling to white undertail. **Adult non-breeding** bill duller red. Lores, forehead, crown whiter than Common, Arctic. Perhaps some grey on underparts. **Size** 40-41 cm. **Juv.** like Common. Upperparts more strongly scaled brown; breast washed brown. Identify from Arctic, Common Terns (all plumages); and perhaps from White-fronted Tern (winter plumage). Vagrant. One recent specimen (SA); a few offshore sightings.
Reading
1985, *Reader's Digest Complete Book of New Zealand Birds*, Reader's Digest Services, Sydney, NSW.

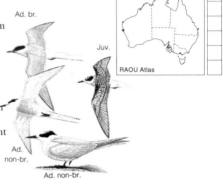

Black-backed Wagtail *Motacilla lugens*

Vagrant to E Aust. (Fraser Is., Qld, May-Sept. 1987; prob. adult female). Recently promoted to full species from *Motacilla alba lugens*. Migratory from its breeding area of Manchuria, Korea, Kurile Islands, Kamchatka, E China, Northern Japan, to winter in S Japan, Taiwan, S China. Distinguish from White Wagtail races, *baicalensis*, *leucopsis*, *ocularis*. **Male breeding** black throat, breast band, collar but white chin; black eyestripe; black crown, nape, back, scapulars, rump. Long black tail edged white. Dorsal wings in flight mostly white. **Male non-breeding** grey back, anterior scapulars; less black on breast but retains narrower black collar. **Female breeding** charcoal-grey crown, nape, breast band, collar. Grey back, scapulars, rump; **Female non-breeding** paler grey, crown, nape, back, rump, scapulars. Greyer, narrower breast band, collar. **Size** 17-18 cm. **Imm./Juv.** (see Howell below). Plumages of wagtails vary greatly with sex, age, season. Be very, very careful with identification.
Reading
Wild Bird Society of Japan (1982), *A Field Guide to the Birds of Japan*, Wild Bird Soc., Japan, Tokyo, pp. 224-5.
Howell, S. (1990), 'Identification of White and Black-backed Wagtails in alternate plumage', *Western Birds* **21**, 41-9. (American article.)

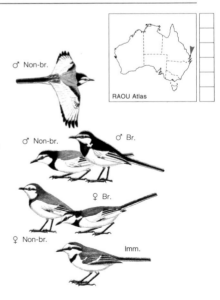

The Handbook

In the pages that follow, you will meet the concept of *order* in the natural world. We commence with a summary of some of the major sequences that comprise a bird's life cycle. When you see a bird, any bird, it is going about one aspect of its day, its year, its life. So, for that matter, are you.

Now, having identified your bird from one of the preceding colour plates, you can begin to learn more about its life and requirements.

The life cycle of a bird

Males and females meet for courtship with the intention of breeding. Pair bonds are established, either for life, for one year, or for brief matings which are followed by solitary nesting and/or brooding by one of the sexes. Elaborate courtship ceremonies occur between the sexes in many birds; in others it is an inconspicuous happening.

Availability of the correct nest site, safely located and typical of its species, is vital for successful breeding. Environmental damage affects this aspect of a bird's life cycle probably more severely than anything else. Nesting may be above or below ground. It may be colonial, where only the immediate nest area is defended, or solitary, often in a defended territory of variable size. Site choice usually dictates nest materials. Some birds build no nest, others have elaborate structures.

Nest and territory defence may be by direct physical attacks and vocalising, by distraction displays designed to lead an attacker away, or by skilful camouflage. The number of broods per season varies. One brood is considered normal for most Australian birds, but many species have demonstrated a capacity to breed from two to four times in a season in which optimum environmental conditions prevail.

Eggs of most bird species are plain white or pastel in colour, and may have darker speckles, spots or blotches. A smaller number have camouflaging patterns on them. Eggs of hollow-breeding species may have a high gloss, and those of a burrow-breeding species may have a chalky surface. Shapes vary between species, from well-rounded to pyriform.

Often eggs are given minimal care until the entire group (clutch) is laid. Then intensive incubation, with covering and heating, commences in earnest. The period of incubation depends, to some extent, on external temperatures, body bulk and egg-size ratios and, to a large extent, on the degree of advancement to be achieved at hatching. Incubation does not last long in species that have naked, blind and virtually helpless young. Birds that have advanced (precocious), largely or entirely independent young, may incubate much longer.

Hatchlings usually have a tiny 'egg tooth'. It is a hard protuberance on the upper-bill tip which helps them chip a hole in the eggshell. Hatching may take from a few minutes to several days, depending on egg size, thickness of shell, external air temperature and degree of parental assistance. Hatchlings must recognise (imprint on) their parents from the moment of hatching and vice versa, so that each knows the other from then on. Cuckoo nestlings may be an exception: do hosts and neighbouring birds imprint on them?

Natal covering of nestlings varies from quite naked to lightly or fully clad in fluffy down, depending on egg size, incubation period and future lifestyle.

For nestling or chick maintenance, suitable food must be brought fairly soon after hatching as the yolk reserves of the baby are soon exhausted. Warmth, shading and protection from predators and territorial neighbours is also required. Education of the baby proceeds by mimicry of adults, observation, and trial and error.

Adult breeding patterns are displayed in **breeding bars** beside the detailed family information on pp 292-370. Most of the information in these is derived from our interpretation of Gordon Beruldsen's (1980) *A Field Guide to Nests and Eggs of Australian Birds*, Rigby, Adelaide, South Australia. Other sources and personal information from many of our contributors were also used.

Every bird species undergoes a series of feather moults. These commence as the natal down is lost and continue throughout life. Usually, all the feathers change once a year, in either a pre-breeding or post-breeding moult. However, there are plenty of exceptions to this. Many have a partial moult, changing either body or wing feathers in turn, or moulting the wing feathers in series, so that flight capacity is not lost. Penguins have a total body moult over a short period for re-waterproofing purposes. Many migratory birds arrive in or leave Australia in a state of partial or complete moult. They moult into, or out of, a drab, less conspicuous winter or eclipse plumage. As you will appreciate, it is important that you work hard to identify the visiting seabird and wader species, gulls and foreign wagtails, because plumages may vary greatly.

Death of birds, as with other animals, may come in many guises: by mechanical means — killing (by shot, trapping, choking or entangling accidents), becoming prey, being tossed out by a cuckoo; or by various physiological (systemic) means — diseases, starvation, exposure, overwhelming parasite load, poison, pollutants, even old age!

In this book, we use the following terminology for the ages of birds.

Nestling (= Hatchling = Downy) In or about the nest. Naked or downy, i.e. *before* true feathers develop.

Fledgling (leaving the nest) Partly or wholly feathered. Flightless or partly flighted, but *before* full flight capacity.

Note These first two categories are dependent on parental care. Exceptions do exist. Both could be called 'chicks'.

Juvenile (= Juvenal) Fledged to free-flying birds, with the feathers which *first* replaced the natal down. May or may not be still under parental care. Plumage duration may be short-lived, a few weeks only in some species.

Immature (= Sub-adult) All plumages which *follow* first moult *until* full breeding capacity and/or plumage is reached.

Adult Birds which breed or are *known to have* breeding capabilities. Adult plumages are those which do not change in appearance in subsequent moults (allowing for alternating eclipse plumages in some species, e.g. waders, fairy-wrens).

Hints for bird-watchers

It is easy to imagine, looking out at the 18-63 bird species in your own garden, or the 47-129 species in the surrounding neighbourhood, that there cannot possibly be any more to discover about any of them. But this is not so. Pick one, any one, of the most common birds and then make a point of looking up as much as you can of its published literature. With very few exceptions you will find that large gaps exist in the printed knowledge of even the most common local species — no matter where you live. So, try it! Observe keenly, report correctly and without any exaggeration, and try to write 'something' for a local newspaper, school magazine, or for the lay or scientific journals.

Take thorough notes on any strange or new birds that you see — try to do a little sketch (see mine on p. 320) and add as many significant details as possible. Include proportions, relative size and comparisons with other bird species about you, the colours of plumage and soft parts (eyes, legs and facial skin). Record behaviour, postures, flight mannerisms and calls. Take notes on *anything* that will help you to identify the bird accurately. The first set of fieldnotes of the recent sighting of a Black-headed Gull at Broome, for example, was not only several pages long but was accompanied by about 15-20 clear sketches and several photographs!

Obtain a two-post binder, a punch, and commence a scrapbook or research file on the bird species you are seeing regularly, that you have decided to study in more detail, or that you see for the first time. Keep your day-to-day bird lists safely too. They may be required as a contribution to habitat or regional surveys, for conservation statements or environmental impact studies. Use the Field Data Sheet supplied on p. 279 — you may photocopy **this single page** — or draw up a suitable sheet of your own. Notes kept in a systematic way are easier to interpret later. Use the official RAOU numbers allocated to each bird species (accompanying the maps in our Field Information section) if you wish a short-hand or computer-based way of handling your data collection.

Do you live near an environmentally sensitive area, a forest likely to be logged, inadvertently burned, or in some way damaged? Start to record the birds (and other animals and plants) in this area and be meticulous with dates and times. Take excellent habitat photographs. If inappropriate development is threatened, you will then have data of great value. Anticipate such a need.

We urge you to see as many bird species as you can in Australia and you may choose to carry your hobby to other countries in due course. Start today! Tick off the species in the tick-boxes provided beside the maps on the pages facing the colour plates. No cheating — treat it like a game of golf; keep a clean scorecard.

Considering that the bird's home environment is of vital importance to its day-to-day and year-to-year survival, we have devoted the succeeding eight pages to describing Australia's habitats. The summaries are brief, far too brief we know, but you can go on building your knowledge of these habitat categories, and what goes on inside each and between each. The bird *in* its habitat, the habitat and its birds, will provide you with a lifetime's study.

The Handbook contains 79 pages of bird Family summaries, some with further reading, some without. The broad plan for each entry is to mention taxonomic and evolutionary

Hint, Hint, Hint, Hint . . .

• Keep the sun behind you when observing.

• Build a bird feeding table and/or a bird bath in a safe place.

• Examine dead birds on roads and beaches — send rare ones to the nearest natural history museum.

• Read the scientific names with close attention. Can you interpret their meanings?

• Learn to read the daily weather map. Try to relate each day's weather to the dispersal of birds.

• Always record locality, date, time of day (state if daylight-saving time) on *all* of your records and notes.

• Look for indirect evidence of birds — scratches, moulted feathers, droppings, pellets, damaged fruits or flowers. Play detective — what did this?

• Keep a notebook in a waterproof cover. Use biro or pencil, *not* felt-tipped pens.

• Use binoculars and/or a small telescope for easier and more satisfying bird-watching.

• Report all banded (ringed) birds to the authority named on band. Never remove a band from a living bird.

• Take a camera into the bush and try to photograph a bird or two — then think about buying a telephoto lens!

• Try to map the territory of several different bird species that live near you.

• Try to tape-record some bird songs in the wild.

• Do you have a space in your garden? Plant a shrub known to provide nectar for birds.

• Take a bag of bread to the beach and feed it to the gulls — then try to interpret all their posturings and calls.

• Report people who are behaving suspiciously to land owners, park rangers or to police — safeguard the bush and its inhabitants.

• Take a torch or spotlight into the bush. Which birds are up and about? Where do the rest roost?

• How do the birds react when rain suddenly falls after a dry spell?

• Make up a chart in the kitchen, recording all the birds that pass before the window, and why.

information first. This is followed by general biology and behavioural information and concludes with breeding information and miscellaneous items. All of the birds which *breed* in Australia have a diagrammatic representation of their breeding seasons, although there are many exceptions and anomalies in this presentation. Several breeding bars are really necessary for some species, because of asynchronous breeding in different parts of the continent, variable numbers of breeding attempts in a season, etc.

Here is the Field Data Sheet for you to photocopy or redraw for yourself.

Field Data Sheet

Species	Date	Time
Number seen	Place (suburb, town, etc.)	
Flight direction (detailed)	Exact locality of record (description of near-by streets, landmarks, distance to nearest town. Draw map if possible).	
Manner of flight (high, low, direct, circling)		
Wind (direction and strength)	Notes on behaviour (feeding, drinking, foods, courtship, calls, enemies, association with other species, alighting, breeding sites, habitat usage, etc.)	
Weather (at time of sighting)		
Weather (on preceding days)		
	Observer's name and address	

Any freshly dead birds should be sent to your state museum or wildlife department. Plastic wrap and freeze birds, then deliver by hand or courier in an airtight container.

Where the birds live: vegetation and landform habitats of Australia

Geology and soils, together with latitude, altitude, surface topography and availability of water, determine the kinds of plants that are found in particular areas. The following pages first give a summary of those habitats in which the vegetation is the dominant visible feature, then those in which the landform is dominant.

The purpose of these descriptions is to amplify the very brief descriptions of habitat given in the Field Information section. Space limitations have meant that the precise terms introduced here have not always been used in the prior section.

The sequence of presentation is broadly based on a structural classification proposed by Professor R. L. Specht during the 1970s and modified since by Walker & Hopkins (1984). The classification looks at identifiable plant habitats and community groups as a whole and analyses, not so much what species are present but how each association exists in terms of spacing, density and heights of its component species. In addition, the number of horizontal layers that the plant species impart to the structure is taken into account (there may be several layers, or just one).

Habitats often merge with each other. Some of the richest bird localities are those where several habitat types meet. You are likely to see the endemic birds of each 'pure' habitat, plus the species which thrive in several habitats or in the fringe zones.

Line drawings, photographs and maps of each vegetation type can be found in Volume 6, *Vegetation*, of *Atlas of Australian Resources*. We are pleased to acknowledge the permission of the General Manager, Australian Surveying and Land Information Group (AUSLIG), Department of Administrative Services, Canberra, ACT, to reproduce these vegetational structural diagrams from this atlas. Likewise, we acknowledge the assistance of Dr Robert Parsons and Dr Keith McDougall, Botany Department, La Trobe University, in the re-writing of these habitat notes.

We urge *all* field observers, ornithological or otherwise, to use the terminology of this atlas, and to identify correctly the vegetational categories they are working in, to improve the quality of their reports.

Vegetation heights in the diagrams are given in metres. The percentage figure above each diagram refers to the amount of foliage coverage afforded by each structural type. Nomenclature is based on Specht (1970).

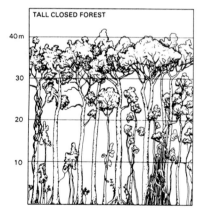

Closed forest

Closed forest (rainforest or monsoon forest) is forest closed in by dense, umbrella-like tree canopies so that little sunlight reaches the ground. Usually luxuriant, often majestic, it occurs in high rainfall areas and is named tropical or temperate depending on the mean annual temperature. Vines are prominent in the tropical types; ferns and mosses become more prominent in the temperate ones. Dense fringes may make physical entry difficult. Once under the canopy, reasonable mobility is possible. Birds can be clearly heard, but to see and identify them in the canopy is often a *real* challenge.

Open forest

Open forest (**wet or dry sclerophyll; eucalypt forest**) consists of trees spaced with *no* continuous canopy. In high

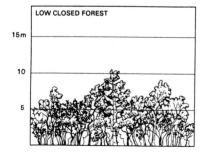

rainfall areas, tall open forest is also called **wet sclerophyll** and often contains tall shrubs and tree ferns.

Most open forest is in drier areas with understories of low shrubs, grasses or both. Eucalypts usually dominate these forests, but some are predominately acacia (e.g. brigalow) or various casuarinas. These may be known as **dry sclerophyll** forests.

Woodland

Once the tree density drops (usually with declining rainfall) so the average distance between tree crowns is more than one-quarter of the average crown diameter, the vegetation is called **woodland**, *not* forest. Eucalypts are usually dominant but *Acacia*, *Banksia*, *Callitris* and *Melaleuca* dominate some types. The ground cover can be grassy or shrubby depending on various factors including soil fertility. Spinifex is the main understorey in parts of northern Australia. In **open woodland**, the distance between tree crowns can be 1-20 metres.

Eucalyptus scrub and tall shrublands

Woody plants 2-8 metres tall, with many stems arising at or near the base, are regarded as shrubs, not trees, and dominate vegetation types called **scrub** or, as shrub density declines, **tall shrublands**. Such types dominated by eucalypts are the well-known 'mallee scrub' of much of semi-arid southern Australia. The soils can range from very infertile deep white sands to fertile calcareous loams and clays. Depending on soils and climate, the understorey can be dominated by:

a tussock grasses like spear grass and wallaby grass
b spiny hummock grasses like spinifex *Triodia*
c low, hard-leaved (sclerophyllous) shrubs like *Leptospermum* and *Hakea* — types with this understorey have been called 'mallee-heath' in South Australia and Victoria
d dense, erect shrubs of the 'broombush' type, e.g. *Melaleuca uncinata*
e semi-succulent low shrubs, especially of the Family Chenopodiaceae (saltbush family).

Mallee vegetation can sometimes be found on rocky, infertile or otherwise unfavourable sites in some wet, mountainous areas.

Acacia scrub and tall scrublands

The most common types are dominated by mulga *Acacia aneura* and a few other wattles. These dominate about 20 per cent of inland Australia, usually in areas drier than the main mallee scrub. Low shrubs such as *Senna* (previously called *Cassia*) and *Eromophila* (emu-bushes) often occur, as do some chenopods. A layer of perennial tussock grasses is often present, along with ephemeral herbs. On some central and north-western Australian sandplains, hummock grasses ('spinifex') dominate the understorey.

Vast areas of these inland scrubland formations are available for sheep and cattle grazing. Stock there rely heavily on top feed, particularly during droughts, resulting in destruction of many mature mulga stands. In addition, rabbits have often prevented seedling growth. Many regions of scrubs and shrublands have been severely degraded and are subject to soil erosion. Huge areas were cleared for wheat production, resulting frequently in over-cropping, over-supply of superphosphate fertiliser and inevitable degradation, leading to erosion and, in some places, rising salinity levels.

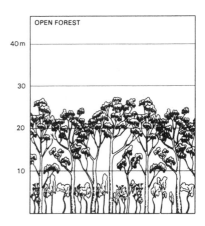

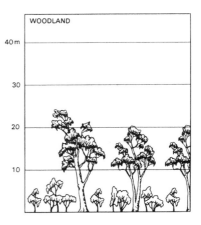

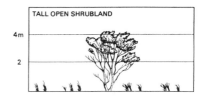

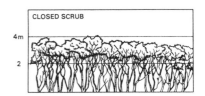

Excess fertilisers can inhibit endemic vegetation growth, favouring introduced pasture grasses.

The scrub known as 'mallee-heath' of southern Australia likewise has suffered from grazing and clearance for often ephemeral wheat farming. In the late 1940s it was discovered that the addition of soil trace elements such as molybdenum and copper allowed pasture growth for sheep in the 'mallee-heaths'. Some of the habitat has been preserved in national parks but a great amount has been lost.

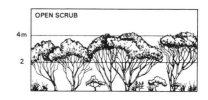

Heath

If the vegetation has its tallest layer dominated by evergreen, hard-leaved (sclerophyllous) shrubs less than two metres high, it is called heath. For many of these shrubs, the leaves are both hard and small (less than 2.5 cm long). Such leaves are called 'ericoid'.

Heaths occur in two distinct habitat types, on coastal lowlands and in some alpine and sub-alpine areas. Heaths, particularly lowland heaths, have very diverse floras, with representatives of many plant families, including Casurinaceae, Proteaceae, Mimosaceae, Myrtaceae, Xanthorrhoeaceae and Epacridaceae. A ground layer of grass-like plants such as sedges and Restionaceae is often present. Heath communities are mostly confined to areas of southern and eastern Australia where mean rainfall exceeds about 300 mm and where soils are very infertile.

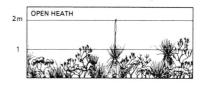

Low nutrient levels in heath soils have meant that comparatively little has been cleared for farming, although the addition of fertilisers does render some areas suitable. Main threats to this formation come from coastal and alpine recreational and housing developments, and also from the increasing amount of sand mining being carried out in coastal heaths on stabilised dune systems. Fire frequency appears to have increased in heaths since white settlement and is degrading some areas.

Fairy-wrens, emu-wrens, scrubwrens and honeyeaters are often well represented in heathlands. The Ground Parrot may be found in a patchy distribution through some coastal heaths.

Low shrubland

Low shrubland (formerly called **shrub steppe**), is dominated by well separated shrubs up to two metres tall of the Family Chenopodiaceae. The plants are semi-succulent, often with hairy leaves, and are well adapted to soils with a high clay content and to periodic drought conditions. The most common dominants are species of *Maireana* (bluebushes) and *Atriplex* (saltbushes). After rains, grasses and ephemeral plants in the families Compositae, Cruciferae and Leguminosae occur, along with lichens and fungi.

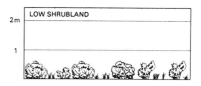

Salt marshes around coastal tide inlets and the salt pans of inland and central Australia are also structurally part of this formation but are discussed separately. Gibber plains are often covered with a very open low shrubland (see below).

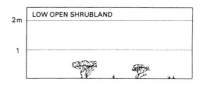

Low shrublands are important sheep grazing areas. The sheep eat the chenopodiacious shrubs in times of drought. Over-stocking has led to the destruction of the flora of many such areas and its replacement by annual grasses. Often there is little shrub regeneration and much top soil erodes.

Parrots, cockatoos, small doves, fairy-wrens, chats, wood swallows and some honeyeaters are seen in low shrubland. Flooding may attract wader species and a variety of waterfowl.

Gibber plains

Gibber plains ('stony deserts') consist of a sheet of continuous small- to medium-sized stones and rocks which effectively determine how the sparse plants are spaced and perhaps to what height they will grow. These deserts have formed over millions of years as widespread regional erosion of an earlier land surface dumped (deflated) the most resistant siliceous rocks (largely quartzites, although other rock types may also be involved). A visit to one of the remaining flat-topped hills will show you how it came about.

A very open low shrubland also occurs on gibber plains; the *Atlas of Australian Resources* maps these areas as **sparse open herbfield**. The most common plants are non-woody species of the chenopods *Atriplex* and *Sclerolaena*; in drier years virtually all vegetation disappears. Cattle graze on gibber plains and erosion problems develop about artificial water sources such as stock tanks, bore drains and dams. Emus, chats, birds of prey, Banded and Australian Plovers and Australian Pratincoles may be seen on gibber plains.

Closed grassland

Closed grassland is dominated by grasses of short or medium height where masses of individual plants are in close contact at their bases and have interlacing leaf canopies. Smaller herbs are also present. These communities are typical of the flood plains of many rivers draining Australia's north coast, where the heavy black soils flood during the monsoon, then dry and crack deeply toward the end of the dry season. In some areas, sedges are dominant or co-dominant with the grasses.

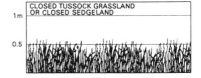

The grazing of cattle, the frequent firings which encourage green grass in the dry season, and destruction by introduced pigs and water buffalo severely damage areas of these grasslands.

Closed grasslands are also found in alpine and sub-alpine areas of south-eastern Australia where tussocks of *Poa* and *Danthonia* merge to form closed tussock grasslands. Some types are rich in perennial daisies and other herbs. The closed grasslands grade into moss-beds or bogs in the wetter hollows. They are covered by snow for several weeks or months each year. Such habitats were previously known as **closed herbfield**. Botanists now classify *all* of the low alpine/sub-alpine vegetation which was called 'herbfield' as grassland.

Fire (which in some areas occurs far too frequently) and also cattle grazing and trampling in the alpine areas of Tasmania, Victoria and New South Wales have caused extensive damage. To a lesser extent, so has the provision of firebreaks, ski runs, tele-communication towers, vehicle access tracks and car parks, lodges and other buildings, and the general trampling of some popular places by humans in the summer season. Exotic weeds are appearing along tracks and in stream courses.

Most of the small number of bird species inhabiting these alpine habitats in summer tend to move out (down) in the winter — altitudinal migration or nomadism.

Tussock grassland

Tussock grassland mostly occurs in northern Australia along the southern edges of the high summer rainfall zone (monsoonal influence) on calcareous, cracking clay soils. Mitchell Grass (*Astrebla*) dominates these rolling treeless plains, the tussocks occurring about one metre apart.

Except in drought years, a dense cover of short grasses and herbs occupies the spaces. The tussocks die back during the dry season or drought, and regenerate from the root stock following rain. In western Victoria, the geologically Recent basalt plain carried a closed tussock grassland dominated by *Themeda* and *Danthonia* species, but most has been destroyed by grazing, improved pastures and land clearance.

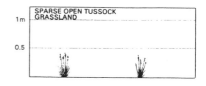

Hummock grassland

Hummock grassland mostly occurs on skeletal or deep sandy soils, in arid or semi-arid areas where mean annual rainfall is 130-350 mm. It is dominated by large, perennial, evergreen, usually pungent-pointed plants of the grasses *Triodia* and *Plectrachne* which form mounds ('hummocks') up to a metre in diameter. These are often dead in the middle, forming a doughnut-shaped ring. Flowering stems may be up to 1.5 metres high. The spaces between the hummocks are often bare; ephemeral plants may appear after rain. Over many years, these mounds enlarge and begin to overlap each other, forming a complex land terrain in some areas. A good example is in the Simpson Desert, where the lower sides of the many parallel dunes have hummock grassland associations.

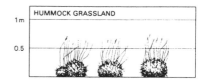

It is noticeable in hummock grassland, and in the habitat descriptions following, that the geology of the land surface becomes more obvious. It is more visual, and is seen to be partly or largely controlling the vegetation structure and spacing.

Salt marshes and mangroves

Salt marshes and mangroves are very often found together along the coastline, occurring on tidally inundated areas of sheltered coasts. Mangroves dominate the seaward fringe of many estuaries and bays. By definition, mangroves are trees and tall shrubs found in sites flooded by tides, and are best developed in tropical areas where a number of different, often well-defined zones occur. Their structure ranges from forest to shrubland, with height and species-richness declining progressively southward. Only one mangrove species, *Avicenna marina*, is found in southern Australia. No single bird species is a specific frequenter of this mangrove, but in the tropics a number of bird species may spend virtually all their lives in the mangrove communities — more work on this aspect of ornithology is needed.

Immediately inland of the mangrove zones, it is quite common to find various zones of salt marsh. These are usually shrublands dominated by nearly leafless chenopods called samphires. Further inland, high soil salinity produces a zone bare of almost all vegetation in many areas. Salt marshes are differently used by varying bird species and many migratory waders enter them at high tide to roost after feeding on tidal mud or sand flats. The Orange-bellied Parrot is in part a frequenter of salt marsh in SE Australia during the winter months.

Salt marshes also occur about inland salt lakes, in basins or hollows in the land from which there is only seepage or evaporative escape for the water, and on land where poor farming practices, over-grazing and tree clearance have radically altered the soil/water relationship.

Coastal dunes

Coastal dunes are readily recognisable. Exposed shorelines are usually backed by a series of sand dunes formed during the recent geological past. A marked plant succession occurs from the seaward fringe of the frontal dune, inland, resulting in a gradual stabilisation of the sand. The zones frequently parallel the coastline for several kilometres inland. The succession is from grasses to low shrubland to woodland. Freshwater lakes or swamps may lie between the dunes.

Coastal dune systems all around Australia are under considerable pressure. Development of coastal resorts has involved destruction of dune vegetation, and building houses and roads, often just above the high-tide mark. As a result, severe beach erosion has occurred. Groynes and sea walls have been built in an attempt to control sand loss or movement in popular areas. More recent threats to other major coastal dune systems are sand mining operations for heavy minerals (for instance rutile, ilmenite, monazite and zircon) and increasing problems posed by dune buggies, trail bikes and rabbits.

Inland waters

Inland waters across the continent are variable, intermittent, or virtually non-existent, because of low and unreliable rainfall, high evaporation and fairly level topography. Perennial streams are confined to the northern and eastern coasts and along small stretches of the southern coast. The largest river system is the Murray/Darling and its tributaries, but even there, flow is very variable as no *permanent* snow fields exist to maintain river levels in summer months.

Major streams in Australia often change within one year from a peak flow that inundates vast areas of flood plain, to a chain of pools and billabongs with little or no flow between them. Rivers in more arid regions generally do not flow every year and drainage is towards the generally extensive playa basin areas rather than towards the coast. The rivers are 'grouped' into catchments or basins of drainage, such as Lake Eyre Basin.

The most extensive areas of **swamp** (wetland) in Australia are associated with the northern coastal rivers and the Murray/Darling Basin. Other smaller swamps are widely scattered through higher rainfall areas where they may occur in natural or man-made depressions. Apart from sub-alpine bogs, most swamps dry out during the summer.

The only extensive **freshwater lakes** in Australia are those of the Tasmanian central plateau. Here, lakes, lakelets and ponds ranging in depth from less than a metre to more than 200 metres resulted from the last glaciation period. Similar lakes occupy glacial basins in the Australian Alps. The remaining freshwater lakes in Australia are confined to the higher rainfall areas; the majority of these either dry out annually or have been dry a number of times since European settlement. Minor exceptions are flooded volcanic craters, such as Lakes Eacham and Barrine in northern Queensland.

Saline lakes vary in character in terms of dissolved salts and the presence or absence of water itself. They include *some* of the volcanic crater lakes of western Victoria, the mound springs south-west of Lake Eyre which are the natural outlets of the subterranean Great Artesian Basin, and the numerous salt pans of arid Australia. In *most* years these lakes, including the vast bed of Lake Eyre, consist of extensive areas of white salt crust supporting no vegetation at all, and with surface temperatures reaching 50°C in the summer.

Pollution from mining waste, industrial and household effluents, uncontrolled boating, conversion of lakes into reservoirs for the generation of hydro-electricity or for water storage — often with release of cold, de-oxygenated bottom water — plus land clearance and creeping salinity levels, pose the main threats to the comparatively small number of our natural freshwater lakes, streams and wetland areas.

Obviously, all of Australia's birds are dependent in one way or another on the limited freshwater complexes of the continent. The nomadic lifestyle of many species reflects their capacity and need to follow the rains, and they breed only if local conditions are right.

Marine habitats

Marine habitats divide into three types, each having their own birds, while sharing some birds with adjacent habitats.

Estuaries occur where freshwater streams meet the tide's influence. These estuarine, or 'mixing of the waters', zones could be said to extend seaward as far as the diluting influence of the freshwater reaches. This will vary with the season, the amount of rainfall or melting snow contributed, the range and reach of normal and king tides, and the width and depth of the embayment into which the freshwater flows. Estuaries are also areas of active sedimentation from the land. Mangroves often fringe the seaward side and salt marshes may develop behind them as new land is formed and edges outward.

Our definition of **coastal seas** includes all of the comparatively shallow seas lying directly on the submerged portions of the continental shelf of the Australian continental plate. By definition, Bass Strait, Torres Strait, Gulf of Carpentaria, Timor and Arafura Seas and the Great Barrier Reef are all *coastal* areas.

The **oceans** include all sea areas beyond the continental plate margin, where the *really* deep water lies. The boundary between these pelagic (oceanic) areas and the edge of the continental shelf is proving a very rich area to visit for seabird watching. Take a bird- or whale-watching trip on a small boat if you possibly can. The rewards can be high. But consult a pharmacist if you are prone to sea sickness — it can be largely overcome!

Cliffs and exposed rock faces

There are thousands of cliffs and exposed rock faces around Australia. Many contain caves or deep joints, faults and crevices; some have vegetation on them, some are bare. Only a fairly small number of bird species *consistently* breed on, or under rock ledges in Australia. These include the Little Penguin, Fairy Prion, Common Diving-petrel, gannets and boobies, Great Cormorant, Black-faced Shag, Red-tailed Tropicbird, Osprey, Wedge-tailed Eagle, White-bellied Sea-Eagle, Peregrine Falcon, Australian Kestrel, Silver, Pacific and Kelp Gulls, Rock-Pigeons, Rock Parrot, Barn and Masked Owls, swallows and martins, Grey and Sandstone Shrike-thrushes, Origma, pardalotes, sparrows, Common Starling and Common Mynah. In south-western Victoria, Long-billed Corellas breed in holes in the tuff, the volcanic crater walls of Tower Hill.

Many other species breed opportunistically in such sites. Quarry faces, open-cut mines, road and railway cuttings, embankments and cave entrances are all used. Large office buildings, silos and factories may be regarded as 'human cliffs'. Birds often use such sites.

We *exclude* from examples of bird species using this habitat, those which nest on telegraph poles, aerials, tele-communication towers and land-line (cable) towers — they are using them as substitute trees.

Islands
Islands may merely be mud banks exposed at low tide in an estuary or bay, or offshore mountain tops or ranges, as are many of the islands of our continental shelf. Sometimes these are enlarged by the growth of coral upward from the floor of the shallow seas, or along the edge of the shelf itself, for example the Great Barrier Reef. Islands may have no vegetation, an individual plant character, or extensions of the flora of the adjacent mainland. Islands usually have fewer land bird species than does the nearby land mass.

Caves
Caves form in many ways: by solution in limestone areas, by rifting and jointing in almost every rock type, by the flowing on of molten lava to form lava tunnels by plucking or grinding of sea or river in cliffs of coastlines or gorges and by the abrasion of windblown sand. Mines, railway- and pipe-line tunnels may be regarded as 'human caves'.

Only one bird species in Australia, the White-rumped Swiftlet, is fully adapted to total blackness and a cave-dwelling way of life. It uses echo-navigating clicks to find its way in the dark (see p.336). Swallows and martins, the Grey Shrike-thrush and the Masked Owl use the twilight zone of caves and mines at times. If exploring, take a torch, leave a note or marker at the entrance of any cave you enter, watch out for snakes, do not smoke, wear a helmet and be very slow, quiet and responsible — caves and their fauna are *extremely* vulnerable to human interference.

Agricultural and pastoral lands
Agricultural and pastoral lands now dominate a huge proportion of the continent. Even those wilderness regions which remain directly uncontaminated by Europeans and their crops, stock, feral plants and animals, receive indirect pollution from airborne or waterborne chemicals. Direct human interference with the land is the rule, not the exception. We urge everyone interested in any way in natural history, at any level, to increase their efforts in the documenting of entire communities and associations and their ecological webs, and in saving and rehabilitating the natural vegetation.

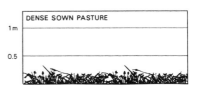

Urbanised land
Urbanised land represents the end of the road for most Australian native birds! But some are able to adapt and hang on in gardens and reserves. They, with introduced bird species, constitute completely new, although usually species-impoverished, communities to be studied.

Relief for birds and other fauna must come in the form of massive green belts, with a linking web of 'green corridors' between these. Selected species plantings, wetland provision and preservation and coastal reserves are needed. So too is a ruthless onslaught against feral animals and weed species, and a far-reaching educational programme for humans.

Reading
Specht, R. L., (1970), 'Vegetation', Leeper, G. W. (editor), *The Australian Environment*, 4th edition, CSIRO, in association with Melbourne University Press, Melbourne.
Walker, J. & Hopkins, M. S. (1984), 'Vegetation', in: McDonald, R. C. et al., *Australian Soil and Land Survey: Field Handbook*, Inkata Press, Melbourne.

Prehistoric birds

Birds evolved from small, running, bipedal reptiles (dinosaurs), which were probably warm-blooded. Their evolution took place in the Late Jurassic period. At that time, the world's land masses were interconnected and vertebrates, including primitive birds and mammals, could probably move across the great northern continent, Laurasia, and the southern continent, Gondwana. It was even possible to move between the two masses on dry land.

After this period, major but very slow rifting and separation began. Seaways widened, breaking the two supercontinents into the fragments that are today's familiar land masses.

The earliest and most primitive bird known is the famous *Archaeopteryx lithographica*. It lay buried for some 140 million years in lime-rich lagoonal rocks that were quarried extensively as lithographic limestone in Bavaria, southern Germany.

In modern Australia, the earliest known evidence of any bird is a series of small feathers from Lower Cretaceous lake sediments, exposed in a road-cutting at Koonwarra, Victoria. The feathers are about 110 million years old.

Birds evidently reached ancestral Australia soon after the origin of their Class. The Orders of birds we know today steadily evolved from Early Cretaceous times onward. Continental separation and drift gave rise to parental stocks, which, continuously dividing themselves, gave rise to ever more Superfamilies, Families, genera, species and subspecies. These characterise today's modern avifaunal regions (see map on p. 290).

Fossils that have been found on each continent indicate *something* of the path of evolution and genetic inheritance of today's bird fauna. Thus it was discovered that giant runners, the dromornithids or mihirungs, existed in Australia but became extinct about 26 000 years ago.

Fossils of palaelodids, a group of long-legged water-birds previously

Early Jurassic
(180 million years)

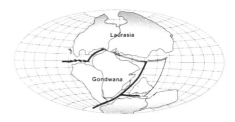

Late Jurassic/Lower Cretaceous
(135 million years)

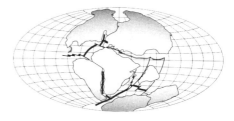

Late Cretaceous
(65 million years)

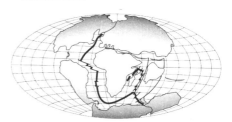

known only from Europe and North America, occur at three sites in South Australia, and probably represent three species. Flamingos of the Family Phoenicopteridae have a long history in Australia, and are known from many South Australian sites and one in Northern Territory. Palaelodids and flamingos are absent from the contemporary avifauna in Australia. Their evolution and demise is linked to the change in climate from a cool temperate one to a warm one with less moisture. This change in climate happened as Australia broke away from its southern 'dock' some 40-50 million years ago and drifted north towards Asia. Eocene forests of Southern Beech which once were known in central Australia gave way to grasslands. Permanent lakes dried or became intermittent. The climate edged into today's environment.

If you would like to assist in fossil research, enlist as a volunteer at the museum in your capital city or ask at the zoology department at a university.

Last Glacial Maximum
(18 thousand years)

Today

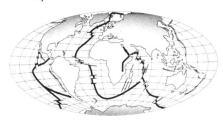

――――	Trench
▬▬▬	Rift
――――	Zones of slippage

Reading

Archer, M., Hand, S. J. & Godthelp, H. (1991) *Riversleigh: The story of animals in ancient rainforests of inland Australia*, Reed Books Pty Ltd, Balgowlah, NSW (especially see pp. 79-84).

Rich, P. V., (1979), 'The Dromornithidae, an extinct family of large ground birds endemic to Australia', *Bull. Bureau Mineral Resources Aust.*, **184**, 1-196.

Rich, P. V., Monaghan, J. M., Baird, R. F. & Rich, T. H. (editors), (1991), *Vertebrate Palaeontology of Australasia*, Pioneer Design Studio, Lilydale, Victoria, in association with Monash University Publications Committee, Melbourne (fossil birds see pp. 721-892).

Rich, P. V. & van Tets, G. F. (editors), (1985), *Kadimakara: Extinct vertebrates of Australia*, Pioneer Design Studios, Lilydale, Victoria.

Steadman, D. W. S. (1985), 'Fossil Birds', in: Campbell, B. & Lack, E. (editors), *A Dictionary of Birds*, T. & A. D. Poyser Ltd, Calton, England, for the British Ornithologists' Union (see pp. 239-42).

Wellnhofer, P., (1990), 'Archaeopteryx', *Scientific American* **262** (5), 42-9.

Modern avifaunal regions

Three major avifaunal regions are recognised in Australia. Each contains a number of sub-divisions. The **Torresian** is in the humid tropical and subtropical area. The **Eyrean** exists right across the semi-arid interior. The **Bassian** occupies the temperate south-eastern and south-western climatic zones, with an isolate in Queensland. There is a certain amount of overlap between the three regions, for example, in the southwest of Western Australia the Bassian overlaps with the Eyrean.

All are areas where much of the endemic fauna form identifiable associations. Each group of birds is broadly discrete from that in the next avifaunal region. However, there is mixing where the overlap zones exist, just as there is in the avifaunal regions of the world, and there are some species which occur across all three regions. Introduced and vagrant birds may occur virtually anywhere.

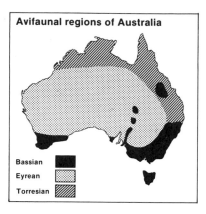

Avifaunal regions of Australia

Bassian
Eyrean
Torresian

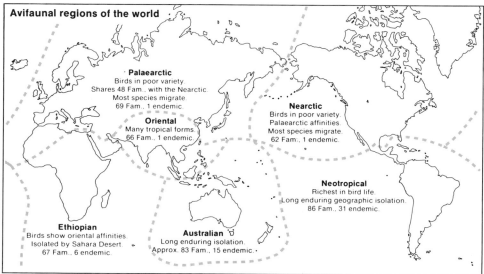

Avifaunal regions of the world

Palaearctic
Birds in poor variety.
Shares 48 Fam., with the Nearctic.
Most species migrate.
69 Fam., 1 endemic.

Oriental
Many tropical forms.
66 Fam., 1 endemic.

Nearctic
Birds in poor variety.
Palaearctic affinities.
Most species migrate.
62 Fam., 1 endemic.

Neotropical
Richest in bird life.
Long enduring geographic isolation.
86 Fam., 31 endemic.

Ethiopian
Birds show oriental affinities.
Isolated by Sahara Desert.
67 Fam., 6 endemic.

Australian
Long enduring isolation.
Approx. 83 Fam., 15 endemic.

DNA-DNA hybridisation

DNA-DNA hybridisation is a recent molecular biology technique where the chromosomes — which are made of DNA — of different species are compared. The extent of the differences between the DNAs is mathematically equivalent to the time that has elapsed since the species had common DNA, that is, since they belonged to the same, prehistoric species. A picture can be built up of how and when each species diverged from a common stock by studying the differences between their DNAs.

Before this molecular technique was available, evolutionary systems were based on geographical and visible evidence — how similar species looked and behaved. This could lead to false conclusions, as species can come from very different stock but look alike because of similar environmental pressures affecting their evolution. DNA-DNA hybridisation cannot mislead like this: two present species may look very similar, but their DNA will be very different if they evolved from different ancestors. This is not just a 'science for the birds'. All organisms are being studied in this way.

Charles Sibley and Jon Ahlquist are pioneers in the use of this technique as applied to birds. Their work, and that of others, has resulted in some controversial conclusions, and fascinating evidence of evolutionary relationships. Their sequence of the world's bird taxonomy, from Class to Family level, is set out in their reference work, Sibley, C. G. & Ahlquist, J. E., (1990), *Phylogeny and Classification of Birds, A Study in Molecular Evolution*, Yale University Press, New Haven and London. A second volume, Sibley, C. G. & Monroe, B. L., (1990), *Distribution and Taxonomy of Birds of the World*, Yale University Press, presents the new findings right down to species level. A readable summary of the new work can be found in Gill, F. B. & Sheldon, F. (1991), 'The birds reclassified', *Science* **252**.

It is not proposed to change the names of species, just their sequence, to show truer evolutionary relationships. This is causing intense excitement, and new fields of comparative anatomy and behavioural studies are being opened up as ornithologists seek to support or refute claims. We present a very abbreviated summary of the proposed arrangement here.

An abridged outline of Sibley & Ahlquist's classification, as it affects mainly Australasian birds
* indicates the **position** of the family or genus does not follow traditional classifications

NON-PASSERINES
  Order Struthioniformes (ostriches; cassowaries; emus; kiwis)
  Order Craciformes (mound-builders)
  Order Galliformes (pheasants; guineafowls; New World quails)
  Order Anseriformes (Magpie Goose; whistling-ducks; ducks and geese)
  Order Turniciformes (button-quails)
  Order Bucerotiformes (hornbills)
  Order Coraciiformes (rollers, kingfishers; kookaburras; bee-eaters)
  Order Cuculiformes (Old World cuckoos)
  Order Psittaciformes (cockatoos, parrots)
  Order Apodiformes (swifts)
  Order Strigiformes (barn owls, hawk owls; owlet-nightjars; frogmouth nightjars)
  Order Columbiformes (pigeons, doves)
  Order Gruiformes (bustards; cranes, Kagu, rails)
  Order Ciconiiformes
    Suborder Charadrii (*Plains-wanderer; curlews, godwits, snipe, sandpipers; *phalaropes; Painted Snipe; jacanas; thick-knees; waders, oystercatchers, plovers, dotterels, stilts, avocets; *pratincoles; gulls, skuas, jaegars, terns, skimmers, Northern Hemisphere auks)
    Suborder Ciconii
      Infraorder Falconides (Osprey, hawks, eagles, Old World vultures; Secretary Bird; falcons)
      Infraorder Ciconiides (grebes; tropicbirds; boobies, gannets, anhingas, cormorants, shags; herons, ibises; *pelicans, Shoebill Stork; *New World vultures; storks; *frigatebirds, *penguins, *loons, *albatrosses, *petrels)

PASSERINES
  Order Passeriformes
    Suborder Tyranni — suboscines (New Zealand wrens; pittas)
    Suborder Passeri — oscines
      Parvorder Corvida (treecreepers; lyrebirds, scrub-birds; *bowerbirds; grass wrens, fairy wrens; honeyeaters; *Australian chats; pardalotes, warblers, thornbills, scrub-robins, robins; babblers; quail-thrushes, sittellas, whistlers, shrike-tits, monarchs, *drongos, *magpie-larks, flycatchers, fantails, cuckoo-shrikes and trillers, orioles, birds of paradise; woodswallows, butcherbirds; *mud-nesters, crows and allies)
      Parvorder Passerida (true thrushes, starlings, swallows, martins, bulbuls, African warblers, Old World Warblers; Old World larks, sunbirds, flowerpeckers; Papuan berrypickers; Old World wagtails and pipits; sparrows, weaverbirds, waxbills, finches and allies)

At the front of this book, pp. 6-15, we have set out the Bird Families. These are in the traditional sequence of the RAOU Checklist, and of most bird books of the last half century or more. A modified — or conservative — version of Sibley & Ahlquist's new sequence is to be employed by the Australian Biological Resources Survey, and we have chosen to adopt it for the Bird Family Accounts and Island Checklists section of The Handbook in this edition.

Remember that the front half of our book is in the traditional Family sequence; the second half is in the new, but conservative, Family sequence.

Bird Families in Australia

In the pages that follow we give more detail about the habits of the birds described in the **Field Information**. Remember that we only cover families with members in the Australasian region: those bird orders and families not occurring here are not discussed.

The RAOU publishes official Checklists of Australian Birds. These not only list species, they also give a classification system that is generally followed by ornithologists. They produced a Checklist in 1911, and another in 1926. One is now in preparation, but while ornithologists await it they have adopted various modifications to the 1926 list.

H. T. Condon produced a non-passerine checklist and R. Schodde published an *Interim List of Passerines*, both in 1975. Some minor changes induced by the new DNA work have been published in the second edition (1986) of *The Reader's Digest Complete Book of Australian Birds*, and in the second of two volumes of B. J. Coate's book *The Birds of Papua New Guinea* (Vol. 1 Non-Passerines, 1985; Vol. 2 Passerines, 1990). Some changes are also incorporated in the first volume of the RAOU's *Handbook of Australian, New Zealand and Antarctic Birds* (Vol. 1 Ratites to Ducks). McAllan, I. A. W. & Bruce, M. D. (1988), *The Birds of New South Wales, A Working List*, Biocon Research Group in Association with the New South Wales Bird Atlassers, Turramurra, NSW, also use the new sequence.

The order we have adopted in the Handbook is the family sequence to be published by the Australian Biological Resources Study in their forthcoming *Fauna of Australia* (Vol. 2 Amphibia, Reptilia and Aves); for logistical reasons we have kept the sequence in the Bird Identification section as before, in the traditional ratites first, crows last, order. We have departed from the ABRS's sequence once or twice, but clearly show when we do so. We would like to thank Dr Richard Schodde and Dr Les Christidis for their help in this area. Our sequence attempts to lay the groundwork for changes which *will* come in the near future.

These further changes are a result of the DNA-DNA hybridisation work of Sibley & Ahlquist. Although we have *not* followed their classification, we consider their work so important we have included a note of how *they* classify each Family we discuss at the beginning of the entry. Sibley & Ahlquist themselves stress their work is unfinished, and further modifications will be made with time.

Ostriches
Family Struthionidae

[Sibley & Ahlquist place the traditional Family Struthionidae in the Parvclass Ratitae, Order Struthioniformes, Suborder Struthioni and Infraorder Struthionides. A second infraorder, Rheides, contains the allied South American rheas. (Compare heads of ostriches and rheas in the zoo or photographs and you will see how similar they appear in profile.)]

One common characteristic of all the ratites is the lack of a deep keel on the breastbone, as modern flying birds have, for the attachment of flight muscles. They have clearly been flightless for a long time. The massive thighs ('drumsticks') of ostriches are almost bare of feathers — a cooling mechanism for these fast-running birds. Speeds of up to 55 kph have been recorded for running ostriches. They are the largest living birds in the world today. Ostriches have only two toes.

Both sexes incubate the large white eggs, unlike the Cassowary and Emu where only the males incubate. Male ostriches are polygamous.

In Australia, several Ostrich-plume farms were established in the late 1800s. Survivors from the original and largest farm became semi-feral, located across several properties near Port Augusta, at the head of Spencer Gulf, South Australia. A few Ostriches were sighted in 1975 near Morgan, South Australia. More recently, farms have again begun producing Ostriches to revive the industry in meat, leather and feathers. Imported feather dusters are perhaps the best-known Ostrich-derived products in Australia today. Read current farm magazines and newspapers to keep abreast of this avi-farming trend.

The Ostrich has two toes on each foot. Only the large inner toe has a nail.

Breeding season
1 Ostrich (*Insufficient information*)

Mihirungs (Giant Runners)
Family Dromornithidae

Extinct ratites in Australia, eight species known; genus *Genyornis* included (see pp. 288-9).

Cassowaries
Family Casuariidae

[Sibley & Ahlquist continue their classification of the Struthioniformes with Suborder Casuarii, containing Family Casuariidae, in two tribes, Casuariini, the cassowaries, and Dromaiini, the emus. A second family, Apterygidae, is for the New Zealand kiwis.]

The Cassowary is a distinctive bird with a vertical helmet (casque) and a large sharp claw on the innermost of its three toes. This large, flightless, dark ratite inhabits tropical rainforests and is considered distantly related to the Emu. The genus is endemic to Australia and New Guinea and there are three species, one in Australia. Interestingly, there are 18 or 19 neck bones in cassowaries, but emus have 20. As with the Ostrich and Emu, there is no keel on the breastbone (sternum).

Fragmentation and destruction of the rainforests in northern Queensland is reducing the population of the Cassowary in the more southerly portion of its range.

The female lays about four large pale green eggs on forest litter. The male incubates them for about two months. It is considered to be a sedentary species, but it gathers food over a wide 'local' range. It eats fallen fruit from trees and vines, as well as dead birds and mammals. It may be dangerous if cornered and provoked, as it kicks out with its feet.

The Cassowary has a large claw on its innermost toe.

Breeding season

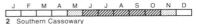

| J | F | M | A | M | J | J | A | S | O | N | D |

2 Southern Cassowary

Emus
Family Dromaiidae

Emus belong to the small, ancient and essentially Southern Hemisphere Order Struthioniformes, also called by the colloquial term, ratites.

Ratites cannot fly. They lack a keel on the sternum (breast bone), which anchors the flight muscles, and do not have the barbules (minute hooked branches) that hold the web of modern bird feathers together.

Only one species of Emu survives. Smaller species once occurred on King Island, Tasmania and Kangaroo Island, South Australia, but were exterminated last century. These are the only Australian bird species *definitely* known to have become extinct in recent times. The race *diemenensis* of mainland Tasmania also became extinct.

The Emu is Australia's national bird emblem. Emus eat mainly herbage and fruit; sometimes insects. They swallow stones to help mechanically grind up (triturate) woody food in the gizzard. In the arid interior of Australia Emus are nomadic and, to some extent, migratory. An extensive Emu-proof fence exists in Western Australia to guide Emus away from crop areas.

Males, which do all the incubation and caring for the young, are smaller and lighter than females. Nine to twelve (occasionally up to 20) large, glossy, dark green eggs are laid on the ground. Goannas, dingoes and feral pigs are nest predators.

Reading

Pople, A., Cairns, S. C. & Grigg, G. C. (1991), 'Distribution and abundance of Emus *Dromaius novaehollandiae* in relation to the environment in the South Australian pastoral zone, *Emu* **91** (4): 222-9.

The Emu is Australia's national bird emblem.

Breeding season

J	F	M	A	M	J	J	A	S	O	N	D

3 Emu

Albatrosses
Family Diomedeidae

[Sibley & Ahlquist have erected Order Ciconiiformes, followed by Suborder Ciconii. The latter includes the storks and *all* their allies. A large number of *previously separate orders* are included. Within the suborder are two new Infraorders, the Falconides and Ciconiides. The Falconides includes all of the diurnal birds of prey — Osprey, hawks, eagles, Old World vultures (Africa, India and Asia) — the Secretary-bird, the falcons and caracaras.

Infraorder Ciconiides is much larger, with four parvorders. Three relatively small ones are Parvorder Podicipedida, grebes, Parvorder Phaethontida, tropicbirds, and Parvorder Sulida, boobies, gannets, anhingas (darters), cormorants and shags. Finally, Parvorder Ciconiida is large, with herons, Hammerkop, flamingos, ibises, pelicans and Shoebill, New World vultures (those of the Americas), storks, frigatebirds, penguins, loons, albatrosses and the many kinds of petrels. Of particular interest here is that the New World vultures are now considered to be close allies of the storks, and not related to the other bird of prey groups. This is an example of convergent evolution at work. Sibley & Ahlquist reduce the families of albatrosses and petrels to subfamilies.]

Albatrosses are related to the three traditional families of petrels. All are united in the traditional Order Procellariiformes. Albatrosses have long, slender, hook-tipped bills with small tubular nostrils placed on each side. A shallow groove (nasal sulcus) runs forward. The 'plate' shape at the top of the upperbill base helps identify 'mollymawks'.

Albatrosses are superb long-winged gliders that consistently fly in a wheeling pattern. Into the wind they rise, wings stiff, to a point of stall. They then steeply glide downwind to pick up speed, turn at right angles across wind on reaching sea level, then repeat the process. If you have an opportunity to take a boat excursion, or stand upon a suitable coastal headland, watch the albatrosses carefully (see also the accompanying diagram). They rarely flap in a strong wind; effortless and graceful gliding may continue for hours.

Observers can look for albatrosses off coastal headlands in temperate or southern regions, usually in winter. Compare their appearance, relative size, flight mannerisms and behaviour with that of other large seabirds in such coastal areas. Boats however, are certainly best for watching albatrosses because they consistently scavenge from boats.

The birds' feet are webbed for swimming, act as air brakes during approach to alight, and act as stabilisers as they soar around cliff-induced updraft currents on breeding islands. Albatrosses also rest on the sea where they must be identified from similarly positioned gannets and white morphs of the Southern Giant Petrel.

For identification, clear views of features like bill colour, and head, underwing and upperwing patterns are needed. The patterns change with maturity from a usually dark plumage to a progressively paler one in the white-bodied albatrosses and mollymawks. There are a number of races and island populations of some species.

Wandering Albatrosses breed in different plumages. The southern populations are whiter and were once called 'Snowy Albatrosses'. The more northern populations may breed whilst in a rather browner body plumage. A colony of great albatrosses breeding at New Amsterdam Island (Indian Ocean) was recently described as a full new species *Diomedea amsterdamensis*. Adults are black- or dark-brown-capped, look like immature Wandering Albatrosses, but have a dark bill with a black cutting edge, like that of the Royal Albatrosses (see diagram p. 22).

The sequence of great albatross plumages on p. 22 is a compilation of 'average stages' of the slow change occurring from fledging to old age. It is also a broad summary of the different races of Wandering and Royal Albatrosses. Treat it as a general guide, not as absolutely defined stages.

The only albatross to breed in Australia is the nominate race of the Shy Albatross, *cauta*, on Albatross Island off north-west Tasmania, and on Pedra Branca and The Mewstone, off southern Tasmania. It also breeds in New Zealand. Earth and faecal material form a raised platform where one large white egg is laid and incubated for several weeks. Dancing courtship displays precede egg-laying. Nestlings are downy and are fed by both parents.

The long-line fishing industry has resulted in deaths of many albatrosses in recent years; new research is improving bait-throwing methods in an attempt to counter this.

Reading

Brothers, N. (1992), 'Longline fisheries', *The Bird Observer* **717**, Bird Observers Club of Australia, Nunawading, Victoria, p. 7.

Harper, P. C. & Kinsky, F. C. (1978), *Southern Albatrosses and Petrels*, Price Milburn and Co., Wellington.

Harrison, P. (1983), *Seabirds: an identification guide*, Croom Helm Ltd, Beckenham, Kent, UK and A. H. & A. W. Reed Ltd, Frenchs Forest, NSW, (see pp. 221-32 and plates 12-17).

Lindsey, T. & The National Photographic Index of Australian Wildlife (1986), *The Seabirds of Australia*, Angus & Robertson Publishers, North Ryde, NSW, Australia and London, England (and see pp. 77-143).

Warham, J. (1990), *The Petrels: Their ecology and breeding systems*, Academic Press, Harcourt Brace Jovanovich, Publishers, London, (pp. 17-46).

Wind direction and strength

Albatross glide-path.

Breeding season

J	F	M	A	M	J	J	A	S	O	N	D

24 Shy Albatross

Petrels, Shearwaters

Family Procellariidae

Albatrosses and petrels are known as fossils from the Oligocene and Miocene and from more modern sediments of marine, estuarine or otherwise coastal and sub-coastal habitats. The fossil record to date does not yet show a common ancestor for the petrels and the penguins. However, the modern technique of DNA-DNA hybridisation indicates that all of the Procellariiformes — albatrosses and the various petrel groups — are a distinctive group (Order) of essentially marine birds. Sibley and Ahlquist and their colleagues suggest an origin in which the petrels collectively have as their nearest relatives the frigatebirds and penguins, and the Northern Hemisphere loons.

The petrels and shearwaters (and storm-petrels) are characterised by nostrils encased in a tube, joined at the bill base. Albatross nostrils are small and separated on the bill sides; diving-petrels also have separated nostrils. In flight, petrels have long wings and in strong winds they can appear very graceful, wheeling and gliding up and down, sometimes in huge arcs; usually singly but sometimes in pairs. Storm-petrels differ in having proportionately longer legs and shorter wings than petrels. Diving-petrels are very short-winged.

Some 55 petrel species are now known to occur in and about Australian seas, not including the ten or eleven albatrosses. The figure is a significant proportion of the approximately 89 species occurring world-wide. Only ten species breed in Australia but the figure is increased when Australian territories (islands and the Antarctic sector) are taken into account.

Fulmarine petrels have very long nostrils and vary in size from the obviously large giant-petrel *Macronectes* to the small Snow Petrel *Pagodroma*. This group consists of several genera including *Fulmarus* (Fulmars), *Thalassoica* (Antarctic Petrel) and *Daption* (Cape Petrel). All have stiff-winged gliding flight interspersed with quick flapping. 'Gadfly petrels' *Pterodroma*, *Halobaena* and *Bulweria* have short, stubby black bills, short heads and long wings. They are perhaps the most graceful of petrels. Blue Petrels (*Halobaena*) are superficially like prions (*Pachyptila*), but bone structure, bill shape and colour suggest they are closer to *Pterodroma*. Other authors have moved this monotypic genus about, variously in and out of *Pterodroma* and *Pachyptila*. Sibley and Ahlquist do not single out *Halobaena* for mention.

Prions are specialised petrels with bluish plumage. Bill shape varies enormously through the range of Broad-billed Prion (width as great as 25 mm), Lesser Broad-billed, Antarctic, to Slender-billed Prion (as narrow as 9 mm). The forms within this group (often known as 'whalebirds') are extremely variable and a paper by Cox treats all but the Slender-billed as one clinal species. Possibly the Slender-billed Prion should also be placed under *Pachyptila vittata* with the 'whalebirds'. A *second* group, Fairy and Fulmar Prions, were also 'joined' (lumped together) by Cox as a single (conspecific) species — *Pachyptila turtur*.

Procellaria, *Calonectris* and *Puffinus* form the other group of petrels, the latter two being known as shearwaters (mutton-birds). The four *Procellaria* are very large, have bulbous, pale bills and range the southern seas. *Calonectris* are large, pale shearwaters. Australia's visiting representative is the Streaked Shearwater. *Puffinus* are a large, variable group of

The nesting site of a Gould's Petrel at Cabbage Tree Island, off the north coast of New South Wales.

Breeding seasons (*variable*)

	J	F	M	A	M	J	J	A	S	O	N	D
33 Great-winged Petrel												
37 Herald Petrel*												
42 Gould's Petrel												

Breeding season

	J	F	M	A	M	J	J	A	S	O	N	D
52 Fairy Prion												

A Fairy Prion nesting in a rock crevice.

petrels with long, slender bills and flattened legs. They are either all dark, or dark and white. Most have fluttering, sometimes gliding flight; all alight to pick up or dive for food.

Nearly all petrels are wanderers; some are migrants of the highest degree. The Short-tailed Shearwater *Puffinus tenuirostris*, or 'Muttonbird', breeds in south-eastern Australia and migrates to the north Pacific every year in millions. Other petrels have similar migratory routes (e.g. Providence, Cook's, Mottled Petrels). Some petrels do almost the opposite, e.g. the Asia-breeding Streaked Shearwater migrates to northern Australia. Fluttering and Hutton's Shearwaters are examples of migrants from New Zealand. Many Antarctic and sub-Antarctic species wander north in winter to Australian waters, including the Cape Petrel, giant-petrels and White-headed Petrel.

Marine animals of varying sizes from small tuna to microorganisms are taken. Prions sift food with the help of lamellae (stiff hair-like membranes) along the inside of the upper mandible (very well developed in the Broad-billed Prion).

Petrels occur solitarily or in extremely large flocks of up to millions as in the Short-tailed Shearwater. Petrels breed mostly in burrows or crevices. Giant-petrels nest in depressions surrounded by dried vegetation. Other fulmarine petrels breed in raised scrapes on the ground, on hillsides and cliffs. One white egg is laid; a clutch of one.

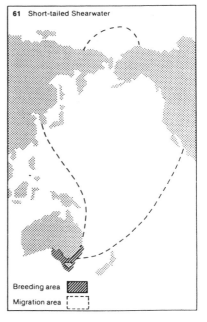

61 Short-tailed Shearwater

Breeding area
Migration area

Reading

Cox, J. B. (1980), 'Some remarks on the breeding distribution and taxonomy of the prions (Procellariidae: *Pachyptila*)', *Rec. S. Aust. Museum* **18** (4), 91-121.

Harper, P. C. (1980), 'The field identification and distribution of the prions (genus *Pachyptila*) with particular reference to storm-cast material', *Notornis* **27**, 235-86.

Harper, P. C. & Kinsky, F. C. (1978), *Southern Albatrosses and Petrels*, Price Milburn and Co., Wellington.

Marchant, S. & Higgins, P. J., (co-ordinators) (1990), *Handbook of Australian, New Zealand and Antarctic Birds*, Volume 1, Ratites to Ducks, Part A: Ratites to Petrels, Oxford University Press, Melbourne (pp. 263-735).

Warham, J. (1990), *The Petrels: Their Ecology and Breeding Systems*, Academic Press, Harcourt Brace Jovanovich, London, (pp. 47-170).

Breeding seasons

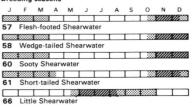

	J	F	M	A	M	J	J	A	S	O	N	D
57 Flesh-footed Shearwater												
58 Wedge-tailed Shearwater												
60 Sooty Shearwater												
61 Short-tailed Shearwater												
66 Little Shearwater												

Storm-Petrels

Family Hydrobatidae

Storm-petrels are closely related to the true petrels but differ in having proportionately longer legs and shorter wings. The bill is small with raised nostrils. Storm-petrels are the smallest petrels.

Wilson's Storm-Petrel is the most wide-ranging species, breeding on islands of the southern oceans and moving to the Northern Hemisphere. Offshore from Australia's continental mass, Wilson's Storm-Petrel is quite common. The White-faced Storm-Petrel is the only known breeding species in Australia. They breed on sandy islands in long narrow burrows. One white egg is laid by these (as for all storm-petrels). Many of them migrate north and west into the Indian Ocean and Arabian Sea in the winter. Many thousands of this species have been banded, but only a few have been recovered, mostly locally. The migratory pattern is still not fully clear.

Grey-backed Storm-Petrels breed on islands south-east of New Zealand and migrate to seas off south-east Australia. White-bellied and Black-bellied Storm-Petrels are difficult to identify from each other. Excellent views are required

Flight mannerisms

Wilson's: purposeful, fast, direct; hovers; patters with feet while wings raised in 'V'.

Grey-backed: like moth; skims low; leaps from side to side, pushing off sea with both feet.

White-faced: bounces up and down on sea, dangling long legs; sways from side to side. Long glides.

Black-bellied & White-bellied: both zig-zag low and smack water with breast every few moments.

Matsudaira's: soars; glides very slowly. A little-known species.

Leach's: deep, slow wing beats, swooping flight; sometimes glides. Rarely patters on water.

but boating conditions do not always provide these. The White-bellied breeds on Lord Howe Island and many other tropical islands; the Black-bellied is a sub-Antarctic island breeder. Birds with intermediate markings also occur in small numbers, which can complicate identification in some ocean areas. The possibility of northern and southern morphs of a single species complex exists in the genus *Fregetta*.

Leach's Storm-Petrel is a Northern Hemisphere-breeding species, of which a few vagrants have reached Australian seas. The first was found dead at Port Fairy, Victoria, in July 1965. Matsudaira's Storm-Petrel may migrate annually to north-west Australia from Japan but sightings are few because of a lack of observers at sea.

Storm-petrels are usually seen in waters over 100 metres in depth. Storm-petrels within the subfamily Oceanitinae generally fly by fluttering and bouncing on the water with their legs extended. In the subfamily Hydrobatinae, birds glide more and have tern-like wingbeats. All species feed on tiny surface organisms.

Reading

Warham, J. (1990), *The Petrels: their ecology and breeding systems*, Academic Press, Harcourt Brace Jovanovich, London, Sydney, (pp. 171-92).

Breeding season

J	F	M	A	M	J	J	A	S	O	N	D

70 White-faced Storm-Petrel

Diving-Petrels — Family Pelecanoididae

Diving-petrels are small, black and white birds. They have short bills with separate nostrils that open upward. They are small and dumpy, with short, rounded wings. All species are closely related and difficult to identify, nostrils and bill shape being the main differences. Diving-petrels superficially resemble, in body and feeding, the Northern Hemisphere auks.

They prefer waters away from the coast but usually not over about 100 metres in depth. When disturbed they fly off the water in a quail-like manner. They fly through waves, using their wings to propel themselves under water. The diet is small fish and crustacea. Common Diving-Petrels breed on some offshore islands of Australia's southern coasts, nesting in tunnels in shallow soil, and lay one white egg. The South Georgian Diving-Petrel was recorded near Sydney, NSW, in 1958.

Reading

Warham, J. (1990), *The Petrels: their ecology and breeding systems*, Academic Press, Harcourt Brace Jovanovich, London, Sydney, (pp. 193-206).

Diving-petrels swim underwater with partly opened wings.

Breeding season

J	F	M	A	M	J	J	A	S	O	N	D

75 Common Diving-Petrel

Penguins — Family Spheniscidae

[Sibley & Ahlquist retain the traditional Family Spheniscidae, penguins, within the Infraorder Ciconiides, Parvorder Ciconiida and Superfamily Procellariioidea. The DNA hybridisation studies indicate that the penguins are members of the procellariiform birds, together with the albatrosses and the many petrels, the loons and the frigate-birds. Thus their classification is very different from taxonomic sequences to date, in that the penguins show a closer affinity with the storks than was previously suspected. We retain the more conservative approach for the time being.]

Penguins have flattened feather shafts and keep their dense plumage waterproof with oil from a tail gland. Each year, *all* penguins *must* leave the sea briefly to completely moult the worn plumage; they stand quietly in a cloud of feathers. Birds forced to swim at this time may drown. Similarly, sick penguins treated for serious fuel oil contamination *must never* be released to sea until the next annual moult is complete. Lightly oiled penguins may be cleaned and released.

Most Australian penguin records are either of winter migrants or those caught out and obliged to come ashore in autumn to moult (Rockhopper, Fiordland, perhaps Royal), or rarer vagrants (Chinstrap, Adelie, Magellan, Erect-crested, Snares). The colour plate (p. 21) is arranged to reflect the approximate proportion of sightings for each species, those for which there are the least number of records and which therefore are *our* rarest species, being in the background.

Within the genus *Eudyptes*, the crested penguin group, there are two divisions possible, based on the position of the origin of the coloured crests. The Macaroni-Royal Penguin species complex has a crest which may be called a 'frontal crest' in that it originates right across the front of the head. The remainder, Rockhoppers, Snares, Erect-crested and Fiordland Penguins, have laterally originating crests, which begin anteriorly as an eyebrow stripe, becoming an expanded crest behind the eye and ear. This may be called a 'superciliary stripe-crest'. The *point of anterior origin* of this is of crucial importance in adult identification. Young birds show incomplete superciliary stripe-crests and are more difficult to identify.

The Little Penguin (of 'Penguin Parade' fame in Victoria) is the only penguin that breeds in Australia. It also breeds in New Zealand. These birds feed on small fish and crustaceans, usually nest colonially in burrows and have one or two young. Adults return at late dusk to feed the nestlings.

Proximity of human habitation, nefarious human activities, predation by dogs, cats, foxes and rats, trampling of burrows by stock, plastic pollution, oil spills, and perhaps pesticide or heavy-metal ingestion are problems of varying importance to some of the birds and colonies.

Reading

Reilly, P. N. (1983), *Fairy Penguins and Earthy People*, Lothian, Melbourne.

Simpson, G. G. (1976), *Penguins, Past & Present, Here and There*, Yale University Press, Connecticut, USA.

Sparks, John & Soper, Tony (1987), *Penguins*, (2nd edition), Macmillan Co. of Australia, Melbourne.

Stahel, Colin & Gales, Rosemary (1987), *Little Penguin: Fairy Penguins in Australia*, NSW University Press.

Stonehouse, Bernard (1975) *The Biology of Penguins*, Macmillan, London; University Park Press, Baltimore, USA.

Little Penguins come ashore at dusk.

Breeding season

J	F	M	A	M	J	J	A	S	O	N	D

17 Little Penguin

Grebes   Family Podicipedidae

[Sibley & Ahlquist conclude that the grebes have no close living relatives and that the Northern Hemisphere loons are not related to them despite a certain superficial likeness. The Grebes have their own Parvorder Podicipedida within the Order Ciconiiformes. Their distant 'sister' groups appear to be the tropicbirds, gannets and boobies and their allies, and the other larger cluster of waterbird and seabird families in the stork assemblage. The grebes are an ancient lineage however.]

Grebes fly well but *prefer* not to in daylight. Migratory or nomadic flights are at night. Birds dive to feed and to escape danger, or fly low, pattering over the water surface and slowly gaining height if disturbed by a raptor.

Breeding plumage differs from non-breeding plumage. Both sexes take part in ritual courtship ceremonies and later in nesting activities. In spectacular displays (see p. 18), Great Crested Grebe partners face each other in the water, shaking erected head crests and ruffs, apparently preening and offering each other nest material. At the climax of the display, they rise up in the 'penguin posture', colliding breast to breast. Copulation later occurs on the hidden, floating or anchored nest-platform or on aquatic vegetation.

In general, the white eggs of grebes (three to nine) stain rapidly. Eggs when freshly laid have a dull, chalky surface. When a grebe leaves its eggs, it covers them with weed. Downy young are brightly marked and striped.

Hatchlings move under the wings into the fur-like back plumage of whichever parent is on the nest. They are fed by parents, which carry them out onto the water on their backs. Older chicks follow parents for food. Small fish, tadpoles, freshwater crayfish and other aquatic invertebrates are eaten. The legs of grebes are set far back on the body, and they use these, not the wings, to swim with. Walking is not a forte of the grebes and they rarely emerge onto dry land.

Reading
O'Donnell, C. F. J. (1981), 'Head plumage variation and winter plumage of the Southern Crested Grebe', *Notornis* **28**, 212-13.

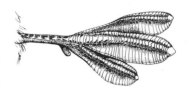

The Hoary-headed Grebe, like other grebes, has a compressed tarsus (leg) and lobed toes.

Breeding seasons

	J	F	M	A	M	J	J	A	S	O	N	D
4 Great Crested Grebe												
5 Hoary-headed Grebe												
6 Australasian Grebe												

Tropicbirds
Family Phaethontidae

Tropicbirds are white with black markings and thick but rather tern-like bills. Adults have very long central tail streamers, either red or white. Some populations have pinkish (Red-tailed) or apricot (White-tailed) hues to the feather tips when the body plumage is freshly moulted. Tropicbirds breed on island cliffs, often in crevices, and lay one white egg.

Juvenile Red-tailed Tropicbirds leave the nest with small, mainly white central tail feathers; the red streamers may take several years to develop fully; the period taken is not yet defined. These juvenile birds have a strongly marked plumage, with black bars on inner dorsal wings, back, rump and mantle. An immature period follows during which the birds slowly whiten on the dorsal surface, as the black bars and sub-terminal marks gradually disappear.

Reading
Stokes, T. (1990), 'The post-juvenal plumage of the Red-tailed Tropicbird *Phaethon rubricauda*', *Aust. Bird Watcher* **13** (8), 259-60.

Breeding season (*variable*)

	J	F	M	A	M	J	J	A	S	O	N	D
92 Red-tailed Tropicbird*												

Frigatebirds
Family Fregatidae

Frigatebirds may be allied to albatrosses, petrels and penguins. Frigatebirds are black, or black and white, with long bills that are strongly hooked at the tip. The adult male has a red gular pouch that resembles a balloon when inflated. Their flight is very graceful; they may soar for long periods at great heights. The birds are piratic, mobbing other seabirds to steal food. Occasionally they catch their own, newly hatched sea turtles being one favoured item. One white egg is laid on a nest of sticks, built usually on low bushes of tropical islands.

Reading
Harrison, P. (1987), *Seabirds of the World, a Photographic Guide*, Christopher Helm, Bromley, UK (see pp. 100-4).

Male gular pouch inflated.

Breeding seasons

	J	F	M	A	M	J	J	A	S	O	N	D
90 Great Frigatebird												
91 Least Frigatebird												

Cormorants, Shags, Darters
Family Phalacrocoracidae

[Sibley & Ahlquist retain the traditional Family Phalacrocoracidae, cormorants and shags, within the Infraorder Ciconiides, Parvorder Sulida and Superfamily Phalacrocoracoidea. Note that they remove the anhingas or darters, once always allied with the above, to Superfamily Suloidea, which allies them with the gannets and boobies.]

Cormorants, Shags

Subfamily Phalacrocoracinae

Shags and cormorants are long-necked birds with hook-tipped bills. All Australian species are black or pied. Two groups are defined: the sea-cormorants or shags (*Leucocarbo*) and the other cormorants (*Phalacrocorax*). The Black-faced Shag, once called White-breasted Cormorant, is Australia's only endemic marine representative of the group.

All catch fish by swimming and diving from the surface. Their eyes are protected underwater by a nictitating membrane. Unlike penguins, which move underwater by 'flying' with their wings (flippers), cormorants and shags use their feet as principal underwater propulsion (see drawing). After fishing, shags and cormorants (and darters) stand with outstretched wings, apparently to dry non-waterproofed feathers, but there may be more complex reasons for this behaviour.

Nesting is generally colonial, sometimes of several species together, and sometimes on the fringes of ibis colonies or heronries. One to five whitish eggs are laid on a tree platform or on the ground. Nestlings have a distinctly 'reptilian' look about them.

Little Pied Cormorant pursuing fish under water.

Breeding seasons (*variable*)

J	F	M	A	M	J	J	A	S	O	N	D

84 Black-faced Shag*

85 Pied Cormorant*

86 Little Pied Cormorant*

87 Great Cormorant*

88 Little Black Cormorant*

Anhingas (Darters)

Subfamily Anhinganinae

[Sibley & Ahlquist retain Family Anhingidae (anhingas or darters) within the Parvorder Sulida and Superfamily Suloidea. The superfamily also includes Family Sulidae, gannets and boobies. Thus, they are indicating that darters are allied more closely to the gannet group than they are to the cormorants, with which they have previously been associated.]

Darters are very long-necked, 'cormorant'-like birds with sharp, pointed bills. Compare the spear-shaped bills of gannets, boobies and darters with the hook-tipped bills of cormorants and shags. When fishing, only the slender neck is visible, leading to its colloquial name of 'snake-bird'. Text books differ in their treatment of the darters — once there were considered to be three species of darter. Today, the three have become one, extending from Africa and Madagascar to India, the Middle East, Indonesia, Australia and New Guinea. The Australasian race *novaehollandiae* has white-breasted females. There is also the American Anhinga, a separate species.

Their habits are generally similar to the cormorants. In the air they are excellent fliers, soaring on thermals across the countryside. Darters may breed adjacent to or mixed in with cormorants and members of the heron family at colonies in inland swamps and river systems of Australia.

Reading

Vestjens, W. J. M. (1974), 'Breeding behaviour of the Darter at Lake Cowal, NSW', *Emu* **75**, 121-31.

Breeding season (*variable*)

J	F	M	A	M	J	J	A	S	O	N	D

83 Darter*

Boobies and Gannets

Family Sulidae

[Sibley & Ahlquist retain the traditional Family Sulidae within the Infraorder Ciconiides, Parvorder Sulida and Superfamily Suloidea. This superfamily also includes Family Anhingidae (anhingas or darters).]

Gannets and boobies are straight-billed birds, adapted to plunging into the sea from considerable heights. Gannets lack the naked gular region and mask of the boobies and have shorter tails. Except when breeding in colonies on land, they are found out at sea. One or two whitish eggs are laid in

Display.

a mound or on a stick nest. One nestling is favoured, the other usually dies. Abbott's Booby of Christmas Island, a rare and endangered species, is illustrated on p. 43 but we have not included a written description of it. Boobies are mostly tropical in their distribution; gannets tend to be in southern temperate waters.

Gannets and boobies feed on live food only, caught by plunging into the sea. If a clean take is not achieved, the birds can chase prey briefly by swimming with half-folded wings. Diving gannets may be followed down by shearwaters, which then attempt to grab fish or take advantage of the disturbance to catch smaller food items adjacent to the gannet.

Around southern Australia, the Australasian Gannet breeds on the islands and rock stacks. It also breeds in New Zealand, where the famous Cape Kidnappers Gannetry is the best-known locality, but birds banded on White Island have been taken in Australian seas.

In 1967, a few Australasian Gannets were discovered breeding on Wedge Light platform, a beacon in Port Phillip Bay, Victoria. The number of nests increased steadily and in the early 1980s the gannets spilled over onto an adjacent man-made islet, Pope's Eye. A small platform was later erected to cater for them but ever more nests were constructed. This is the first known occurrence of gannets breeding on artificial structures.

In August 1980 a Cape Gannet was identified on Wedge Light. It subsequently mated with an Australasian Gannet, occupying a nest site. This Cape Gannet has been present ever since and is still there (March 1992). Successful breeding between the pair prior to 1991-92 needs verification. A well-grown fledgling was present on 23 February 1992, with the Cape Gannet in attendance. The hybrid, which shows a long dark gular stripe, is darker in body plumage than the many surrounding Australasian Gannet fledglings and is also possibly larger. Three adult Cape Gannets were recorded on the Lawrence Rocks, off Portland, Victoria, during February 1992, the third confirmed record for Australia. The second record was an immature, banded in South Africa, caught off Cape Leeuwin, WA, 18 October 1986.

Reading

Marchant, S. & Higgins, P. J. (co-ordinators) (1990), *Handbook of Australian, New Zealand and Antarctic Birds*, Volume 1, Ratites to Ducks, Part B: Australian Pelican to Ducks, Oxford University Press, Melbourne (see pp. 748-97).

Nelson, J. B. (1978), *The Sulidae, Gannets and Boobies*, Oxford University Press, London.

Reville, B., Tranter, J. & Yorkston, J. (1987), 'Monitoring the endangered Abbott's Booby on Christmas Island, 1983-86', *Occasional Pap.* no. 11, ANPWS, Canberra, 1-18.

Venn, D. R. (1982), 'The Cape Gannet (*Sula capensis*), a new record for Australia', *Victorian Naturalist* 99, 56-8.

Breeding seasons (*variable*)

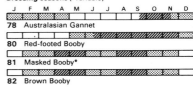

78 Australasian Gannet

80 Red-footed Booby

81 Masked Booby*

82 Brown Booby

Pelicans   Family Pelecanidae

[Sibley & Ahlquist have removed the traditional Family Pelecanidae from its 'normal' or prior position with the gannets, boobies, cormorants and shags, and placed it in the Infraorder Ciconiides, Parvorder Ciconiida and Superfamily Pelecanoidea. Their Superfamily has two subfamilies, Pelicaninae, the pelicans as expected, and Subfamily Balaenicipitinae, the Shoebill (Shoebill Stork or Whale-headed Stork) of Africa. The DNA hybridisation study has pointed in this direction for the relationship, carrying the pelicans into a far closer liaison with the true storks than was previously realised. Sibley & Ahlquist recognise that this is, at the moment, controversial and urge more study to clarify the situation.]

Pelicans   Subfamily Pelecaninae

Pelicans are very distinctive members of the traditional Order Pelecaniformes, a group characterised by four toes joined by webs, the hind toe directed forward, and sealed nostrils.

In pelicans the gular region is naked and expanded into a large pouch. In extremely hot weather, pelicans open their bills and rapidly vibrate the soft skin of the pouch. This radiates heat from the numerous blood vessels in the tissue. This behaviour is known as 'gular fluttering'. Cormorants and the Darter also do it, but less conspicuously. As a cooling mechanism it must be quite effective, for pelicans are able to breed in hot-arid and hot-humid areas, as well as in more temperate zones.

Pelicans are affected by pesticides and related chemicals concentrated in the fish that they eat. As 'top-of-the-food-chain' piscivores, the result is egg-shell thinning, leading to egg loss during breeding. Australian Pelicans are nomadic and, when breeding, colonial. One to four white eggs are laid in a ground hollow or scrape; young are naked when hatched and need protection from fierce sunlight. When birdwatching, please do not linger in or near the nests of ground-nesting colonial bird species, as disturbances usually lead to egg and nestling losses.

Reading

Vestjens, W. J. M. (1977), 'Breeding behaviour and ecology of the Australian Pelican *Pelecanus conspicillatus* in NSW', *Aust. Wildl. Res.* **4**, 37-58.

Co-operative fishing.

Breeding season (*variable*)

J	F	M	A	M	J	J	A	S	O	N	D

77 Australian Pelican*

Herons, Bitterns, Egrets   Family Ardeidae

[Sibley & Ahlquist retain the traditional Family Ardeidae and place it within the Infraorder Ciconiides, Parvorder Ciconiida and Superfamily Ardeoidea.]

Accurate field observations, particularly of plumage, soft-part colours, and behavioural changes which occur just before egg-laying, are insufficient for a surprising number of heron species. Detailed study and reporting by bird-watchers is needed in Australia.

Herons are adapted to capture prey such as insects, crustaceans, frogs and fish in water, and insects and other prey on land, using four main feeding techniques: standing and waiting, slow stalk, active pursuit, and (sometimes) hovering and plunging. The first three techniques use modified wing and leg movements to attract, disturb or confuse prey. Some (such as Striated Heron, Little Egret) will spread one or both wings, then search for prey in their shadows. This reduces glare and may attract small fish, as does shade from an overhanging branch. One or both wings may be flicked to startle prey; a foot is treadled either to disturb prey or, possibly, in the case of the Little Egret, to attract prey to its yellow sole.

Colonial nesting species are monogamous, pairing only for the duration of the breeding season. Ornamental plumes and soft-part colour changes are important in establishing the pair bonds. The nest site is vigorously defended. On the other hand, the Australasian Bittern may not defend its nest site. It is so far little studied but is related to the polygamous European Bittern. Several females nest in the male Australasian Bittern's territory. Heron feeding areas are not defended and spectacular concentrations may form when food is abundant. The Eastern Reef Egret is exceptional in that pairs defend the feeding area when it is exposed at low tide.

'Changeover' display at nest.

Breeding seasons (*variable*)

J	F	M	A	M	J	J	A	S	O	N	D

94 Great-billed Heron

95 Pacific Heron

96 White-faced Heron

97 Pied Heron

98 Cattle Egret

99 Great Egret*

100 Little Egret*

101 Intermediate Egret*

102 Eastern Reef Egret

103 Striated Heron

Until the beginning of this century, heron species that acquired spectacular plumes were ruthlessly killed to supply the millinery trade. Populations of many species were severely reduced because breeding adults were shot just as egg-laying commenced. Today, with no such hunting, effective conservation is possible but depends on rigorous preservation of suitable wetland habitats, which must be maintained completely undisturbed during the breeding seasons of the heron, egret and bittern species of Australia.

Reading

Hancock, J. & Elliott, H. (1978), *The Herons of the World*, London Editions, London, UK; Harper & Row, New York.

Hancock, James & Kushlan, James (1984), *The Herons' Handbook*, Croom Helm Ltd, London and Sydney; Harper & Row, New York.

Breeding seasons

	J	F	M	A	M	J	J	A	S	O	N	D
104 Rufous Night Heron												
105 Little Bittern												
107 Black Bittern												
108 Australasian Bittern												

Flamingos Family Phoenicopteridae

[Sibley & Ahlquist retain the traditional Family Phoenicopteridae and place it within the Infraorder Ciconiides, Parvorder Ciconiida and Superfamily Phoenicopteroidea.]

Extinct in Australia; see **Prehistoric birds**, pp. 288-9.

Palaelodids Family Palaelodidae

Extinct in Australia; see **Prehistoric birds**, pp. 288-9.

Storks Family Ciconiidae

[Sibley & Ahlquist retain the traditional Family Ciconiidae and place it within the Infraorder Ciconiides, Parvorder Ciconiida and Superfamily Ciconioidea. There are two subfamilies, the Ciconiinae containing the true storks, i.e. storks, open-bills, adjutants and Black-necked Stork (= Jabiru), and the Cathartinae, which contains the New World vultures (condors).]

The Black-necked Stork (formerly known as Jabiru) feeds on small mammals, frogs, lizards, insects, large bivalves and carrion. Birds are sedentary and remain paired for many years. They only occur in groups of more than four or five when severe drought reduces suitable habitat. Nests are large stick-and-reed platforms in tall trees, low bushes or on the ground, but surrounded by water. The birds lay two to four eggs. Rarely do all the nestlings survive the 100-115 days to nest departure.

Breeding season

	J	F	M	A	M	J	J	A	S	O	N	D
109 Black-necked Stork												

Ibises, Spoonbills Family Threskiornithidae

[Sibley & Ahlquist retain the traditional Family Threskiornithidae in the Infraorder Ciconiides and Superfamily Threskiornithoidea.]

Both ibises and spoonbills probe in water for hidden prey: spoonbills sweeping their bills from side to side repeatedly, ibises probing and plucking. On land, both kinds of birds also hunt visible prey — insects, frogs, small mammals at times.

Huge mixed breeding colonies may occur. Ibises' nests are packed close together on reeds, bushes or muddy islands; only rarely in trees. Spoonbills may nest low, intermingled with ibises, or high in outer branches of large trees. Other species may breed in loose association with them — cormorants, darters, egrets, herons, night herons and various ducks. The mix of species may vary with location and seasonal factors.

Ibises frequently travel 30-40 kilometres from colonies to feed, and may use thermals to gain height in arid regions, either when coming or going to the nests. Unlike herons,

Breeding seasons (*variable*)

	J	F	M	A	M	J	J	A	S	O	N	D
110 Glossy Ibis*												
111 Australian White Ibis*												
112 Straw-necked Ibis*												
113 Royal Spoonbill*												
114 Yellow-billed Spoonbill*												

ibises and spoonbills always fly with their necks extended. Stragglers of the Yellow-billed Spoonbill have reached New Zealand, and the Royal Spoonbill breeds there in small numbers.

Osprey, Hawks, Eagles   Family Accipitridae

[Sibley & Ahlquist erected Order Ciconiiformes, including the storks and *all* their allies. Within it are two new Infraorders, the Falconides and Ciconiides. The Falconides is divided in two also, the first of the divisions being a Parvorder Accipitrida including all of the diurnal birds of prey — Osprey, hawks, eagles, Old World vultures (the vultures of Africa, India and Asia) — plus the Secretary-bird. The falcons and caracaras are in the second Parvorder Falconida. The New World vultures (those of the Americas), however, fall into the Infraorder Ciconiides, and thus are now considered to be closely allied to the storks, and not related to the other diurnal bird of prey groups. Sibley & Ahlquist retain the traditional subfamilies of the Family Accipitridae.]

Osprey   Subfamily Pandioninae

This subfamily contains only one genus, *Pandion*, with one species, the Osprey. Usually coastal dwelling, it is a highly specialised fish catcher. It has some unique (probably adaptive) anatomical features: a reversible outer toe, spicules under the foot, and closable nostril (see drawings).

Ospreys construct a stick nest in trees, on rocky outcrops or on the ground. Nests may be used for many years and may attain massive proportions, even acting as navigation aids for local boats in Western Australia and the Northern Territory. Flying foxes (fruit-bats — Megachiroptera) are caught and eaten by some Ospreys in the tropics.

Reading
Poole, A. F. (1989), *Ospreys*, Cambridge University Press, Cambridge, UK.

Breeding season

J	F	M	A	M	J	J	A	S	O	N	D

138 Osprey

Hawks, Eagles   Subfamily Accipitrinae

This subfamily consists of 12 Australian genera and 17 species. The genera are listed below.

Elanus Australia's two elanid kites are specialist hunters of small rodents. The Letter-winged Kite hunts the nocturnal Long-haired Rat *Rattus villosissimus* in central Australia. When rats reach plague numbers (often after flooding), the Letter-wings breed continuously in colonies — the only Australian raptor to do so. When rat populations subsequently fall, the kites must either leave or starve. Large-scale dispersal to coastal regions may occur. Black-shouldered Kites hunt from perches or by hovering and seem to have increased numerically in coastal areas this century, possibly due to larger populations of the introduced House Mouse. They build small stick nests in tree canopies; they may breed in spring and again in autumn.

Aviceda The Pacific Baza is the only local example of its genus. Bazas have a short head crest, a long tail and relatively weak feet. Largely insectivorous, they crash into tree tops to take phasmids (leaf and stick insects). A small nest of twigs is built high in a forest tree.

Milvus Two species; one, the Black Kite, occurs in Australia. Tens of thousands inhabit northern Australia during the dry season but six months later they have gone, along with the slightly less numerous Whistling Kite. Many may migrate to the inland to breed, others may go north to Asia

These Black Kites are soaring in a thermal.

Breeding seasons (*variable*)

J	F	M	A	M	J	J	A	S	O	N	D

139 Black-shouldered Kite*

140 Letter-winged Kite*

141 Pacific Baza*

— only a large-scale banding operation will tell. Ever an opportunist and scavenger, the Black Kite is attracted to bushfire smoke and is often the first of the predatory birds to take fire victims. Primarily a carrion feeder, it is often displaced at the carcass by more aggressive species. It breeds in a fairly large stick nest — newly built or a disused existing one.

Lophoictinia and *Hamirostra* These genera contain two monotypic Australian endemic species — Square-tailed Kite and Black-breasted Buzzard respectively. The two are related, but their relationship to other raptors is obscure. Detailed behavioural, anatomical and biochemical studies of both would be invaluable. The buzzard is more common in northern and central Australia, the kite more coastal-dwelling. Both feed on nestling birds, and both build large stick nests. Pairs of buzzards share incubation, nest guarding and hunting almost equally — an unusual phenomenon. Even more unusual is their habit of feeding their nestlings and one another, at the same time.

Haliastur Two species, both in Australia: the widespread Whistling Kite, and the north coastal Brahminy Kite. They are similar in important respects: both use a distinctive, slow, wheeling flight to locate carrion (live prey is also taken); both generally nest high in tree forks, lining the stick nests with green leaves (Brahminy Kites sometimes use seaweed).

Accipiter About 50 species, of which three occur in Australia: the Brown Goshawk, Collared Sparrowhawk and Grey Goshawk. They have short, rounded wings, long tails and fairly long yellow legs. Long toes and claws facilitate prey capture. They take birds, small mammals, reptiles and insects. Birds are likely to be the main food of the Collared Sparrowhawk and probably the Grey Goshawk. Rabbits are an important prey of Brown Goshawks. These species generally construct stick nests high in trees, lining them with green leaves. Each nest may be used several times. The two colour morphs of the Grey Goshawk interbreed freely, producing offspring of either colour. On rare occasions, Grey Goshawks have interbred with Brown Goshawks.

Erythrotriorchis The Red Goshawk has been regarded as sufficiently different from the accipiters to warrant its own monotypic genus. It has comparatively long wings, a fairly short tail and extremely powerful legs and feet. One of Australia's rarest raptors, it appears restricted to remote woodlands of northern Australia. Historical records suggested its range was shrinking; a recent survey regards it 'safe' for now.

Haliaeetus The White-bellied Sea-Eagle is the only Australian representative of this genus. It has long, broad wings, well suited to soaring and lifting prey, and powerful legs, feet and talons. Spectacular dives secure fish, while other foods — mammals, reptiles and birds — are often taken as carrion.

Aquila The Wedge-tailed Eagle is Australia's only *Aquila* species. It is a very large eagle with long 'fingered' wings, extremely powerful legs, feet and talons, and a deep, sharply hooked bill. It is predominantly a carrion-eater across the continent, although live prey, rabbits, small macropods and birds are also taken by diving attacks or rapid pursuit. Wedge-tailed Eagles have a long history of human persecution, mainly as a consequence of alleged stock predation. Research shows the allegation to be very largely unfounded.

Hieraaetus This genus shares feathered tarsi (lower legs) with the *Aquila* eagles, but is usually smaller, more slender, and

Sexual dimorphism in the Brown Goshawk: large female (left); small male (right).

Breeding seasons (*variable*)

	J	F	M	A	M	J	J	A	S	O	N	D
142 Black Kite*												
143 Brahminy Kite*												
144 Whistling Kite*												
145 Square-tailed Kite*												
146 Black-breasted Buzzard*												
147 Brown Goshawk*												
148 Collared Sparrowhawk*												
149 Grey Goshawk*												
150 Red Goshawk* (*not well known*)												
151 White-bellied Sea-Eagle												
152 Wedge-tailed Eagle												
153 Little Eagle												

has long toes and powerful talons more like the *Accipiter* hawks. The Little Eagle is Australia's sole example. Rapid, powerful flight secures prey, both birds and mammals (especially rabbits where available). All the eagle genera build large stick nests, lined with fresh green leaves. Nests may be used repeatedly, in rotation over several years if there are several in a territory, or new ones constructed.

Circus Harriers have long tails and wings, and very long legs. Their prey, small rodents, rabbits and waterfowl, are sought by a characteristic low quartering flight over grasslands and swamps. An owl-like facial disc gives acute hearing for prey location. In Australia, the Swamp Harrier engages in spectacular diving displays above the chosen breeding site — a platform trampled in long grass, crops or swampland.

The Swamp Harrier's nest is a platform in long grass, crops or swamplands.

Sometimes the species is polygamous; invariably it is very sensitive to nest disturbance. After breeding, many Tasmanian Swamp Harriers migrate to the mainland. Spotted Harriers are the world's only tree-nesting harriers. A nomadic bird, they are monogamous, defending large, exclusive territories. Females do most nest building, incubation and guarding of the young; males hunt. Females hunt again after chicks reach two weeks old.

Reading

Badman, F. J. & Debus, S. J. (1987), 'Field identification of the Black-breasted Buzzard and Square-tailed Kite', *Aust. Bird Watcher* **12** (4), 112-17.

Cupper, J. & Cupper, L. (1981), *Hawks in Focus*, Jaclin Enterprises, Mildura, Australia.

Czechura, G. V., Debus, S. J. S. & Mooney, N. J. (1987), 'The Collared Sparrowhawk *Accipiter cirrhocephalus*: a review and comparison with the Brown Goshawk *Accipiter fasciatus*', *Aust. Bird Watcher* **12** (2), 35-62.

Debus, S. J. S. (1991), 'The Square-tailed Kite *Lophoictinia isura* in South Australia', *Sth Aust. Ornithologist* **31**, 57-71.

Debus, S. J. S. & Czechura, G. V. (1988a), 'Field identification of the Red Goshawk *Erythrotriorchis radiatus*', *Aust. Bird Watcher* **12** (5), 154-9.

Debus, S. J. S. & Czechura, G. V. (1988b), 'The Red Goshawk *Erythrotriorchis radiatus*: a review', *Aust. Bird Watcher* **12** (6), 175-99.

Hollands, D. (1984), *Eagles, Hawks and Falcons of Australia*, Thomas Nelson Australia, Melbourne.

Weick, F., et al. (1980), *Birds of Prey of the World*, A Coloured Guide to Identification of all the Diurnal Species, Order Falconiformes, Verlag Paul Parey, Hamburg and Berlin.

The owl-like facial disc of the Spotted Harrier assists hearing and thus prey location.

Breeding seasons

	J	F	M	A	M	J	J	A	S	O	N	D
154 Spotted Harrier												
155 Swamp Harrier												

Falcons

Family Falconidae

Falcons are powerful birds with long, narrow, pointed wings and fairly short tails. Unlike the Accipitridae, they *lack* a spasmodic clutching foot mechanism; prey is generally killed by severing the neck vertebrae with a bite. To this end they have powerful bills, with a tomial tooth in the upper mandible and a corresponding notch below.

The family has one genus in Australia, *Falco*, and six species: Black Falcon, Peregrine Falcon, Australian Hobby, Brown Falcon, Australian Kestrel (the smallest), and the rare arid-zone species, Grey Falcon. While Black, Grey and Brown Falcons prey on birds and mammals, the Peregrines and Australian Hobby seem to rely more completely on birds and insects, often taken in spectacular stoops or by rapid pursuit. Australian Kestrels hover or perch in search of ground-dwelling small vertebrates and insects.

Peregrine Falcons have powerful bills with tomial teeth in the upper mandible and corresponding notches below.

Falcons generally nest on cliff ledges, in tree hollows or in disused stick nests of other species. Peregrines and Kestrels sometimes nest on ledges of city high-rise buildings, although not always successfully. No reliable published reports exist to indicate that any of the Australian falcons build their own nests, despite assertions to the contrary. Falcons are among birds most severely affected by pesticides. DDT affects the shell gland, causing egg-shell thinning, leading to breakages and therefore lowered reproductive success. Falcon populations may serve as environmental-quality guides or indicators.

Reading

Cade, T. J. (1982), *The Falcons of the World*, William Collins Sons, London.

Czechura, G. V. & Debus, S. J. S. (1986), 'The Australian Hobby *Falco longipennis*: a review', *Australian Bird Watcher* 11 (6), 185-207.

Metcalf, E. C., (1989), 'The breeding biology of the Australian Hobby', *Australian Bird Watcher* 13 (1), 20-9.

Paull, D. (1991), 'Foraging and breeding behaviour of the Australian Kestrel *Falco cenchroides* on the Northern Tablelands of New South Wales', *Australian Bird Watcher* 14 (3), 85-92.

See also: Cupper & Cupper (1981); Hollands (1984); Weick et al. (1980) in Reading about Accipitrinae.

Breeding seasons

J	F	M	A	M	J	J	A	S	O	N	D

157   Black Falcon

158   Peregrine Falcon

159   Australian Hobby

160   Grey Falcon

161   Brown Falcon

162   Australian Kestrel

Magpie Goose   Family Anseranatidae

[Both Sibley & Ahlquist and Marchant & Higgins, co-ordinators of the comprehensive work on Australian birds for Oxford University Press, accept the very different characters of the Magpie Goose as worthy of a family of its own. The taxonomic position of Sibley & Ahlquist is: 'Order Anseriformes, being then divided into two Infraorders. The first, Anhimides, has two superfamilies: Anhimoidea contains Family Anhimidae — the screamers of South America; Anseranatoidea contains only the Magpie Goose.]

The Magpie Goose is a waterfowl of course, and the general remarks under Family Anatidae below concerning waterfowl requirements and conservation apply also to this unusual genus and species. The Magpie Goose moults its flight feathers sequentially, so that flight is never lost. Other waterfowl have a total wingmoult; thus for them a vulnerable period ensues (usually soon after breeding) of six to eight weeks in swans and three to four weeks in ducks.

This goose of the far north plains and swamps of Australia and of southern New Guinea was more widely distributed before 1900. Breeding colonies existed as far south as Westernport Bay, Victoria, and Bool Lagoon, South Australia. In NSW it occurred on the Lachlan and Murrumbidgee Rivers. By 1911 it had disappeared from the southern parts of its range.

Magpie Geese have a semi-palmated foot, a knob on the crown, which is very distinctive in the field, and a hooked bill. Inside the neck there is a peculiarly looped windpipe. Both sexes incubate the eggs and sometimes pairs of females accompany one male, sharing both nest duties and care of young.

The Magpie Goose has a semi-palmated (partly webbed) foot.

Breeding season (*variable*)

J	F	M	A	M	J	J	A	S	O	N	D

115   Magpie Goose

Ducks and allies   Family Anatidae

[Sibley & Ahlquist have two families and four subfamilies in their Infraorder Anserides of the Order Anseriformes. Family Dendrocygnidae contains only the Whistling-Ducks. Family Anatidae is divided into Subfamily Oxyurinae (stiff-tailed ducks, which are the Blue-billed and Musk ducks), Subfamily Stictonettinae (Freckled Duck), Subfamily Cygninae (swans) and Subfamily Anatinae. This last is divided into two tribes, Anserini (geese), and Anatini (typical ducks).]

Closely associated with water, most waterfowl possess webbed feet, dense waterproof plumage, and usually rather broad, flat bills with lamellae (a fine series of grooves) that act as sieves or gripping surfaces for feeding. Waterfowl also display great diversity in size (35-cm-long pygmy-geese to the 150-cm Mute Swan). Diverse feeding habitats are utilised. Some are mainly terrestrial, grazing on open plains or in shallow billabongs, others utilise rivers, deep lakes, coastal estuaries and the seashore.

Courtship displays vary in Anatidae, ranging from simple 'haughty' posturing in geese to elaborate animated displays by brightly coloured male dabbling ducks. Geese and swans usually mate for life; ducks take a new partner every year.

Waterfowl nest in many habitats, from isolated rocky islands to swamps, among crops, in Arctic tundras and in flooded woodlands. Nests can be on the ground, or high in tree hollows, varying from basic scrapes lined with down (ducks) to large bulky nests of vegetation (swans). Typical clutch sizes are eight or more in ducks, and from five to six in swans. Incubation varies from 21-28 days for stiff-tailed and dabbling ducks, and up to 35-40 days for swans.

All waterfowl have a covering of thick, waterproof down on hatching and may enter the water almost immediately. The fledging period is from 35 days for teal to 100 days for swans. The attainment of nuptial plumage may be at only six months in dabbling ducks. Some species, however, assume an immature plumage after the juvenile stage and do not reach nuptial plumage until 12 months.

Male ducks usually enter an eclipse plumage after breeding, but others (some tropical species) do not.

Southern Hemisphere waterfowl do *not* perform regular seasonal migrations. In Africa and Australia, large, irruptive, nomadic movements occur in some species due to the widely fluctuating water regimes resulting from irregular rainfall patterns over large areas of these continents.

Twelve of the 19 Australian waterfowl species are endemic to Australia and New Guinea. The Mallard and Mute Swan are introductions.

The flight feathers of the Black Swan are moulted simultaneously. This leaves the bird flightless for a short period.

Black Swans at their nest.

Swans — Subfamily Cygninae

Black Swans are numerous in southern Australia, and have been introduced to New Zealand, where large numbers now occur.

Breeding seasons (*variable*)

	J	F	M	A	M	J	J	A	S	O	N	D
118 Black Swan*												
119 Mute Swan*												

Whistling-Ducks — Subfamily Dendrocygninae

[Marchant & Higgins place the whistling-ducks in the subfamily named above. Sibley & Ahlquist erect a Family Dendrocygnidae for them.]

These differ from true ducks by being monomorphic (sexes the same colour) and have long legs and necks. Both sexes incubate, the calls are whistles as distinct from 'quacks', they dive for food, and there is mutual preening within a pair.

Breeding seasons (*variable*)

	J	F	M	A	M	J	J	A	S	O	N	D
116 Wandering Whistling-Duck												
117 Plumed Whistling-Duck*												

Geese and Ducks — Subfamily Anatinae

It appears there may be no true geese — Tribe Anserini — endemic to Australia.

The typical ducks fall into the Tribe Anatini. Notes on some of the most interesting endemics follow.

Cape Barren Goose The taxonomy of this strange goose is still confused. Some taxonomists have suggested a relationship to the South American Kelp Goose *Chloephaga*. Others placed it tentatively with the shelducks Tadornini. Affinities with *both* true geese and shelducks are acknowledged and it is sometimes placed in its own Tribe Cereopsini.

Freckled Duck   This primitive species is considered to be related to the swans due to the similar plumages, swan-like voice, simple courtship display and grey, downy young. An inhabitant of large, permanent inland cumbungi swamps and dense coastal tea-tree swamps; nomadic during droughts, sometimes occurs in large numbers near the coast.

Chestnut Teal   This species is less common than the Grey Teal and more coastal in distribution. Its population has probably declined since European occupation due to the elimination of its optimum habitat, thought to have been brackish tea-tree swamps. It readily uses nest boxes for breeding, but it is questionable whether this truly benefits the species. Courting males perform attractive communal 'whistling' and also 'burp-whistling' displays. Males have a drab winter (eclipse) plumage.

Pink-eared Duck   This aberrant member of the Anatini is well-suited to Australian conditions, utilising extensive, shallow, temporary, inland floodwater pools at any time of the year. The highly specialised bill is fringed with very fine lamellae to filter out microscopic plants and animals, which comprise the bulk of the species' diet.

Reading

Corrick, A. (1982), 'Records of Freckled Duck in Victoria from Dec. 1980 to July 1981 and of the number shot on opening day of the 1981 duck season', *Aust. Bird Watcher* **9**, 260-8.

Frith, H. J. (1982), *Waterfowl in Australia*, Angus & Robertson, Sydney.

Fullagar, P. (1982), 'Freckled Duck', *Australian Natural History* **22** (10), 472-3.

Kingsford, Richard (1991), *Australian Waterbirds, a Field Guide*, Kangaroo Press, Kenthurst.

Marchant, S. & Higgins, P. J. (co-ordinators) (1990), *Handbook of Australian, New Zealand and Antarctic Birds*, Volume 1, Ratites to Ducks, Part B: Australian Pelican to Ducks, Oxford University Press, Melbourne, (pp. 1112-363).

National Photographic Index of Australian Wildlife (1985), *The Waterbirds of Australia*, Angus & Robertson, Sydney.

Courting Chestnut Teal males (bottom) attract a female (top) with their communal whistling displays.

Breeding seasons (*variable*)

J F M A M J J A S O N D

- 120 Freckled Duck*
- 121 Cape Barren Goose
- 122 Australian Shelduck
- 123 Radjah Shelduck
- 124 Pacific Black Duck*
- 125 Mallard
- 126 Grey Teal*
- 127 Chestnut Teal*
- 128 Australasian Shoveler*
- 131 Pink-eared Duck*
- 132 Hardhead
- 133 Maned Duck*
- 134 Cotton Pygmy-Goose
- 135 Green Pygmy-Goose

Stiff-tailed Ducks   Subfamily Oxyurinae

The Musk Duck is named for the musky odour of the males, resulting from secretions of the uropygial gland (a small oil gland at the tail base). The strange lobe of the male's throat varies in size with age and sexual activity. When breeding, the lobe is engorged with blood and is part of the bird's bizarre splashing courtship display.

Breeding seasons (*variable*)

J F M A M J J A S O N D

- 136 Blue-billed Duck*
- 137 Musk Duck*

Mound-builders (Megapodes)   Family Megapodiidae

[Sibley & Ahlquist place the megapodes early in the evolution of birds, in the Infraclass Neoaves, Parvclass Galloanserae, Superorder Gallomorphae and Order Craciformes. This has two suborders. One, the Craci, contains a group of birds including the curassows; the other, Megapodii, contains the traditional Family Megapodiidae.]

Megapodes are considered to be most closely related to pheasants (Phasianidae). These big-footed birds scratch and pile sand, soil and vegetation litter into a large mound. Their eggs are laid in tiers in a deep hole in the mound's top. A combination of the sun's direct heat and the heat generated by the composting litter incubates the eggs. In some areas of New Guinea and some W Pacific islands, incubation of the local Scrubfowl's eggs is assisted by volcanic heat.

A diagrammatic cut-away of a Malleefowl mound showing the egg chamber and leaf litter.

Mated for life, a pair inhabits a large territory. Normally only one of the pair operates the mound; the Scrubfowl is an occasional exception. Males usually manage the mound and control the incubating temperature. The Malleefowl is able to maintain total temperature control; the Australian Brush-turkey and Scrubfowl have less control.

The chicks are quite independent. They dig their own way out of the mound and fly within hours of surfacing. Apart from humans, mound and chick predators include goannas, pythons, carnivorous marsupials and introduced pigs and foxes.

If pressed, megapodes fly well but heavily. They usually roost in trees. All are omnivorous. The Scrubfowl is widespread from the Philippines across to New Guinea, Australia and Western Pacific islands. The other species are local endemics. Plumage colours suit their varied habitats quite closely. The jungle-dwelling Australian Brush-turkey is very dark; the Scrubfowl is medium-brown and lives in a range of dense to lightly vegetated, sometimes rocky, terrains. In the open scrubby country of inland Australia, Malleefowls are camouflaged; the black chest line breaks up the bird's outline and colour pattern as it stands quietly among small mallee, eucalypt boughs and litter.

Fossil skeletal elements of a very much larger megapode (*Progrura gallinacea*) have been found in Pleistocene deposits of south-east Queensland.

Reading

Frith, H. J. (1962), *The Malleefowl*, Angus & Robertson, Sydney.
Stone, T. (1991), 'Megapode mounds and archaeology in northern Australia', *Emu* **91** (4), 255-6.

Megapode hatchlings

Australian Brush-turkey

Malleefowl

Orange-footed Scrubfowl

Breeding seasons

	J	F	M	A	M	J	J	A	S	O	N	D
163 Orange-footed Scrubfowl												
164 Malleefowl												
165 Australian Brush-turkey												

Pheasants and allies — Family Phasianidae

[Sibley & Ahlquist continue their classification of the gallinaceous birds with the Order Galliformes and two parvorders. Parvorder Phasianida contains two superfamilies: the Phasianoidea, with Family Phasianidae, the pheasants, grouse and Old World quail; and Numidoidea, with Family Numididae, the guineafowls. The other parvorder, Odontophorida, contains Family Odontophoridae, the New World quails.]

Two subfamilies occur in Australia: Phasianinae, the native quails and introduced pheasants, and Odontophorinae, the introduced California Quail. All introduced species are rare, or confined to islands.

Pheasants and quails are dumpy ground birds with long necks, small heads, short bills, strong legs and feet. Quails have short tails. Pheasants are large, with long tails that are often decoratively coloured.

Native quails are fairly nomadic, wandering wherever conditions are suitable and breeding in large numbers in some seasons. The Stubble Quail prefers open grassy areas; the King Quail prefers rank grasslands, often near swamps; the Brown Quail occurs in grassy regions near forests and bracken. Quails hide in grass until nearly walked upon, then flush with a rapid whirring flight, low to the ground.

Nests are simple, located on the ground under bushes or grass; 4-11 eggs are laid. They are pale in colour and dark-spotted. At times, open hunting seasons on these birds are declared. Helmeted Guineafowls, from Africa, have been introduced to a few Great Barrier Reef islands and are feral.

Reading

Delacour, J. (1977), *The Pheasants of the World*, 2nd edition, Spur Publications and World Pheasant Association, Hindhead, U.K.

Breeding seasons (*variable*)

	J	F	M	A	M	J	J	A	S	O	N	D
166 Stubble Quail												
167, 168 Swamp and Brown Quails*												
169 King Quail												
170 Peafowl												
171 Feral Chicken*												
172 Common Pheasant (*Insufficient information*)												
173 California Quail												

Button-quails (Hemipodes)　　　Family Turnicidae

[Sibley & Ahlquist recognise this family as a group with no known or close living relatives. Previously placed in the Gruiformes, it appears they may represent a distinct and now isolated group of birds, with its own Parvclass Turnicae, Order Turniciformes and family as above. More research needs to be done.]

The button-quails used to be allied to the Plains-wanderer (p. 315), but no longer are. Most button-quail species prefer to live in grassland and appear to be nomadic. The first indication of their presence comes as they 'explode' from near an observer's feet. Button-quails feed on seeds and insects. Females lay about four eggs in a cup-shaped ground nest near a tussock or shrub. Males incubate the eggs for about 14 days and care for the young.

Two species are particularly rare. Habitat clearance has diminished the Black-breasted's numbers. The Buff-breasted Button-quail is locally restricted and rarely reported.

Reading

Sibley, C. G., Ahlquist, J. E. & Monroe, B. L., Jr (1988), 'A classification of the living birds of the world based on DNA-DNA hybridization studies', *Auk* **105**, 409-23.

Squire, J. E. (1990), 'Some southern records of the Buff-breasted Button-quail *Turnix olivei*', *Aust. Bird Watcher* **13**, 149-52.

Breeding seasons (*variable*)

J	F	M	A	M	J	J	A	S	O	N	D

174　Red-backed Button-quail*
175　Painted Button-quail
176　Chestnut-backed Button-quail
177　Buff-breasted Button-quail
178　Black-breasted Button-quail
179　Little Button-quail*
180　Red-chested Button-quail*

Cranes　　　Family Gruidae

[Sibley & Ahlquist divide the Order Gruiformes into three suborders. They place the Suborder Otididi (bustards) first, but we have not done so in this section of the book.

The Suborder Grui contains Superfamily Gruidodea in which there are two families. The traditional Family Gruidae contains Subfamily Balearicinae, the crowned-cranes of Africa, and the Subfamily Gruinae, the 'typical' cranes of the Holarctic region, and Africa to Australia, within which the Sarus Crane and Brolga are included.]

Fossil cranes date back 40-60 million years. Four of the world's 15 modern and widespread species are endangered.

The Sarus Crane of India and Asia has two races but only the race *sharpei* occurs in Australia. It has naturally colonised Australia, first being recorded in Queensland in 1967, and has established breeding populations.

Brolgas and Sarus Cranes are alike in behaviour and biology. Their food includes insects, fresh- and salt-water invertebrates, small vertebrates and plants. Bulkuru sedge *Eleocharis dulcis* is a preferred Brolga food. Brolgas are considered non-migratory but move long distances for food and water. Both cranes are monogamous, probably forming life pairs, and breeding at traditional sites during each year's wettest months. A drought may halt breeding.

Nests are of coarse grass, sticks and leaves, usually formed into a raised mound, either above water, or on dry land. One to three (usually two) eggs are laid. Both sexes incubate for a total of 29-32 days. Brolga hatchlings are grey, Sarus Crane hatchlings tawny. They can run and swim hours after emerging but are fed by their parents. Families may persist for up to ten months.

Reading

Walkinshaw, L. H. (1973), *The Cranes of the World*, Winchester Press, New York.

An incubating Brolga on a raised nest.

Breeding seasons (*variable*)

J	F	M	A	M	J	J	A	S	O	N	D

199　Brolga*
200　Sarus Crane*

Rails, Gallinules, Coots
Family Rallidae

[Sibley & Ahlquist indicate that within the Order Gruiformes, Sub-order Ralli forms a distinct cluster apart from the cranes and their allies. They recognise at present only the rails, gallinules and coots in this suborder, for the material studied in this group is less than complete, and some associations remain to be examined. The DNA evidence supports skeletal evidence that the New Zealand Takahe *Notornis* is congeneric with *Porphyrio*, the swamphens of Australia and New Zealand.]

The rails, gallinules (swamphens, moorhens) and coots are a large cosmopolitan family of mainly aquatic birds. Sixteen species are represented in Australia, two of them vagrants. Rails superficially resemble fowls, but are unrelated. In Australia they range from sparrow-sized (Baillon's Crake) to rooster-sized (Purple Swamphen). All rails are characterised by: short wings; fairly long powerful legs with unwebbed toes; short tails; general shortness and stoutness of body. Bill shape ranges from long and slender in Lewin's Rail to short (majority of rails) and sometimes stout (Purple Swamphen and its huge New Zealand relative, Notornis or Takahe *Porphyrio mantelli*).

Swamphens, moorhens and coots have large frontal shields (skin extended from the bill onto the frons), but crakes, bush-hens and water-hens range from vestigial frontal shields to none. Coots are characterised by flaps of skin on their toes that help to propel them through water. Manner of flight in rails varies from rapid fluttering, which is like the quails but weaker, to flightlessness in some island forms, for instance Tasmanian Native-hen, Woodhen (*Tricholimnas [Gallirallus] sylvestris*) of Lord Howe Island and, in New Zealand again, Notornis and the Wekas (*Gallirallus* species).

Rails have a characteristic habit of flicking their tail up and down when swimming or walking, especially noticeable in those with white markings on their undertail coverts. The function of this is not well understood. Many rails are notorious for their secretive habits. Except for the coots, moorhens, swamphens and native-hens, which feed in the open much of the time, the rest spend their time in dense vegetation, especially reeds and in associated habitats. The only way to see some species is to wait beside suitable waterside habitat until one appears. Because some species are nocturnal to a degree, spotlighting may help under some situations, but care must be taken not to panic other diurnal waterfowl.

The voice of rails generally consists of harsh, hoarse squeaking, repetitive 'pumping' calls, nasal noises and clicking. Their voices often give away their presence, as each species has a distinctive call. Rail food varies from small invertebrates and vertebrates to plant food. Some species rob other bird nests. Australian rails are nomadic. They build up their numbers in wet years and disperse to the coast and remaining waterholes in dry years. Nests are deep and cup-like, well lined with fibrous material. Except for the coots, which have large floating nests anchored to reeds or nests built on tops of bushes standing in water, nests are usually well-concealed in thick vegetation. Egg clutches vary from three to 10. When hatched, nestlings are downy, often have colourful heads and soon can walk, then run. Coots and moorhen hatchlings can swim from their first day.

Reading
Ripley, S. D. (1977), *Rails of the World*, David R. Godine, Boston, Mass., USA.

Purple Swamphen
Dusky Moorhen
Red-necked Crake
Australian Crake
Spotless Crake
Lewin's Rail

The size and shape of bills and frontal shields varies in the Family Rallidae.

Breeding seasons (*variable*)

	J	F	M	A	M	J	J	A	S	O	N	D
182 Buff-banded Rail*												
183 Lewin's Rail												
184 Chestnut Rail												

Breeding seasons (*variable*)

	J	F	M	A	M	J	J	A	S	O	N	D
186 Red-necked Crake												
188 Baillon's Crake*												
189 Australian Crake												
190 Spotless Crake												
191 White-browed Crake												
192 Bush-hen												
193 Tasmanian Native-hen												
194 Black-tailed Native-hen*												
195 Dusky Moorhen*												
196 Purple Swamphen*												
197 Eurasian Coot*												

Bustards
Family Otididae

[Sibley & Ahlquist place the Otididae in Order Gruiformes, ahead of the cranes (our Brolga and Sarus Crane), now considered a sub-family within the Family Gruidae, and the rails, gallinules and coots.]

The 11 genera of Old World bustards are all very similar in appearance and biology. Genus *Ardeotis* occurs in Australia, and it is now believed that we have the very same Kori Bustard as occurs in Africa, Arabia, India and New Guinea.

Nomadic omnivores (insects, small vertebrates, plant material), bustards seek areas abundant in food after rain but can survive long periods without drinking.

The onset of breeding is closely allied to the amount and intensity of rain and the number of wet days. Bustards are probably polygamous. Only females incubate and care for the young. Males can breed at 5-6 years, females at 2-3 years. One or occasionally two eggs are laid in a ground scrape and incubated for 23-24 days. Young are precocial.

Bustards were killed in thousands until fully protected in 1935. Foxes and habitat destruction reduced their range to northern monsoonal Australia where heavy rains prevent human access during breeding. Population recovery is slow. A rehabilitation programme operates in Victoria.

When courting, the male Australian Bustard inflates its throat sac and gives roaring calls.

Reading
Frith, H. J. (1986), 'Kori Bustard', *Reader's Digest Complete Book of Australian Birds*, Reader's Digest Services, Surry Hills, NSW (see p. 183).

Breeding season (*variable)

J	F	M	A	M	J	J	A	S	O	N	D

198 Kori Bustard*

Waders (Shorebirds)

[Sibley & Ahlquist indicate that Order Ciconiiformes is enormous, and includes large suborders. The first, Charadrii, includes all the waders or shorebirds, through to the gulls and terns, and also the auks, murres, puffins and guillemots of the Northern Hemisphere. The position of each family is outlined in the pages following. The second large suborder is the Ciconii, discussed earlier.]

Reading
Coates, B. J. (1985), *The Birds of New Guinea*, Vol. I, *Non-Passerines*, Dove Publications Pty Ltd, Alderly, Queensland.

Hayman, P., Marchant, J. & Prater, T. (1986), *Shorebirds: an identification guide to the waders of the world*, Christopher Helm Ltd, Bromley, UK.

Johnsgard, P. A. (1981), *The Plovers, Sandpipers and Snipes of the World*, University of Nebraska Press, Lincoln, Nebraska, USA and London.

Lane, B. A. & Davies, J. (1987), *Shorebirds in Australia*, Thomas Nelson Australia, Melbourne.

Prater, T. & Marchant, J. (1977), *Guide to the Identification and Ageing of Holarctic Waders*, British Trust for Ornithology Field Guide **17**, BTO, Tring, Hertfordshire, UK.

Pringle, J. D. & The National Photographic Index of Australian Wildlife (1987), *The Shorebirds of Australia*, Angus & Robertson, North Ryde, NSW.

Schodde, R. & Tidemann, S. C. (editors) (1986), *The Reader's Digest Complete Book of Australian Birds*, 2nd edition, Reader's Digest Services Pty Ltd, Sydney.

Soothill, E. & Soothill, R. (1989), *Wading Birds of the World*, 2nd edition, Blandford Press, Cassells, London.

A mixed flock of waders roosting at high tide. The flock includes Grey-tailed Tattlers, Bar-tailed Godwits, Terek Sandpipers, Eastern Curlews and Whimbrels (sleeping).

Jacanas
Family Jacanidae

[Sibley & Ahlquist have determined that the jacanas are fairly, but not *very*, closely related to the Painted Snipe. They place them in Super-family Jacanoidea next to Superfamily Scolopacoidea (which contains the families of seedsnipe, Plains-wanderer, snipe, sandpipers and their allies), and retain the traditional Family Jacanidae.]

Jacanas *appear* more akin to rails (Rallidae) than waders. Until recently they were considered an early wader development. In Australia, they are often called lily-trotters or lotusbirds.

They occur in tropical or sub-tropical areas of South America, Africa, India, South-east Asia and Australia. Our resident species is possibly locally nomadic or migratory. The Pheasant-tailed Jacana, of South-east Asia, *may* eventually be confirmed for Australia — unreliable records exist.

Jacanas have small spurs on their wings. Their heads bob back and forth as they walk over floating vegetation. In flight, their long legs and toes trail. They have 10 tail feathers. They nest during rainy/monsoon periods on a damp pile of floating herbage. Small chicks are sometimes carried under the wings of an adult, as they move about the aquatic vegetation.

Breeding season (*variable*)

| J | F | M | A | M | J | J | A | S | O | N | D |

201 Comb-crested Jacana*

Painted Snipe   Family Rostratulidae

[Sibley & Ahlquist found that the Painted Snipe is fairly, but not *very*, closely related to the jacanas. They position it in Superfamily Jacanoidea, next to the Superfamily Scolopacoidea and they retain the traditional Family Rostratulidae.]

Family Rostratulidae has two genera, each with one species. One genus (*Nycticryphes*) and its species is South American; the other occurs through central and southern Africa, and southern Asia, to China, Japan and Australia. The local breeding race seems non-migratory but nomadic. It is mainly crepuscular and difficult to find. Birds favour broad shallow swamps; these are becoming less common as settlement proceeds.

Males incubate eggs and care for young, and so are smaller and less brightly coloured than females. The oesophagus is enlarged into a crop-like organ for food storage, and the birds have 14 tail feathers.

Reading

Lowe, V. J. (1963), 'Observations on the Painted Snipe', *Emu* **62**, 221-37.

Breeding season (*variable*)

| J | F | M | A | M | J | J | A | S | O | N | D |

205 Painted Snipe*

Plains-wanderer   Family Pedionomidae

[Sibley & Ahlquist, like Olson & Steadman (1981) (below), have determined that the Plains-wanderer is a wader. Thus these two recent studies bear each other out, although totally different means, DNA hybridisation and skeletal comparisons, were used.

Within the large Order Ciconiiformes of Sibley & Ahlquist, the sandpipers are included under Infraorder Charadriides, Parvorder Scolopacida and Superfamily Scolopacoidea. This superfamily includes three families: the Thincoridae (American seedsnipes), Pedionomidae (Plains-wanderer) and Scolpacidae (the snipe, sandpipers, godwits, curlews and phalaropes). A second superfamily in the same parvorder contains the Rostratulidae (Painted Snipe) and Jacanidae (jacanas). Thus, the Plains-wanderer is now considered to have its greatest affinities with the seedsnipes, and the sandpipers and their allies.]

Following Olson & Steadman's new evidence (1981), based on skeletal comparisons, it became necessary to remove this monotypic family from its former proximity to the Button-quails (Turnicidae) to a position 'in amongst' the order comprising the waders (Charadriiformes). Where should it be placed? Olson & Steadman recommend that 'in any sequential listing, it should precede the American seedsnipes (Thinocoridae)'. Their study compared the osteology, the skeletal structure, of the Plains-wanderer with button-quails and with members of the waders. Differences showed up in bones, muscles and the presence of a hind toe. Other differences are in the shape of the eggs and flight mannerisms. The Plains-wanderer's flight is weak and fluttering, more like that of an immature song-lark than the fast, whirring wing-beats of a quail.

The Plains-wanderer is a cryptically coloured, upright little bird that will 'freeze' or run rather than fly. The bird runs erect and has a wide range of vision, covering close to 360°. Its foot-scent is readily followed by a trained gun-dog, and always follows a meandering course in the grassland of its plains or sheep paddock habitat. Introduced grasses, clearing and grazing have almost certainly had a deleterious effect on its populations, which are more restricted than 30 years ago. There are few recent reports of the species in southern Victoria, a former stronghold, but it remains relatively plentiful in some Riverina grasslands of NSW; perhaps less so in northern central Victoria. Early concern was expressed (D'Ombrain, 1926), and continues today.

Although said to be nomadic, it remains in a limited area of grasslands for most of the year, and appears to lose or suppress its body- and foot-scent, as do quail, during the breeding season. The nest is a ground scrape, lined with grass, and the four eggs are pale green-buff, blotched and spotted with brown, grey and olive. The smaller, more cryptically coloured male incubates the eggs and cares for the young.

Reading

Baker-Gabb, D. J. (1990), 'An annotated list of records of Plains-wanderers *Pedionomus torquatus*, 1980-89', *Aust. Bird Watcher* **13** (8), 249-52.

Bennett, S. (1983), 'A review of the distribution, status and biology of the Plains-wanderer *Pedionomus torquatus*, Gould', *Emu* **83** (1), 1-11.

Crome, F. H. J. & Rushton, D. K. (1975), 'Development of the plumage in the Plains-wanderer', *Emu* **75** (4), 181-4.

D'Ombrain, E. A. (1926), 'The vanishing Plains-wanderer', *Emu* **26** (1), 59-63.

Olson, S. L. & Steadman, D. W. (1981), 'The relationships of the Pedionomidae (Aves: Charadriiformes)', *Smithson. Contribut. to Zool.* no. **337**, 1-15.

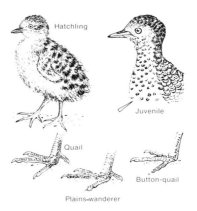

The Plains-wanderer resembles button-quails in appearance and in that the female is the brighter and dominant bird, but it has a hind toe like true quails.

Breeding season

J	F	M	A	M	J	J	A	S	O	N	D

181 Plains-wanderer

Oystercatchers   Family Haematopodidae

[Sibley & Ahlquist place the oystercatchers, and the avocets and stilts, in Tribe Haematopodini and Recurvirostrini respectively, under a common Subfamily Recurvirostrinae, within Family Charadriidae. A second subfamily, Charadriinae, the plovers and dotterels (see p. 317-18), is also included. The Charadriidae, together with the traditional Family Burhinidae (thick-knees and stone curlews), form a superfamily, the Charadriodea, the 'plover-like birds'.]

Oystercatchers are non-migratory but locally nomadic. The Pied is a local race of a world-wide species, including New Zealand; the Sooty is an endemic Australian species of rocky coastlines. The Pied is common, the Sooty less so.

Their food is obtained by cutting the adductor muscles of bivalve mollusc shells, by prising limpets and other gastropods from rocks, or by dismembering crustaceans.

Oystercatchers are social, possibly due to a relatively long period before maturity and pair formation. Pair bonds may persist over a long period. Some interbreeding occurs, producing hybrid offspring with variable mixtures of characters, but these birds may be infertile.

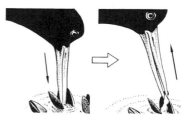

The feeding technique of Oystercatchers is shown here.

Breeding seasons (*variable*)

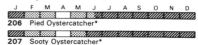

J	F	M	A	M	J	J	A	S	O	N	D

206 Pied Oystercatcher*

207 Sooty Oystercatcher*

Stilts and Avocets

Family Recurvirostridae

Stilts and avocets (like oystercatchers) probably evolved from a common plover-like stock. Australia is the only country with three species, all nomadic. The Black-winged Stilt ranges world-wide; the Banded Stilt and Red-necked Avocet are endemic Australian species. Black-winged Stilts are fairly common in suitable habitats and are vagrants to Tasmania. The Banded Stilt is more restricted to parts of the west and south-west of Western Australia, across to South Australia and Victoria, occasionally in New South Wales. Avocets are fairly common in suitable areas but are sparse in eastern Victoria, northern Queensland to Cape York Peninsula, and northern Northern Territory.

The front toes of stilts are partly *or* fully webbed; they are *always* fully webbed in avocets. The Banded Stilt, unlike other stilt species, can swim but feeds in a pecking, stilt-like manner when wading. Avocets mostly feed by sweeping with their bills. Occasionally they swim, up-ending like ducks, for food.

Reading

Phillips, H. (1990), 'A tale of three species: the stilt, the shrimp and the scientist . . .', *Australian Natural History* **23** (4), 322-9.

Breeding seasons (*variable)

	J	F	M	A	M	J	J	A	S	O	N	D
225 Black-winged Stilt*												
226 Banded Stilt*												
227 Red-necked Avocet*												

Thick-knees (Stone Curlews)

Family Burhinidae

Two sedentary species occur in Australia. The Bush Thick-knee is not uncommon in temperate and tropical mainland Australia, especially in the north, but is becoming rare in settled southern areas. The Beach Thick-knee is uncommon but widespread in the tropics. They are largely crepuscular and nocturnal in habit.

Reading

Anderson, G. J. (1991), 'The breeding biology of the Bush Thick-knee *Burhinus magnirostris* and notes on its distribution in the Brisbane area', *The Sunbird* **21**, no. 2, 33-61.

Breeding seasons (*variable)

	J	F	M	A	M	J	J	A	S	O	N	D
203 Bush Thick-knee*												
204 Beach Thick-knee												

Lapwings, Plovers, Dotterels

Family Charadriidae

[These species comprise Subfamily Charadriinae of Sibley & Ahlquist.]

Lapwings

Subfamily Vanellinae

Lapwings of the Subfamily Vanellinae are medium-sized, with bills shorter than head length and wing length greater than 15 cm. Two species are local, the Banded and Masked Lapwings. Some of the world's 23 species are migratory but not to Australia.

Banded Lapwings are nomadic, usually occurring in drier lands, preferring areas with little cover. They tend to breed in localised colonies and breeding tends to follow rains. Banded Lapwings are fairly common in suitable habitats, more so in temperate Australia.

Masked Lapwings are common, particularly on cleared grazing lands. Two races occur: one across northern Australia, the 'Masked Plover' of earlier literature; one across southern regions, the 'Spur-winged Plover'. The two races overlap in mid-Queensland where interbreeding occurs. During breeding, solitary pairs are very territorial. At other times non-breeding birds may form large flocks. They are non-migratory but are locally nomadic up to 150 kilometres.

Masked Lapwings will vigorously defend their territory and young.

Breeding seasons (*variable)

	J	F	M	A	M	J	J	A	S	O	N	D
208 Masked Lapwing*												
209 Banded Lapwing*												

Plovers, Dotterels
Subfamily Charadriinae

The name 'dotterel', although previously embracing the smaller plovers in Australia, is now preferred only for the Inland and Red-kneed Dotterels which do not belong to the genera *Pluvialis* (greater plovers) or *Charadrius* (lesser plovers).

Some 38 species of the traditional subfamily breed in various climatic conditions, from Arctic Siberia and North America to the temperate areas of North America, and also in central Asia, South America, South Africa, Australia and New Zealand. Some are found in tropical-subtropical regions of Australia, Africa, central and South America. Generally, the species breeding farthest north, in Arctic areas, then migrate furthest south to escape the northern winter. Those breeding in temperate to tropical areas migrate lesser distances and include some virtually sedentary or only partially nomadic species. Of the 13 species recorded for Australia, five are endemic and eight migrate here regularly or are vagrants.

The Inland Dotterel (formerly 'Australian Dotterel') is uncommon, nomadic and virtually the only species adapted for inland arid areas. The other residents are common, but the Hooded Plover is becoming less so, apparently because its habitats of southern open ocean beaches and grassy dunes are becoming more accessible to humans and there is much disturbance, particularly in the summer breeding period.

The Double-banded Plover, which breeds in New Zealand, is the only known east-west migratory wader species. The other migrant species coming here all breed in the Northern Hemisphere. On arrival, there may be traces of the colourful breeding plumage but this is moulted to a plain wintering (eclipse) plumage. Birds may begin to colour-up again before departure in autumn. Lesser Golden and Grey Plovers are moderately common; the American Golden Plover *Pluvialis apricaria* is *not* confirmed yet for Australia. Of the smaller migrant plovers, only the Oriental, Mongolian and Large Sand Plovers are common, mainly in northern Australia. Ringed Plovers are vagrants.

Breeding

Moulting

Non-breeding

Lesser Golden Plover
Puvialis dominica fulva

Many of the migratory plovers have colourful breeding plumage and drab non-breeding plumage. Birds can often be seen with irregular blotches of colour when moulting into or out of their breeding plumage.

Breeding seasons (*variable*)

	J	F	M	A	M	J	J	A	S	O	N	D
213 Red-kneed Dotterel*												
214 Hooded Plover												
222 Red-capped Plover*												
223 Black-fronted Plover*												
224 Inland Dotterel*												

Curlews, Godwits, Snipe, Sandpipers and allies
Family Scolopacidae

[Sibley & Ahlquist place the snipe in Subfamily Scolopacinae, the curlews, godwits and sandpipers in Subfamily Tringinae of Family Scolopacidae — one of several families in Superfamily Scolopacoidea.]

This is the largest wader family. Its species mostly breed in northern temperate to Arctic areas. Those migrating to Australia tend to breed in north-eastern Siberia and Alaska rather than western Siberia or Canada. They vary in size from the world's smallest wader, the Red-necked Stint, to the world's largest, the Eastern Curlew. Most are believed to migrate over established species' routes and generally between the same areas each year. Many instances have been recorded of ringed birds being seen in the same locations after one or more overseas migratory flights to breed. Because breeding areas of many different species overlap, there have been occasional Australian sightings of rare vagrant species that normally migrate to Africa or South America.

Juveniles hatch in the northern summer and, arriving from spring to early summer in Australia, do not return to their

Curlew Sandpipers and Red-necked Stints fly in a mixed flock.

breeding areas until they are more than a year old. They either stay for the southern summer or migrate relatively small distances northwards. Usually only juveniles remain in Australia during winter, but very occasionally adults in breeding plumage that may not have put on enough body fat for overseas migration can be seen locally during the southern winter.

Abbreviated notes on the species migrating to Australia from the Palaearctic follow.

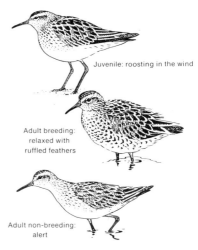

Postures of the Sharp-tailed Sandpiper

Juvenile: roosting in the wind

Adult breeding: relaxed with ruffled feathers

Adult non-breeding: alert

Ruddy Turnstone   Migrates to Southern Hemisphere continents. In Aust. common on our rocky coasts; some overwinter.

Eurasian Curlew   Migrates to Europe and Africa. Very rare vagrant in Aust.

Eastern Curlew   Migrates to Taiwan, Philippines, PNG, Aust. Common in suitable areas, especially NE and SE Aust. coasts.

Whimbrel   Migrates to India, China, SE Asia, and Southern Hemisphere areas. A race breeding in NE Siberia migrates to Aust. where common around N and E coasts.

Little Curlew   Migrates to NZ, PNG, N Aust.; rare in S of Aust.

Upland Sandpiper   Migrates to S America. Rare vagrant to Aust.

Wood Sandpiper   Migrates to S Africa, S Europe, India, SE Asia, S China, Japan, PNG and Aust. Reasonably common in N Aust.; uncommon but regular in S Aust. on or near coasts.

Green Sandpiper   Migrates to Africa, SE Asia. Rare vagrant in Aust.

Grey-tailed Tattler   Migrates to China, Taiwan, Australasia. Common N coast of WA, around to NSW.

Wandering Tattler   Migrates to Pacific coasts of America, Pacific islands, Australasia. Rare.

Common Sandpiper   Migrates to S Europe, Africa, S Asia, and Aust. where fairly common on N and E Aust. coasts.

Greenshank   Migrates to S Africa, S Europe, Persian Gulf, India, SE Asia, E China, and Aust. Common some areas; widespread around our coastline.

Spotted Greenshank   Migrates to SE Asia. Rare vagrant to N Aust.

Redshank   Migrates to Africa, S and SE Asia. Rare, but regular to N Aust. coasts.

Spotted Redshank   Migrates to central Africa, India, SE Asia. Recent sight records in Aust.; one confirmed SE Aust.

Lesser Yellowlegs   Migrates to central and S America. Rare vagrant in S of Aust.

Marsh Sandpiper   Migrates to central Asia, Mongolia, Aust. Regular but less common migrant to Aust.

Terek Sandpiper   Migrates to S Africa, S and SE Asia, Aust. Fairly common to rare here, but widespread.

Latham's (Japanese) Snipe   Migrates to Aust. where fairly common E and SE.

Pin-tailed Snipe   Migrates to S and SE Asia. An uncommon migrant here.

Swinhoe's Snipe   Migrates to India, SE Asia. Uncommon in N Aust.

Asiatic (Asian) Dowitcher   Migrates to India, SE Asia. Very rare migrant to Aust.

Black-tailed Godwit   Race seen here migrates to SE Asia, Aust. Common on coasts of WA and from N Aust. to NSW.

Bar-tailed Godwit   Migrates to China, Japan, Philippines, PNG; common in Aust. except WA.

Hudsonian Godwit   Migrates to central and S America. Rare vagrant in E Aust.

Red Knot   Migrates to America, Africa, S Europe, Asia, Australasia. Fairly common Aust. coastal areas; some overwinter.

Great Knot   Migrates to India, Burma, Aust. More common in N Aust. on the coast; some do overwinter.

Sharp-tailed Sandpiper   Very common; seldom overwinter in Aust.

Pectoral Sandpiper   Migrates to S America. Vagrant elsewhere, including Aust.

Cox's Sandpiper   Source of birds not known. Appears rare in Aust. Dispute exists over identity and variation of characters of this recently recognised and named bird. The possibility it is a hybrid must be considered. We have illustrated it as *Calidris paramelanotus* (p. 107) and await more details. Some Dunlin records have been rescinded; identify also from Pectoral Sandpiper; their behaviours are different. Two or three specimens; more than 30 sightings.

Baird's Sandpiper   Migrates to S America. Accidental vagrant to Aust.

White-rumped Sandpiper   Migrates to central and S America. Rare vagrant to Aust.

Western Sandpiper   Migrates to N and central America. Not confirmed for Aust. Submit any sightings to Records' Appraisal Committee, RAOU.

Little Stint   Migrates to Africa, SE Asia. Uncommon vagrant to Aust.

Red-necked Stint   Migrates to China, Taiwan, Philippines, Australasia. Very common here; many overwinter.

Long-toed Stint   Migrates to China, India, SE Asia. Rare migrant here.

Curlew Sandpiper   Migrates to Africa, Persian Gulf, India, SE Asia, Australasia. Common; some overwinter.

Dunlin   Rarely migrates S of Equator. Very rare in Aust. Some supposed records of the Dunlin prior to 1981 have been voluntarily rescinded (see Cox's Sandpiper).

Sanderling   Migrates to N and S America, Europe, Africa, India, China, Australasia. Widespread in coastal areas here, especially in N Aust.

Buff-breasted Sandpiper   Migrates to S America. Uncommon vagrant in Aust.

Broad-billed Sandpiper   Migrates to S Europe, India, China, SE Asia, Aust. — a few reach Aust. annually.

Ruff (Reeve)   Migrates to UK, S Europe, S India, SE Asia. Rare but possibly regular migrant to Aust.

Stilt Sandpiper   Migrates to central and S America. Rare vagrant in Aust.

Reading

Hayman, P., Marchant, J. & Prater, T. (1986), *Shorebirds: an identification guide to the waders of the world*, Christopher Helm Ltd, Bromley, UK (see pp. 311-87).

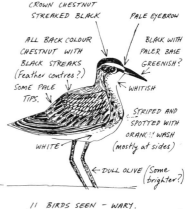

SNAPPER POINT, PORT ADELAIDE.
15/10/83   Light overcast.

CROWN CHESTNUT STREAKED BLACK

PALE EYEBROW

ALL BACK COLOUR CHESTNUT WITH BLACK STREAKS (Feather centres?)

BLACK WITH PALER BASE GREENISH?

SOME PALE TIPS.

WHITISH

WHITE

STRIPED AND SPOTTED WITH ORANGE WASH (mostly at sides)

DULL OLIVE (Some brighter?)

11 BIRDS SEEN — WARY.
(SOME MORE CHESTNUT THAN OTHERS)
IN FLIGHT { PALE WING STRIPE / BLACK STRIPE ON PALE RUMP

One page from a bird observer's notebook.

Phalaropes   Family Phalaropodidae

[Sibley & Ahlquist include the phalaropes in the wader Subfamily Tringinae, of Family Scolopacidae. Thus the traditional Family Phalaropodidae is removed from their classification.]

Phalaropes are small sandpiper-like waders with long necks, long legs and thin, sharp, straight bills. Their toes are not webbed but lobed. They turn in circles ('spin') whilst feeding.

Red-necked Phalaropes breed in most circumpolar Arctic areas and in northern Canada. They migrate mostly to the tropical coasts of the Pacific Ocean and Persian Gulf. Vagrants are occasionally seen in Australia, less often in New Zealand and at widely spread locations, on lakes or at sea.

Grey Phalaropes breed in arctic Siberia and North America. They migrate to the southern oceans, mainly the SE Pacific and southern Atlantic, where they remain at sea, their habit being pelagic. Extremely rare vagrant in Australia.

Wilson's Phalarope breeds in western Canada and northwest USA, normally migrating to coastal and inland waters of South America. Vagrants are occasionally seen in Australia at widely scattered locations, on lakes or at sea.

The Red-necked Phalarope spins around in circles when feeding (below). The lobed foot of the Red-necked Phalarope (above).

Pratincoles   Family Glareolidae

[Sibley & Ahlquist retain the traditional Family Glareolidae, with its two subfamilies: Dromadinae, the Crab Plover of East Africa and some Indian Ocean islands; and Glareolinae, the coursers of the Afro-Indian region and the pratincoles.

However, the fascinating news is that the Glareolidae moves into the Superfamily Laroidea; its other family is the Laridae, which comprises the gulls, skuas, jaegers, terns, skimmers, as well as the Northern Hemisphere Subfamily Alcinae, the auks, murres, puffins and guillemots.]

Pratincoles have usually been considered aberrant waders of drier areas. But sometimes they were *not* included with waders because their evolutionary relationships were uncertain. They fly like terns, feeding on insects caught on the wing or from the ground. The work summarised in Sibley & Ahlquist (1990) now seems to have finally settled their evolutionary background as allies of the gull/tern complex and their tern-like flight is explained.

The Oriental Pratincole breeds in central and southern Asia, migrating to the Philippines, Sunda Island and Australia. It is common in the north during October-May; rare in the south.

The partly migratory, partly nomadic Australian Pratincole has long legs, long wings and a short tail, something like the coursers (*Cursorius*) of the same Family Glareolidae. It behaves more like a courser than a pratincole. Sporadic breeding occurs in inland Australia from the Kimberley of Western Australia to northern Queensland and south to South Australia, Victoria and western New South Wales. In the winter dry season, it visits Australian northern coasts, also Indonesia and Papua New Guinea. From October to March it may be seen in south-eastern, south and west Australia. Drought years may see irruptions closer to southern coasts.

Reading

Hayman, P., Marchant, J. & Prater, T. (1986), *Shorebirds: an identification guide to the waders of the world*, Christopher Helm Ltd, Bromley, UK (see pp. 78-9, 253, 255).

Despite temperatures exceeding 45° Celsius, Australian Pratincoles continue to incubate their eggs. They face their backs to the sun and pant.

Hatchling sheltering from the sun.

Breeding season (*variable*)

J	F	M	A	M	J	J	A	S	O	N	D

273   Australian Pratincole*

Skuas, Gulls, Terns and allies   Family Laridae

[Sibley & Ahlquist place the gulls and allies in the Superfamily Laroidea, one of three within the Parvorder Charadriida. In Family Laridae, Subfamily Larinae contains four tribes, one each of jaegers and skuas combined, gulls and terns. The fourth is Tribe Rynchopini, the skimmers (not represented in Australia). A second subfamily, Alcinae, contains the Northern Hemisphere auks, murres, puffins and guillemots.]

Jaegers, Skuas   Subfamily Larinae, Tribe Stercorariini

Of the six world species, five are recorded for Australia. Only the Chilean Skua *Catharacta chilensis* is not.

Skuas are characterised by sheaths covering the base of the upper bill. There are two skua groups: the great skuas *Catharacta*, chunky brown birds with very short central tail feathers, barely longer than the tail; and jaegers, *Stercorarius*, smaller, and with specialised long central tail feathers.

Most species probably pass through Australian waters annually, some less than others. The South Polar Skua *Catharacta maccormicki* has not often been recorded. The Long-tailed Jaeger is probably much more common than once thought;

numbers vary annually — October to March is their season in Australian waters. Up to 20 birds were recorded off NSW on one day in 1985; lesser numbers in recent years. The other species are common.

The jaegers migrate southward after breeding in the Northern Hemisphere. Great and South Polar Skuas migrate from the sub-Antarctic and Antarctic respectively, the South Polar Skua migrating to the northern Pacific in winter. Thus jaegers tend to be in Australian seas in our summer; great skuas during our winter.

Both skuas and jaegers are piratic, chasing other seabirds (for instance, shearwaters, gulls, terns) and forcing them to drop or disgorge their food. Aerobatics, the very quick directional changes performed during the chase, are often spectacular. Skuas are also scavengers and readily take refuse from ships.

At sea, great skuas tend to be solitary or in pairs. Groups form to scavenge, but are competing hard with each other. Jaegers may form loose flocks of up to 100 birds in the wintering period. All skuas and jaegers are strongly territorial on their breeding grounds, fiercely attacking anything they feel is a threat to their young.

Great skuas have no well-defined differences in plumage throughout the year. Jaegers, by contrast, have complicated plumage sequences which are not yet fully understood. They leave the north as barred juveniles with short tail streamers, moulting into first winter plumage when they arrive in Australia. They then slowly acquire adult plumage over three or four years. Adults moult their body feathers twice annually and have both breeding and non-breeding plumage. They only moult the wing feathers once a year. All jaeger species also have differently coloured morph plumages, generally described as 'pale, medium (or intermediate) and dark' morphs.

Reading

Lewis, M. J. (1991), 'The status of the Long-tailed Jaeger *Stercorarius longicauda* in Australian waters', *Aust. Bird Watcher* **14**, 119-22.

Reader's Digest Services (1985), *Reader's Digest Complete Book of New Zealand Birds*, Reader's Digest Services Pty Ltd, Surry Hills, NSW, pp. 217-20.

Wood, K. A. (1989), 'Seasonal abundance, marine habitats and behaviour of skuas off central New South Wales', *Corella* **13**, 97-104.

Pomarine Jaeger

Fully developed tail streamers

Juvenile (blunt)

Arctic Jaeger

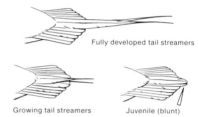

Fully developed tail streamers

Juvenile (pointed)

Long-tailed Jaeger

Fully developed tail streamers

Growing tail streamers   Juvenile (blunt)

Great Skua

Small and pointed tail streamers

Gulls   Subfamily Larinae, Tribe Larini

The world has about 45 gull species. Relationships are not well defined. Some authors emphasise behavioural (ethnological) traits, others consider physical (morphological) features more stable and reliable. The darkest in colour of plumage, bill, foot and eye may well be the *least*-evolved type, as in pigmentation and lack of pronounced pattern these dark gulls resemble the young of others which later develop highly specialised colours and patterns.

Gulls generally moult completely once a year and have a partial moult of head and body feathers twice a year. (Franklin's Gull moults completely twice a year.) Adults usually undergo the full moult after completing breeding. Northern vagrants have different summer and winter plumages, but local species do not. Relatively long-lived, gulls have, however, a sequence of plumages and moults from dark mottled juveniles to typical adult forms. Smaller gulls attain adult

A Pacific Gull incubating.

plumage in their second year, but the larger species take three or four years. The Pacific Gull, Australia's only endemic species, and the Kelp Gull both fall in this latter category. Variation can occur between fast and slow-developing individuals. Unusual plumages may sometimes be attributed to moult or feather wear.

Bill and leg colour, shape and size, behaviour and mode of flight are all important characteristics for recognition.

The sexes are similar except that females are usually smaller and more finely built.

Gulls are generally coastal in habit. They tend to be omnivorous scavengers, mainly along the coast, riverflats and nearby tips. They will feed inland on insects and worms in paddocks, and will follow a plough. They also follow ships at sea, feed on the eggs and young of other bird species, and even small adult seabirds. In turn, gull eggs and chicks are predated by other gulls, skuas, corvids and raptors. Humans eat gull eggs in some countries.

Gulls breed only once a year but if the nest, eggs or young are lost, a new start is often made. An exception is in Western Australia, where individual Silver Gulls may lay and successfully raise a second clutch, although this is not so in the eastern states. Larger gulls tend to breed along shorelines, either by inlets or on offshore islands. Smaller species tend to breed in marshes or swamps. Gulls may nest alone, though most kinds are social breeders to a variable extent. The degree of colony formation usually depends on the local food supply. A series of calls and postures is associated with courtship, nest-building, mating and change-over for incubation, and nest defence. To begin a study of birds, new observers could do no better than to take a bag of bread or other food scraps and feed gulls. Observe their behaviour and try to estimate their ages from the varying plumages they exhibit.

Gull nests are mostly on the ground, usually well-formed and constructed of whatever material is locally available. The clutch size is usually two or three, but sometimes just one egg. Clutches that are laid later in the season are almost always smaller than early ones. Eggs are usually a tapered oval shape, light brown, green or blue in ground (background) colour, and evenly spotted or blotched with black, brown or grey. Incubation varies from 21 days for small gulls to 29 days for large gulls. Newly hatched chicks are heavily covered with down and are capable of leaving the nest within a few days to hide. Older chicks may take to the water for protection. Both parents care for and feed chicks. They are fed partly digested food, sometimes until they are five to six weeks old and are free-flying.

Silver Gulls have had something of a population explosion in recent years about Australia's cities, due to the excessive provision of scraps at municipal tips. The species has become very urbanised indeed. Pacific Gulls in southern Australia may find themselves competing with the recently colonising Kelp Gull, should the population of the latter suddenly increase. More observers in the field have resulted in several rare/vagrant gull records in recent years.

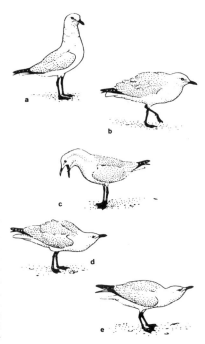

The behavioural postures of the Silver Gull: (a) upright and aggressive; (b) hunched and ready to pursue; (c) arched and aggressive; (d) forward attitude (often both c and d appear together at the conclusion of other displays); (e) submissive (similar to begging posture of juveniles).

The downy hatchlings of gulls are grey and/or buff with black blotches: Pacific Gull (upper); Silver Gull in a cryptic posture (lower).

Reading

Grant, P. J. (1981), *Gulls: a guide to identification*, T. & A. D. Poyser, Calton, UK.

Harrison, P. (1983), *Seabirds: an identification guide*, A. H. & A. W. Reed, Sydney, NSW.

Breeding seasons (*variable*)

	J	F	M	A	M	J	J	A	S	O	N	D
279 Silver Gull*												
280 Pacific Gull												
281 Kelp Gull												

Terns

Subfamily Sterninae, Tribe Sternini

Australia has 22 species of terns and noddies (including the recently added Antarctic Tern *Sterna vittata*) from a world subfamily (Sterninae) of 42 species. Terns are related to gulls but have generally straighter, more pointed bills, slenderer wings, more delicate flight and weaker legs. Noddies (*Anous*) are a fairly distinctive group of terns, being dark with pale caps. They are gliding birds with broader wings, fluttering less than other terns. Their feet and legs are stronger and their tails are broad, rounded and deeply notched. The Grey Ternlet (*Procelsterna*) is a small, pale noddy with longer legs. It has a distinctive habit of sometimes pattering on the water like a storm-petrel when feeding. The White Tern (*Gygis*) is the only nearly all-white tern. An upturned bill and different nesting habits seem to set it apart from other terns.

The migratory marsh terns (*Chlidonias*) occur mostly in inland waters and sometimes on the coast. All are short-tailed with distinctive breeding and non-breeding plumages. Black and White-winged Terns are blackish in breeding plumage, and grey and white in non-breeding plumage. Whiskered Terns are local breeders, White-winged Terns migrate from east-central Asia, and Black Terns are vagrants (sighted once at Sydney, once at Newcastle, both NSW).

The genera *Sterna*, *Hydroprogne* and *Gelochelidon* are all so closely related that recently they were placed in the one genus — *Sterna*. Sizes vary widely, from the starling-sized Little Tern to the gull-sized Caspian Tern (formerly *Hydroprogne*). Several natural 'groupings' are clearly recognised: Caspian Tern, Gull-billed Tern (formerly *Gelochelidon*); the 'commic' terns — Arctic, Antarctic, Common, White-fronted, Roseate and Black-naped; the Bridled and Sooty Terns; the small 'least' terns — Fairy and Little; and the crested terns (formerly *Thalasseus*).

Identifying many of the terns is very difficult, none more so than the 'commic' terns. All have blackish bills (sometimes with hints of red) in non-breeding plumage, some attaining red bills in breeding plumage. All are middle-sized, white-bellied in non-breeding plumage and grey, white or pinkish in breeding plumage, varying in duration from species to species.

Identification *relies on a combination of features*, such as plumage, size, shape, bill and leg length, primary feather patterns, amount (degree) of translucency in the underwing. One characteristic useful for separating two notoriously difficult species, Common and Arctic Terns, is the wing-moult sequence. Common Terns moult the inner half of the primaries (inner four to six) twice a year and moult the other primaries once. Since tern feathers wear from fresh silver-grey to worn blackish at certain times of year (abraded by use and faded by sunlight) Common Terns show a strong contrast between the inner and outer primaries. The inners are fresh and silvery; the outers are old and blackish. Adult Arctic Terns moult primaries once a year in the Southern Hemisphere and usually have uniformly grey upperwings (except when in moult, in which case there are gaps between old and new primaries in the wing).

Care should be taken with this feature because Common Terns undergo a complete wing moult in autumn before migrating. Before they leave for the north they have uniform upperwings. First-year birds arriving from the north

A flock of roosting terns, including the Crested, Lesser Crested, Common, and the Little.

A Whiskered Tern hatchling.

Whiskered Terns at their nest.

in the spring *also* have uniform upperwings for some time. Birds remaining for the southern winter can have a complete primary moult as late as August and *again* have uniform upperwings. Subsequently they follow the same sequence as adults that finish moulting in autumn. As a rule, if a bird is seen before autumn with contrasting grey and blackish primaries *without* gaps between the 'contrast', then the bird is a Common Tern. Roseate Terns, like Common Terns, moult the inner primaries twice annually and the outer three, once.

Arctic Terns are perhaps the most travelled birds in the world. They breed in northern Asia, Europe, North America and up into the Arctic Circle, migrating south in August through the tropics to the Antarctic, to wander throughout the southern seas from September to April (immatures remain to overwinter). Birds banded in northern Europe have been recovered in Australia.

Black Noddies nest in trees.

Two main migration routes are known. One population from east Asia and western North America migrates down the west coast of the Americas. The other, from Europe and eastern North America, migrates down the east coast of Africa. It is possible that small numbers of Arctic Terns also migrate via east Asia and eastern Australia as some recent sightings in eastern Australia in spring suggest.

Common Terns are also strongly migratory; Australian birds (*Sterna hirundo longipennis*) come from north-east Asia and migrate via east Asia to Australia. It is certain (though hard to prove, even from specimens) that the other northeast Asian race *minussensis* migrates to Australia, because red-billed Common Terns with large amounts of black on the bills and red legs are annually seen in east Australia. Common Terns banded in Europe (nominate race *hirundo*) have sometimes been found dead in Australia. Most White-fronted Terns migrate from New Zealand in the winter, but recently a small population was found breeding on Battery Island in Bass Strait. Geologically Recent fossils in the soil suggest prior breeding.

The Antarctic Tern *Sterna vittata* has recently been identified from a specimen in South Australia. It breeds on sub-Antarctic islands, and *some* populations migrate north in the winter (the birds breeding closest to Australia do *not* migrate). It is identified from other 'commic' terns by its pale grey outer tail streamers (dark grey in Common and Arctic) and its short, stout black and red bill in winter (red in summer). In winter it has as much white on the crown as does the Arctic Tern. It lacks a carpal bar, and is larger and stockier than the Artic Tern (see p. 257 for description).

Two populations of Little Terns occur in Australia. One migrates from Asia and is here in non-breeding plumage in summer. The other population breeds in northern and eastern Australia. Fairy Terns breed in western and southern Australia. Gull-billed Terns (race *macrotarsa*) mostly breed here, but there are also a small number of birds from Asia of the race *affinis* (smaller and darker above than the local race). Crested Terns disperse widely throughout Australia; banded South Australian birds have been found as far away as south-east Queensland. Grey Ternlets and White Terns breed in the Pacific (as near as Lord Howe Island) and occasionally wander into coastal waters — there have been about six sightings of each species off Wollongong, NSW, between 1984 and 1990. The movements of most other Australian terns are poorly understood.

Food is made up mainly of aquatic animal life, the size of

Fairy Terns attending to their chicks.

the tern correlating with the size of its prey. Some terns occasionally hawk for insects. Unlike gulls, terns rarely eat scraps. Food is gathered by hovering (quick fluttering in smaller terns; slow flapping in larger terns) and then either picking it off the surface or plunging partly into the water. Most terns are gregarious, feeding in flocks, breeding colonially. Congregations of feeding terns (also shearwaters, gannets and gulls) may guide fishermen to fish shoals in coastal seas.

Before mating, terns usually have paired flight displays, sometimes flying in perfect unison, spiralling, zig-zagging and flapping together. Terns usually breed on islands, often on ground scrapes in sandy regions. These are sometimes lined with sticks. Some inland-breeding terns construct vegetation platforms floating on or placed near water.

Terns such as the Sooty Terns and Common Noddies often breed communally in thousands. Lesser and Black Noddies breed in trees. White Terns build no nest, but lay an egg on tree branches or palm fronds. Grey Ternlets nest on cliff ledges. Eggs range from dull white to brown, greenish or grey with varying amounts of small blotches and spots. Clutches consist of one or two eggs, sometimes up to three or four. Soon after hatching, tern chicks are downy and fairly mobile.

Reading

Hulsman, K. & Langham, N. P. E. (1985), 'Breeding biology of the Bridled Tern *Sterna anaethetus*', *Emu* **85**, 240-9.

Smith, P. (1990), 'The biology and management of the Little Tern (*Sterna albifrons*) in NSW', Species Management Report no. **1**, NSW National Parks and Wildlife Service, Hurstville, NSW.

Whinray, J. S. (1980), 'The Australian breeding record of the White-fronted Tern', *Aust. Bird Watcher* **8**, 137-46.

Breeding seasons (*variable)

	J	F	M	A	M	J	J	A	S	O	N	D
286 Whiskered Tern*												
289 Gull-billed Tern*												
290 Caspian Tern*												
294 Roseate Tern*												
295 White-fronted Tern												
296 Black-naped Tern*												
297 Sooty Tern*												
298 Bridled Tern*												
299 Little Tern*												
300 Fairy Tern*												
301 Crested Tern*												
302 Lesser Crested Tern*												
303 Common Noddy*												
304 Lesser Noddy												
305 Black Noddy												

Pigeons, Doves   Family Columbidae

[Superorder Passerimorphae of Sibley & Ahlquist contains three orders. They place the pigeons and doves, Family Columbidae, in the traditional Order Columbiformes, immediately following the Family Raphidae, the now extinct dodos and solitaires. Following are the other Orders, Gruiformes and Ciconiiformes.]

Of the 290-odd pigeon and dove species found across the world, 44 occur in the New Guinea region and New Zealand has one. Australia has 25 species (three are introduced). Some have evolved to fill the ecological niche occupied by pheasants, grouse and partridges on other continents.

Many Australian species are old endemics that have developed with the changes to the Australian environment. The Wonga Pigeon is one, as is the Topknot — the latter once spread over much more of the continent than it does now. Others, notably the fruit-doves, are recent invaders from the northern islands and from Asia, where many additional species are found.

Although little physical difference exists between pigeons and doves, we tend to use the former name for larger species while 'doves', by popular usage, refers to the smaller birds with generally longer tails.

The need to obtain food has caused many Australian pigeons and doves to become nomads, although the range of their wandering seems rather restricted. The Superb Fruit-Dove, and to a lesser degree the Rose-crowned, are 'local nomads' with a difference — periodically an individual bird will stray enormous distances down the east coast. Both are recorded as vagrants in Victoria and Tasmania. The Flock

The Bar-shouldered Dove raises its wings while sun-bathing.

Many pigeons, including this Peaceful Dove, drink by sucking.

Bronzewing and Diamond Dove, inhabitants of a dry, inland environment, are both highly nomadic. The former, in particular, occasionally irrupts into areas far from its generally accepted habitat. By contrast, the Spinifex Pigeon is mostly sedentary, an unusual trait for an inland bird.

The two 'big movers' are the migratory Torresian Imperial-Pigeon whose flights into northern Australia from New Guinea are one of Australia's most spectacular ornithological events, and the Topknot Pigeon, in its long-range search for fruits. Torresian Imperial-Pigeons arrive on Cape York Peninsula in late July and by late August they appear in Darwin. Their return flight takes place mainly in February and early March. The bulk of the Australian population goes to southern Papua New Guinea, and Irian Jaya contains areas frequented by the birds.

Pigeons have long been hunted, first by Aborigines who used nets and throwing sticks, then by the early seamen who made the birds a welcome addition to their diet. As the continent was opened up by settlers, pigeons were hunted more systematically, mainly for food, less frequently for sport. Even now some species, particularly the Topknot and Wompoo, are hunted, but mainly by pot hunters or 'sportsmen'. Small numbers are trapped, often illegally, for aviaries.

Despite casual persecution, the far graver threat is habitat loss. Fruit-doves, as rainforest inhabitants, are greatly at risk, for this irreplaceable resource has been, and still is being, cleared or damaged at an alarming rate. In other areas, mining activities, with the incidental problems of hunters and cats that stray from the mining towns, pose a threat to the Squatter and Rock-Pigeons. Foxes, feral cats and straying station dogs are *always* a danger to ground-dwelling and feeding pigeons and doves, and other birds. The Banded Fruit-Dove has a restricted range in Arnhem Land, an area subjected to intense mining exploration work.

Some species are apparently secure. These include the Common Bronzewing and a trio of doves — Bar-shouldered, Peaceful and Diamond. Only the Crested Pigeon has gained markedly by European settlement. It has been able to extend its range as grain-growing was established and watering places for stock increased. It may now be considered an urban resident about many country towns.

The map we show for the Spinifex Pigeon is simplified. A more detailed map of the distribution is given by Johnstone (1981). We have used the terminology 'race *leucogaster*' and 'race *ferruginea*' for the two main colour varieties, white-bellied and red-bellied birds respectively. Johnstone has shown that in reality a cline of discordant belly colour variation exists across the continent. Iris colour varies a little too. Johnstone delineates eight populations across northern Australia. He retains true races (sub-species) for the Partridge Pigeon however.

Pigeons and doves are either granivorous (grain-eaters) or frugivorous (fruit-eaters) although some are plant grazers. The Crested Pigeon, for example, feeds extensively on leaves of medicks, plants of the semi-arid plains. Because pigeons can quickly gather large quantities of food in a short time, less time than is taken for its digestion, a storage pouch (crop) has evolved on the wall of the oesophagus. The crop is essential, particularly for the Crested Pigeon for its medick leaves. The Topknot Pigeon swallows the fruits of the bangalow palm. These contain a large seed, with a comparatively thin flesh over it — little digestible food from

Breeding seasons (*variable*)

J	F	M	A	M	J	J	A	S	O	N	D

308 Banded Fruit-Dove

309 Superb Fruit-Dove

310 Rose-crowned Fruit-Dove

311 Wompoo Fruit-Dove

312 Torresian Imperial-Pigeon

314 Topknot Pigeon

315 White-headed Pigeon

316 Feral Pigeon

317 Spotted Turtle-Dove

318 Laughing Turtle-Dove

319 Brown Cuckoo-Dove

320 Peaceful Dove*

321 Diamond Dove*

322 Bar-shouldered Dove*

323 Emerald Dove

324 Common Bronzewing

325 Brush Bronzewing*

326 Flock Bronzewing

327 Crested Pigeon*

328 Squatter Pigeon*

329 Partridge Pigeon*

330A White-quilled Rock Pigeon

330B Chestnut-quilled Rock Pigeon

331 Spinifex Pigeon

332 Wonga Pigeon

An incubating Superb Fruit-Dove — note the very flimsy nest.

327

such large volumes of material. Once again, the pigeon's crop comes into its own.

The crop has one other vital use, the production of 'pigeon-milk'. In breeding adults, a cheese-like secretion fills certain lining cells of the crop and these are shed into the crop where they remain. Newly hatched young are fed on regurgitated 'milk', and as they grow, other food is regurgitated with it. By the time they leave the nest, the young are fed almost entirely on normal adult food.

Many pigeons when drinking are able to suck water up so they do not need to throw back their head to let it run down their throat. This reduces their vulnerability to predators at drinking places. Many pigeon species in arid regions make quite long flights to water, giving an opportunity to observe them in flight, as locating them otherwise can be difficult.

Pigeons' nests are not elaborate, usually a meagre platform of sticks. The nest site is variable, depending on the species. Some nest on the ground, others on a rock ledge or in a crevice. Most select the fork of a tree or shrub. One or two eggs form the clutch and they are white or off-white, often glossy, oval in shape and not large considering the bird's body size.

The bowing displays of the Feral Pigeon (left) and the Crested Pigeon (right).

Reading

Coates, B. J., (1985), *The Birds of New Guinea, Volume II, Non-Passerines*, Dove Publications, Alderley, Queensland (pigeons pp. 232-309).

Crome, Frank, Shields, James & The National Photographic Index of Australian Wildlife (1992), *Parrots and Pigeons of Australia*, Collins Angus & Robertson, Pymble, NSW.

Frith, H. J. (1982), *Pigeons and Doves of Australia*, Rigby, Adelaide.

Goodwin, D. (1970), *Pigeons and Doves of the World*, 2nd edition, Trustees of the British Museum (Nat. Hist.), London.

Johnstone, R. E. (1981), 'Notes on the distribution, ecology and taxonomy of the Partridge Pigeon (*Geophaps smithii*) and Spinifex Pigeon (*Geophaps plumifera*) in Western Australia', *Records of the WA Museum*, **9** (1), 49-63.

The nest site and eggs of a Rock-Pigeon.

Cockatoos, Parrots — Family Psittacidae

[Sibley & Ahlquist present a series of six Parvclasses within the Infraclass Neoaves. We have met the Parvclass Galloanserae (pheasants, waterfowl and allies) and Parvclass Turnicae (button-quails). Three others are Parvclass Picae (woodpeckers and allies), Parvclass Coraciae (jacamars, puffbirds, hornbills, hoopes, trogons, rollers, motmots, todies, kingfishers, bee-eaters and allies), and Parvclass Coliae for the colies. Finally, there is another very large one, Parvclass Passerae. This contains *all* the rest of the living birds of the world other than those included in the five Parvclasses listed.

This Parvclass has five Superorders: Superorder Cuculimorphae (cuckoos and allies); Superorder Psittacimorphae (parrots, macaws and allies); Apodimorphae (swifts, hummingbirds and allies); Strigimorphae (owls, oilbird, nightjars and allies); and finally the Superorder Passerimorphae, which contains *all* the rest of the living birds of the world. Because the Sibley & Ahlquist list is *not* in the same sequence as the conservative list for the family sequence we are following, it appears as though their list is badly fragmented. Such however is not the case, as is clear in their book.

Their Superorder Psittacimorphae contains the traditional Order Psittaciformes and Family Psittacidae. Within their evolutionary position, they are a very discrete group, with cuckoos and the Hoatzin before them, and swifts and hummingbirds following. Although the parrots have previously been difficult to place, it appears now that they have no close living relatives. A divergence in the DNA evidence suggests that three sub-units of parrots exist, in Africa, Australasia and the Americas, but inadequate data at present leaves this to be resolved.]

A Yellow-tailed Black-Cockatoo extracts beetle larvae from a tree trunk. Note the foot, bill, cere and tongue anatomy.

The Order Psittaciformes, which embraces the cockatoos and parrots, forms one of the most well-defined groups of birds. Collectively, we call them 'The Parrots', a term in wide use. They are characterised by: a short, strongly hooked bill; bulging cere; a toe arrangement with two forward and two back; interesting intestinal looping and the lack of an appendix; the presence of a feather aftershaft; a diastatic wing (no secondary feather corresponding to the fifth feather of the greater wing coverts); naked young that are fed by the parent holding the nestling's bill inside its own.

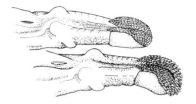

Lorikeets have specialised brush-tipped tongues. This illustration shows a Rainbow Lorikeet's tongue in two positions: normal and relaxed (top); erect for feeding (bottom).

Their short neck and legs, prominent eye, large head and compact, bulky body, combined with bright plumage dominated by primary colours, give cockatoos and parrots a distinctive and engaging appearance. The ability of many species to mimic human words makes them even more attractive as cage birds.

Parrots form a large, uniform group distributed throughout the inter-tropical zone as well as the sub-tropical and colder parts of the Southern Hemisphere. Great diversity and endemism (occurrence of species peculiar to a locality and with the most basic evolutionary traits) occur in Australia and New Guinea. This fact, combined with continental drift evidence, suggests that parrots originated and radiated from the southern continents.

Within Australia the general direction of evolutionary adaptation has been radiation from Tertiary rainforests through eucalypt woodlands to colonisation of the central deserts. Today, the diversity of species is greatest in the drier eucalypt open forests and woodlands, and declines towards both the deserts and wetter areas.

Only one family is now recognised in Australia, with six subfamilies, 23 genera and about 50 species. The number of species recognised is 'reduced' because the rosellas with white cheeks (Eastern, Northern, Pale-headed) as well as the two ringnecks (Mallee Ringneck, Port Lincoln), interbreed where they meet. Therefore the birds in each group are best considered as a single variable species. Three species of Black-Cockatoo occur in south-west Australia: the White-tailed Black-Cockatoo, previously considered a race (*latirostris*) of the Yellow-tailed Black-Cockatoo, the Red-tailed Black-Cockatoo and the Long-billed Black-Cockatoo which in recent years has been intensively studied and better defined.

Except for lorikeets and the Swift Parrot, most Australian parrots are primarily seed-eaters; fruits, berries, flowers and insects are also eaten to varying extents. It seems incongruous that one of the largest cockatoos, the Red-tailed Black-Cockatoo, is largely dependent on the minute seeds of bloodwood eucalypts and she-oaks. Obviously when the food consists of tiny seeds, large quantities must be consumed. It has been estimated that individual Ground Parrots and Orange-bellied Parrots consume in the order of 10 000 seeds per day to meet their requirements.

Bill-shape variations have resulted from specialisation to particular foods. For example, the straighter, elongated bill of the Long-billed Corella is used to dig up corms; the elongated, down-curved bill of the Red-capped Parrot enables efficient removal of seeds from large-fruited eucalypts, particularly marri (*Eucalyptus calophylla*).

Yellow-tailed Black-Cockatoos have learned to extract insect larvae from tree trunks and exposed roots, from *Banksia* cones and from grasstree flower spikes (*Xanthorrhoea* spp.).

Lorikeets feed on pollen and nectar from flowers; they

have specialised brush-tipped tongues and comparatively long, narrow bills. Some also regularly eat fruit. Nectar and pollen are also important in the diet of the brush-tongued Swift Parrot. This species also eats insects and often gleans psyllid plant-bugs, which have a sugary coating, from eucalypt foliage.

Most Australian parrots nest in tree hollows, especially those formed in broken limbs of eucalypts. However, Golden-shouldered and Paradise Parrots breed only in tunnels excavated in certain types of termite mounds. Ground and Night Parrots construct nests of coarse grass in dense tussocks. Rock Parrots nest in crannies between boulders on coastal islands. Most hollow-nesting species, with the exception of Galahs which line their hollows with fresh eucalypt leaves, chew woodchips from inside the hollow to form a soft layer on which the eggs are laid.

Parrots' eggs are rounded, white and often lustrous, in common with most species whose eggs are safely concealed in a hollow. The chicks are altricial (naked and helpless at birth) and must be cared for by the parents for an extended period (from 30 days for *Neophema* species to 100 days for black-cockatoos). Chicks of the Ground Parrot, however, are covered in dense blackish down, presumably as a protection from cold and damp in their open nests. Chicks of black-cockatoos have long yellow down, the function of which is not clear.

In most species, nests are widely spaced, for instance, Pink Cockatoo nests are usually more than two kilometres apart. However, in agricultural districts the uneven dispersion of trees containing suitable hollows may lead to the concentration of breeding birds into habitat remnants. In Western Australia up to seven cockatoo species were recorded breeding at densities of seven nests per hectare.

In eastern and southern Australia most species breed in spring and summer (August-January) while in the tropical north breeding tends to occur in the dry season (May-August). Species adapted to the arid centre usually have a breeding peak between August and October, but may breed at other times, especially March to June, following rain. When conditions are suitable some species, such as the Budgerigar, may raise several broods in succession.

Most species of Australian parrots are sedentary although in some species, for example the Galah, flocks of non-breeders may travel widely. Several arid country species (Cockatiel, Budgerigar, Night Parrot, Alexandra's Parrot and Scarlet-chested Parrot) are nomadic and are able to exploit sudden availability of food resulting from unpredictable and often patchy rainfall. Lorikeets are also nomads, their feeding movements and range determined by blossom availability.

Migration is undertaken by two species of *Neophema* and the Swift Parrot, all of which breed in summer in Tasmania and spend the winter on the mainland. The Orange-bellied Parrot is a migrant which breeds in coastal south-west Tasmania, wintering along the coast of central Victoria, and south-eastern South Australia. The Swift Parrot is also a migrant breeding only in Tasmania. Most individuals winter in southern and central Victoria, but with irregular irruptions to the north and west. Blue-winged Parrots, by contrast, are partial migrants because only the Tasmanian-breeding portion of the population migrates. In March and April birds from Tasmania travel north across Bass Strait and Victoria

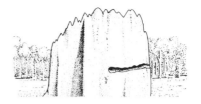

The illegal trapping of highly prized Australian parrots for aviculture is threatening the survival of some species. This nest of the Golden-shouldered Parrot has been excavated by trappers.

Breeding seasons (*variable)

	J	F	M	A	M	J	J	A	S	O	N	D
333 Palm Cockatoo												
334 Red-tailed Black-Cockatoo*												
335 Glossy Black-Cockatoo												
336A Yellow-tailed Black Cockatoo*												
336B White-tailed Black Cockatoo*												
337 Long-billed Black-Cockatoo												
338 Gang-gang Cockatoo												
339 Galah*												
340 Long-billed Corella												
341 Little Corella*												
342 Pink Cockatoo*												
343 Sulphur-crested Cockatoo*												
344 Eclectus Parrot												
345 Red-cheeked Parrot												
346 Rainbow Lorikeet												
347 Red-collared Lorikeet												
348 Scaly-breasted Lorikeet												
349 Varied Lorikeet												
350 Musk Lorikeet												
351 Purple-crowned Lorikeet												
352 Little Lorikeet												
353 Double-eyed Fig-Parrot												
354 Australian King-Parrot												
355 Red-winged Parrot*												
356 Superb Parrot												
357 Regent Parrot												
358 Alexandra's Parrot												
359 Cockatiel*												

to New South Wales and Queensland, returning in September and October to breed. Blue-winged Parrots breeding in southern Victoria are probably a sedentary population.

Threats to the survival of Australian parrots include: (*i*) changes induced by frequent fires and the grazing of stock to the plant species' composition, and hence seed production, of the grassy understorey in eucalypt woodlands; (*ii*) diminishing availability of hollow trees for breeding sites and widespread lack of regeneration of eucalypts to replenish the stock of hollow trees; (*iii*) patchy dispersion of food and nesting sites in the remaining natural vegetation across much of southern Australia; (*iv*) gross destruction of the habitat of specialised species such as those restricted to rainforest (Palm Cockatoo, Eclectus Parrot, Red-cheeked Parrot and Double-eyed Fig-Parrot) or to coastal heath and salt-marsh (Ground Parrot, Orange-bellied Parrot); (*v*) unrelenting, illegal seizing of highly prized wild birds and young, for the interstate and international avicultural trade, and with it the frequent destruction of nest hollows by chainsaw or axe, rendering the site useless for future breeding.

The first cause may have hastened the Paradise Parrot's decline, as well as probably contributing to the apparent continuing decline of the Golden-shouldered Parrot. The situation of the latter has been aggravated by severe illegal trapping. Rapid decline of available nest hollows potentially threatens most species, including seemingly common ones, for example the Galah, which mainly breeds in agricultural districts. A study of a remnant population of Yellow-tailed Black-Cockatoos revealed that patchy food dispersion, due to unsympathetic clearing of native vegetation, meant that the parents could not provide enough food for their young. Thus the population declined.

Because parrots are often long-lived, continual breeding failure may not become apparent until it is too late to take corrective action. Degradation of coastal salt marshes in Victoria may be a major cause for the steep decline of the Orange-bellied Parrot to its present critical level of about 200 wintering individuals. Even now, the two most important wintering areas, both in Port Phillip Bay, are continuing to be threatened by major land-use changes. Despite an increased government research effort, volunteer censusing and commencement of habitat enhancement by selective weeding out of an invasive plant which competes for space with the favoured food of the parrot, the long-term survival of this species is by no means certain at the present time (1992). Bird observers and other sympathetic people could do a huge amount to improve the habitats of Australia. Why not establish your own regular programme of selective planting, weeding and litter collection in your district?

Reading

Boles, W., Longmore, W. & Thompson, M. (1991), 'The fly-by-Night Parrot', *Australian Natural History* **23** (9), 689-95.

Coates, B. J. (1985), *The Birds of Papua New Guinea*, Vol. 1 Non-Passerines, Dove Publications, Alderley, Queensland.

Crome, Frank, Shields, James & The National Photographic Index of Australian Wildlife (1992), *Parrots and Pigeons of Australia*, Collins Angus & Robertson, Pymble, NSW.

Forshaw, J. M. (1981), *Australian Parrots*, 2nd (revised) edition, Lansdowne Editions, Melbourne.

Forshaw, J. M. & Cooper, W. T. (1978), *Parrots of the World*, 2nd (revised) edition, Lansdowne Editions, Melbourne.

Julian, R. (1989), 'Paradise Parrot', *Australian Natural History* **23** (1), 78-9.

Breeding seasons (*variable*)

J F M A M J J A S O N D

360 Ground Parrot
361 Night Parrot (*Insufficient information*)
362 Budgerigar*
363 Swift Parrot
364 Red-capped Parrot
365 Green Rosella
366 Crimson Rosella
367 Eastern Rosella
368 Pale-headed Rosella*
369 Northern Rosella
370 Western Rosella
371 Mallee Ringneck*
372 Port Lincoln Ringneck*
373 Red-rumped Parrot
374 Mulga Parrot
375 Golden-shouldered Parrot
376 Hooded Parrot
377 Paradise Parrot (*Insufficient information*)
378 Blue Bonnet
379 Bourke's Parrot*
380 Blue-winged Parrot
381 Elegant Parrot
382 Rock Parrot
383 Orange-bellied Parrot
384 Turquoise Parrot
385 Scarlet-chested Parrot

Rowley, Ian (1990), *The Galah: behavioural ecology of the galah in the wheatbelt of Western Australia*, Surrey Beatty & Sons, Chipping Norton, NSW.

Saunders, D. A. (1979), 'Distribution and taxonomy of the White-tailed and Yellow-tailed Black-Cockatoos *Calyptorhynchus* spp.', *Emu* **79**, 215-17.

Saunders, D. A., et al. (editors) (1987), *Nature Conservation: the role of remnants of native vegetation*, Surrey Beatty & Sons, with CSIRO and WA Department of Conservation and Land Management, Chipping Norton, NSW.

Saunders, D. A. & Hobbs, Richard J. (editors) (1991), *Nature Conservation 2: the role of corridors*, Surrey Beatty & Sons, with CSIRO and WA Department of Conservation and Land Management, Chipping Norton, NSW.

Schodde, R. & Mason, I. (1980), *Nocturnal Birds of Australia*, Lansdowne Editions, Melbourne.

Stephenson, L. H. (1991), 'The Orange-bellied Parrot Recovery Plan: Management Phase'. Department of Parks, Wildlife and Heritage, Hobart, Tasmania.

Veerman, P. A. (1991), 'The changing status of the Rainbow Lorikeet *Trichoglossus haematodus* in South-east Australia: the role of wild and escaped birds', *Aust. Bird Watcher* **14** (1), 3-9.

Old World Cuckoos Family Cuculidae

[Sibley & Ahlquist have two superfamilies, Cuculoidea and Centropoidea, within the Order Cuculiformes. In its superfamily, Family Cuculidae has the Old World Cuckoos, which includes the parasitic true cuckoos and bronze-cuckoos, and also the koels, among which is the New Zealand Long-tailed Cuckoo. The Family Centropidae has only the coucals. The order also includes American cuckoos, the interesting Hoatzin, anis, Guira Cuckoo, and also ground cuckoos and roadrunners; of course none of these occur in Australia.]

Parasitic Cuckoos Subfamily Cuculinae

DNA comparisons indicate that the cuckoos have no close living relatives, but are one of the sister groups that comprise about half of the living birds of the world. It is concluded they are an ancient lineage with wide genetic diversity within their own superorder. It is doubtful that the owls and nightjars are closely related, nor the parrots, as has often previously been proposed.

This group of birds presents a real challenge to observers, who will need to learn cuckoo plumages and calls with care; many are difficult to identify. Much remains to be discovered about breeding and other behaviour and we can present only a fraction of what is known. Take detailed notes of cuckoo behaviour, of all species, whenever you see them. Special care needs to be used at nests of small birds, because no interference must be caused to the host passerine species whilst observations are made. Please be meticulous at all times.

The Black-eared Cuckoo's egg (right) closely resembles the chocolate-coloured egg laid by its host, the Speckled Warbler (left).

Parasitic cuckoos often lay small eggs by comparison with their own body weight, for their eggs must resemble their hosts' in size, as well as in colouration. Once hatched, the naked baby cuckoo ejects all objects with which it comes in contact in the nests, including the host's eggs and nestlings. By making begging postures and juvenile calls, even well after it is fledged, the juvenile cuckoo then ensures that a constant food supply is brought by the hosts and sometimes by other birds of the same *and* different bird species.

Cuckoos are vocal mainly during the breeding season. At other times they may be silent and very difficult to observe. They may call by day or night. Repetitious nocturnal calling

The Black-eared Cuckoo nestling begs from its foster parent, a Speckled Warbler.

by the Pallid Cuckoo has earned it the colloquial name of 'brain fever bird'.

All Australian species (except the Pheasant Coucal) are parasitic on a wide variety of native birds. Most cuckoos are insectivorous. The Fan-tailed and bronze-cuckoos (except Horsfield's) select dome-shaped nests for egg-laying. The other species may use such nests but conventionally select open or cup-shaped nests.

The Pallid, Brush, Fan-tailed, Horsfield's and Little Bronze-Cuckoos, Channel-billed Cuckoo and Common Koel all breed in Australia, and at least part of their populations migrate to northern Australia and New Guinea in the winter. The south-east Queensland and northern New South Wales populations of the Little Bronze-Cuckoo (race *barnardi*) migrate to Cape York Peninsula in winter. The New Zealand Shining Bronze-Cuckoo (the green-headed nominate race *lucidus*) breeds in New Zealand, then winters in western Pacific islands and a portion of the population reaches eastern Australia.

A recent discovery that Little and Gould's Bronze-Cuckoos hybridise has resulted in their contraction to one species.

Reading

Brooker, M. G. & Brooker, L. C. (1991), 'The identification of nestling cuckoos in the Canberra region', *Canberra Bird Notes* **16**, 61-4.

Brooker, M. G., Brooker, L. C. & Rowley, I. (1988), 'Egg deposition by the Bronze-Cuckoos *Chrysococcyx basalis* and *Ch. lucidus*', *Emu* **88** (2), 107-8.

Breeding seasons (*variable*)

J	F	M	A	M	J	J	A	S	O	N	D

387 Pallid Cuckoo
388 Brush Cuckoo
389 Chestnut-breasted Cuckoo
390 Fan-tailed Cuckoo
391 Black-eared Cuckoo
392 Horsfield's Bronze-Cuckoo*
393 Shining Bronze-Cuckoo
394 Little Bronze-Cuckoo
395 Gould's Bronze-Cuckoo
396 Common Koel
397 Channel-billed Cuckoo

Coucals — Subfamily Centropodinae

The Pheasant Coucal of northern Australia is the only Australian cuckoo which does, in fact, build its own nest, incubate and raise its own family and does not indulge in the parasitic habit. The coucals inhabit areas of very dense vegetation through which they make small tunnels they run along in a pheasant-like manner. Observers will cause them to clamber to a vantage point in a tall tree, from which they may fly heavily away. Their deep hooting calls are very distinctive.

Coucals feed on live insects and small vertebrates. They build open, cup-shaped nests and average three to five white (but rapidly stained) eggs. Hatchlings are covered in a long, white, hairy covering. There are some 26 other species of the genus *Centropus* in the world.

A Pheasant Coucal at its nest.

Breeding season

J	F	M	A	M	J	J	A	S	O	N	D

398 Pheasant Coucal

Barn Owls — Family Tytonidae

[Sibley & Ahlquist place owls and nightjars in the same superorder and order because the DNA evidence points to that. Within Suborder Strigi, Barn Owls remain discrete in Parvorder Tytonida and traditional Family Tytonidae.]

There is no doubt that the two owl Families — barn owls and hawk owls — are much more closely related to each other than they are to any other group. But barn owls have been distinct at least since the Miocene (7-26 million years). The barn owls have: a sternum (breast bone) fused to the furcula (wish bone); reduced slotting of the primaries, which are also moulted in an irregular sequence; a pectinate (comb-like) middle claw and an inner toe equal in length to the middle toe. The general lack of correlation between these features and their functions tends to add weight to separation from the Strigidae, the hawk owls.

Barn Owl talons and detail of middle claw.

Breeding seasons (*variable*)

J	F	M	A	M	J	J	A	S	O	N	D

404 Barn Owl*
405 Masked Owl*
406 Eastern Grass Owl*
407 Sooty Owl*
408 Lesser Sooty Owl

Tyto is the only Australian genus. Unlike hawk owls, barn owls generally defend nest territories not with regular calling but with postures. Some are not territorial at all. The general trend towards opportunistic breeding seems to be correlated to these other tendencies. When they do breed they lay more eggs than *Ninox*; the males feed the females *at* the nest; the fledglings are not downy. They also regurgitate mucous-coated pellets of indigestible portions of the food. Cave deposits of fossilised prey species in pellets occur where Masked Owls once inhabited the sites.

Reading

Burton, John A. (1973), *Owls of the World: their evolution, structure, and ecology*, Peter Lowe, Netherlands.

Fleay, D. (1968), *Nightwatchmen of Bush and Plain*, Jacaranda Press, Brisbane.

Hollands, D. (1991), *Birds of the Night: owls, frogmouths and nightjars of Australia*, Reed Books, Balgowlah, NSW (pp. 71-141).

Olsen, P. (1988), 'Night stalker — the remarkable Barn Owl', *Australian Natural History* **22** (8), 376-80.

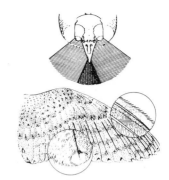

Two adaptations for nocturnal hunting as seen in the Barn Owl: large forward-pointing eyes for bifocal vision (above); a comb-like leading edge and softened trailing edge for quiet flight (below).

Hawk Owls (Typical Owls)　　　　Family Strigidae

[Within the Suborder Strigi, Sibley & Ahlquist keep the Typical Owls discrete in Parvorder Strigida and traditional Family Strigidae. It appears owls are not closely related to the hawks, but there is a real, though distant, relationship with the swifts and hummingbirds.]

This and the Family Tytonidae share many features unique to their Order, Strigiformes. Most authorities now agree that the nightjars and frogmouths (Caprimulgiformes) are the closest relatives of the owls and that the two groups shared a common ancestor prior to the Palaeocene (54-65 million years ago).

Owls are linked to nightjars and frogmouths on the basis of similar egg-white protein distributions, similarities in structures such as intestinal caeca, oil glands, voice boxes, a lack of the ambiens muscle in the leg, a lack of a crop or throat pouch in which food would normally be stored, and a tendency to have zygodactylous toes (two forward and two back). Other common features, such as large eyes, nightly routines, plumage patterns and, in some groups, feather structure, could be a result of nocturnal life, that is, convergence rather than shared evolution.

The hawks (Order Falconiformes) share many traits with owls as a result of similar diets rather than any close relationship. Members of both orders have strong, hooked bills with ceres, and powerful feet with large talons for catching, killing and ripping prey apart. Both also regurgitate pellets containing indigestible remnants of victims — bone, fur, scales, feathers, etc. However, convergence is at work here.

There is a general trend for the females of the two orders to be larger than their males, in order to reduce competition for food between partners, particularly during the breeding season. Unique among raptors, Australian hawk owl species display a tendency towards larger *males*.

Finally, there are characteristics unique to owls, including an advanced pelvic muscle system, although the obvious characteristics are adaptations for nocturnal hunting. Large, forward-pointing eyes give fine binocular vision, especially under low light conditions. The size of the eyes, though, renders them almost immovable in the skull, but owls overcome this by having extraordinarily flexible neck muscles that allow the head to be rotated through a maximum of 270°.

All owls regurgitate pellets containing indigestible remains of victims. These are pellets of the Powerful Owl, showing hair, bristles, bones, beetle wings etc.

In order to fly but to listen for prey whilst doing so, most owls have developed near-silent flight. This is made possible by large, broad wings with softened trailing edges to the flight feathers, a comb-like leading edge to the foremost primary, and loose, soft, body feathers. Most owls have well-developed hearing via large, sometimes asymmetrically positioned ear-openings, and facial discs formed by one or more special types of feathers. The facial discs direct sound waves to the ears as do the 'dishes' of radio telescopes. It is the nature of the facial disc which serves most conveniently to distinguish between the living representatives of the two families of owls.

It is clear from the fossil record and the number of extant species (100-134, depending on the authority) that the Family Strigidae represents the main line of owl evolution. The family has several structural features separating it from the barn owls, including shorter, broader skulls, larger eyes and broader pelvic girdles. However, the Australian species, all in the genus *Ninox*, are most distinctive in their behavioural traits. All form pairs which vigorously defend territories with monotonous 'hooting'; all have downy fledglings; all males feed incubating females by calling them *from* the nest.

Reading

Burton, John A. (editor) (1973), *Owls of the World: their evolution, structure, and ecology*, Peter Lowe, Netherlands.

Fleay, D. (1968), *Nightwatchmen of Bush and Plain*, Jacaranda Press, Brisbane.

Hollands, D. (1991), *Birds of the Night: owls, frogmouths and nightjars of Australia*, Reed Books, Balgowlah, NSW (pp. 11-69).

Breeding seasons

J F M A M J J A S O N D

399 Rufous Owl

400 Powerful Owl

401 Southern Boobook

402 Barking Owl

Australian Frogmouths — Family Podargidae

[Within Sibley & Ahlquist's Order Strigiformes and Suborder Caprimulgi, the Infraorder Podargides is divided into the Family Podargidae, Australian Frogmouths, and Family Batrachostomidae, Asian Frogmouths.]

These noctural birds capture arthropods, snails and small vertebrates by flying from a vantage perch to the ground. Consequently they have relatively broad wings, being strong fliers only over short distances. Heavy mortality is caused by motor traffic, because the frogmouths are slow to rise from road surfaces. The leading edge of the first primary feather is fringed for silent flight. The inside of the mouth is yellowish or apple-green in colour; the tongue is thin like a scrap of paper. Gaping at potential predators, and a hissing sound, are part of their defence mechanisms. At night, when active, they may also dive from a branch at potential predators, 'clopping' their beak very loudly. Such an attack has been known to deter a cat and was probably a defence against large marsupial predators before feral animals were introduced to Australia. They roost by day on exposed branches, relying on stillness and excellent cryptic camouflage to avoid predators. Their 'stretched-out' static posture when alarmed, which then resembles a branch stub, is well known and frequently observed by day. They nest on horizontal forks, building a tiny and apparently inadequate nest. They have two eggs; nestlings are downy-white.

Reading

Hollands, D. (1991), *Birds of the Night: owls, frogmouths and nightjars of Australia*, Reed Books, Balgowlah, NSW (pp. 143-63).

Schodde, R. & Mason, I. J. (1980), *Nocturnal Birds of Australia*, Lansdowne Editions, Melbourne.

Threat display.

Breeding seasons

J F M A M J J A S O N D

409 Tawny Frogmouth

410 Papuan Frogmouth

411 Marbled Frogmouth

Owlet-Nightjars — Family Aegothelidae

[Within Sibley & Ahlquist's Order Strigiformes and Suborder Aegotheli, the traditional Family Aegothelidae contains the Owlet-Nightjars. Six species in PNG.]

Australia's single but very widespread species occurs in many habitat types, but is more common in arid regions. It breeds (and roosts by day) in tree hollows or stumps; lays two to four white, oval eggs; often lands on the ground to feed.

Fossils of the genus are known from Australia. New Zealand has fossils of a large Pleistocene to sub-Recent owlet-nightjar, tending to gigantism. With large hind limbs and reduced wings, it may have tended toward flightlessness. It is *Megaegotheles novaezeelandiae*, related to Australia's genus *Aegotheles*.

Reading

Hollands, D. (1991), *Birds of the Night: owls, frogmouths and nightjars of Australia*, Reed Books, Balgowlah, NSW (pp. 165-9).

Rich, P. V. & Scarlett, R. (1977), 'Another look at *Megaegotheles*, a large owlet-nightjar from New Zealand', *Emu* 77 (1), 1-8.

Breeding season (*variable*)

J	F	M	A	M	J	J	A	S	O	N	D

412 Australian Owlet-nightjar*

Nightjars and allies — Family Caprimulgidae

[Within the Order Strigiformes and Suborder Caprimulgi, Sibley & Ahlquist place the traditional Family Caprimulgidae, with two subfamilies, one of which, Caprimulginae, contains the typical Nightjars (one species inhabits Australia and New Guinea), and the American Whip-poor-wills. A new Family Eurostopodidae is introduced for the genus *Eurostopodus*, separate from Caprimulgidae; two in Australia, three in PNG.]

Nightjars — Subfamily Caprimulginae

Nightjars hawk evening- and night-flying insects for food. One or two pale eggs are laid in a ground-scrape, the superbly camouflaged incubating adults protecting them. Loose concentrations of presumably migrating nightjars may be encountered roosting over a wide area in bushland. Many foreign nightjar species hibernate to escape low temperature periods but this is not proven for Australia's two genera and three species. Our three birds superficially look alike.

Breeding seasons

J	F	M	A	M	J	J	A	S	O	N	D

413 White-throated Nightjar

414 Spotted Nightjar

415 Large-tailed Nightjar

Typical Swifts — Family Apodidae

[Sibley & Ahlquist place the typical swifts in the traditional Order Apodiformes and Family Apodidae. A division of their superorder, Apodimorphae, leads to the hermits and the hummingbirds.]

The White-rumped Swiftlet *Aerodramus spodiopygius chillagoensis* breeds in the total darkness of eastern Queensland caves in which tiny, scoop-shaped nests, partly of saliva, are glued to the walls. One egg is laid; nestlings are naked. A second egg is often then laid and incubated by the first nestling. Adults use echo-locating clicks to navigate in the caves.

The two large swifts are annual non-breeding summer migrants to Australia from northern Asia. On arrival, White-throated Needletails slowly disperse along the whole length and on each side of the Eastern Highlands mountain chain, including Tasmania; occasionally some reach New Zealand. Fork-tailed Swifts disperse widely, mainly across the western half of the continent. Both species become nomadic in response to broad-scale weather-pattern changes. They rely entirely on aerial insects, especially nup-

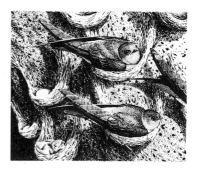

Part of a White-rumped Swiftlet nesting colony in a cave.

tial swarms of beetles, ants, termites and native bees, for food. If standing beneath a feeding flock of White-throated Needletails, a rain of abdomen-less ants may fall on you; the birds manipulate the flying queen ants and nip off the soft, nutrient-rich abdomen, dropping the less palatable remainder.

Other Asian and Melanesian swiftlets and swifts may be expected as occasional vagrants. Field identification of the Uniform Swiftlet is so far considered unreliable.

Reading
Crouther, M. M. (1983), 'Observations on White-rumped Swiftlets breeding at Finch Hatton Gorge, 1981-82', *Aust. Bird Watcher* **10**, 1-11.
Tarburton, M. K. (1988), 'Breeding biology of the White-rumped Swiftlet at Chillagoe', *Emu* **88** (4), 202-9.

Breeding season

J	F	M	A	M	J	J	A	S	O	N	D

417 White-rumped Swiftlet

Alcedinid Kingfishers — Family Alcedinidae

[Sibley & Ahlquist retain the Family Alcedinidae within Parvorder Alcedinida of Order Coraciiformes. However, in Order Coraciiformes they also establish Parvorder Cerylida, divided into Superfamily Dacelonoidea and Family Dacelonidae for the kookaburras and allies, which include Australo/Papuan members, and a second superfamily, Ceryloidea, and Family Cerylidae (non-Australian).]

Kingfishers perch upright, are large-headed, short-necked, and have long, stout bills. Their flight is swift, strong and direct. All are carnivorous, piscivorous and insectivorous. Two main groupings are recognised.

True Kingfishers — Subfamily Alcedinae

The aquatic kingfishers are represented by the genus *Alcedo* (formerly named *Ceyx*), and feed entirely on aquatic life.

Breeding seasons

J	F	M	A	M	J	J	A	S	O	N	D

422 Azure Kingfisher

423 Little Kingfisher

Kookaburras — Subfamily Daceloninae

The more terrestrial 'tree-kingfishers' are represented by several genera: *Dacelo*, *Todirhamphus*, *Syma* and *Tanysiptera*. Kookaburras (*Dacelo*) are among the largest kingfishers in the world. They feed mostly by flying to the ground from a vantage point and catching insects and small vertebrates. The Laughing Kookaburra's call is known world-wide.

Todirhamphus kingfishers (formerly *Halcyon*) are a large, world-wide group with four species in Australia. The Collared Kingfisher is confined to mangroves, feeding on marine, aquatic and terrestrial life. The other species are less aquatic: the Red-backed is found in arid inland but may move to the coast in drought years. Sacred Kingfishers nest in Australia, including the south, then migrate to northern Australia, New Guinea, Timor and the Solomon Islands in winter. Many of the eastern Australian Forest Kingfishers also migrate to New Guinea.

Those in the genus *Syma* have distinctive saw-edged bills but otherwise resemble *Todirhamphus* kingfishers in many aspects of ecology and movement.

As adults, paradise-kingfishers *Tanysiptera* have long, thin central tail feathers, sometimes with racquet-shaped tips. The Buff-breasted breeds in tropical north Queensland in the wet season, then migrates to New Guinea in the dry. The Common Paradise-Kingfisher has occurred once at Boigu Island, off the New Guinea coast but a part of Australia.

Kingfishers nest in tree-holes (*Dacelo*, *Todirhamphus*), termite mounds (*Tanysiptera*, *Todirhamphus*) or banks (Redbacked, sometimes Sacred Kingfishers).

Breeding seasons

J	F	M	A	M	J	J	A	S	O	N	D

424 Laughing Kookaburra

425 Blue-winged Kookaburra

426 Forest Kingfisher

427 Red-backed Kingfisher

428 Sacred Kingfisher

429 Collared Kingfisher

430 Yellow-billed Kingfisher

431 Buff-breasted Paradise-Kingfisher

Bee-eaters   Family Meropidae

[Sibley & Ahlquist retain the Family Meropidae in their Order Coraciiformes.]

Most Rainbow Bee-eaters breed in southern Australia, moving to northern Australia, New Guinea and Indonesia in winter. They are insectivorous, sit on exposed perches and, with swift and undulating flight, catch insects. They tunnel into sandy banks (or flat ground) to lay four to five white eggs, incubated and tended by both sexes. As many as eight adults have been seen in attendance at one nest hole.

In some regions of Australia they may be shot under permit because of their habit of catching bees around commercial hives. This ought to be investigated.

Reading

Fry, C. H. (1984), *The Bee-eaters*, T. & A. D. Poyser, Calton, UK; Buteo Books, Vermillion, S Dakota, USA.

Section of nest burrow.

Breeding season

J	F	M	A	M	J	J	A	S	O	N	D

433 Rainbow Bee-eater

Typical Rollers   Family Coraciidae

[Sibley & Ahlquist also maintain the traditional Family Coraciidae Typical Rollers, within their Order Coraciiformes.]

All rollers perform acrobatic aerial twisting and rolling during their very vocal courtship flights.

The Dollarbird is a regular summer breeding migrant to northern and eastern Australia from southern Asia. During migration they fly at high altitudes. They hunt, usually early or late in the day, for insects and even small birds. Dollarbirds hawk from high bare branches. The nest is usually in a hollow in a tree; several glossy white eggs are laid.

Breeding season

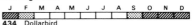

J	F	M	A	M	J	J	A	S	O	N	D

434 Dollarbird

ORDER PASSERIFORMES (Traditional)

[Sibley & Ahlquist's Order Passeriformes commences here, as does the traditional. Their Suborder Tyranni is also known as the Suboscines. There are four superfamilies of Old World Suboscines: of these two families are of interest to Australasia — Family Acanthisittidae, New Zealand wrens (not dealt with further), and Family Pittidae, an Asian family with Australasian representatives.

There is also a large group of South American Suboscines, not dealt with in this book.

Collectively the Suboscines may be regarded as 'more advanced' in an evolutionary sense than the previously discussed non-passerines, but 'less advanced' than the Oscines — true song birds of the Suborder Passeri — which follow on pages 339-70. There are anatomical as well as DNA differences between the groups.]

Pittas   Family Pittidae

[Sibley & Ahlquist suggest that the rather uniform external morphology of the world's pittas in fact hides a more complex genetic diversity. They do not further subdivide the pittas but suggest that investigation will see more taxa emerge from within the present family.]

The Order Passeriformes commences with the suboscine pittas. They are brilliantly plumaged birds that are superficially thrush-like. Stout, longish legs reflect a ground-dwelling existence, but they perch in trees to give territorial calls and to roost.

With their bodies in a crouching attitude parallel to the ground, pittas sometimes bend their legs and alternately raise and lower their back and head.

They feed on insects, other invertebrates and reptiles;

A Rainbow Pitta feeds its nestling.

probably on fallen fruit and berries as well. Land snails are smashed open on anvils of roots or stones, leaving a tell-tale litter of empty shells.

Pittas' nests are bulky, and normally close to the ground on logs, branch debris or between diverging or emergent tree roots. They are partly or wholly domed, with a large side entrance.

The Blue-winged Pitta's range is from eastern India to the Philippines; two have straggled to Australia.

Breeding seasons

	J	F	M	A	M	J	J	A	S	O	N	D
435 Red-bellied Pitta												
437 Noisy Pitta												
438 Rainbow Pitta												

Suborder Passeri (Oscines)

[The Oscines, *all* of the 'true song birds', are divided by Sibley & Ahlquist into two great groupings, the parvorders Corvida and Passerida respectively. Parvorder Corvida contains *all* of the birds now known to have evolved locally and radiated outward from the Australasian avifaunal region. They include the entire complement of the world's crow family, and many birds with which we in Australia are not familiar — vireos, fairy-bluebirds, leafbirds, true shrikes, jays, nutcrackers, Old World Orioles, bushshrikes, helmetshrikes, vangas, puffbacks and their allies, and New Zealand wattlebirds.

The Parvorder Passerida contains *all* of the rest of the 'true song birds' of the Old and New Worlds. It will be noted that several groups of these passerines that we know well in Australasia are in fact representatives of Old World species that did *not* evolve in the Australasian avifaunal region.

The Parvorder Corvida starts here.]

Lyrebirds   Family Menuridae

[Within Parvorder Corvida, Sibley & Ahlquist have erected Super-family Menuroidea, containing the lyrebirds and scrub-birds, in their Family Menuridae, *and* bowerbirds in the separate Family Ptilinorhynchidae. In discovering close DNA links between lyrebirds and bowerbirds, they also have established that bowerbirds and the birds-of-paradise are not nearly so closely related as often previously considered. The birds-of-paradise are most closely related to the Australo-Papuan magpies, currawongs and butcherbirds, with the next nearest being the orioles and cuckoo-shrikes, and then the crows, jays and true magpies, most of which now live elsewhere in the world. Work is continuing and much further refinement is necessary. We continue to be conservative!]

The name 'lyrebird' stems from the resemblance of the male Superb Lyrebird's tail to a Greek lyre. The tail comprises 16 highly modified tail feathers: two lyrates, two medians and 12 filamentaries which are all thrown forward over the head in a drooping fan during courtship display. The tail of Albert's Lyrebird lacks lyrates and consists of 14 feathers.

Lyrebirds rake the forest floor constantly for soil-dwelling invertebrates. The sharp claws on their powerful feet rip away bark, exposing invertebrates beneath.

The Superb's courtship display takes place on or near earth mounds, the Albert's from vine and twiggy platforms, and both sing loudly. Although the Superb's territorial song contains a short species-specific component (a phrase unique to its species), it is largely a repertoire of mimicked sounds, including duetting of other bird species and wing beats and calls of flying parrot flocks. During close pursuit of females, males have a quieter song which may contain mimicry.

Male Superb Lyrebirds are polygamous and perform no parental duties. Some females visit more than one male before mating, but male-female association is brief and limited, so that pair-bonding seems to be absent. Breeding commences in winter. The female lays a single stone-grey

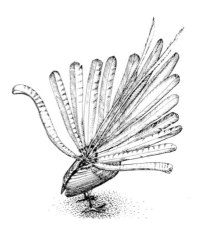

The Superb Lyrebird's tail has 16 tail feathers. The tail feathers of the immature male (shown here) are not fully modified as in the adult.

coloured egg in the large, side-entranced nest chamber. Incubation takes 50 days, probably because the female deserts the egg for three to six hours each morning during which time the embryonic temperature falls to the low ambient temperature generally prevailing in eastern and southern winter months, and this interrupts development.

Nestling development takes 47 days, the chick being fed about three times hourly. Its weight increases twelvefold to a fledgling weight of some 63 per cent of that of the adult female. Estimates of nesting success vary widely (11-20 per cent to 65-79 per cent); the main nest predators are probably native birds, cats, dogs, foxes; perhaps goannas. Fledglings accompany their mothers and are partly fed by them for up to eight months.

The biology of Albert's Lyrebird is broadly similar to that of the Superb, but is poorly documented. There is an outstanding need for a detailed, long-term study of the ecology and breeding biology of this species.

Reading

Reilly, P. (1988), *The Lyrebird: a natural history*, NSW University Press, Kensington, NSW.

Sibley, C. G. (1974), 'The relationships of the Lyrebirds', *Emu* **74**, 65-79.

Smith, L. H. (1968), *The Lyrebird*, Lansdowne Press, Melbourne.

The Superb Lyrebird builds a large, side-entranced nest chamber.

Breeding seasons

	J	F	M	A	M	J	J	A	S	O	N	D
439 Albert's Lyrebird												
440 Superb Lyrebird												

Scrub-birds   Family Atrichornithidae

[This is an ancient Australian family. The closest allies are the Lyrebirds. Previously, the two families have frequently been placed in a suborder, Menurae, of the Passeriformes. The recent work of Sibley & Ahlquist indicates that within Parvorder Corvida and Superfamily Menuroidea, both Lyrebirds and Scrub-birds are in Family Menuridae, with a lyrebird Subfamily Menurinae and a scrub-bird Subfamily Atrichornithidae. The other families in this complex are believed to be the bowerbirds Ptilinorhynchidae and Australo-Papuan treecreepers Climacteridae. We are keeping them separate for the present.]

The males of these two rare species display rather like immature lyrebirds with elevated and fanned tails, lowered wings, and with the body quivering from the effort of sustained, loud, melodious song and mimicry.

The birds live in dense cover, are 'ground-hugging' species that run fast; are camouflaged by virtue of being brown and in the shadows. Domed nests are close to the ground with small side-entrances and are lined with thin, papery wood pulp. One egg is laid (Noisy Scrub-bird), or two (Rufous Scrub-bird).

Much recent research has been centred on the Noisy Scrub-bird of the south-west of Western Australia, a species with a radically reduced range since European settlement. It is now restricted to a few localities centred on Two Peoples Bay. Census attempts involve counting singing males in order to estimate distribution and numbers. An increase in male population numbers, from around 40-45 in 1962-66, to around 157 in 1985, is encouraging. The world population at 1986 was perhaps 400 Noisy Scrub-birds.

Reading

Burbidge, A. A., Folley, G. L. & Smith, G. T. (1986), 'The Noisy Scrub-bird', *Wildlife Management Program* no. 2, Department of Conservation and Land Management, Como, WA.

Breeding seasons

	J	F	M	A	M	J	J	A	S	O	N	D
441 Rufous Scrub-bird												
442 Noisy Scrub-bird												

Australo-Papuan Treecreepers   Family Climacteridae

[In 1984, Sibley and others assigned the Treecreepers to the Super-family complex Menuroidea which contains the lyrebirds and scrub-birds and which, in Sibley & Ahlquist's work, also includes the Bowerbirds, Ptilinorhynchidae.

Although still included in their systematic list in this position, the 1990 publication now *questions* the placing of the Climateridae in the Menuroidea. Sibley & Ahlquist indicate that although their results show that treecreepers are most closely allied to lyrebirds and bowerbirds, they have some reservations, and suggest that continuing research and re-evaluation of the true relationships of the Climacteridae is required.]

The White-throated Treecreeper differs from other Australian treecreepers in so many respects that different ancestry is conceivable. It has shorter legs, and the foot's sole has scaly ridges rather than broad pads. Its bill is thinner, straighter and has a grey-white lower mandible base; other climacterids have an all-black bill. Its forecrown is distinctly scalloped and the lores have a white line; by contrast, the other species have a uniform crown and dark lores. Patterns of sexual dimorphism and juvenile plumage also show a strong dichotomy.

In the White-throated, females have an orange cheek spot; females of the other species have rufous chest stripes. White-throated juveniles have black-edged whitish scapular streaks, and a bright chestnut rump patch (only in females); nestlings have yellow patches behind the 'knees', on the soles, and the tips of the toenails. These features are lacking in the other species.

Other peculiarities of the White-throated may relate to its probable rainforest origin. It has a more complex vocal repertoire, including sexually diagnostic calls, an audible tail-flicking territorial display and an elaborate pre-mating display, all of which may assist contact in closed habitats with reduced visibility. Its little-marked white eggs may enhance their visibility under such conditions; they differ strikingly from the heavily-marked pinkish eggs of the other species.

The female White-throated builds the nest and incubates for 22-3 days, whereas in the Red-browed and Brown, both sexes build the nest and the incubation period is much shorter, (16-18 days). Moreover, the White-throated roosts externally on tree-trunks, just inside burned-out stumps, or sometimes on man-made structures. The other species usually roost inside hollow dead branches. A suggestion of invoking an earlier generic name, *Cormobates*, for the White-throated is adopted. A new race *intermedia* was described in 1983.

Orenstein published a summary of the treecreepers: White-throated Treecreepers breed in solitary pairs, raising their young alone, whereas Red-browed, Black-tailed, Brown and Rufous Treecreepers breed communally, in that extra birds, mostly males, help feed the young.

The breeding biology of the Rufous and Black-tailed has yet to be examined in detail, and the plumages of their juveniles described.

Reading

Noske, R. A. (1980), 'Cooperative breeding by treecreepers', *Emu* 80, 35-6.

Sibley C. G., Schodde, R. & Ahlquist, J. E. (1984), 'The relationships of the Australo-Papuan treecreepers Climacteridae as indicated by DNA-DNA hybridisation', *Emu* 84, 236-41.

The pale wing bars of the White-throated Treecreeper are exposed in flight (top); a White-throated Treecreeper's foot (bottom).

Breeding seasons

	J	F	M	A	M	J	J	A	S	O	N	D

602 White-throated Treecreeper

603 Red-browed Treecreeper

604 White-browed Treecreeper

605 Brown Treecreeper

606 Rufous Treecreeper

607 Black-tailed Treecreeper

Fairy-wrens, Emu-wrens, Grasswrens Family Maluridae

[Sibley & Ahlquist's work clearly indicates that the fairy-wrens, emu-wrens and grasswrens are part of the ancient Australo-Papuan bird group, which evolved locally and spread through Australasia. This finally excludes the Old World Sylviidae and Muscicapidae, the warblers, thrushes and flycatchers, from any possible close relationship.]

Restricted to Australia and New Guinea, the malurids' affinities are somewhat disguised, because their external morphology does not indicate a clear relationship with other species. They have variously been linked with Old World warblers (Sylviidae), with babblers (Timaliidae), and with a hybrid mixture of bird families loosely bundled together in (previously) an ever-changing family known as the Muscicapidae, a family now better defined, containing the typical thrushes and the Old World flycatchers and their allies.

The behavioural postures of the Superb Fairy-wren: (a) clumping and allopreening; (b) territorial singing; (c) rodent-like display.

Fairy-wrens Subfamily Malurinae, Tribe Malurini

In Australia, fairy-wrens are found in every terrestrial habitat. Characteristically, they keep their tails cocked when hopping on the ground or through bushes. Their bills are short, their legs long or thick. They usually fly low over the ground or hop. An elaborate distraction display is given if an intruder approaches a nest: the bird scuttles away in a rodent-like manner, the 'rodent-run' display.

The fairy-wrens are well-known for the beauty of the male's plumage, where blues and mauves predominate. The females, juveniles and non-breeding males are much duller, being mostly brown-bodied, but males always have blue or dark blue tails.

All fairy-wrens are social, living in groups that maintain their own territory. These co-operative groups consist of a dominant male, one female, subordinate non-breeding birds of both sexes and first-year birds.

Breeding seasons (*variable*)

	J	F	M	A	M	J	J	A	S	O	N	D
542	Purple-crowned Fairy-wren*											
543	Superb Fairy-wren											
544	Splendid Fairy-wren											
545A	Variegated Fairy-wren											
545B	Lovely Fairy-wren											
546	Blue-breasted Fairy-wren											
547	Red-winged Fairy-wren											
548	White-winged Fairy-wren											
549	Red-backed Fairy-wren											

Emu-wrens Subfamily Malurinae, Tribe Stipiturini

Emu-wrens are brown and streaked, the males having blue on the face, throat and breast. They have distinctive, filamentous, emu-feather-like tail feathers (hence their name) and are among the smallest of Australian birds; only the Weebill is smaller.

Emu-wrens live in groups like fairy-wrens, are often very difficult to see and will retreat deep into undergrowth for protection. Eggs and nests are generally similar to those of fairy-wrens but 'helpers at the nest' seem to be the exception, not the rule.

Three species are now recognised in this book. The Rufous-crowned Emu-wren occurs in spinifex and the Southern Emu-wren in heathlands. The Mallee Emu-wren is now considered a full species, similar in habitat requirement to the Rufous-crowned but geographically isolated.

Breeding seasons

	J	F	M	A	M	J	J	A	S	O	N	D
550A	Rufous-crowned Emu Wren											
550B	Mallee Emu-wren											
551	Southern Emu-wren											

Grasswrens Subfamily Amytornithinae

Grasswrens include some of the most difficult Australian passerines to see, occurring as they do in remote arid or rocky regions. They can be very shy and will hide in vegetation. They are beautifully streaked brown, rufous, black and white, and vary in size from as large as the Common

Starling to as small as the fairy-wrens. When escaping from the observer they often run rather than fly; they are excellent runners.

Grasswrens eat seeds as well as insects. Two to three eggs, which are white to pink and spotted brown-red, are laid in a dome-shaped nest hidden in low vegetation. Grasswrens have only one brood per year.

Entrepreneurs now run tours which criss-cross the country, specifically to see as many grasswrens as possible (of course, sightings of other birds are made!).

Reading

Schodde, R. (1982), *The Fairy-wrens — A Monograph of the Maluridae*, Lansdowne Editions, Melbourne.

Sibley, G. C. & Ahlquist, J. E. (1982), 'The relationships of the Australo-Papuan fairy-wrens *Malurus* as indicated by DNA-DNA hybridisation', *Emu* **82**, 251-5.

National Photographic Index of Australian Wildlife (1982), *The Wrens and Warblers of Australia*, Angus & Robertson, London, Sydney, Melbourne.

Breeding seasons (*variable)

J F M A M J J A S O N D

552 Black Grasswren
553 White-throated Grasswren
554 Carpentarian Grasswren
555 Striated Grasswren*
556 Eyrean Grasswren
557 Grey Grasswren
558 Thick-billed Grasswren*
559 Dusky Grasswren*

Honeyeaters
Family Meliphagidae

[Within the Parvorder Corvida, Sibley & Ahlquist have erected a Superfamily Meliphagoidea to include the closely related families of Maluridae, Meliphagidae and Pardalotidae. In Meliphagidae, the honeyeaters, they also include the Australian chats (genus *Epthianura*) and Gibberbird (genus *Ashbyia*).]

Honeyeaters are mainly found in Australia and New Guinea but their geographic range extends from Bali to the Bonin Islands (where there is one species), Micronesia, Polynesia as far as Tonga and Samoa and through to Hawaii, and New Zealand. Evidence clearly suggests that the family evolved in and radiated from Australia and New Guinea. At least one species occurs in every terrestrial habitat in Australia, from tropical rainforest to arid shrublands, from mangroves to suburbia.

The principal and most striking anatomical feature of the family is the brush-tipped tongue, which functions in the same way as a paint brush, collecting fluids (like nectar) by capillarity. Most honeyeaters can protrude their tongues well beyond their bill tips, enabling nectar collection from the base of long tubular flowers or honeydew extraction from deep narrow cracks in bark. Most can lap up these fluids at rates of 10 or more licks per second and can empty a flower in less than one second.

In Australia, 67 honeyeater species occur. Classification of these into genera and species is still in a state of flux. The degree of variation in the genera varies. For example, genus *Phylidonyris* with five species shows considerable variation (compare Tawny-crowned with New Holland Honeyeater) but elsewhere in the family an equivalent (or less) variation results in two genera (for instance, *Acanthagenys* and *Anthochaera*; *Lichenostomus* and *Meliphaga*). Some taxonomists do not consider that *Lichenostomus* is a separate genus from *Meliphaga*. Thus the most recently described species, the Eungella Honeyeater, was described as a species of *Meliphaga*, yet its closest ally is the Bridled Honeyeater *Lichenostomus frenatus*. In the classification followed here, we use *Lichenostomus*.

The distributions shown on the maps need to be explained to avoid misinterpretation. Broadly, they demarcate the regions in which each species has been seen since European occupation. It would be incorrect to assume that a

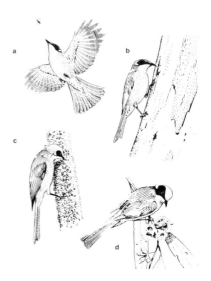

The Yellow-tufted Honeyeater feeding: (a) insects; (b) honeydew; (c) blackboy; (d) gum blossom.

species is equally abundant throughout its range. In fact, many species are unlikely to be seen in the extremities of their geographic range. For example, Regent Honeyeaters are now virtually absent from the Mt Lofty Ranges and Kangaroo Island of South Australia. Mobile species, such as Black, Scarlet, Pied and Painted Honeyeaters, are irregular visitors to southern parts of their range. 'Fuscous' (Yellow-tinted) and Yellow-tufted Honeyeaters are also very infrequent visitors to South Australia. And further, many of the mobile species could easily appear in areas *outside* the marked distribution.

Honeyeaters feed mainly on nectar, fruit and sugary secretions of herbivorous insects (honeydew or lerp), which are rich in carbohydrates (sugars) but low in nutrients. Although they provide most of the food for many honeyeaters, no species feeds entirely on them. All honeyeaters include at least a few insects in their diets to satisfy protein and nutrient requirements.

In southern temperate Australia, honeyeaters may be divided into three groups. 'Nectarivorous' genera, such as *Anthochaera, Phylidonyris, Lichmera* and *Acanthorhynchus*, feed mainly on nectar. So-called 'insectivorous' genera, such as *Melithreptus, Manorina* and many species of *Lichenostomus*, feed mainly by gleaning foliage or probing bark for honeydew, lerps or insects. 'Frugivorous' species, such as Spiny-cheeked and Singing Honeyeaters, eat large amounts of fruit 'in season', at least in parts of their range. These groupings are not *rigid*. In fact, almost all species have been observed taking nectar, fruit and honeydew.

The groupings, however, highlight the morphological specialisation within the family. Nectarivorous species are generally longer-beaked, enabling them to probe a greater variety of flowers. The most specialised are the slender-beaked species such as spinebills. Their long, decurved bills match the equally long, decurved flowers of many native plants (for instance, the heath *Epacris longiflora*). Short-beaked honeyeaters can extend their tongues to reach nectar at some of the flower bases, but the further the tongue is extended, the less efficient it becomes. Sometimes birds pierce the sides of such tubular flowers, or instead, visit the less specialised flowers (e.g. of *Eucalyptus*) where nectar is more readily accessible.

Little is known about the ecology of honeyeaters of the inland or tropical regions of Australia. The long-beaked *Myzomela* and *Certhionyx* are undoubtedly nectarivorous; shorter-beaked rainforest species are probably frugivorous. The Painted Honeyeater specialises on mistletoe fruits.

Honeyeaters are one of the most successful Australian bird families. Ten or more species may occur in one area; honeyeaters can account for more than half of all birds living in such an area. In part, this success can be attributed to the quantity and diversity of their food. In some areas sufficient nectar is produced to support more than 20 individuals per hectare. A single ironbark tree, *Eucalyptus sideroxylon*, can support 15 New Holland Honeyeaters for a period of 1-2 months during peak flowering.

Australian melaphagid movements are therefore often associated with the flowering of native plants. In areas with a year-round nectar or honeydew supply, honeyeaters are usually resident, switching from one plant species to another as each blooms. Where food is only available for part of the year, honeyeaters show regular seasonal movements.

The brush-tipped tongue of the White-plumed Honeyeater.

The brush-tipped tongue of a honeyeater functions in the same way as a paint brush.

A male Western Spinebill pollinates a *Grevillea wilsonii*. Note the pollen grains on its crown.

An Eastern Spinebill feeding on the heath *Epacris longiflora*.

The nest of a Black Honeyeater is bound to twigs on a fork of a tree. It is not slung beneath a branch. The eggs are buff in colour with grey and dark green speckles.

In the inland, where flowering is irregular, nectarivorous honeyeaters are described as 'blossom nomads'. Only Yellow-faced and White-naped Honeyeaters, and perhaps the Red Wattlebird, are considered to be migratory, but their movements are poorly understood. Large, restless flocks of these birds can be seen moving through areas in south-eastern Australia during autumn. Large numbers winter in coastal regions of New South Wales and parts of South Australia. Their origin is not known, but the movements may be altitudinal, birds avoiding cold mountain winter weather.

Honeyeaters are pugnacious and are often seen chasing other birds. This aggression is associated with their food supply defence. Wattlebirds and New Holland Honeyeaters frequently defend nectar sources from members of their own species and other smaller honeyeater species. Regent Honeyeaters were recently recognised as mimicking the calls of larger honeyeater species, e.g. wattlebirds, friarbirds, Spiny-cheeked Honeyeater and perhaps miners, to avoid being chased from shared food resources. When two or more nectarivorous species co-occur, nectar sources are then usually partitioned. The larger wattlebirds, for example, use the richest and most dense nectar sources (*Banksia*, *Eucalyptus*) and aggressively exclude smaller species from these. Smaller species exploit any rich sources not so monopolised and also poorer, more scattered nectar sources (*Lysiana*, *Correa*, *Epacris*). Although less is known about the insectivorous species, they too, probably partition resources along a gradient of food density, with the largest species, *Manorina*, excluding smaller species from the richest sources (such as outbreaks of lerp).

Breeding seasons of Australian honeyeaters also depend largely on the availability of carbohydrate food and the locality. Most species breed between late winter (July/August) and early summer (December) but a number of species also breed during autumn and occasionally during winter. Honeyeaters usually moult during summer after spring breeding. Juveniles often have an incomplete post-juvenile moult during summer or autumn.

Female honeyeaters build the cup-shaped nest in either a fork of a shrub or tree, or suspend it in pendulous foliage, often in a eucalypt. Nest location depends on the honeyeater species. Nests are usually constructed of small twigs and strips of bark held together by spiders' webs, and often lined with mammal hair, soft plant material and the occasional feather. Fine moss may sometimes be used in the cup.

Clutches usually consist of two or three pinkish-buff (sometimes whitish) eggs, with darker spots or blotches. Eggs are laid on consecutive days. Incubation normally takes about two weeks. Chicks remain in the nest for a similar period. In nearly all species, only the female incubates but both sexes feed the nestlings.

Males of many species give display flights during the breeding season, in which they flap up at an angle into the air, often giving a piping call, then steeply glide back to a perch. Many species breed as monogamous pairs but some species, for example *Manorina* and *Melithreptus*, may breed communally when non-breeding individuals assist the breeding pair by feeding chicks. Miners, in particular, live in distinct colonies and have a complex social system. Some species, notably *Manorina*, but also *Lichenostomus* and *Phylidonyris*, gather for group displays or 'corroborees'. The purpose of these is not known.

Breeding seasons (*variable*)

J F M A M J J A S O N D

608 Red Wattlebird*
609 Yellow Wattlebird
610A Little Wattlebird*
610B Brush Wattlebird*
611 Spiny-cheeked Honeyeater*
612 Striped Honeyeater*
613 Helmeted Friarbird*
614 Silver-crowned Friarbird*
615 Noisy Friarbird*
616 Little Friarbird*
617 Regent Honeyeater
618 Blue-faced Honeyeater*
619 Bell Miner*
620 Noisy Miner*
621 Yellow-throated Miner*
622 Black-eared Miner
623 Macleay's Honeyeater
624 Tawny-breasted Honeyeater
625 Lewin's Honeyeater
626 Yellow-spotted Honeyeater
627 Graceful Honeyeater
628 White-lined Honeyeater (*Insufficient information*)
629 Eungella Honeyeater (*Insufficient information*)
630 Yellow-faced Honeyeater
631 Bridled Honeyeater
632 Singing Honeyeater*
633 Varied Honeyeater*
634 Mangrove Honeyeater
635 White-gaped Honeyeater*
636 Yellow Honeyeater
637 White-eared Honeyeater

Honeyeaters have a close mutual association with the Australian flora and are important pollinators and seed dispersers. Among the plants pollinated by honeyeaters are various *Eucalyptus, Banksia, Callistemon, Grevillea, Correa, Eremophila, Epacris* and mistletoes, to name a few only, many plants depending on birds for pollination. Planting suitable nectar-producing plants attracts honeyeaters to suburban gardens. Honeyeaters also disperse the seeds of various acacias, chenopods, mistletoes and epacrids. The genera of honeyeaters are listed here.

Acanthochaera 4 species, the wattlebirds. Recent separation of Little Wattlebird *lunulata* (SW of WA), from the Brush Wattlebird *chrysoptera* (SE Aust. and Tas.) as they are two totally isolated species.

Acanthagenys 1 species, the Spiny-cheeked Honeyeater.

Plectorhyncha 1 species, the Striped Honeyeater. Monotypic genus.

Philemon 4 species in Aust., the friarbirds. 7 species in PNG.

Xanthomyza 1 species, the Regent Honeyeater. No geographic variation of significance found in the Regent Honeyeater. Brightness of the yellow in the wing may vary with season. On the endangered list of Australian birds.

Entomyzon 1 species, the Blue-faced Honeyeater. Resembles the white-naped group of honeyeaters *Melithreptus* but is much larger. 3 races in Aust.; 1 race in PNG. Monotypic genus.

Manorina 3 or 4 species, the miners, depending on whether the Black-eared Miner (now also on the endangered list because of a critically low population) is regarded as a full species.

Xanthotis 2 species in Aust. Macleay's and Tawny-breasted Honeyeaters of far N Qld. The latter, and another species, also in PNG.

Meliphaga 4 species in Aust. Dark birds, favouring dense, wet forests, and mainly tropical in distribution. Discussion continues about relationships between this genus and *Lichenostomus*.

Lichenostomus About 18 species of generally yellowish honeyeaters. A rehabilitation programme is underway for the Helmeted Honeyeater (a race of the Yellow-tufted Honeyeater), also on the endangered list, with a critical population east of Melbourne.

Melithreptus 6 species, dark-headed honeyeaters, all but 1 species having a white or pale nape line.

Glycichaera 1 species, Green-backed Honeyeater. Also in PNG.

Lichmera 1 species, Brown Honeyeater in Aust.

Trichodere 1 species, White-streaked Honeyeater. Monotypic genus.

Phylidonyris 5 species, mainly black and white striped honeyeaters, the 'New Holland' group of Aust.

Grantiella 1 species, Painted Honeyeater, a specialist on mistletoe fruits, flowers. Monotypic genus.

Ramsayornis 2 species, Brown-backed and Bar-chested Honeyeaters of N. Aust. Brown-backed also occurs in PNG.

Conopophila 3 species, Rufous-banded, Rufous-throated and Grey Honeyeaters. A race of Rufous-banded also in PNG.

Acanthorhynchus 2 species, the spinebills, with considerable dimorphism between the sexes.

Certhionyx 3 species. Nomadic; sexually dimorphic — black and white males; brown females.

Myzomela 3 species in Aust.; the 'Scarlet Honeyeater' group. 14 species in PNG, including Red-headed and Dusky Honeyeaters.

Reading

Clarke, M. F. (1988), 'The reproductive biology of the Bell Miner *Manorina melanophrys*', *Emu* **88** (2), 88-100.

Ford, H. A. & Paton, D. C. (1982), 'Partitioning of nectar sources in an Australian honeyeater community', *Aust. J. Ecol.* **7**, 149-59.

Longmore, N. W. & National Photographic Index of Australia (1991), *Honeyeaters and Their Allies of Australia*, Collins/Angus & Robertson, North Ryde, NSW.

Menkhorst, P. & Middleton, D. (1991), 'The Helmeted Honeyeater Recovery Plan: 1989-1993', Dept of Conservation & Environment, East Melbourne, Victoria.

Schodde, R., Mason, I. J. & Christidis, L. (1992), 'Regional, age and sexual differentiation in the Regent Honeyeater', *Corella* **16**, 23-8.

Breeding seasons (*variable)

	J	F	M	A	M	J	J	A	S	O	N	D

638 Yellow-throated Honeyeater
639 Yellow-tufted Honeyeater
640 Purple-gaped Honeyeater
641 Grey-headed Honeyeater*
642 Yellow-plumed Honeyeater*
643 Grey-fronted Honeyeater*
644 Fuscous Honeyeater
645 Yellow-tinted Honeyeater
646 White-plumed Honeyeater*
647 Black-chinned Honeyeater*
648 Strong-billed Honeyeater
649 Brown-headed Honeyeater
650 White-throated Honeyeater
651 White-naped Honeyeater*
652 Black-headed Honeyeater
653 Green-backed Honeyeater (*Insufficient info.*)
654 Brown Honeyeater*
655 White-streaked Honeyeater
656 Tawny-crowned Honeyeater*
657 Crescent Honeyeater*
658 New Holland Honeyeater*
659 White-cheeked Honeyeater*
660 White-fronted Honeyeater*
661 Painted Honeyeater*
662 Brown-backed Honeyeater
663 Bar-breasted Honeyeater*
664 Rufous-banded Honeyeater
665 Rufous-throated Honeyeater
666 Grey Honeyeater (*Insufficient information*)
667 Eastern Spinebill
668 Western Spinebill
669 Banded Honeyeater*
670 Black Honeyeater*
671 Pied Honeyeater*
672 Dusky Honeyeater*
673 Red-headed Honeyeater*
674 Scarlet Honeyeater*

Australian Chats
Family Epthianuridae

[The molecular biology work of Sibley & Ahlquist indicates the chats *are* true honeyeaters and they include them in the prior Family Meliphagidae. We separate them in this classification for the present.]

This is an endemic family of brightly coloured species in which the females are similar to but generally duller in plumage than the males. They are among the few small birds which walk and do not hop. While doing so, they eat insects and seeds gathered on the ground. They have brush-tipped tongues, presumably for feeding on nectar when flowers bloom in the arid inland and which also show their close anatomical affinity with the honeyeaters. Their nests are cup-shaped, made of fine twigs and grasses, and have a fine lining of vegetable matter and hairs. They are usually placed on a low bush, in a spinifex clump, or on the ground. Some chats breed in loose colonies, but each nest territory is strongly defended. In the non-breeding season small, highly nomadic flocks form, which may consist of mixed chat species. These tend to irrupt and breed after desert rains. Some species appear to have the capacity to go into torpor in response to extreme cold.

Reading

Major, R. E. (1991), 'Breeding biology of the White-fronted Chat *Ephthianura albifrons* in a saltmarsh near Melbourne', *Emu* **91** (4), 236-49.

The brush-tipped tongue of the Crimson Chat.

Breeding seasons (*variable*)**

	J	F	M	A	M	J	J	A	S	O	N	D
675 Crimson Chat*												
676 Orange Chat*												
677 Yellow Chat*												
678 White-fronted Chat*												
679 Gibberbird*												

Pardalotes, Bristlebirds, Scrubwrens, Thornbills and allies
Family Pardalotidae

[This once small family has now been enlarged by Sibley & Ahlquist, with its amalgamation with other former families and then the reduction of these to subfamily status. They have a Family Pardalotidae — the Australo-Papuan warblers and allies — within their Superfamily Meliphagoidea (fairy-wrens, honeyeaters and chats).]

Pardalotes
Subfamily Pardalotinae

The pardalotes have one genus and four to five species. Their nearest relatives were debatable and for a long time pardalotes were placed with the flowerpeckers, Dicaeidae. Recent evidence from molecular biology suggests their origins lie with an old Australian endemic group which includes the bristlebirds, scrubwrens, thornbills and their allies.

The Yellow-rumped Pardalote is a drier-country representative of the Spotted Pardalote. Where they meet they may interbreed, so may best be considered conspecific. Taxonomic treatment of the Striated Pardalote has also been controversial. Some authors suggest that *Pardalotus striatus* may be divided into four or five species.

Pardalotes are distinctive: small and colourful with short tails and short blunt beaks. They resemble only one other species, the Weebill (*Smicrornis brevirostris*), which is duller, smaller and more active than any mainland pardalote.

All pardalotes glean arthropods from tree foliage, frequently hanging upside down to do so. Many also feed specifically on the sugary lerps exuded by psyllids, small plant-sucking insects living on *Eucalyptus* trees. Clicking sounds made by the bills of these birds when removing lerps is a characteristic of their feeding.

The Red-browed Pardalote inhabits inland and northern Australia, mainly in trees lining watercourses. Other species are found in a wide range of eucalypt forests; often two species occur together.

A black-headed form of the Striated Pardalote about to enter a nest hole in a dead tree.

Striated and Spotted Pardalotes may have substantial seasonal movements. Birds travel in winter from wetter (mountain) forests to both inland and more northerly coastal areas. Most Striated Pardalotes from Tasmania leave in autumn and may travel as far north as Queensland. During this dispersal, both species may form very large flocks. Many birds may die. The Forty-spotted Pardalote is restricted to the coastal eucalypt forests of eastern Tasmania and offshore islands; it may have a minor winter dispersal within Tasmania.

All species build characteristic cup or domed nests in tree hollows or burrows drilled in the ground. Like other burrow-nesting birds, their eggs are plain white. The clutch size (about four) is higher than for most other Australian insectivorous birds; incubation and fledging times are relatively long. Both parents work at hole and nest construction. Several other individuals may help to feed the young: another example of co-operative breeding.

There are, however, interesting differences in the nests each species builds. Spotted Pardalotes nest in loose soil and, because each pair defends its feeding territory, nest holes are widely spaced. By contrast, Forty-spotted Pardalotes and Striated Pardalotes nest in hollows in trees and in earth banks. Sites for both of these species are often close together — a factor which assists in defending nest sites from other birds. Striated Pardalotes, as a result, nest in large loose colonies, in sandhills, river banks, sand quarries, road cuttings and old hollow trees or limbs. They may nest solitarily. But the Forty-spotted Pardalote, it seems, can only nest successfully in small colonies which it defends against the more dominant local Striated Pardalotes, competing with it for nesting holes. No detailed studies exist for the nesting habits of the Red-browed Pardalote.

To observers, pardalotes are most noticeable when breeding in the ground. They fly to and from the nest hole and may ignore the approach of a bird-watcher. Otherwise, they tend to feed high in eucalypts and may be recognised only through their frequent calling or bill-clicking.

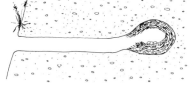

A diagrammatic cut-away showing the lined nest chamber at the end of a Spotted Pardalote's burrow.

Breeding seasons (*variable*)

	J	F	M	A	M	J	J	A	S	O	N	D
682 Spotted Pardalote												
683 Yellow-rumped Pardalote												
684 Forty-spotted Pardalote*												
685 Red-browed Pardalote*												
686 Striated Pardalote*												

Bristlebirds — Subfamily Dasyornithinae

[In the new Sibley & Ahlquist classification, bristlebirds *Dasyornis* are now in Subfamily Dasyornithinae of Family Pardalotidae.]

Bristlebirds are terrestrial, long-tailed and rufous-brown. The three species, widely separated in Australia, suggest that they represent part of an older, once wider-spread species complex, and now are 'hanging on' as a series of relict populations. The western species is confined to just a few sites. It is officially listed as 'Rare'; the Eastern Bristlebird as 'Vulnerable'.

Bristlebirds have forward-curving (rictal) bristles at the bill base and pleasant, squeaky songs. Domed nests have a side entrance; clutch is two brownish to pinkish eggs, dark-spotted.

Breeding season

	J	F	M	A	M	J	J	A	S	O	N	D
560, 561, 562 Bristlebirds												

Scrubwrens — Subfamily Acanthizinae, Tribe Sericornithini

[Sibley & Ahlquist place the scrubwrens in Tribe Sericornithini, Subfamily Acanthizinae of Family Pardalotidae, these all being in the Superfamily Meliphagoidea of Parvorder Corvida, but suggest some minor juggling within the genus *Sericornis* may be necessary in the future.]

The genus *Sericornis* is a diverse group of controversial taxonomic interest. At present it includes the prior genera

Breeding seasons (*variable*)

	J	F	M	A	M	J	J	A	S	O	N	D
563 Pilotbird												
564 Origma												
565 Australian Fernwren												
566 Atherton Scrubwren												
567 Large-billed Scrubwren												

Hylacola, the 'heath-', or 'groundwrens', *Pyrrholaemus*, the Redthroat, *Calamanthus*, the former 'fieldwrens', *Acanthornis*, the Scrubtit, and *Chthonicola*, the Speckled Warbler. In addition, three other genera, *Pycnoptilus*, the Pilotbird, *Origma*, the Origma (formerly Rock Warbler) and *Crateroscelis*, the Australian Fernwren, are all included. The Tropical (Beccari's) Scrubwren is shared with PNG.

Breeding seasons (*variable*)

J F M A M J J A S O N D

568	Yellow-throated Scrubwren*
569	Tropical Scrubwren*
570	White-browed Scrubwren*
571	Scrubtit
572	Chestnut-rumped Hylacola
573	Shy Hylacola
574	Redthroat
575A	Striated Calamanthus*
575B	Rufous Calamanthus*
576	Speckled Warbler

Weebill, Thornbills, Gerygones and White-faces
Subfamily Acanthizinae, Tribe Acanthizini

[Within Family Pardalotidae, Sibley & Ahlquist discuss Subfamily Acanthizinae and clearly isolate these birds from the Old World Sylviidae, the warblers. The name Pardalotidae has taxonomic priority over the name Acanthizidae, and so has been adopted for the name of this family of Australo-Papuan warblers and allies. The subfamily is divided into two tribes; the genera *Smicrornis*, *Acanthiza*, *Gerygone* and *Aphelocephala* are included in Tribe Acanthizini.]

These small birds are frequently difficult to identify in the field and are sometimes loosely categorised by bird watchers as being 'too hard', or 'wretched little brown birds'. There are some 40 or 41 species in Australia. They have twelve tail feathers, often with a dark to black subterminal band, and ground-feeding species often have paler eyes.

Females tend to nest-build and incubate alone, but males and perhaps other birds in the local group may assist to feed the young — co-operative breeding activity. Acanthizids are often sought out by the smaller cuckoos as hosts for their young.

The Weebill *Smicrornis* is the smallest Australian bird. It is thornbill-like but has a small, short and pale bill. A hanging, domed nest contains two to three white to buff-white, finely flecked eggs. A regular nesting association in south-western New South Wales between Weebills and a communal-nesting spider named *Badumna candida* is described and discussed by Hobbs (1990). Weebills frequently accompany thornbills and other small bush birds in mixed-species feeding flock associations. Whistlers, shrike-thrushes, robins, honeyeaters, treecreepers, fairy-wrens and fantails may be present in small numbers around the basic Weebill-thornbill core of birds.

Eleven gerygones (fairy-warblers), genus *Gerygone*, occur in Australia. Since many species sing beautiful songs, the generic name is *Gerygone*, meaning 'born of sound'. They are dainty birds and actively feed singly or in pairs in the outer foliage of woodland trees. Many occur in mangroves and rainforests. Two to three eggs are laid in a dome-shaped suspended nest. The entrance is protected by a spout. The north-east Australian species, the Fairy Warbler, often constructs its nest close to a 'wasp's' (hornet's?) nest.

Twelve thornbills, genus *Acanthiza*, are recognised. Thornbills are smaller and plumper than gerygones and feed in

Breeding seasons (*variable*)

J F M A M J J A S O N D

577	Weebill*
578	Brown Gerygone
579	Large-billed Gerygone*
580	Dusky Gerygone*
581	Mangrove Gerygone*
582	Western Gerygone
583	Green-backed Gerygone
584	Fairy Gerygone
585	White-throated Gerygone
586	Mountain Thornbill
587	Brown Thornbill
588	Inland Thornbill
589	Tasmanian Thornbill
590	Chestnut-rumped Thornbill*
591	Slaty-backed Thornbill*
592	Western Thornbill
593	Buff-rumped Thornbill
594	Slender-billed Thornbill*
595, 596, 597	Yellow-rumped, Yellow & Striated Thornbills
598	Southern Whiteface*
599	Chestnut-breasted Whiteface (*Insufficient info.*)
600	Banded Whiteface*

small groups. Identification relies on facial and chest striations, rump colours and calls. The pale-eyed thornbills are mainly terrestrial feeders, while the dark-eyed members are mostly arboreal. All build domed nests and lay two to four eggs. The Yellow-rumped Thornbill constructs an extra cup on top of the main domed nesting chamber. Speculation exists as to the purpose of this little structure.

The three whitefaces, genus *Aphelocephala*, are larger than thornbills. They are dumpy, terrestrial feeders with a white face. Whitefaces occur in the dry country of southern Australia where seeds and insects are included in their diet. The Chestnut-breasted Whiteface of the South Australian arid, stony environment, is classified as 'Rare', is known only from about 30 localities within its range and is little studied.

Australo-Papuan Robins, Scrub-Robins
Family
Eopsaltriidae

[Within the Superfamily Corvoidea, Sibley & Ahlquist place the Family Eopsaltriidae first. They point out that the very first division in corvoid evolution separated the ancestral Eopsaltriidae from all other corvoids. This, then, is the group of Australo-Papuan robins and scrub-robins which includes the following genera: *Eopsaltria*, *Petroica*, *Melanodryas*, *Microeca*, *Tregellasia*, *Poecilodryas*, *Drymodes* in Australia, and all of those plus *Monachella*, *Amalocichla*, *Peneothello* and *Pachycephalopsis* in PNG. An additional genus, *Eugerygone*, a bird until recently usually assigned to the gerygone warblers, has affinities with *Petroica* and is included by Coates (1990) in the Eopsaltriidae. The Mangrove Robin of PNG has been given the name *Penoenanthe* (as an alternative to *Eopsaltria*; if the alternative name is adopted, *Eopsaltria* will not be represented in PNG. Secondly, *Heteromyias*, an early generic name for the Grey-headed Robin of NE Australia, has recently been used by Boles (1988) for that species and apparently by Sibley & Ahlquist. Some genera extend into the Pacific, *Eopsaltria* to New Caledonia and *Petroica* through New Zealand to Samoa, Fiji and other islands.

Anatomical work on the scrub-robins *Drymodes*, in 1975 and 1976, indicated differences from the typical thrushes of the now Subfamily Turdinae and from the typical (Old World) flycatchers, now Tribe Muscicapini of the Subfamily Muscicapinae. The DNA work has confirmed these results, showing no close relationship of the scrub-robins to these birds, and indicating that their closest affinities are with the genera *Eopsaltria*, *Heteromyias* and *Microeca*.]

The genus *Petroica* includes four red-breasted robins endemic to Australia. The Rose Robin, the most arboreal and acrobatic, catches flying insects in outer canopies of trees. The Red-capped Robin, like other inland birds, may undergo nocturnal torpor; it breeds after good rains. Recent observations show that some females in the population have a pink wash or flush to the breast feathers, a feature perhaps not previously published. Note that *only* Flame Robins occur in *winter* flocks, as distinct from travelling autumn or spring birds. In the field, check throat and abdomen of coloured males and look for the company kept by 'brown birds'. Are they *all* females?

All species build cup-shaped nests, untidily or neatly decorated with grass and lichen. Females build the nest and incubate two or three eggs. Both parents feed the young and may raise several broods in a season. All are parasitised by cuckoo species. Pairs of 'brown birds' (the male in immature plumage) may successfully rear young. All species show some autumn-winter dispersal or migration. During this migration birds may be seen feeding over open ground, perhaps many in a restricted area, for instance, Flame Robins.

All juvenile *Petroica* robins are mottled and streaked brown and buff. The patterns may vary between species. This one is a juvenile Scarlet Robin.

Future studies (Flame Robin research is already in progress) will include not only banding but probably telemetry, to discover dispersal routes. A 'general consensus' of opinion does not yet support the idea of a trans-Bass Strait crossing by Flame Robins, although Silvereyes make the journey twice each year. Banding studies have apparently not produced any individuals on the 'wrong side' of the Strait so far, but Flame Robins do occur on the major Bass Strait islands — further developments must be awaited.

New Zealand has three species of *Petroica*: the Black Robin *P. traversi* (now very rare and the subject of a prolonged and successful rehabilitation programme), Robin *P. australis* and Tit *P. macrocephalus*. Each of the latter species has undergone subspecific (race) radiation in the islands of New Zealand, with three races of the Robin, and five of the Tit.

Microeca flycatchers are nomadic. They are more like 'typical' flycatchers and catch flying insects. They have the smallest nests of any Australian birds, usually on small forks or horizontal branches. Nests are of fine vegetation and covered with cobwebs, mosses and lichens. The clutch size is one to four. Eggs are shaded green, blue, sometimes cream, buff or white, and are marked brown or grey. Birds have up to three broods per season. Both parents build nests and rear young. Cuckoos parasitise some species. Adults feign injury to distract attention away from their nest or young if an intruder approaches.

Leaving out *Drymodes*, there are six or seven other genera of 'robins and flycatchers' apart from *Petroica* in Australia, seven if *Heteromyias* is again accepted as the name for the Grey-headed Robin. These are all small, stout, active birds often seen perched on branches or stumps, or clinging to the sides of vertical trunks. They show much body, tail and wing movement. Tails in particular are variously fanned, waved, carried cock-up or swivelled from side to side, depending on the genus. They may be located by calls — penetrating, monotonous piping or plaintive whistles — which contrast with those of the whistler and shrike-thrush group, although songs of *Microeca* can be quite melodic. Their diet is mainly insects; robins feed from the ground and surfaces of trunks and branches. Crustaceans form part of the Mangrove Robin's diet.

Melanodryas, the Dusky Robin of Tasmania and the Bass Strait islands, is monochromatic, both sexes being alike in plumage. By contrast, the Hooded Robin of most of arid Australia is strongly dichromatic, as are the *Petroica* red-breasted robins. The sexes of the other 'robins', *Eopsaltria*, *Microeca*, *Tregellasia* and *Poecilodryas*, are all basically similar, and sexes cannot readily be identified on plumage characters.

In the NW of Australia, the Kimberley Flycatcher is now regarded as a race of the wider-spread Lemon-bellied Flycatcher.

The Yellow Robin complex is interesting because there is a colour cline in the eastern states, with the bird formerly known as the 'Northern Yellow Robin' being a brighter yellow on the rump than the dull green-rumped bird formerly called the 'Southern Yellow Robin'. The distribution of the two colour forms is continuous and they are now regarded as one species, the Eastern Yellow Robin. The Western Yellow Robin has two distinct races, with the eastern one *rosinae* not being very far to the west of the westernmost populations of Eastern Yellow Robins. Once again, the isolating barriers of arid country are at work. What was probably a

Breeding seasons (*variable)

J F M A M J J A S O N D

467	Northern Scrub-robin
468	Southern Scrub-robin
469	Rose Robin
470	Pink Robin
471	Flame Robin
472	Scarlet Robin
473	Red-capped Robin
474	Hooded Robin*
475	Dusky Robin
476	Mangrove Robin*
477	White-breasted Robin
478	Eastern Yellow Robin
479	Western Yellow Robin
480	Yellow-legged Flycatcher (*Insufficient infor.*)
481	Lemon-bellied Flycatcher
482	Kimberley Flycatcher (*Insufficient information*)
483	Jacky Winter*
484	Pale-yellow Robin
485	White-faced Robin
486	White-browed Robin
487	Grey-headed Robin

continuous population of the Yellow Robin complex across perhaps a wetter, more humid landscape in prehistoric times has become fragmented, and so we see the development of isolates which have little hope of joining up again unless we get a radical climatic change.

The two species of Scrub-robin *Drymodes* have long been separated from each other by arid country. They too were probably once far more widespread, and represent today an antique group of the radiation of corvid passerines in Australia. The Southern Scrub-robin is widely accessible to observers in Australia, but the Northern Scrub-robin is confined to the tip of Cape York Peninsula and Papua New Guinea.

Reading

Boles, W. E. & National Photographic Index of Australian Wildlife (1988), *The Robins and Flycatchers of Australia*, Angus & Robertson, London, Sydney, Melbourne, for the Australian Museum Trust, Sydney (see pp. 35-181).

Coates, B. J. (1990), *The Birds of Papua New Guinea*, Vol. II, Dove Publications Pty Ltd, Alderley, Queensland (see pp. 178-202).

Hobbs, J. N. (1986), 'Pink-breasted females in a population of Red-capped Robins *Petroica goodenovii*', *Aust. Bird Watcher* **11** (5), 150-2.

Reader's Digest Services Pty Ltd (1985), *Reader's Digest Complete Book of New Zealand Birds*, Reader's Digest Services Pty Ltd, Surry Hills, NSW (see pp. 281-5).

Reader's Digest Services Pty Ltd (1986), *Reader's Digest Complete Book of Australian Birds*, Reader's Digest Services Pty Ltd, Surry Hills, NSW (see pp. 382-98).

Sibley, C. G. & Ahlquist, J. E. (1982), 'The relationships of the Australo-Papuan scrub-robins *Drymodes* as indicated by DNA-DNA hybridisation', *Emu* **82**, 173-6.

Log-runners, Chowchillas   Family Orthonychidae

[Sibley & Ahlquist place the Logrunner and Chowchilla (genus *Orthonyx*) in the Family Orthonychidae, within the Parvorder Corvida. By doing so, they sever the link with the whipbirds and quail-thrushes, where they have frequently been assigned in recent years. They have also been shaken free of the Old World Family Timaliidae (Old World Babblers). In the past, when actually assigned to their own Family Orthonychidae, they have always had other genera and species included with them, and only recently has it become clear that the Chowchilla and Logrunner are sufficiently distinct to warrant a family to themselves.]

The genus *Orthonyx* are ground-dwelling birds of the rainforests. The Chowchilla (*Orthonyx spaldingi*) inhabits northern highlands. The Logrunner (*O. temminckii*) inhabits more southerly coastal and mountain areas. Females build side-entranced domed nests made of sticks. These are placed on the ground or close to it in low vegetation. Territories are defended and used annually by these sedentary species.

Both species have protruding feather shafts in the tail; the name 'Spine-tailed Logrunner' was in use until recently. Small groups of Chowchillas call very loudly during the 'dawn chorus', making it relatively easy to discover them.

Reading

Boles, W. E. & National Photographic Index of Australian Wildlife (1988), *The Robins and Flycatchers of Australia*, Angus & Robertson, North Ryde, NSW (see pp. 389-402).

Breeding seasons (*variable)

| J | F | M | A | M | J | J | A | S | O | N | D |

518 Logrunner*

519 Chowchilla*

Australo-Papuan Babblers   Family Pomatostomidae

[Subfamily Cinclosomatinae is within Family Corvidae of the DNA-based hierarchy. It has also been removed from the Old World Family Timaliidae (Old World Babblers), with which they were often assigned, as taxonomists searched for the most suitable relationship in which to place them.]

Three species of the genus *Pomatostomus* are endemic; one other reaches southern New Guinea. They are omnivorous, and live in highly sociable, mainly sedentary, territorial groups. They build domed stick nests and erect similar constructions for communal roosting. These large bundles of sticks, usually in dead or only partly living trees, are a feature of the Australian outback.

Very vocal, babblers typically fly low from cover to cover or 'bounce', running away along the ground. Group activities are common in babblers; they travel, dust-bathe, feed and preen as a family or association of families.

Grey-crowned Babblers have declined alarmingly in some southern areas; a new research programme is to begin.

Reading

Boles, W. E. & National Photographic Index of Australian Wildlife (1988), *The Robins and Flycatchers of Australia*, Angus & Robertson, North Ryde, NSW (see pp. 449-75).

Schulz, M. (1991), 'The Grey-crowned Babbler *Pomatostomus temporalis* — a case for concern in southern Victoria', *Aust. Bird Watcher* **14** (2), 37-43.

Breeding seasons (*variable*)

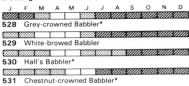

528 Grey-crowned Babbler*
529 White-browed Babbler
530 Hall's Babbler*
531 Chestnut-crowned Babbler*

Quail-thrushes and allies — Family Cinclosomidae

[Whipbirds and wedgebills (genus *Psophodes*) are grouped by Sibley & Ahlquist as allies of the quail-thrushes in Subfamily Cinclosomatinae, together with three species of Papuan jewel-babblers (genus *Ptilorrhoa*) and the Malaysian Rail-babbler (*Eupetes macrocerus*). The Subfamily Cinclosomatinae is within the Family Corvidae of the DNA-based hierarchy.]

The genus *Cinclosoma*, the quail-thrushes, includes four endemics. Shy, elusive, ground dwellers, they usually flush away with a quail-like 'whirr'. At times, they perch on fairly low branches, and may then be viewed clearly from a short distance.

The cup-shaped nest of leaves and bark is built in a shallow ground scrape. The birds' food includes insects, seeds and probably small reptiles. The Chestnut, Chestnut-breasted and two races of the Cinnamon Quail-thrush inhabit arid or semi-arid country. They are closely related and their taxonomy is still debatable. The Spotted Quail-thrush of east and south-east Australian woodland is declining with slowly encroaching settlements.

The two arid country whipbirds (wedgebills), genus *Psophodes*, are almost identical in plumage, but are easily identified by their calls. These insectivores run fast, fly low, often with their tail fanned. They may be solitary or in small flocks. The onset of breeding depends on suitable desert rains; nests are shallow, cup-shaped and low to the ground.

Reading

Boles, W. E. & National Photographic Index of Australian Wildlife (1988), *The Robins and Flycatchers of Australia*, Angus & Robertson, North Ryde, NSW (see pp. 403-47).

Schodde, R. & Mason, I. J. (1991), 'Subspeciation in the Western Whipbird *Psophodes nigrogularis* and its zoogeographical significance, with descriptions of two new subspecies', *Emu* **91** (3), 133-44.

Smith, G. T. (1991), 'Ecology of the Western Whipbird *Psophodes nigrogularis* in Western Australia', *Emu* **91** (3), 145-57.

Breeding seasons (*variable*)

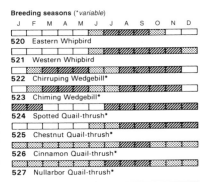

520 Eastern Whipbird
521 Western Whipbird
522 Chirruping Wedgebill*
523 Chiming Wedgebill*
524 Spotted Quail-thrush*
525 Chestnut Quail-thrush*
526 Cinnamon Quail-thrush*
527 Nullarbor Quail-thrush*

Sittellas — Family Neosittidae

[DNA hybridisation studies show sittellas are closely related to Australo-Papuan whistlers, monarchs and flycatchers of the Family Pachycephalidae. Sibley & Ahlquist place them in the Family Corvidae, Subfamily Pachycephalinae and, finally, their own Tribe Neosittini. Family similarities exist also in nests, eggs and immature plumages of sittellas when compared with whistlers, as noted by other workers.]

The five main Australian sittella forms (races) hybridise wherever they overlap. They avoid rainforests, but occur in most other wooded habitats. Often the first sign of the species is the sight of a group of small birds at canopy height, flying into the next large tree as a loose group.

All forms except *leucocephala* are sexually dimorphic in plumage, females having more black on the face (in *striata* also on the breast). First-year birds seem more dimorphic than older birds. White spots on the back of the juvenile disappear at about three months after fledging.

Average sittella group size is about five; some groups merge after breeding. Members huddle together when roosting; they sometimes allopreen by day and often the whole group forages in the same tree concurrently. Males have longer bills than females and forage lower in trees. Sittellas breed communally; young from earlier broods attend later broods in same season. Only females incubate. Nests in deep forks.

The nest of the Varied Sittella is usually located in an upright fork of a tree.

Reading

Sibley, C. E. & Ahlquist, J. E. (1982), 'The relationships of the Australo-Papuan sittellas *Daphoenositta* as indicated by DNA-DNA hybridisation', *Emu* 82 (3), 173-6.

Breeding season

J	F	M	A	M	J	J	A	S	O	N	D

601 Varied Sittella

Whistlers, Shrike-thrushes and allies   Family Pachycephalidae

[Like a number of birds previously discussed, Sibley & Ahlquist place the whistlers and their allies in Subfamily Pachycephalinae, within the Family Corvidae. Subfamily Pachycephalinae is worth considering for a moment. It contains the wide-ranging whistlers, the shrike-tits, Crested Bellbird, the six pitohuis of PNG, sittellas, shrike-thrushes, and the New Zealand Whitehead, Yellowhead and Brown Creeper. Most occur in Australia, PNG or New Zealand, with the whistlers spread out into the Pacific islands, Java and the Moluccas as well, but not into New Zealand.]

Shrike-tits   Subfamily Falcunculinae

[Within Subfamily Pachycephalinae, Sibley & Ahlquist use a Tribe Falcunculini in which are placed the shrike-tits (genus *Falcunculus*), the Crested Bellbird (*Oreoica gutturalis*) and the New Guinea endemic Mottled Whistler (*Rhagologus leucostigma*).]

Crested Shrike-tits feed mainly in upper branches, prising invertebrates from bark with their robust bills. They give distinctive chuckling calls or drawn-out plaintive whistles. The female constructs a deep cup-shaped bark nest; two or three white eggs with olive or brown markings are laid.

Breeding seasons (*variable*)

J	F	M	A	M	J	J	A	S	O	N	D

488 Crested Shrike-tit

501 Crested Bellbird*

Whistlers, Shrike-thrushes   Subfamily Pachycephalinae

The DNA studies show that the whistlers and shrike-thrushes are closely allied, as are the whistler group to the monarchs. The whistlers and shrike-thrushes as a group have often been given full Family status. They are robust birds with relatively large heads, hence the vernacular name 'thickheads'. They also have distinctive voices — some are among Australia's most beautiful songsters, with variable repertoires of rich, melodic phrases. Most feed on arboreal and ground-dwelling insects and other invertebrates. Berries are also included. A large portion of the food of the White-breasted Whistler is small crabs taken from the muddy substrate of tropical mangroves at low tide.

Slightly shorter but stouter, whistlers differ most obviously from shrike-thrushes in their often striking sexual dimor-

Grey Shrike-thrush nest

phism. The male appears in contrasting combinations of yellow, black, white, rufous, cinnamon and green. Shrike-thrushes are plain and drab by comparison, with little or no sexual dimorphism. In this regard, the Crested Bellbird is most akin to whistlers.

All build open cup-shaped nests of twigs, bark, grasses, roots and leaves. In *Pachycephala* these are shallow, usually low down in small forks and foliage, except for the Grey Whistler which nests high in the canopy, in keeping with its lifestyle. Shrike-thrushes and the Crested Bellbird's nests are deeper, usually in the forks of a trunk or large branch. Grey Shrike-thrushes may nest on top of a stump, on an overhanging bank or over a cave or old mine entrance. The Sandstone Shrike-thrush builds on ledges and crevices of the sandstone boulders and cliffs on which it lives. The Crested Bellbird habitually places paralysed hairy processional or bag caterpillars around the nest rim. These are apparently not eaten by the nestlings, and may be a defence measure.

All species (in Australia) have two to three white, cream or buff eggs with brown markings toward the larger end. Some develop breeding territories, become particularly vocal and engage in courtship and territorial display. Both sexes take part in nest construction and care of the young. After breeding some species may become nomadic, with small movements north and inland in autumn and winter. Habitat clearance may ultimately limit the future distribution of the Red-lored and Gilbert's Whistlers.

Breeding seasons (*variable*)

J	F	M	A	M	J	J	A	S	O	N	D

489 Olive Whistler

490 Red-lored Whistler

491 Gilbert's Whistler

492 Golden Whistler

493 Mangrove Golden Whistler

494 Grey Whistler*

495 Rufous Whistler

496 White-breasted Whistler*

497 Little Shrike-thrush

498 Bower's Shrike-thrush

499 Sandstone Shrike-thrush

500 Grey Shrike-thrush*

Drongos, Monarchs, Fantails   Family Monarchidae

[Within their Family Corvidae, Sibley & Ahlquist utilise seven sub-families. Six of these are relevant to Australasia. Their Subfamily Dicrurinae is more embracing than the conservative approach we are still maintaining, as it includes all the drongos, monarchs, magpie-larks and flycatchers. We use the same subfamily name (below), where we restrict it just to drongos.]

Drongos   Subfamily Dicrurinae

Drongos form a fairly uniform group — mainly glossy black, often with ornamental, curved tail feathers. There are about 20 species in the world, ranging from Africa through Iran and India, south-east Asia and southern China, to Papua New Guinea and Australia. Until recently, their evolutionary relationships were uncertain. A degree of clarification has been achieved with their inclusion, close to the monarchs, within the recently defined and very large Australo-Papuan 'corvid' complex.

The migratory Spangled Drongo eats fruits, insects and nectar. Occasionally one is reported well outside its accepted tropical range. Detailed records of movements, ecology and behaviour are needed.

Breeding season

J	F	M	A	M	J	J	A	S	O	N	D

722 Spangled Drongo

Flycatchers, Monarchs, Magpie-larks   Subfamily Monarchinae

[Sibley & Ahlquist indicate that the Australian Magpie-lark and New Guinea Torrent-lark are monarchs, closely allied to the others in this large Australo-Papuan group. There are some 18 species in Australia; 28 or so in PNG, some of which are shared with Australia; the group extends right across to Africa through India, and is in some of the Pacific islands. They indicate that *Grallina* is barely a genus, so close is it to *Monarcha*. Their work also shows no relationship between magpie-larks and other 'mud-nesters' (our Family Corcoracidae; their Subfamily Corcoracinae).]

Monarch flycatchers are a group of forest- and woodland-dwelling insectivorous birds (four genera and 12 or 13 species in Australia). All are sexually dimorphic to a varying degree. Bill width varies from the proportionately 'huge' bill of the Yellow-breasted Boatbill, to the slender bills of *Arses*, *Monarcha* and *Myiagra*.

Insects are taken either in flight, or in foliage or branches. *Arses* flycatchers have a habit of flitting up tree trunks and probing under bark; they are also distinctive in having erectile frills on their napes. Many monarchs are territorial and may respond immediately to imitations of their calls in the breeding season. All of our species breed in Australia. Some migrate northwards to north Queensland and New Guinea in winter (Black-faced, Black-winged and Spectacled Monarchs; Leaden and Satin Flycatchers). All construct cup-shaped nests, have two to three pale, spotted eggs, sometimes brown-tinged.

One of our most widespread birds, the distinctively patterned, black and white Australian Magpie-lark (Peewee or Murray Magpie), builds cup-shaped mud nests as do the Corcoracidae, White-winged Chough and Apostlebird, and was once placed in the same family. Later, plumage, social and anatomical differences led to it being placed in a new Family Grallinidae, together with the New Guinea Torrent-lark *Grallina bruijni*. Now the Magpie-larks have again been 'shifted' taxonomically. Note that the juvenile plumage pattern of face and neck of the Magpie-lark closely resembles that of the much smaller adult of the White-eared Monarch (see p. 188). Three to five pink eggs, blotched purple and brown, are laid. Pairs sing antiphonally, raising and closing their wings as they do so.

Breeding seasons (*variable*)

	J	F	M	A	M	J	J	A	S	O	N	D
502 Yellow-breasted Boatbill												
503 Black-faced Monarch												
504 Black-winged Monarch												
505 Spectacled Monarch												
506 White-eared Monarch												
507 Frilled Monarch												
508 Pied Monarch												
509 Broad-billed Flycatcher												
510 Leaden Flycatcher												
511 Satin Flycatcher												
512 Shining Flycatcher												
513 Restless Flycatcher*												
738 Australian Magpie-lark*												

Fantails
Subfamily Rhipidurinae

[Sibley & Ahlquist utilise a Tribe Rhipidurini for the fantails, a homogeneous group of birds, within their larger Subfamily Dicrurinae and indicate they are the sister group of the monarchs, from which they diverged.]

Fantails have long, fan-shaped tails which they wave from side to side in an upward arc, with the wings held downwards. The genus *Rhipidura* occurs widely in Australia, PNG, New Zealand, many Pacific islands and into south-east Asia. There are now five fantails in Australia, with the elevation of the Mangrove Fantail to a full species. The familiar, mis-named Willie Wagtail is a fantail, not a wagtail (Motacillidae); it occurs throughout Australia but is rare in Tasmania. Fantails build cup-shaped nests, some with 'wine-glass stems' underneath. Two to three eggs are laid, variable in colour and spotted.

Reading

Coates, Brian J. (1990), *The Birds of Papua New Guinea*, Vol. II, *Passerines*, Dove Publications, Alderley, Queensland (pp. 132-3).

Schodde, R. & Tidemann, S. (editors) (1986), *The Reader's Digest Complete Book of Australian Birds*, 2nd edition, Reader's Digest Services, Surry Hills, NSW (p. 419).

Sibley, C. G. & Ahlquist, J. E. (1982), 'The relationships of the Australasian whistler *Pachycephala* as indicated by DNA-DNA hybridisation', *Emu* **82** (4), 199-202.

White, F. W. G. (1987), 'A comparison of the whip-crack calls of the Olive Whistler and Eastern Whipbird', *Aust. Bird Watcher* **12** (1), 28-9.

Breeding season (*variable*)

	J	F	M	A	M	J	J	A	S	O	N	D
514 Rufous Fantail												
515 Grey Fantail												
516 Northern Fantail												
517 Willie Wagtail*												

Cuckoo-shrikes and Trillers   Family Campephagidae

[Subfamily Corvinae within Family Corvidae of Sibley & Ahlquist contains (at first appearances) a diverse group of birds. The molecular biology research indicates that the world's 'crow family' — crows, ravens, rooks, jackdaws, jays, magpies, choughs (but not the Australian chough), nutcrackers, birds of paradise, Australian magpies and currawongs, butcherbirds and woodswallows, *Peltops* of PNG, the Borneo Bristlehead, the Old World orioles and the cuckoo-shrikes and trillers — are all closely related. They represent an ancient, endemic, basically Australasian group which not only radiated far beyond Australia but, more recently geologically speaking, recontributed members of the genus *Corvus* back into Australia. For example, DNA hybridisation studies on the Little Raven show it is very close to other *Corvus* species outside Australia.

It was a surprise to Sibley & Ahlquist that orioles and cuckoo-shrikes, which are morphologically different in appearance, were also closely related. They too, so far as the Australian-Papuan populations go, seem to have recolonised the region in recent geological times. They place them in a Tribe Oriolini.]

The campephagids include two genera of Asian 'shrikes' and also the genus *Pericrotus*, the Asian minivets, none of which are represented in Australia. Cuckoo-shrikes are neither 'cuckoos' nor 'shrikes', but superficially resemble the cuckoos in plumage colouration and slender physique, and the shrikes in bill appearance.

The flight of cuckoo-shrikes and trillers is undulating. Trillers often sing loudly when flying through forest canopy and must then be identified from the Rufous Songlark. Many campephagids refold their wings upon alighting. Members of these genera forage for insects over the outer foliage of trees. Sometimes they flop or 'crash' with outstretched wings and tail to grab an insect and to disturb others. They also hawk flying insects from a static perch or alight on the ground to feed. Some berries and soft fruits are eaten.

Campephagids are mainly arboreal, although the Ground Cuckoo-shrike is more frequently seen on the ground in small social groups. This species is also known to be a co-operative breeder; several adults help at the nest.

Cuckoo-shrikes and trillers build their small nests on horizontal branches or forks. They sometimes use the empty nests of other bird species; the mud nest of the Magpie-Lark is a favoured choice. Nests of cuckoo-shrikes are so shallow that eggs or young may be lost in high winds.

Reading

Rogers, K., Rogers, A. & Rogers, D. (1986), *Bander's Aid — A Guide to Ageing and Sexing Bush Birds*, The Authors, St Andrews, Victoria (see pp. 44-5).

Schodde, R. & Tidemann, S. C. (editors) (1986), *The Reader's Digest Complete Book of Australian Birds*, Reader's Digest Services, Sydney (see pp. 372-7).

Breeding seasons (*variable)

	J	F	M	A	M	J	J	A	S	O	N	D

456 Black-faced Cuckoo-shrike*

457 Yellow-eyed Cuckoo-shrike

458 White-bellied Cuckoo-shrike

459 Cicadabird

460 Ground Cuckoo-shrike

461 White-winged Triller*

462 Varied Triller*

Orioles and Figbirds   Family Oriolidae

[Sibley & Ahlquist include the orioles, cuckoo-shrikes and trillers in a Tribe Oriolini, for the reasons explained under our Family Campephagidae (above). We retain two separate families for the present.]

The Oriolidae are thought to be comparatively recent colonists in Australia. The two orioles, Olive-backed and Yellow, are principally forest-dwelling insect- and fruit-eaters, and are migratory or nomadic, perhaps responding to seasonal food supplies. The Figbird, confined to Australasia, is very dependant on figs and other fruit. It eats fewer insects and is unusual among the Oriolidae in being very gregarious.

An Olive-backed Oriole at its cup-shaped suspended nest.

Orioles and figbirds build strong, deep, cup-shaped, suspended nests; the Yellow Oriole's nest is often placed over a stream or pool.

Figbirds were once separated as two species on the basis of regional dimorphism, but because there is a hybrid zone with interbreeding they are now considered a single species.

Reading

Crouch, H. W. (1970), 'Olive-backed Oriole in South Australia', *S. Aust. Orn.* **25**, 195-200.

Ford, J. (1975), 'Systematics and hybridisation of figbirds *Specotheres*', *Emu* **75**, 163-71.

Liddy, J. (1982), 'The Olive-backed Oriole: an occasional disseminator of mistletoe', *Corella* **6**, 93.

Breeding seasons (*variable*)

J	F	M	A	M	J	J	A	S	O	N	D

719 Yellow Oriole

720 Olive-backed Oriole*

721 Figbird

Bowerbirds Family Ptilinorhynchidae

[Sibley & Ahlquist, in one of their most interesting findings, demonstrate that the bowerbirds are more closely allied to the lyrebirds than either group is to any other. They place them in the Oscines, in the Parvorder Corvida, the great group of Australo-Papuan-evolved birds.

Within the Corvida, they are placed in the Superfamily Menuroidea and the discrete bowerbird family name of Ptilinorhynchidae is preserved. Thus Sibley & Ahlquist sever the time-honoured tradition of placing the bowerbirds and birds of paradise next to each other.

At present, this research still has not gained full recognition and other studies do not agree with all aspects of it. For example, anatomical work by Feduccia & Olson concluded that lyrebirds and bowerbirds were unrelated.

Maintaining our stand of broadly reporting the trends developing, rather than acting on them totally, we retain the two families of bowerbirds and birds of paradise next to each other for the time being, as does the List of the Australian Biological Resources Study that we have adopted as our guide].

A bower of the Great Bowerbird.

Bowerbirds have been considered by some people to be the most advanced of all birds because of their remarkable bower-building and associated activities. The spectacular behaviour of most male bowerbirds has attracted much attention, resulting in considerable scientific and popular literature. The Fawn-breasted Bowerbird, relative to other species in Australia, has lacked field study.

Bowerbirds are predominantly local-living forest birds that actively feed when not calling or perched at bowers. Promiscuous males of all Australian bowerbirds (except the Spotted Catbird and Tooth-billed Bowerbird) build bowers or clear a court, decorated in various ways to impress many females. Bower- or court-owning males call much of the day at their display site to attract females and deter rival males. Some have call notes given almost exclusively at the bower, which helps potential mates (and bird-watchers) locate them.

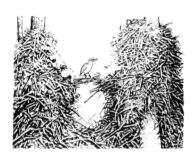

A very well-established bower of the Golden Bowerbird.

A hide (concealed observatory) is invaluable at a bower if you are to observe male behaviour and the elusive female-plumaged visitors. Females perform all nest building, egg incubation and feeding of young without male help. Most of the avenue bower-building species form locally mobile winter flocks, often quite large, whereas other species remain sedentary and relatively solitary.

Male catbirds do not build bowers and are not promiscuous. They pair with one female, defend an all-purpose territory and assist in feeding their offspring.

Bowerbirds are predominantly frugivorous but their young are fed various percentages of animal items. Catbirds frequently kill other birds' nestlings to feed their own young. Figs are particularly important, notably to the catbirds. Buds,

The court of the Tooth-billed Bowerbird.

flowers, fresh succulent stems and leaves are also eaten, more so in winter by some species (Satin, Tooth-billed Bowerbird). The latter bird becomes quite folivorous (foliage-eating) in winter, using its peculiar bill to tear and masticate leaves and shoots, whilst perching inconspicuously.

Nests are bulky cups of twigs, leaves and tendrils, usually placed in a shrub or tree fork, a vine, or low tree. Eggs usually number one or two; catbirds sometimes lay three. Incubation takes approximately 19-25 days, nestlings fledge at 18-22 days and may become independent of parents 60-80 days after fledging.

Reading

Bradley, J. M. (1987), 'Vocal behaviour and annual cycle of the Western Bowerbird *Chlamydera guttata*', *Aust. Bird Watcher* **12** (3), 83-90.

Chaffer, Norman (1984), *In Search of Bowerbirds*, Rigby Publishers, Adelaide.

Coates, B. J. (1990), *The Birds of Papua New Guinea*, Vol. 2, *Passerines*, Dove Publications, Alderley, Qld (see pp. 417-538).

Cooper, W. T. & Forshaw, J. M. (1977), *The Birds of Paradise and Bowerbirds*, Collins, Sydney.

Diamond, J. M. (1982), 'Evolution of bowerbirds' bowers: animal origins of the aesthetic sense', *Nature* (UK) **297**, 99-102.

Feduccia, A. & Olson, S. L. (1982), 'Morphological similarities between the Menurae and the Rhinocryptidae, relict passerine birds of the Southern Hemisphere', *Smithsonian Contributions to Zoology* no. **366**.

Frith, C. B. & Frith, D. W. (1990), 'Notes on the nesting biology of the Spotted Bowerbird *Chlamydera maculata* (Ptilinorhynchidae)', *Aust. Bird Watcher* **13** (7), 218-25.

Gilliard, E. T. (1969), *Birds of Paradise and Bower Birds*, Weidenfeld & Nicolson, London.

Breeding seasons

	J	F	M	A	M	J	J	A	S	O	N	D
723 Golden Bowerbird												
724 Satin Bowerbird												
725 Regent Bowerbird												
726A Spotted Bowerbird												
726B Western Bowerbird												
727 Great Bowerbird												
728 Fawn-breasted Bowerbird												
729 Tooth-billed Bowerbird												
730 Spotted Catbird												
731 Green Catbird												

Birds of Paradise
Family Paradisaeidae

[As explained under the bowerbird entry (p. 358), Sibley & Ahlquist have determined that birds of paradise are *not* related so closely to bowerbirds as has been thought, but are members of the 'crow complex'. They place them in their Family Corvidae and Subfamily Corvinae. Some suggestions are made that the present large number of bird-of-paradise genera (about 18 or 20) could be reduced by as many as ten or more in the future, following further research.]

Forty-three birds-of-paradise species form 18 genera through the Moluccas, New Guinea and Australia. Australia's four species are members of two genera. *Manucodia keraudrenii*, the Trumpet Manucode of northern Cape York Peninsula, Queensland, also occurs in New Guinea, and the three riflebirds, *Ptiloris* species, form a 'super-species' of broken distribution along the central and northern sections of the east Australian coast. The Magnificent Riflebird of northern Cape York is also in New Guinea; the two smaller riflebirds are endemic to Australia. Unlike the Manucode, which is somewhat drab and a monogamous breeder, the males of the three riflebirds are splendidly plumaged and, like so many birds of paradise, are promiscuous. Each adult displays alone on defended dead branches and displays with many females.

The Australian birds of paradise are medium- to large-sized. The whole family includes some which are only starling-sized, and some about 25 per cent larger than our Magnificent Riflebird.

Riflebirds are typical of their family and very closely related to the genera *Lophorina*, *Epimachus* and *Astrapia* of New Guinea. The larger Magnificent Riflebird is clearly a race of the New Guinea species and is distinctly different from Victoria's Riflebird and the Paradise Riflebird. These two smaller

The Magnificent Riflebird waves its head during its courtship display.

birds are very similar and are considered by some ornithologists as forms of a single species.

Often described as the most beautiful or spectacular group of birds on earth, the birds of paradise have long been admired and studied. Most species are more colourful and ornately plumaged than the Australian representatives although the plumage and courtship displays of our male riflebirds are an impressive indication of what awaits the adventurous bird-watcher in New Guinea.

Birds of paradise are strong-footed and vocal forest birds with typically, cryptically coloured, often ventrally barred females. Brightly plumaged adult males exhibit much iridescent and metallic colouration. Bill shape is extremely varied relative to the feeding ecology of each species. Most are predominantly frugivorous and, like the Trumpet Manucode, have an all-purpose starling- or crow-like bill. Some, like the riflebirds, are mainly insectivorous and have long decurved bills for probing into dead wood and beneath moss and bark of large tree boughs and trunks.

Males of some species display solitarily, like the riflebirds. Other New Guinea species congregate in groups or 'clans' at 'leks' and there display communally in one or several tree tops, providing a fine avian spectacle. At such noisy and colourful leks, visiting females are attracted to the one or two dominant, often central, males which perform most or all of the matings.

Apart from the harsh advertising calls of male riflebirds given at their display area, these birds may be located as they actually display, or as they fly through the forest, because the oddly modified outer primary feathers produce a strange loud rustling sound during these activities.

The trumpet-like blast of the Trumpet Manucode call is considerably enhanced by a peculiar elongation of the trachea. This is positioned as a greatly convoluted structure just beneath the breast skin and over the pectoral muscles.

Riflebirds sometimes add cast snake-skins to the rims of their nests, perhaps for decoration or to deter predators.

Reading

Coates, B. J. (1990), *The Birds of Papua New Guinea*, Vol. 2, *Passerines*, Dove Publications, Alderley, Qld (see pp. 417-538).

Cooper, W. T. & Forshaw, J. M. (1977), *The Birds of Paradise and Bowerbirds*, Collins, Sydney.

Gilliard, E. T. (1969), *Birds of Paradise and Bower Birds*, Weidenfeld & Nicolson, London.

The cup-shaped nest of the Paradise Riflebird is decorated with cast snake-skins.

Breeding seasons

	J	F	M	A	M	J	J	A	S	O	N	D
732 Paradise Riflebird												
733 Victoria's Riflebird												
734 Magnificent Riflebird												
735 Trumpet Manucode												

Woodswallows Family Artamidae, Subfamily Artaminae

[Within the Subfamily Corvinae, Sibley & Ahlquist establish a Tribe Artamini which is the equivalent in content of the Family Cracticidae of many prior authors. It contains the woodswallows, butcherbirds and currawongs, Australian magpies, the genus *Peltops* of PNG (previously considered as 'probably monarchs') and the Borneo Bristlehead *Pityriasis gymnocephala*.

We include the same group of species, so far as Australia is concerned, in the Family Artamidae, with a subfamily for each group represented here.]

Although woodswallows have bifurcated (divided) tongues and are often observed taking nectar and pollen, they are considered most closely related to the butcherbirds. Both subfamilies have a similar skull structure and black-tipped blue bills.

There is a clear relationship between the nature of the movements of the Australian woodswallows and their geographical races. At one end of the scale, wide nomadic

A female White-browed Woodswallow on its nest.

movements of the Little, Masked and White-browed Woodswallows facilitated gene flow which in turn accounts for the lack of variation. At the other end, the very sedentary Black-faced Woodswallow has developed two markedly different races, while the migratory Dusky and White-breasted Woodswallows are intermediate in their development of minor races.

Woodswallows' movements are in response to the availability of their main food item, flying insects. They also eat terrestrial insects and, as previously mentioned, nectar and pollen. All species build flimsy nests of fine twigs in tree forks and angles of broken bark.

In line with their gregarious tendencies they rear their young co-operatively, mob predators and may roost in tight clusters on the sides of trees or on branches. This last activity may sometimes occur in the daytime and then is frequently a consequence of sudden storms or a marked fall in temperature. Other distinctive features of woodswallows include tail-swivelling and plumages that are soft in colour and texture due to the presence of powder-down.

Breeding seasons (*variable*)

J F M A M J J A S O N D

739 White-breasted Woodswallow*

740 Masked Woodswallow*

741 White-browed Woodswallow

742 Black-faced Woodswallow

743 Dusky Woodswallow

744 Little Woodswallow

Butcherbirds, Currawongs, Magpie Family Artamidae, Subfamily Cracticinae

As a family, cracticids are omnivorous as well as partial scavengers, feeding on invertebrates, reptiles, small birds, mammals and fruits and seeds. They utilise many niches within their territories and also cache food for later use.

Three distinct species of Australian Magpie were once recognised but are now considered races of the one species because they interbreed (hybridise) where their geographic ranges intersect. The Australian Magpie has been intensively studied and its behaviour of living in family groups and aggressively defending breeding territory is well known. Five different kinds of groups are formed for feeding and breeding activities. Butcherbirds and magpies are mostly sedentary or partly nomadic. Butcherbirds form only family groups, although they do defend their territory. However, some currawongs are annual altitudinal migrants. After breeding as pairs in mountain forests, they migrate to more open lowland country in winter, forming large, noisy, foraging flocks. The Grey Currawong tends to be more sedentary than the Pied.

Breeding occurs throughout the distributional range of the cracticids. Nests, mainly made of sticks and twigs, then lined with dry grasses and rootlets, are usually placed in tree forks. Two to five oval-shaped eggs are laid (currawongs' eggs are more tapered). Egg colouring varies considerably. Magpie eggs are mostly bluish-green, butcherbirds are greenish-grey, and currawong eggs are brownish. All eggs have darker streaks and spots.

The Black Currawong, once considered a race of the Pied by some, now has full species status based on differing plumage and call. The Silver-backed Butcherbird of the north is now considered a race of the Grey Butcherbird; the Black-backed Butcherbird of Cape York Peninsula *may* also be one.

Australian Magpies have been introduced into New Zealand and are found widely in the North Island, less so in the South. In northern Australia, Australian Magpies are distinctly smaller, those of Groote Eylandt once even being named as a separate subspecies or race.

Butcherbirds cache food in forks of trees. This nestling will be eaten later.

Breeding seasons

J F M A M J J A S O N D

745 Black Butcherbird

746 Grey Butcherbird

747 Black-backed Butcherbird

748 Pied Butcherbird

749 Australian Magpie

750 Pied Currawong

751 Black Currawong

752 Grey Currawong

Reading

Burton, T. C. & Martin, A. A. (1976), 'Analysis of hybridisation between Black-backed and White-backed Magpies in south-eastern Australia', *Emu* **76**, 30-6.

Ford, J. (1979), 'A new subspecies of Grey Butcherbird from the Kimberley, Western Australia', *Emu* **79**, 191-4.

Crows and allies
Family Corvidae

[Sibley & Ahlquist preserve the traditional name Family Corvidae, but use a Tribe Corvini to 'house' what may be called the traditional members of the Family Corvidae. The Corvidae are now considered to have evolved in the Australasian region, then spread widely.]

The best clue to a corvid's identity is the pitch, tone and tempo of its territory advertisement calls, and characteristic behaviour patterns. The three large territorial species call from high perches or during a high advertisement flight, which has exaggerated, jerky wing beats. The two endemic crows perform dipping, 'currawong flight' aerial displays. Knowledge of corvid ecology is also useful in identification. Usually, at least two species live together. They avoid competition by differences in ecology and social organisation. Usually, one is a large resident species, the other a small nomad. Inspect the colour of the neck feather bases of any dead birds you may find along highways (paying due heed to other traffic and your safety). All raven species have grey neck feather bases; both crows have white neck feather bases. Then examine the small hackle feathers from the throat and compare their relative length, shape and colour pattern with the drawings on p. 270. Sketch your findings in your field notebook. Gradually you will achieve a reference note collection for use in future travels.

Corvids are omnivorous, eating carrion and also caching (hiding) surplus food. To some extent they specialise: flesh (Australian, Forest Ravens), insects (Little Raven), grain (Torresian Crow). The desert-dwelling Little Crow has a broad diet, using food sources not available to the larger species.

Regurgitated pellets under perches or nests (all predators including corvids) can provide diet information. Check these at weekly intervals. Tease pellets apart in a warm *disinfectant* solution for release of their contents. Sort into relative proportions of plant and animal matter; record that; then divide each fraction up into further suitable groups or units for detailed identification and record again.

Preserve desired material in 70 per cent alcohol (methylated spirits) and label each container accurately with place, date, nest or perch number, and your name as a minimum requirement. Such work is very useful but check the wildlife possession laws — contact a wildlife authority, seek advice and a permit and work with them.

The Little Raven and Little Crow move in large nomadic flocks except when breeding. In south-east and south-west Australia they move from inland to coastal areas for summer. Little Ravens breeding in alpine areas move to lower altitudes in autumn and winter.

The Forest Raven and newly separated Relict Raven are the least studied, yet their mainland populations may be declining. In Tasmania Forest Ravens adapt well to some human-induced landscape changes. When mainland forest is cleared for agriculture, the Australian Raven moves in, displacing both Forest and Relict Ravens.

Little Crows, like other corvids, build large nests of sticks.

Corvids build a large, bowl-shaped stick nest in a tree or man-made structure. The Little Crow's nest contains a layer of mud or clay under the lining. Corvids are monogamous. Females incubate eggs and tend chicks; males supply food.

The Little Raven and Little Crow are flexible in choice of nest sites and breeding season, have a shorter breeding cycle, and forage in areas unsuitable for nesting. They breed semi-colonially in habitats unsuitable for the large territorial species. In courtship displays a pale nictitating membrane is drawn over the eyes.

Reading

Rowley, I., et al (1973), 'The comparative ecology of the Australian corvids', *CSIRO Wildl. Res.* **18**, 1-169.

Breeding seasons

	J	F	M	A	M	J	J	A	S	O	N	D
753 Australian Raven												
754A Forest Raven												
754B Relict Raven												
755 Little Raven												
756 Little Crow												
757 Torresian Crow												

Mud-nesters Family Corcoracidae

[Sibley & Ahlquist (1990) place these two species in a subfamily of their own, Corcoracinae, in the larger Family Corvidae. The two mud-nester species are very closely related.]

The Australian mud-nesters are most notable for their communal way of life, perhaps more complex than any other Australian birds'. Basic is a close-knit family party, usually of about 7 in the White-winged Chough, 10 in the Apostlebird. The groups consist of a 'breeding unit' of a dominant male, several mature females and some immature birds (progeny from previous seasons). Nest construction, brooding and feeding of the young are shared more or less equally. Incubation appears to be left to adults.

The nest, a distinctive bowl of mud and plant fibre, is placed on a limb which is horizontal or almost so. Building is in several distinct stages. A solid base of mud is formed over the branch, and grass stem or bark coated in mud form the walls. First-year birds join in, but are less dextrous.

The normal clutch is 3-5 pale, lustrous eggs, with a variable pattern of grey, brown and maroon spots. Clutches double this size are not uncommon and form when more than one female lays in the same nest. However, only four chicks reach the fledgling stage. The rigidity of the nest is an obvious restriction. Usually, only one Chough brood is raised in a season but a second may be stimulated by heavy summer rain and consequent mud. Second broods often fail. Two broods per season *may* occur in the Apostlebird.

During breeding a Chough nest territory is heavily defended. Later, defence is dropped and birds wander within a 'home range' of up to several square kilometres.

Much time is spent foraging on the ground for insects or small vertebrates. In autumn and winter the birds move to more open country and then seeds become a significant part of their diet. Large concentrations (up to 100 individuals) may occur where food is abundant (such as grain crops). Such groupings are merely the result of a rich food source and have no unity — each family is independent.

An Apostlebird on its mud nest.

The construction of the bowl-shaped mud nest of the White-winged Chough is in several stages. (Modification of Ian Rowley's sketches.)

Breeding seasons

	J	F	M	A	M	J	J	A	S	O	N	D
736 White-winged Chough												
737 Apostlebird												

Swallows, Martins Family Hirundinidae

[The Parvorder Passerida of Sibley & Ahlquist commences here.

Sibley & Ahlquist place the swallows and martins in the Parvorder Passerida, the Superfamily Sylvioidea, and retain the traditional Family Hirundinidae. Swallows and martins resemble swifts (Apodidae) and woodswallows (Artamidae) but all are unrelated.]

This cosmopolitan family has six or seven representatives in Australia (the Pacific Swallow *Hirundo tahitica* has yet to be confirmed). Martins are generally dumpier versions of swallows. Australia's martins have white rumps and square tails; swallows have deeply forked tails. All have long wings and graceful, often erratic, flight. Their bills are short and broad for insect capture. The White-backed Swallow is a nomadic (mainly) inland species that roosts and nests in tunnels in sandy banks or eroded dunes.

Welcome Swallows breed in a half-cup mud nest, usually under roof-eaves, bridges or culverts in southern and eastern Australia. The Barn Swallow migrates from the Northern Hemisphere to northern Australia — stragglers have reached Victoria. More observers and better knowledge is also resulting in more sightings of the Red-rumped Swallow in northern Australia.

Fairy Martins build bottle-shaped mud nests, often under bridges, culverts or cliff overhangs; occasionally in hollow, leaning trees. House Sparrows sometimes move into empty nests in suburban areas of eastern Australia. Bats, lizards, and invertebrates may also utilise abandoned nests. Tree Martins nest in tree- or cliff-holes, lined with mud. All of the family are gregarious, often congregating on telegraph wires or fences. They roost as well as breed in their nests. Eggs are pale in colour; often spotted reddish-brown. Two to six eggs are laid. Fledglings have conspicuous pale fleshy gapes for several weeks after leaving the nest.

Reading

Turner, Angela & Rose, Chris (1989), *A Handbook to the Swallows and Martins of the World*, Christopher Helm (Publishers), UK.

Welcome Swallows breed in a half-cup mud nest, usually under roof-eaves or bridges in southern and eastern Australia.

Breeding seasons (*variable*)

	J	F	M	A	M	J	J	A	S	O	N	D
445 White-backed Swallow*												
447 Welcome Swallow*												
449 Tree Martin*												
450 Fairy Martin*												

Bulbuls — Family Pycnonotidae

[Sibley & Ahlquist place the Bulbuls in the Parvorder Passerida, Superfamily Sylvioidea, and retain the traditional Family Pycnonotidae.]

Genus *Pycnonotus* contains most species; one in Australia, *P. jocosus*, was introduced from China in the early 1900s; a second, Red-vented Bulbul (*P. cafer*) was brought in but appears to have died out.

Wing size and structure precludes non-migratory bulbuls from being strong fliers, but they are lively, energetic feeders with cheerful calls. Their foods are fruit, insects, and young shoots. Research is needed on this little-studied bird in Australia. Reported as pest of fruit in NSW.

Breeding season

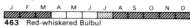

	J	F	M	A	M	J	J	A	S	O	N	D
463 Red-whiskered Bulbul												

African Warblers — Family Cisticolidae

[We depart from the ARBS List of Families at this point, and introduce Family Cisticolidae. In doing so we reflect Sibley & Ahlquist's position. They place the African Warblers in the Parvorder Passerida, Superfamily Sylvioidea, and then use a family which has been proposed at different times, Cisticolidae.]

Australia has two cisticolas, one of which is shared with Africa. Both also occur in India, Asia and south-east Asia. Africa has 39 species, one of which is the Zitting Cisticola. Only the Golden-headed is not found in Africa.

Breeding seasons (*variable*)

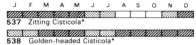

	J	F	M	A	M	J	J	A	S	O	N	D
537 Zitting Cisticola*												
538 Golden-headed Cisticola*												

Old World Warblers — Family Sylviidae

[Sibley & Ahlquist place the Old World Warblers in the Parvorder Passerida, Superfamily Sylvioidea and retain the traditional Family Sylviidae. There are four subfamilies, two in Australia.]

Leaf, Reed Warblers   Subfamily Acrocephalinae

This subfamily contains the reed-warblers, genus *Acrocephalus*, of which Australia has two species. The Great Reed-warbler is a rare vagrant into the north of the continent. The Clamorous Reed-warbler is widespread, an annual north-south migrant, breeding in reed and bullrush beds in south-east Australia, where it binds several stems together and builds a deep nest to prevent eggs being lost on windy days. The voice is strong, melodious, and a feature of the reed beds in summer in south-east Australia.

The subfamily also includes the Arctic Warbler, genus *Phylloscopus*, recent Australian records of which tend to remind us of the propensity of small birds to move widely about the world's surface.

Breeding seasons (*variable)

J	F	M	A	M	J	J	A	S	O	N	D

532   Clamorous Reed-Warbler*

Grass Warblers   Subfamily Megalurinae

This subfamily contains the Tawny and Little Grassbirds, genus *Megalurus*, the Spinifexbird of inland Australia, genus *Eremiornis*, and the two aptly named songlarks, the Brown and the Rufous, genus *Cinclorhamphus*.

Breeding seasons (*variable)

J	F	M	A	M	J	J	A	S	O	N	D

534   Tawny Grassbird*

535   Little Grassbird*

536   Spinifexbird*

540   Rufous Songlark*

541   Brown Songlark*

White-eyes   Family Zosteropidae

[Sibley & Ahlquist conclude that the White-eyes are members of the Superfamily Sylvioidea. The brush-tipped tongue is a convergent feature, and the similar Honeyeaters Meliphagidae, Sunbirds Nectariniidae and White-eyes Zosteropidae are independently evolved lineages, with convergent morphology but no common recent ancestry.]

These olive-green and yellow birds, usually with white eye-rings, are found in the Old World and in Australia.

Pale White-eyes are restricted to islands off far north-east Queensland and are seen by few ornithologists. Little is know of their habits, or those of the mangrove-dwelling Yellow White-eye of northern Australia.

By contrast, the Silvereyes of eastern and southern Australia have been studied intensively for over two decades. Well over 100 000 individual birds have been banded to discover their migratory movement. It is now known that in autumn some populations undertake lengthy journeys. The Tasmanian race is perhaps most notable: large numbers cross Bass Strait and winter from Adelaide through to southern Queensland. The birds search foliage for insects, seeds, nectar (they have a brush-tipped tongue) and fruit (which sometimes makes them orchard pests).

Two to four pale blue eggs are laid in a small, neat cup of fine grasses, rootlets and cobwebs. Pale White-eyes use leaves but little is known of their breeding and behaviour.

The series of papers variously written over many years by G. F. Mees and J. Kikkawa ought to be consulted for further information on the genus *Zosterops* in general.

Banding studies have been initiated and results published largely in the *Australian Bird Bander*, now retitled as the journal *Corella*. Read the early articles by S. G. Lane for an excellent entry into Silvereye population studies.

A Silvereye feeding on nectar.

The brush-tipped tongue of the Silvereye.

Breeding seasons

J	F	M	A	M	J	J	A	S	O	N	D

687   Pale White-eye (*Insufficient information*)

688   Yellow White-eye

689   Silvereye

True Thrushes Family Muscicapidae, Subfamily Turdinae

[Within the Passerida, Superfamily Muscicapoidea of Sibley & Ahlquist contains four families. These are the Bombycillidae (waxwing group), Cinclidae (dippers), Muscicapidae (true thrushes, Old World flycatchers and wheatears) and the Sturnidae (starlings and mockingbirds). The last two families are represented in Australasia. Over the last 200 years or so, vast numbers of passerine birds have been assigned to the 'Muscicapidae' in its various forms but the clearest definition yet achieved seems to be with us now.]

In Australia the genus *Zoothera*, the ground or mountain thrushes, are typical thrushes, and were recently overhauled taxonomically to provide two species, White's Thrush with two races, and the Russet-tailed Thrush of north-central Queensland. The Blackbird and Song Thrush of Europe have been introduced to Australia and are well established in the south-east of the continent.

Reading
Ford, J. (1983), 'Speciation in the Ground-Thrush complex *Zoothera dauma* in Australia', *Emu* **83** (3), 141-51.

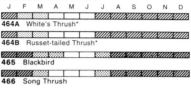

Breeding seasons (*variable)

464A White's Thrush*
464B Russet-tailed Thrush*
465 Blackbird
466 Song Thrush

Starlings and allies Family Sturnidae

[Sibley & Ahlquist include the true starlings in a Tribe Sturnini of traditional Family Sturnidae. Their work tends to eliminate any close link with the corvids, to which starlings have been traditionally assigned. They conclude that the closest relatives of the starlings *may be* the American region's mockingbird group, Tribe Mimini, but this is yet to be proved.]

Metallic Starlings (*Aplonis*) are migratory and fruit-eating. They maintain traditional nest colonies in tall trees, often isolated or taller than the surrounding forest canopy. Nests are pendulous and vermin-ridden, mites usually being present.

The Common Starling and Common Mynah are introductions, to some degree commensal with humans, but not completely dependent on them for shelter and food. The Common Starling in particular occurs well away from settlements, and is still extending its range. Both compete with native birds for nesting holes and for food. Starlings are significant agricultural pests in some districts, especially where fruit is grown.

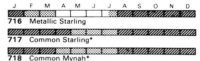

Breeding seasons (*variable)

716 Metallic Starling
717 Common Starling*
718 Common Mynah*

Old World Larks Family Alaudidae

[Sibley & Ahlquist's Superfamily Passeroidea contains six families. Four are represented in Australia: Alaudidae, Nectariniidae, Passeridae and Fringillidae. They are not precisely in this sequence in our Handbook however. Sibley & Ahlquist also prove there is no direct link between larks and swallows; most books traditionally place them together.]

Larks are widespread in the world and are one of the most clearly defined songbird families. The Singing Bushlark naturally colonised Australia. The Skylark was introduced in 1857. Both feed on seeds, insects and small molluscs. Both build nests on the ground; cup-shaped (Skylark) or can be fully domed (Bushlark). Most incubation is by females; the males feed them at the nest and help to feed the young. The birds may be found in open grassland, crop and salt-marsh areas.

Reading
Mayr, E. & McEvey, A. R. (1960), 'The distribution and variation of *Mirafra javanica* in Australia', *Emu* **60**, 155-92.

Breeding seasons (*variable)

443 Singing Bushlark*
444 Skylark

Old World Wagtails and Pipits Family Motacillidae

[Sibley & Ahlquist place the wagtails and pipits of the Old World in their Superfamily Passeroidea and assign them a subfamily, Motacillinae, in the traditional Family Passeridae.]

Most pipits are grassland birds, a bit like larks, but have different mannerisms, flight and song. Richard's Pipit, Australia's only breeding member of this family, builds a cup nest of grass in a depression, usually in the shelter of a stone or tussock. It lays three to four finely freckled off-white eggs (and see p. 5 for the newly recorded Red-throated Pipit).

The wagtails have evolved into a number of well-defined races inhabiting separate parts of their vast breeding range. Wagtails are non-breeding visitors or rare vagrants to Australia from the Northern Hemisphere. Two races of Yellow Wagtail, *simillina* and *taivana*, are regular visitors. However, a bird collected in eastern Australia was identified as race *tschutschensis*. These three wintering races cannot always be reliably separated in the field.

Reading
Wild Bird Society of Japan (1983), *A Field Guide to the Birds of Japan*, Wild Bird Society, Tokyo, Japan (pp. 222-4).

Breeding season (*variable*)

| J | F | M | A | M | J | J | A | S | O | N | D |

451 Richard's Pipit*

Sunbirds and allies Family Nectariniidae

[Sibley & Ahlquist place the sunbirds and allies in Superfamily Passeroidea, retaining the traditional Family Nectariniidae and Subfamily Nectariniinae. They then erect two tribes, one, Nectariniini for the sunbirds and allies, and the other, Dicaeini, for the flower peckers.]

This Old World insectivorous and nectivorous family (about 104 species) extends from Africa to Asia, New Guinea and Australia. There is one Australian species: the Yellow-bellied Sunbird. In Asia the same species is named the Olive-backed Sunbird. Active, pugnacious and noisy, these birds behave rather like honeyeaters. The sexes have different plumages. Yellow-bellied Sunbirds build a spectacular suspended nest with a side entrance. Preferred habitat is lush tropical growth of coastal lowlands and offshore islands. They frequent gardens; may enter houses.

Reading
King, Ben, Woodcock, Martin & Dickinson, E. C. (1976), *A Field Guide to the Birds of South-East Asia*, William Collins, Glasgow, UK.
Maher, W. J. (1991), 'Growth and development of the Yellow-bellied Sunbird *Nectarinia jugularis* in north Queensland', *Emu* **91** (1); 58-61.

Breeding season (*variable*)

| J | F | M | A | M | J | J | A | S | O | N | D |

680 Olive-backed Sunbird*

Flowerpeckers Family Dicaeidae

[Sibley & Ahlquist place the flowerpeckers in the traditional Family Nectariniidae, Subfamily Nectariniinae, in their own Tribe, Dicaeini. The flowerpeckers include our Mistletoebird *Dicaeum hirundinaceum*. Now that pardalotes have their own family, the Mistletoebird is the only Australian representative of the Asian Dicaeidae.]

The range of the Mistletoebird extends to the Aru Islands and western Papua New Guinea; not to Tasmania.

Ripe parasitic mistletoe berries are their main food (insects are eaten when feeding young). The birds are an important agent in dispersal of the fruits. The Mistletoebird does not have a muscular gizzard as do other birds. Its digestive system is an even duct through which large numbers of mistletoe berries quickly pass. The fleshy outer pericarp is digested and the sticky seed is deposited on a branch, the

The Mistletoebird perches lengthwise along branches and defecates mistletoe seeds onto them. If the seeds stick to a suitable branch they usually germinate. In this way the Mistletoebird helps the mistletoe plant to spread.

bird usually standing lengthways to accomplish this. The seed germinates quickly and parasitises another host.

The nest is made of plant-down and spiderweb matted to a silken consistency, and hangs from a level twig. It is a neat pear-shaped 'purse' with a slit-like entrance. The female usually builds it and incubates alone. Non-breeding birds are highly nomadic. Torpidity has been recorded in cold.

Breeding season (*variable*)

J	F	M	A	M	J	J	A	S	O	N	D

681 Mistletoebird*

Sparrows, Weaverbirds, Waxbills and allies
Family Passeridae

[Sibley & Ahlquist have six families within their Superfamily Passeroidea. One is the traditional Family Passeridae, the sparrows, wagtails, weaverbirds, waxbills and allies, and it is divided into five subfamilies. These are Subfamily Passerinae (sparrows, rock sparrows and snowfinches); the Motacillinae (Old World wagtails and pipits); the Prunellinae (the accentors and hedge-sparrows); the Ploceinae (weaverbirds); and, finally, the Estrildinae, the group of beautifully coloured waxbills (grass finches) and indigobirds. There are no indigobirds in Australia, but the waxbill group is well represented. The DNA evidence produced a basically expected result in the Passeridae, but the inclusion of Motacillinae and Prunellinae was a 'surprise' to the investigators.]

Old World Sparrows
Subfamily Passerinae

Two species were introduced into Australia between 1862 and 1872. House Sparrows were released in Sydney, Melbourne, Brisbane and Hobart; Tree Sparrows only in Melbourne. Both eat seeds, grain, flower and leaf buds, insects up to the size of the large green cicadas, and food scraps, and are considered to be pest species.

In spring, winter flocks break up as males find territories and nest sites. With loud 'chirrup' songs they attract females, then adopt a stiff, head-up, tail-up posture, and hop around bowing before the female.

Bulky spherical grass nests with side entrances and inner cups lined with feathers are built in dense bushes, hollows and building crevices. In the latter they may block drains and air ducts, and become a fire hazard or a rat refuge.

House Sparrows lay three to six grey-white eggs blotched brown. Tree Sparrows lay four to six brown-white eggs with fine brown dots. Incubation lasts 14-15 days; females may spend more time than males incubating the eggs. Both sexes feed the nestlings. Young birds fledge 15 to 16 days after hatching. Parents may feed juveniles for a period after fledging.

House Sparrows are pests of grain crops in some rural areas of eastern Australia. Destruction campaigns are occasionally carried out. Attempts by the species to colonise the Northern Territory and Western Australia have been contained to date by shooting any individuals seen. House Sparrows often roost in large flocks in dense reed beds beside swamps and rivers.

A nest hollow of the Tree Sparrow (left); House Sparrows during courtship (right).

Breeding seasons

J	F	M	A	M	J	J	A	S	O	N	D

692 House Sparrow

J	F	M	A	M	J	J	A	S	O	N	D

693 Tree Sparrow

Weaverbirds
Subfamily Ploceinae

The taxonomy of this group of Old World seed-eaters has frequently been rearranged. Groups have been included or excluded depending on current nomenclature trends. The 'true weavers' were *always* included but representation of other groups varied.

The Subfamily Ploceinae (11 genera; 96 species) includes weavers, bishops and wydahs. They weave grass into neat, roofed nests in many beautiful shapes. They have a reduced tenth primary (outer flight feather), strong seed-eating bills and eggs of blue and green colours. They are often polygamous.

The genus *Euplectes* (16 species) typically inhabits swampy African grasslands, eating seeds, grains, insects. Two species were introduced into Australia: the Red Bishop was established on the Murray River at Murray Bridge, South Australia in the 1930s but has not been seen since the 1950s. The White-winged Wydah was established on Hawkesbury River, near Windsor, NSW, in 1931; it was seen until the late 1960s but not since. Both were in small, loose colonies in reed beds beside the rivers.

Breeding seasons

	J	F	M	A	M	J	J	A	S	O	N	D
694 White-winged Wydah												
695 Red Bishop												

Waxbills, Grass-finches, Mannikins Subfamily Estrildini

Subfamily Estrildini (28 genera; 126 species) consists of three tribes: waxbills, grass-finches and mannikins. Smaller than weavers and sparrows, they have only nine primaries, build a roofed unwoven grass nest and lay pure white eggs. Nestlings beg uniquely with their head down to one side and also have intricate palate and tongue patterns. The estrildid song is very soft and non-territorial in function; females solicit with quivering tails, *not* wings.

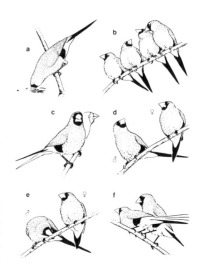

The fledgling of the Gouldian Finch begs for food.

It is believed that the gape markings of a Gouldian Finch nestling stimulate the parent to feed it.

Estrildids evolved in Africa, spreading to Asia and Australia. Waxbills remained in Africa but three separate invasions to Australia gave rise to the grass-finches and mannikins, our only indigenous seed-eating passerines. The first invasion produced the crimson-rumped grass-finches (*Emblema, Neochmia*), the second the white-rumped grass-finches (*Poephila*), and the last wave produced the *Lonchura* and the *Erythrura*. The arrangement of Australian finches into genera remains controversial. All eat seeds and, when breeding, eat insects, especially flying termites. All flock throughout the year except the firetails and the Crimson Finch.

All Australian finches are monogamous, probably for life. Most use pre-copulatory courtship for pair formation. The more primitive *Emblema-Neochmia* group use an ancestral 'stem dance' at courtship. The male holds a long grass stem by the thick end and with stiff legs bobs up and down on a branch. Plumage is fluffed and the bill is pointed up in all except the Diamond Firetail, which holds its head down. A soft, simple song of repetitive phrases is given. Throughout both sexes bow and beak-wipe and twist their heads and tails towards one another.

The *Poephila* group have lost the 'stem dance' but waltz together on branches until the female stops. The male, in a fluffed upright posture, then sings to her. With tail quivers she invites mating. In the mannikin group, the males sing an extremely soft song with bill wide open and pointed down; both sexes pivot, bow and shake.

Most species are colonial nesters except the Beautiful and Red-eared Firetails, and the Crimson Finch, which establish large individual territories. Males show possible nest sites to the female but she ultimately decides. A nest ceremony confirms the decision. Thick, thorny bushes are the most suitable sites. However, some *Lonchura* nest in reeds or grass. Red-eared Firetails prefer tree-tops; Painted Firetails, Pictorella Mannikins and Masked Finches nest on the ground. Gouldian Finches nest in hollow trees and termite mounds. Both sexes build; the male carries most of the chosen materials. The domed grass and twig nest is entered by a lateral tunnel. The egg chamber is lined with feathers and plant

Aspects of grass-finch behaviour: (a) drinking by sucking; (b) clumping and allopreening; (c) singing posture (undirected); (d) waltzing with tails twisted during courtship; (e) bill wiping during courtship; (f) soliciting of male by tail quivering female.

'wool'. Nest dimensions vary: Zebras and Beautiful Firetails build the largest; Painted Firetails the smallest.

Normally, four or five pure white eggs are laid. Incubation begins with the fourth egg. Both sexes take turns for one to two hours. Hatching takes 12-16 days, depending on the weather. The young are brooded for 12 days and fed by both parents on half-ripe seeds and regurgitated insects. Loud, raucous cries accompany the strange begging posture of nestlings in which the wings are *not* quivered. Gouldian Finch nestlings have two large luminous tubercles at each corner of the gape. Nestlings have black patterns of spots or stripes on the mouth and tongue, unique to their species.

The young fledge about 22 days after hatching, and are independent at 40 days. Zebra and Gouldian Finches and Painted Firetails become sexually mature at 70-80 days, which places them among the fastest sexually maturing bird species known. Extensive research has been conducted on physiology and behaviour of Zebra Finches.

All species possess a variety of calls: begging, distress, close-contact, nest-attracting, alarm and courtship. It may be possible for observers to learn the principal calls by studying zoo- or aviary-held birds before entering the field.

Reading

Clayton, N. S., Hodson, D. & Zann, R. A. (1991), 'Geographic variation in Zebra Finch subspecies', *Emu* **91** (1), 2-11.

Goodwin, D. (1982), *Estrildid Finches of the World*, Oxford University Press, London.

Immelmann, K. (1982), *Australian Finches in Bush and Aviary*, 4th (revised) edition, Angus & Robertson, Sydney.

Breeding seasons (*variable*)

	J	F	M	A	M	J	J	A	S	O	N	D
696 Diamond Firetail												
697 Beautiful Firetail												
698 Red-eared Firetail												
699 Painted Firetail*												
700 Star Finch*												
701 Crimson Finch*												
702 Red-browed Firetail												
703 Plum-headed Finch												
704 Zebra Finch*												
705 Double-barred Finch*												
706 Masked Finch*												
707 Long-tailed Finch												
708 Black-throated Finch												
709 Pictorella Mannikin												
710 Chestnut-breasted Mannikin*												
711 Yellow-rumped Mannikin												
712 Black-headed Mannikin												
713 Nutmeg Mannikin												
714 Blue-faced Finch												
715 Gouldian Finch												

Finches and allies
Family Fringillidae

[Sibley & Ahlquist retain the traditional Family Fringillidae within Superfamily Passeroidea. Their family contains three subfamilies, one of which, Fringillinae, contains three tribes. Tribe Fringillini has the chaffinches and brambling; Tribe Cardeulini has the two species introduced into Australia, Goldfinch and Greenfinch; and Tribe Drepanidini contains the remarkable Hawaiian honeycreepers. This is a large, widespread, N. Hemisphere family. All have 12 tail feathers, 9 primaries and a stout conical bill.]

The Goldfinch and Greenfinch are the only 'true' finches in Australia and were introduced last century. Both initially were fairly sedentary and urban-living, but Goldfinches in particular have moved well out into the towns and farmland of south-eastern Australia, including Tasmania. Greenfinches colonised Tasmania from the early 1940s onward. Both species are common also in New Zealand, from where stragglers have reached some outlying islands.

The Greenfinch eats seeds, small fruits and buds and is often seen in association with conifer trees of many varieties. Goldfinches are thinner-billed, eating small seeds, especially of scotch thistle. Both eat many insects in summer.

Greenfinches lay four to six whitish eggs with brown spots; the Goldfinch lays three to seven pale blue eggs spotted brown. Females incubate for 12-14 days; young birds fledge 12-14 days after hatching.

The cup-shaped nest of the European Goldfinch in a gorse bush.

Breeding seasons

	J	F	M	A	M	J	J	A	S	O	N	D
690 European Goldfinch												
691 European Greenfinch												

Australian island territories' checklists

Recent work around the continent indicates a need to study and conserve the fauna and flora of the island territories administered by the Commonwealth of Australia. The RAOU's new *Handbook* series (HANZAB), is dealing with most of the Australo-Papuan, New Zealand and Antarctic region. We feel it important for mainland Australian bird-watchers to be aware of what is on our islands, to promote their study and protection, and to feel that these birds too are part of our avifaunal region and our responsibility. Not everyone can get to every island, but all islands, even Heard Island, are being visited more frequently at present. Lists and some understanding of what each island contains in the way of bird populations are thus being gathered.

Names of the birds We use only the accepted common name, unless the species is not represented on the Australian and Tasmanian continental list, when the Latin name is also provided.

Codes used The coding has been kept as simple as possible. You are asked to see the papers and books listed as references for each island to obtain far more details of each bird species and its status at each locality. Measures of abundance have not been given except in a few cases.

Br.   breeding species
Vagr.   vagrant species
IE   island endemic species or subspecies (race), not found anywhere else
Intro.   introduced species — implication of a real or possible pest species
R   resident all year round
AM   annual migrant
SR   summer resident — leaves for winter months
WR   winter resident — leaves for summer months

We also use the general terms 'Visitor' and 'Irregular visitor' depending on a bird's status above that of 'vagrant/straggler/occasional visitor', all of which we term 'Vagrant'. Birds known to have become recently extinct, whether endemic or introductions which subsequently died out, have not been entered in these lists.

Norfolk Island (and adjacent Nepean, Philip Islands)

Lies 1 367 kilometres off the east coast of Australia: latitude 29°02′S; longitude 167°57′E. An oceanic island of volcanic origin. Situated 675 km S of New Caledonia, 900 km NE of Lord Howe Island, and 772 km NW of New Zealand. Norfolk Island is about 8 km long, 5 km wide and rises to two peaks, 316 and 318 m respectively. Nepean Island is 1 km S; Philip Island is 6 km S. Both are uninhabited. There is a resident human population on Norfolk. Tourist destination. Direct air flights.

Wandering Albatross	unconfirmed; Vagr.			
Laysan Albatross	Vagr.			
Black-browed Albatross	Vagr.			
Giant Petrel	Vagr.; species not determined			
Black-winged Petrel	Br.; AM; SR			
Flesh-footed Shearwater	Vagr.			
Wedge-tailed Shearwater	Br.; AM; SR			
Little Shearwater	Br.; AM?; WR			
Australasian Grebe	Vagr.			
Red-tailed Tropicbird	Br.; AM?; SR			
White-tailed Tropicbird	Vagr.			
Least Frigatebird	Vagr.			
Little Pied Cormorant	Vagr.			
Great Cormorant	Vagr.			
Little Black Cormorant	Vagr.			
Australasian Gannet	Br.; rare SR			
Masked Booby *Sula datcylatra fullagari*	Br.; SR			
Brown Booby	Vagr.			
Australian Pelican	Vagr.			
Pacific Heron	Vagr.			
White-faced Heron	Br.; R			
Cattle Egret	Vagr.			
Great Egret	Vagr.			
Little Egret	Vagr.			
Australian White (Sacred) Ibis	Vagr.			
Straw-necked Ibis	Vagr.			
Royal Spoonbill	Vagr.			
Yellow-billed Spoonbill	Vagr.			
Brown Goshawk	Vagr.			
Marsh Harrier	Vagr.			
Australian Kestrel	Br.?; R			
Black Swan	Vagr.			
Australian Shelduck	Vagr.			
Pacific Black Duck	Br.; Vagr.?; R?			
Mallard	Vagr.			
Hardhead	Vagr.			
Feral Chicken	Extinct or nearly so; Br.; Intro.; R			
California Quail	Br.; Intro.; R			
Buff-banded Rail	Br.; R			
Spotless Crake	Br.; Vagr.? or R?			
Purple Swamphen	Br.; Vagr.			
Eurasian Coot	Vagr.			

South Island Pied Oystercatcher
  Haematopus finschi   Vagr.

Black-winged Stilt   Vagr.

Masked Lapwing   Vagr.

Lesser Golden Plover   AM; SR

Mongolian Plover   Irregular visitor

Double-banded Plover   AM; WR

Ruddy Turnstone   AM; SR

Eastern Curlew   Irregular visitor

Bristle-thighed Curlew
  Numenius tahitiensis   Vagr.

Whimbrel   AM; SR

Grey-tailed Tattler   Irregular visitor

Wandering Tattler   Irregular visitor

Common Sandpiper   Vagr.

Greenshank   Unconfirmed; Vagr.

Terek Sandpiper   Irregular visitor

Latham's Snipe   Irregular visitor

Bar-tailed Godwit   AM; SR

Hudsonian Godwit   Irregular visitor

Red Knot   Irregular visitor

Sharp-tailed Sandpiper   Irregular visitor

Red-necked Stint   Irregular visitor

Skua (*Stercorarious* sp.) Irregular visitor

Silver Gull   Vagr.

White-winged Black Tern   Vagr.

White-fronted Tern   Vagr.

Sooty Tern   Br.; SR

Little Tern   ? Unconfirmed; Vagr.

Common Noddy   Br.; SR

Black Noddy   Br.; SR

Grey Ternlet   Br.; SR

White Tern   Br.; R

Rose-crowned Fruit-Dove   Vagr.

Feral Pigeon   Br.; Intro.; R

Emerald Dove   Br.; Self-intro.; R

Crimson Rosella   Br.; Intro.; R

Red-fronted Parakeet (Green Parrot)
  Cyanoramphus novaezelandiae Br.; IE; R

Pallid Cuckoo   Vagr.

Shining Bronze-Cuckoo
  (Greenback)   Br.; AM; SR

Long-tailed Cuckoo (Long-tailed Koel)
  Eudynamys taitensis Irregular visitor; Br.

Barn Owl   Vagr.

Norfolk Island Boobook Owl
  Ninox undulata
  (or ? *N. novaeseelandiae*)   Br.; IE; R

White-throated Needletail   Irregular
                                      visitor'

Fork-tailed Swift   Irregular visitor

Sacred Kingfisher   Br.; R

Dollarbird   Irregular visitor

Grey Gerygone
  Gerygone igata modesta   Br.; IE; R

Scarlet Robin *Petroica multicolor*
  multicolor   Br.; IE; R

Golden Whistler *Pachycephala pectoralis*
  xanthoprota   Br.; IE; R

Grey Fantail *Rhipidura fuliginosa*
  pelzelni   Br.; IE; R

Welcome Swallow   Br. not confirmed; R

Fairy Martin   ? Unconfirmed

Silvereye   Br.; Self-intro.; R

White-breasted White-eye *Zosterops*
  albogularis Facing extinction; Br.; IE; R

Long-billed White-eye *Zosterops*
  tenuirostris   Br.; IE; R

Grey-headed Blackbird (Guava Bird)
  Turdus poliocephalus
  poliocephalus Extremely rare; Br.; IE; R

Blackbird   Br.; Intro.?; R

Songthrush   Br.; Intro.?; R

Common Starling   Br.; Self-intro.; R

Common Mynah   Vagr.

Richard's Pipit   ? Unconfirmed

House Sparrow   Br.; Intro.?; R

European Goldfinch   Br.; Self-intro.?; R

European Greenfinch   Br.; Self-intro.?; R

Reading

ANPWS Planning Section, Norfolk Island (1989),
'Philip Island, Revised Draft Plan of Management',
Australian National Parks and Wildlife Service,
Canberra.

ANPWS (1984), 'Plan of Management, Norfolk Island
National Park and Norfolk Island Botanic Garden',
Australian National Parks and Wildlife Service,
Canberra.

Bell, Brian D. (1990), 'The status and management of
the White-breasted White-eye and other birds on
Norfolk Island, a report for the ANPWS, May 1990',
RAOU, Moonee Ponds, Victoria.

Hermes, N. (1985a), *Birds of Norfolk Island*, Wonderland
Publications, Norfolk Island.

Hermes, N. (editor), (1985b), *An Annotated Checklist of
Vascular Plants and Vertebrate Animals of Norfolk Island*,
Flora and Fauna Society of Norfolk Island/Australian
National Parks and Wildlife Service, Norfolk Island.

Schodde, R., Fullagar, P. & Hermes, N. (1983), 'A review of Norfolk Island birds: past and present', *Special Publication* **8**, Australian National Parks and
Wildlife Service, Canberra.

Lord Howe Island (and associated Balls Pyramid)

Lies 570 kilometres off the eastern coast of New South Wales: latitude 31°33'S; longitude 159°05'E. Norfolk Island is 800 km to the NE. New Zealand is 1 350 km to the SE and New Caledonia is 1 250 km to the NNE. Administered by the Government of New South Wales. Permanent resident human population. Tourist destination. Direct air flights. The island is about 11 km long, and up to 2.8 km wide; total land area is about 1 455 hectares. Two mountains, Mt Lidgbird 777 m and Mt Gower 875 m, are the highest points. The island is subtropical and of submarine volcanic origin. Balls Pyramid, a volcanic stack or spire, rises to 551 m and is 23 km to the SE.

Wandering Albatross	Vagr.			
Giant Petrel (species not known)	Vagr.			
Cape Petrel	Vagr.			
Great-winged Petrel	Vagr.			
White-headed Petrel	Vagr.			
Providence Petrel	Br.; AM; WR			
Kermadec Petrel	Br. (Balls Pyramid); AM; SR			
Gould's Petrel	Vagr.			
Black-winged Petrel	Br.; AM; SR			
Mottled Petrel	Vagr.			
White-necked Petrel	Vagr.			
Antarctic (Dove) Prion	Vagr.			
Fairy Prion	Vagr.			
Flesh-footed Shearwater	Br.; AM; SR			
Wedge-tailed Shearwater	Br.; AM; SR			
Buller's Shearwater	Vagr.			
Sooty Shearwater	Vagr.			
Short-tailed Shearwater	Vagr.			
Fluttering Shearwater	Vagr.			
Hutton's Shearwater	Vagr.			
Little Shearwater	Br.; AM; WR			
White-bellied Storm-Petrel	Br.; AM: SR			
Little Penguin	Vagr.			
Australasian Grebe	Vagr.			
Hoary-headed Grebe	Vagr.			
Red-tailed Tropicbird	Br.; R			
White-tailed Tropicbird	Vagr.			
Least Frigatebird	Vagr.			
Pied Cormorant	Vagr.			
Little Pied Cormorant	Vagr.			
Great Cormorant	Vagr.			
Little Black Cormorant	Vagr.			
Australasian Gannet	Regular visitor			

Red-footed Booby	Vagr.			
Masked Booby	Br.; R			
Brown Booby	Vagr.			
White-faced Heron	Br.; Self-intro.; R			
Cattle Egret	Regular visitor			
Great Egret	Vagr.			
Rufous Night Heron	Vagr.			
Australasian Bittern	Vagr.			
Little Bittern	Vagr.			
Glossy Ibis	Vagr.			
Australian White (Sacred) Ibis	Vagr.			
Straw-necked Ibis	Vagr.			
Royal Spoonbill	Vagr.			
Yellow-billed Spoonbill	Vagr.			
Black-shouldered Kite	Vagr.			
Swamp Harrier	Regular visitor			
Brown Falcon	Vagr.			
Australian Kestrel	Br.; Self-intro.; R			
Black Swan	Vagr.			
Canada Goose *Branta canadensis*	Vagr.			
Paradise Duck *Tadorna variegata*	Vagr.			
Pacific Black Duck (many hybrids between Pacific Black Duck and Mallard on the island)	Br.; R			
Mallard	Vagr.			
Grey Teal	Vagr.			
Chestnut Teal	Vagr.			
Buff-banded Rail	Br.; Intro.? or Self-intro.; R			
Baillon's Crake	Vagr.			
Dusky Moorhen	Vagr.			
Purple Swamphen	Br.; Self-intro.; R			
Woodhen *Tricholimnas (Gallirallus) sylvestris* (subject of rehabilitation programme)	Br.; IE; R			
Eurasian Coot	Vagr.			
Painted Snipe	Vagr.			
Black-winged Stilt	Vagr.			
Pied Oystercatcher	Vagr.			
Masked Lapwing	Br.; Self-intro.; R			
Banded Lapwing	Vagr.			
Pacific (Lesser) Golden Plover	AM; SR			
Grey Plover	Vagr.			
Mongolian Plover	Vagr.			
Double-banded Plover	AM; SR			
Large Sand Plover	Vagr.			
Oriental Plover	Vagr.			

Ruddy Turnstone	AM; SR		
Eastern Curlew	Irregular visitor		
Whimbrel	AM; SR		
Little Curlew	Vagr.		
Grey-tailed Tattler	Visitor		
Wandering Tattler	Visitor		
Common Sandpiper	Vagr.		
Greenshank	Visitor		
Marsh Sandpiper	Vagr.		
Terek Sandpiper	Vagr.		
Latham's (Japanese) Snipe	Irregular visitor		
Bar-tailed Godwit	AM; SR		
Black-tailed Godwit	Vagr.		
Red Knot	Vagr.		
Sharp-tailed Sandpiper	Vagr.		
Pectoral Sandpiper	Vagr.		
Red-necked Stint	Irregular visitor		
Curlew Sandpiper	Vagr.		
Buff-breasted Sandpiper	Vagr.		
Oriental Pratincole	Vagr.		
Australian Pratincole	Vagr.		
Long-tailed Jaeger	Vagr.		
Silver Gull	Vagr.		
Kelp Gull	Vagr.		
White-winged Black Tern	Vagr.		
Common Tern	Vagr.		
Arctic Tern	Vagr.		
Black-naped Tern	Vagr.		
Sooty Tern	Br.; AM; SR		
Little Tern	Vagr.		
Crested Tern	Vagr.		
Common Noddy	Br.; AM; SR		
Black Noddy	Br.; AM?; SR		
Grey Ternlet	Br.; R		
White Tern	Br.; AM; SR		
Torresian Imperial-Pigeon	Vagr.		
Feral Pigeon	Br.; Intro.; R		
Spotted Turtle-Dove	Vagr.		
Peaceful Dove	Vagr.		
Emerald Ground-Dove	Br.; R		
Brush Bronzewing	Vagr.		
Oriental Cuckoo	Vagr.		
Pallid Cuckoo	Vagr.		
Brush Cuckoo	Vagr.		
Fan-tailed Cuckoo	Vagr.		

Shining Bronze-Cuckoo	Irregular visitor		
Long-tailed Cuckoo (Long-tailed Koel) *Eudynamys taitensis*	Irregular visitor		
Masked Owl (subject of control programme)	Br.; Intro.; R		
White-throated Needletail	Vagr.		
Fork-tailed Swift	Vagr.		
Sacred Kingfisher	Br.; SR		
Rainbow Bee-eater	Vagr.		
Dollarbird	Vagr.		
Noisy Friarbird	Vagr.		
Golden Whistler *Pachycephala pectoralis contempta*	Br.; IE; R		
Australian Magpie-Lark	Br.; Intro.; R		
Leaden Flycatcher	Vagr.		
Grey Fantail	Vagr.		
Black-faced Cuckoo Shrike	Vagr.		
Masked Woodswallow	Vagr.		
Lord Howe Currawong *Strepera graculina crissalis*	Br.; IE; R		
Australian Raven	Vagr.		
Welcome Swallow	Br.; R		
Fairy Martin	Vagr.		
Lord Howe White-eye *Zosterops tephropleura*	Br.; IE; R		
Blackbird	Br.; Self-intro.; R		
Songthrush	Br.; Self-intro.; R		
Common Starling	Br.; Self-intro.; R		
Richard's Pipit	Vagr.		
Yellowhammer *Emberiza citrinella*	Vagr.		
Chaffinch *Fringilla coelebs*	Vagr.		
European Goldfinch	Vagr.		
European Greenfinch	Vagr.		
Redpoll (Lesser Redpoll) *Carduelis flammea*	Vagr.		

Reading

Hindwood, K. A. (1940), 'The birds of Lord Howe Island' *Emu* **10**, 1–86; (also reprinted separately and widely distributed).

Hutton, Ian (1991), *Birds of Lord Howe Island Past and Present*, The Author, Coffs Harbour Plaza, NSW.

Knight, B. (1989) 'Report on Lord Howe Island observations', *Australian Birds*, **22** (1&2), 41-3.

Miller, B. & Muellette, K. J. (1985), 'Rehabilitation of an endangered Australian bird: the Lord Howe Woodhen *Tricholimnas sylvestris* (Sclater)', *Biological Conservation* **34**, 55-95.

Reader's Digest Services (1985), *Reader's Digest Complete Book of New Zealand Birds*, Reader's Digest, Sydney.

Recher, H. F. (1974), 'Colonisation and extinction', *Australian Natural History* **18** (2), 64-8.

Cocos (Keeling) Islands

Lies 3 685 kilometres due west of Darwin, 2 768 kilometres north-west of Perth, in the Indian Ocean: latitude 12°07'S; longitude 96°55'E. Small resident human population. Air and sea access.

Wedge-tailed Shearwater	Br.	
Red-tailed Tropicbird	Br. (few)	
White-tailed Tropicbird	Br.	
Great Frigatebird	Br.	
Least Frigatebird	Br.	
Red-footed Booby	Br.	
Masked Booby	Br.	
Brown Booby	Br.	
White-faced Heron	Vagr.	
Cattle Egret	Vagr.	
Eastern Reef Egret	Br.?; R	
Rufous Night Heron	Br.?	
Feral Chicken	Br. (declining); Intro.	
Helmeted Guinea Fowl	Br. (few); Intro.	
Cocos Buff-banded Rail *Rallus phillippensis andrewsi* Br. (common locally, declining on some islands, considered endangered); IE		
Lesser Golden Plover	Vagr.	
Ruddy Turnstone	Vagr.	
Little Curlew	Vagr.	
Common Sandpiper	Vagr.	
Greenshank	Vagr.	
Pin-tailed Snipe	Vagr.	
Sanderling	Vagr.	
Oriental Pratincole	Vagr.	
White-winged (Black) Tern	Vagr.	
Sooty Tern	Br.; few — declining?	
Common Noddy	Br.	
White Tern	Br.	
Dove	Unidentified	
Nightjar	Unidentified	
White-throated Needletail	Unconfirmed	
Barn Swallow	AM; SR	
Wagtail	Unidentified	
Christmas Island Silvereye *Zosterops natalis* Intro.; few; may be declining		
Christmas Island Thrush *Turdus poliocephalus erythropleurus* Intro.; common 1941; declining 1948; probably now extinct		
Java Sparrow *Padda oryzivora* Intro.; common 1909, 1941, 1949; now believed extinct		

Reading

Covacevich, Jeanette (1983) 'The Cocos Islands', *Wildlife in Australia* **20**, (1), 6-9.

Gibson-Hill, C. A. (1950), 'Notes on the birds of the Cocos-Keeling Islands', *Bulletin of the Raffles Museum* **22**, 212-270 (and see also his prior papers, 1947, 1948, 1949).

House of Representatives Standing Committee on Environment, Recreation and the Arts (1990), 'Tourism in the Indian Ocean Territories', The Parliament of the Commonwealth of Australia, Aust. Government Publishing Service, Canberra.

Stokes, Tony, Sheils, Wendy & Dunn, Kevin (1984), 'Birds of the Cocos (Keeling) Islands, Indian Ocean', *Emu* **84** (1), 23-8.

Wood-Jones, F. (1909), 'Fauna of the Cocos-Keeling Atoll', *Proceedings of the Zoological Society of London* **1909**, 132-59.

Christmas Island

Lies 1 400 kilometres north-west of Western Australia in the Indian Ocean, 900 km NE of the Cocos (Keeling) Islands; and 360 km SE of Java: latitude 10°25'S; longitude 105°40'E. Resident human population. Air and sea access.

Wedge-tailed Shearwater	Vagr.			
Matsudaira's Storm-Petrel	Vagr.			
Red-tailed Tropicbird	Br.; R			
White-tailed Tropicbird *Phaethon lepturus fulvus*	Br.; IE; R			
Christmas Frigatebird	Br.; IE; R; small population — endangered			
Great Frigatebird	Br; R			
Least Frigatebird	Regular visitor			
Great Cormorant	Vagr.			
Little Black Cormorant	Vagr.			
Abbott's Booby	Br.; IE; R			
Red-footed Booby	Br.; R			
Brown Booby	Br.; R			
Australian Pelican	Vagr.			
White-faced Heron	Br.?; Self-intro.; R			
Cattle Egret	Vagr.			
Great Egret	Vagr.			
Little Egret	Vagr.			
Intermediate Egret	Vagr.			
Eastern Reef Egret	Br.?; R			
Striated Heron	Vagr.			
Rufous Night Heron	Vagr.			
Malayan Night Heron *Gorsachius melanolophus* Irregular visitor?; Vagr.				
Yellow Bittern	Vagr.			
Black Bittern	Vagr.			
Brown Goshawk *Accipiter fasciatus natalis*	Br.; IE; R			

White-bellied Sea-Eagle	Vagr.	
Peregrine Falcon	Vagr.	
Australian Kestrel	Br.; Self-intro.; R	
Grey Teal	Vagr.	
Garganey	Vagr.	
Feral Chicken	Br.; Intro.; R; few	
Ruddy Crake *Porzana fusca*	Vagr.	
Watercock *Gallicrex cinerea*	Vagr.	
Sooty Oystercatcher	Vagr.	
Black-winged Stilt	Vagr.	
Masked Plover	Vagr.	
Grey Plover	Vagr.	
Lesser Golden Plover	Regular visitor	
Little Ringed Plover	Vagr.	
Mongolian Plover	Regular visitor	
Oriental Plover	Irregular visitor	
Ruddy Turnstone	Regular visitor	
Whimbrel	Regular visitor	
Little Curlew	Vagr.	
Wood Sandpiper	Regular visitor	
Grey-tailed Tattler	Irregular visitor	
Common Sandpiper	Regular visitor	
Greenshank	Regular visitor	
Redshank	Vagr.	
Marsh Sandpiper	Vagr.	
Terek Sandpiper	Vagr.	
Pin-tailed Snipe	Vagr.	
Bar-tailed Godwit	Vagr.	
Sharp-tailed Sandpiper	Vagr.	
Long-toed Stint	Vagr.	
Curlew Sandpiper	Vagr.	
Sanderling	Regular visitor	
Oriental Pratincole	Irregular visitor	
Australian Pratincole	Regular visitor	
Arctic Jaeger	Vagr.	
Whiskered Tern	Vagr.	
Sooty Tern	Vagr.	
Common Noddy	Br.; AM?; SR	
White Tern	Vagr.	
Torresian Imperial-Pigeon	Vagr.	
Christmas Island Imperial-Pigeon *Ducula whartoni*	Br.; IE; R	
Emerald Ground-Dove *Chalcophaps indica natalis*	Br.; IE; R	
Rose-ringed Parakeet *Psittacula krameri*	Intro. (pet birds); R	
Parrot	Unidentified	

Christmas Island Hawk-Owl *Ninox squamipila natalis*	Br.; IE: R; rare	
Oriental Cuckoo	Vagr.	
Pallid Cuckoo	Vagr.	
Horsfield's Bronze-Cuckoo	Vagr.	
Christmas Island Glossy Swiftlet *Collocalia esculenta natalis*	Br.; IE: R	
Swiftlet	Unidentified	
Fork-tailed Swift	Vagr.	
Sacred Kingfisher	Vagr.	
Collared Kingfisher	Vagr.	
Dollarbird	Vagr.	
Blue-winged Pitta	Vagr.	
Barn Swallow	Regular visitor	
Red-rumped Swallow	Vagr.	
Tawny Pipit *Anthus campestris*	Unconfirmed	
Richard's Pipit	Vagr.	
Yellow Wagtail	Vagr.	
Grey Wagtail	Vagr.	
Christmas Island White-eye *Zosterops natalis*	Br.; IE; R	
Christmas Island Thrush *Turdus poliocephalus erythropleurus*	Br.; IE; R	
Java Sparrow *Padda oryzivora*	Br.; Intro.; R	
Tree Sparrow	Br.; Intro.; R	

Reading

Gray, H. S. (1981), *Christmas Island — Naturally*, The Author, Geraldton, WA.

Phillips, D. J., et al. (1991), 'Observations on the diet of the Christmas Island Hawk-Owl *Ninox squamipila natalis*', *Emu* **91** (4), 250-1.

Stokes, T. (1988), 'A review of the birds of Christmas Island', *Occasional Paper* no. **16**, Australian National Parks and Wildlife Service, Canberra.

Stokes, T., et al. (1987), 'Additional records of birds from Christmas Island, Indian Ocean', *Aust. Bird Watcher* **12** (1), 1-7; (adds 31 new species for the island; extra records of 14 species described as *rare* to the island).

Van Tets, G. F. (1974), 'List of bird species found at Christmas Island', in *Conservation of Endangered Species on Christmas Island: A Report of the House of Representatives Standing Committee on the Environment and Conservation*, Aust. Govt. Publishing Service, Canberra.

Van Tets, G. F. (1983), 'List of bird species found at Christmas Island, Annexe E' in *The Preservation of Abbott's Booby on Christmas Island, Report of the Senate Standing Committee on Science, Technology and the Environment*, Aust. Govt. Publishing Service, Canberra.

Heard Island (and associated McDonald Islands)

Latitude 53°S; longitude 73°30′E. Lies some 4 450 km off the south-western Western Australian coast. Nearest significant land is French-administered Kerguelen Islands (Isles de Kerguelen), 520 km to NW. No resident human population. Intermittent scientific presence; permits required. Administered by Australian Federal Government through Antarctic Division, Tasmania. Research personnel most likely visitors at present. A source for many seabirds in Australian seas.

Black-browed Albatross	Br.; SR	
Light-mantled Sooty Albatross	Br.; SR	
Southern Giant-Petrel	Br.; SR	
Southern Fulmar	Irregular visitor; Vagr.?	
Antarctic Petrel	Rare visitor; Vagr.?	
Cape Petrel	Br.; R	
Snow Petrel	Vagr.	
Blue Petrel	Irregular visitor; Vagr.?	
Antarctic (Dove) Prion	Br.; SR	
Fulmar Prion	Br.; R	
White-chinned Petrel	Irregular visitor; Vagr.?	
Wilson's Storm-Petrel	Br.; SR	
Black-bellied Storm-Petrel	Vagr.	
Common Diving-Petrel	Br.; R	
South Georgian Diving-Petrel	Br.; SR	
Emperor Penguin	Rare visitor; Vagr.?	
King Penguin	Has bred; uncommon	
Gentoo Penguin	Br.; R	
Chinstrap Penguin	May Br.; Vagr.	
Adelie Penguin	Vagr.	
Macaroni Penguin	Br.; AM; SR	
Rockhopper Penguin	Br.; AM; SR	
Heard Shag *Phalacrocorax nivalis*	Br.; R	
Heard Island Sheathbill *Chionis minor nasicornis*	Br.; R	
Great Skua	Br.; AM; SR	
Kelp Gull	Br.; R	
Antarctic Tern	Br.; AM?; SR	
Arctic Tern	AM; passes island on way south	

Reading

(Few published bird lists; no recent lists.)
Downes, M. C., et al. (1959), 'The Birds of Heard Island', *ANARE Reports*, Series B, Vol. 1, Zoology, Australian National Antarctic Research Expeditions, Antarctic Division, Department of External Affairs, Melbourne.

Macquarie Island (now called Macquarie Island Nature Reserve and includes Judge and Clerk Rocks, and Bishop and Clerk Rocks)

Latitude 54°30′S; longitude 159°E. Lies approx. 1 500 km SSE of Tasmania and 1 100 km SSW of New Zealand. The island is about 34 km long and 5 km wide at its widest point. Area is approx. 12 785 hectares. Several peaks rise to 400 m and highest point is 433 m. The nearest islands are the Auckland Islands (640 km) and Campbell Island (700 km). Administered by Tasmanian National Parks and Wildlife Service, and serviced by the Antarctic Division, Tasmania. Ship access only. Permits required. A source area for many seabirds in Australian and New Zealand seas.

Wandering Albatross	Br.; AM; SR; declining	
Black-browed Albatross	Br.; AM; SR	
Grey-headed Albatross	Br.; AM; SR	
Light-mantled Sooty Albatross	Br.; AM: SR	
Sooty Albatross	Vagr.	
Southern Giant-Petrel	Br.; AM; SR	
Northern Giant-Petrel	Br.; AM; SR	
Southern Fulmar	Vagr.	
Antarctic Petrel	Vagr.	
Cape Petrel	Vagr.; few	
White-headed Petrel	Br.; AM; SR	
Blue Petrel	Br.; SR	
Antarctic (Dove) Prion	Br.; AM; SR	
Slender-billed Prion	Br.?; rare	
Fairy Prion	Br. (few); AM; SR	
Grey Petrel	Br.?; few	
Sooty Shearwater	Br.; AM; SR	
Short-tailed Shearwater	Vagr.	
Little Shearwater	Vagr.; very rare	
Grey-backed Storm-Petrel	Br.; rare; poor data	
Common Diving-Petrel	Br. (few); rare	
King Penguin	Br.; R; abundant	
Gentoo Penguin	Br.; R; abundant	
Chinstrap Penguin	Vagr.	
Adelie Penguin	Vagr.	
Royal (Macaroni) Penguin	Br.; AM; SR; abundant	
Rockhopper Penguin	Br.; AM; SR; abundant	
Erect-crested Penguin	Irregular visitor/Vagr.	
Snares Penguin	Vagr.	
Great Cormorant	Vagr.	

Macquarie Shag *Phalacrocorax*
  purpurascens   Br.; IE; R; small
  population

Bird	Status			
Australasian Gannet	Vagr.			
White-faced Heron	Vagr.			
Cattle Egret	Vagr.			
Great Egret	Vagr.			
Little Egret	Vagr.			
Pacific Black Duck	Br.; R; common			
Mallard	Br.; Self-intro.; R; few			
Grey Teal	Vagr.			
Swamp Harrier	Vagr.			
Baillon's (Marsh) Crake	Vagr.			
Eurasian Coot	Vagr.			

Stewart Island Weka   Br.; Intro.; was R;
  Gallirallus australis scotti   now extinct
    following eradication programme

Bird	Status			
Grey Plover	Vagr.			
Black-winged Stilt	Vagr.			
Ruddy Turnstone	Vagr.			
Greenshank	Vagr.			
Latham's Snipe	Vagr.			
Bar-tailed Godwit	Vagr.			
Red Knot	Vagr.			
Red-necked Phalarope	Vagr.			
Great Skua	Br.; AM; SR; common			
Kelp Gull	Br.; R; common			
Antarctic Tern	Br.; R; few			
Arctic Tern	Vagr.			
White-throated Needletail	Vagr.			
Fork-tailed Swift	Vagr.			
Welcome Swallow	Vagr.			
Silvereye	Vagr.			
Blackbird	Br.; was R — now Vagr.?			
Songthrush	Vagr.			
Common Starling	Br.; R; common			
European Goldfinch	Vagr.			

Redpoll *Acanthis (Carduelis)*
  flammea   Br; R; common

Reading

Gillham, M. E., 1967, *Subantarctic Macquarie Island*, A. H. & A. W. Reed, Wellington, New Zealand.

Mawson, Sir Douglas, (1915), *Home of the Blizzard*, London.

National Parks and Wildlife Service, Tasmania, 1987, *Macquarie Island Nature Reserve: Visitor's Handbook*, Nat. Parks & Wildlife Service, Hobart, Tasmania.

Glossary

Abrasion Wearing down of the feathers.

Adult Birds which breed or are known to have breeding capabilities. Adult plumages are those which do not change in appearance in subsequent moults (allowing for alternating eclipse plumages in some species, e.g. waders, fairy-wrens).

Allopatric The geographical range of one species does not overlap with that of another, similar, species.

Allopreening Preening of one bird by another.

Alula Four small feathers found on a bird's 'thumb'. They control airflow over the leading edge of the wing — the 'bastard wing'.

Antiphonal song Two birds contribute to the same song, taking a different part each, e.g. Eastern Whipbird, Australian Magpie-lark.

Asynchronous hatching A clutch of eggs which hatch progressively, not all together (synchronous), e.g. megapodes.

Auricular patch A distinct colour patch of feathers over or about the ear, e.g. King Penguin, Musk Lorikeet, Black-eared Miner, Spotted Catbird.

Axilla The area where the underwing joins the body. The feathers in this area are known as 'axillaries' or the armpit, e.g. Grey Plover.

Bar A fine, transverse mark.

Carpal joint (flexure) The joint found between the 'arm' and the 'hand' of the wing.

Casque A helmet-like structure on the skull or bill, e.g. Southern Cassowary, Helmeted Friarbiard.

Cere Bare, wax-like or fleshy structure at the base of the upper beak, containing the nostrils, e.g. Cape Barren Goose, Peregrine Falcon, Budgerigar.

Chevrons V-shaped stripes, usually on breast, e.g. Powerful Owl.

Cline A graded series of changes in the character of a bird across a geographic area., e.g. Varied Sittella, Figbird.

Colour morph Different colouring within a single interbreeding population, unrelated to season, sex or age (and formerly known as 'colour phase'). e.g. Eastern Reef Egret.

Commensalism When a species benefits from an activity or aspect of a second species, but the second species derives no benefit from, and is often indifferent to, the actions of the first, e.g. Yellow-rumped Thornbill nesting in base of a Whistling Kite's nest.

'Commic' terns Collective name sometimes applied to the group of terns typified by e.g. Arctic, Common and Black-naped. Derivation of word not known to us; probably British.

Conspecific Of the same species.

Coverts Small feathers hiding/protecting the bases of larger ones.

Crepuscular Appearing or flying at dusk, e.g. nightjars, frogmouths.

Cryptic Having protective colouring or camouflage, e.g. Bush Thick-knee, Australasian Bittern.

Culmen The ridge along the whole length or top of the upper mandible.

Diagnostic Having value in a description for the purpose of classification or for positive identification.

Dimorphism (sexual) The occurrence of two distinct types of plumage colour and/or patterns between the sexes of the same species, also shape and size.

Dorsal Pertaining to the upper surface of the body. (see *Upperparts*).

Ear tufts Feathers protruding from near ears, e.g. Yellow-tufted Honeyeater.

Eclipse (plumage) Dull, seasonal plumage assumed by many bird species during late summer, autumn or winter, e.g. ducks, waders, malurid wrens.

Egg tooth A tiny scale-like protrusion on the upper bills of many baby birds to help them chip through the egg shell.

Endemic Native to or peculiar to a particular or defined area.

Extant Living as a species at the present day.

Extinct No individuals of a species left alive today; gone forever; no longer extant.

Facial disc A bird's face, disc-like in form, being well-defined and comparatively flat, e.g. owls, harriers.

Family The division of classification into which an Order is divided and which has one or more genera, i.e. the next taxonomic rank below Order.

Feral Having returned to the wild after domestication. An introduced animal foreign to an environment.

Fingers Term used when a bird spreads its primary wing feathers in flight, e.g. Little Eagle, corvids.

Flank Area on the bird's side, located directly below the forepart of the closed (folded) wing, e.g. strong colour of Tasmanian race of Silvereye.

Fledgling (leaving the nest) Partly or wholly feathered. Flightless or partly flighted, but *before* full flight capability.

Foreneck The whole front section of the neck.

Frons The forehead or feathered front of the crown, immediately above the base of the upper bill, e.g. Common Bronzewing.

Frontal shield Distinctive, unfeathered, horny or fleshy forehead which extends down to the base of the upper bill. Does *not* include nostril, e.g. Eurasian Coot.

Gape The fleshy corner of the beak which is often yellow, cream or pinkish in young birds.

Genus (plural genera) The division of classification into which a Family is divided and which has one or more species, i.e. the next taxonomic rank below Family.

Gular Of the throat. A gular pouch is distendible skin in the central area of the throat, e.g. Great Cormorant, Australian Pelican.

Hackles Neck feathers which are longer than normal, e.g. Trumpet Manucode, corvids.

Hatchling see **Nestling**

Hibernation Over-wintering in a reduced animation state; dormancy (see *Torpidity*).

Hood Colour mass covering the head, e.g. Hooded Robin, Australian Hobby.

Hybridisation Interbreeding of different species, the offspring of which are infertile and known as 'hybrids', e.g. offspring of Pacific Black Duck and Mallard.

Immature (= sub-adult) All plumages which *follow* first moult *until* full breeding capacity and/or plumage is reached. Birds are usually independent of adults.

Infraorder The taxonomic level above Parvorder and below Suborder; a higher taxonomic category.

Iridescence Play of colours (in feathers) by light on feather structure; not a pigment (colour), e.g., speculum of ducks, sheen of Straw-necked Ibis, throat of Magnificent Riflebird.

Irruption Sudden appearance of large numbers of a bird in an area where not normally present, e.g. Black-tailed Native-hen, woodswallows.

Isolating mechanisms Biological or physiographic features which split populations into widely spread and eventually discrete entities; may lead to new races, then to speciation.

'Jizz' A word used by 'twitchers' — avid birdwatchers — to describe everything about a bird in one, all-embracing term; the 'essence' or 'character' of a bird in the field.

Juvenal A bird's first covering of true feathers, i.e. plumage after moult of natal down. An American term adopted in Australia and has same definition as *Juvenile* (below).

Juvenile (= Juvenal) Fledging to free-flying birds, with the feathers which *first* replaced the natal down. May still be under parental control.

Lamella A small layer of stiff hairs (membranes) on the inner edge of the bill, used to sieve food particles from water, e.g. prions, ducks.

Lanceolate Spear-like in shape. Usually used in describing feather shapes.

Leading edge The front edge of a wing or flipper.

Lores Area between the bill and the eye, e.g. Little Tern, Red-lored Whistler.

Malar stripe Cheek stripe of, e.g. Superb Fairy-wren.

Mandible The upper, or the lower, half of the bird's bill.

Mantle Feathers forming a covering of upper back and base of wings, e.g. Paradise Riflebird.

Mask Black or dark area which encloses the eyes and part of the face, e.g. Masked Woodswallow.

Migratory Of regular geographical movement.

Mirror White circles (spots) in the primary feathers of gulls, e.g. Silver Gull.

Nail The hooked tip of the upper mandibles of albatrosses and petrels; also of ducks (*sensu stricta*).

Nape The back of the bird's neck (and see *Nuchal crest*).

Nestling (= Hatchling = Downy) In or about the nest. Naked or downy, i.e. *before* feathers develop.

Nictitating membrane A third 'eyelid' that can be drawn across the eye from the nasal side for protection, lubrication and cleaning the eye. Some are translucent, some have clear central window so vision not seriously impaired.

Nomadic Of variable, often erratic movement with regard to time and area (place).

Nominate If there is more than one race in a species, the race that takes the sub-specific name identical to the specific name of that species is known as the nominate race and should always be named first.

Non-passerine Birds which are not sub-oscines or oscines. Birds placed systematically between grebes and Dollarbird in our book (pp. 18-163).

Nuchal crest 'Of the nape', e.g. Spotted Bowerbird's nuchal crest is positioned on nape.

Nuptial Of or pertaining to breeding, e.g. nuptial plumage; nuptial behaviour.

Orbit The space on each side of the skull filled by the eyeball.

Orbital ring A circular colour patch, fleshy or feathered, surrounding the eye, e.g. Silvereye.

Order The division of classification into which a Class is divided and which has one or more Families, i.e. the next taxonomic rank below Class.

Oscines The true song birds. Previously often used synonomously with 'passerine birds'; now

defined by Sibley & Ahlquist (1990) to include all birds in the Suborder Passeri.

Osteology The study of the skeleton and related elements of a vertebrate.

Palmate The three forward toes connected by webbing, e.g. petrels, ducks, gulls (the fourth toe is free; small).

Parasite An organism exploiting another, frequently inconveniencing it, and not returning a benefit to the host. Chiefly applies to invertebrates parasitic upon vertebrates in the context of this book.

Parasitic behaviour A method by which an organism obtains its living, or part thereof, by living on, in, or around another organism, or 'steals' from that organism, giving nothing in return. Invertebrates infesting vertebrates are best-known examples — fleas, lice, flat-flies, worms, protozoans, etc. Other usage of the term in Australia, e.g. robbing or stealing behaviour of skuas, frigatebirds, etc., probably better called *piracy*. Egg-laying by cuckoos in other birds' nests is better known as *brood-parasitism*.

Parvorder The taxonomic level above Superfamily, the next level below Infraorder; a higher taxonomic category.

Passerines (passeriform) An Order which includes all of the so-called 'song birds', 'perching birds' or 'passerine birds'. Used synonomously in Europe; in Australasia *previously* excluded pittas, lyrebirds and scrub-birds. Sibley & Ahlquist (1990) define as all those species in the Suborder Passeri, ie. Parvorders Corvida and Passerida.

Pelagic Oceanic. Living far from land except when nesting.

Pellet The regurgitated and indigestible remains of prey — usually feathers, hair, bone, scales. Produced by raptors, owls, swifts, corvids, others.

Piratic Stealing food from other species, e.g. frigatebirds, jaegers and skuas.

Plumage The whole layer of feathers and down covering a bird's body.

Plume A long, showy, display feather, e.g. egrets.

Powder-down A fine white powder produced by feathers of some species (a) by disintegration of parts of some feathers or (b) by shedding cells which enclose portion of a newly growing feather's barbules.

Precocial Birds mobile soon after hatching.

Primaries The main or outer flight feathers which control the manoeuvrability of the bird — an old term is 'quill'.

Pyriform Pear-shaped.

Race A group sharing common characteristics that distinguish them from other members of the same species. Often they form a geographically isolated group. In this book, the term is used instead of 'subspecies'.

Rectrice The main feathers of a bird's tail.

Relict population (or species, race, morph) A word used for an isolated population, genus, species, etc., which may now represent a population with a previously much greater range or distribution, e.g. Relict Raven of north-east NSW.

Rictal bristles Stiff whisker-like protrusions about the base of the bill, e.g. Australian Owlet-nightjar.

Roost A resting or sleeping place; perch for birds.

Rump The squarish area between the lower back and base of the tail, e.g. Yellow-rumped Thornbills.

Scapular Feathers which lie along the dorsal shoulder (base of the wing) of a bird.

Secondaries The inner flight feathers attached to the forearm.

Sedentary Locally living; not travelling far.

Shaft The main stem (rachis) of any feather.

Shoulder General term for upperwing coverts.

Soft parts Unfeathered areas of the body — bill, eyes, legs, feet and any bare skin, wattles, etc.

Species The division of classification into which a genus is divided, the members of which can interbreed among themselves, i.e. the next taxonomic rank below genus.

Speculum Iridescent, reflective dorsal patch on a duck's wing; contrasts with the rest of the wing.

Spur Sharp bony projection on the wing or leg.

Striated (striations) Streaked. Usually dark marks aligned along birds long axis, e.g. Calamanthus.

Sub-adult see **Immature**.

Sub-oscines Passeriform birds with different, supposedly more primitive, syringeal (voice-box) anatomy from the remainder of the songbirds, or perching birds, the Oscines.

Sub-terminal 'Near the end', e.g. dark tail band of Australian Kestrel, Pacific Gull, Scrubtit.

Sulcus Groove along bill of albatrosses and some petrels.

Superciliary The eyebrow stripe of some birds, e.g. Pacific Black Duck, White-browed Robin, Hall's Babbler.

Superfamily A grouping of taxonomically related bird Families. The level below Suborder.

Talon Sharply hooked claw used for holding and killing prey e.g. all birds of prey.

Tapetum A reflecting layer behind the eye's retina which permits the better utilisation of dim or low light levels; many nocturnal animals have this feature.

Tarso-metatarsus Fused tarsal and metatarsal leg elements; the 'lower leg' of birds, just above the toes. This is commonly called the *tarsus*. May be feathered, partly so, or not at all.

Terminal 'At the end', e.g. white tail tips of Spiny-cheeked Honeyeater; black tail tips of Australian Magpie.

Tertiary (feather) Row of inner flight feathers on a bird's 'upper arm'; (also the third geological Era Palaeocene to Pleistocene).

Tomial tooth (teeth) A notch and protrusion on the edge of the mandible for killing prey, e.g. Peregrine Falcon. This is not a true tooth.

Torpidity Lowering of body temperature to overcome adverse weather or cold and to conserve energy. May be daily, or for longer periods. Nightjars, swifts capable of it, but may rarely do it in Australia. Other species reported as entering torpor, e.g. Mistletoebird (see *Hibernation*).

Totipalmate *All* four toes completely linked by webbing e.g. Australian Pelican, cormorants, gannets and boobies.

Trailing edge The back or hind edge of a wing or flipper, e.g. Little Penguin, Hardhead, Hooded Plover.

Underparts (ventrum) The chin, throat, breast, belly, underwing, flank, vent and undertail; the ventral surface of a bird (see *Ventral*).

Upperparts (dorsum) Frons, lores, face, crown, nape, mantle, back, upperwing, rump, base of tail, uppertail; the dorsal surface of a bird (see *Dorsal*).

Vagrant A bird found in an area which is not its usual habitat, having strayed there by mistake, e.g. disorientation, or forced by adverse winds.

Vent The cloaca — includes anus, oviduct and sperm duct openings. Also refers to patch of feathers around this.

Ventral Pertaining to the undersurface of the body (see *Underparts*).

Vermiculated Densely patterned with fine winding or wavy lines, e.g. Wandering Albatross, Maned (Wood) Duck.

Wattle Paired fleshy lobes or appendages, often brightly coloured, hanging from the throat or neck of certain birds, e.g. Southern Cassowary, Masked Plover, Yellow Wattlebird.

Wing load (loading) Relates the total body weight to the wing area.

Wingspan The shortest distance between the wingtips; the greatest extent of the spread wings.

Index of Latin names

Common names

Writers and their contributions to the First, Second and Third Editions

All changes and additions to the text of this Fourth Edition have been made by Ken Simpson.

Tom Aumann, B.Sc., B.Ed.
Species 147-50. Families Pandionidae, Accipitridae, Falconidae.
Australasian Wader Study Group
Principal Contributors: Angela Jessop, B.Sc.(Hons), Brett Lane B.A., Clive Minton Ph.D., Mick Murliss.
Contributing members: John Bransbury, Peter Curry, Peter Dann, Berrice Forest, Stephen Garnett, David Henderson, Marilyn Hewish, Roger Jaensch, Tom Lowe, Alan McBride, Jim McNamara, Mike Newman, Danny Rogers.
David Baker-Gabb, B.Ag., Dip.Sc., M.Sc., Ph.D.
Species 139-40, 142-6, 154-6. Families Pandionidae, Accipitridae, Falconidae.
Kevin Bartram
Species 20-32, 47-52, 63-93, 166-73, 182-97, 275-307, 386-98, 416-21, 464-8, 502-17. Families Procellariidae, Oceanitidae, Pelecanoididae, Pelecanidae, Sulidae, Anhingidae, Phalacrocoracidae, Fregatidae, Phaethontidae, Phasianidae, Pedionomidae, Rallidae, Stercorariidae, Laridae, Cuculidae, Muscicapidae (genera *Machaerirhynchus, Monarcha*).
Simon Bennett, B.App.Sc.
Species 174-80. Family Turnicidae.
Ron Brown (deceased)
Species 115-37. Family Anatidae.
Margaret Cameron, B.A.
Species 68-76. Families Oceanitidae, Pelecanoididae.
Mike Carter, C.Eng.
Species 18-19. Family Diomedeidae.
Andrew Corrick, B.Sc.(Hons)
Species 94-114. Families Ardeidae, Ciconiidae, Plataleidae.
Stephen Debus, B.A., Dip.Nat.Resources, Dip.Ed.
Species 138, 141, 151-3, 157-62, 753-8. Families Pandionidae, Accipitridae, Falconidae, Corvidae.
Denise Deerson
Species 115-37. Family Anatidae.
Xenia Dennett B.Sc., Ph.D.
Species 469-73. Family Muscicapidae (genus *Petroica*).

Peter Fell, B.Sc.
Species 608-74. Family Meliphagidae.
Kate Fitzherbert, B.Sc.(Hons), Ph.D.
Species 198-200. Families Gruidae, Otididae.
Cliff Frith
Species 723-35. Families Ptilonorhynchidae, Paradiseidae.
Geoff Gayner
Species 545-59. Family Maluridae.
Belinda Gillies, B.A., Dip.Ed.
Species 745-52. Families Grallinidae, Cracticidae.
Marc Gottsch
Species 163-5, 399-403, 409-15, 680-1. Families Megapodidae, Strigidae, Podargidae, Aegothelidae, Caprimulgidae.
Murray Grant
Species 518-31. Families Orthonychidae, Pomatostomidae.
John Hatch, B.A., Ph.D.
Species 44-6, 53-6. Family Procellariidae.
Victor Hurley, B.Sc.
Many species in Families Dromaiidae, Casuariidae, Struthionidae, Megapodidae, Orthonychidae, Maluridae, Ephthianuridae, Dicaeidae.
Jack Hyett, T.P.T.C.
Species 181. Family Pedionomidae.
Andrew Isles, B.Sc.
Species 333-85. Family Psittacidae.
Jaroslav Klapste
Species 4-6, 422-34, 443-55, 532-41. Families Podicipedidae, Alcedinidae, Alaudidae, Motacillidae, Hirundinidae, Sylviidae.
Peter Klapste (deceased)
Species 4-6, 422-34, 443-55, 532-41. Families Podicipedidae, Alcedinidae, Alaudidae, Motacillidae, Hirundinidae, Sylviidae.
Tess Kloot
Species 463, 716-22. Families Pycnonotidae, Sturnidae, Oriolidae, Dicruridae.
Alan Lill, B.Sc., Ph.D.
Species 439-40. Family Menuridae.
Gordon McCarthy
Species 577-600. Family Acanthizidae.
Ellen McCulloch
Species 456-62, 716-22. Families Campephagidae, Sturnidae, Oriolidae, Dicruridae.

Peter Mason, B.Ed., Dip.T.
Species 1-3, 456-62. Families Dromaiidae, Casuariidae, Struthionidae, Campephagidae.
Peter Menkhorst, B.Sc.
Species 333-85. Family Psittacidae.
Richard Noske, Ph.D.
Species 601-7. Families Neosittidae, Climacteridae.
Ian Norman, Ph.D.
Species 115-37. Family Anatidae.
David Paton, B.Sc.(Hons), Ph.D.
Species 608-74. Family Meliphagidae.
Paul Peake, B.Sc.
Species 399-415, 739-44. Families Strigidae, Tytonidae, Podargidae, Artamidae.
Trevor Pescott, Dip.Civ.Eng., M.Sc.
(*Honoris Causa*)
Species 308-32. Family Columbidae.
Des Quinn
Species 399-415, 560-76, 675-9. Families Megapodidae, Strigidae, Podargidae, Aegothelidae, Caprimulgidae, Acanthizidae, Ephthianuridae.
Pat Rich, Ph.D.
Modern avifaunal regions, Prehistoric birds.
Bruce Robertson, B.Sc., B.V.Sc.
Species 280-6. Family Laridae.
Len Robinson
Species 392-8, 435-8. Families Cuculidae, Pittidae.
Tony Robinson, B.Sc.(Hons), Ph.D.
Where the birds live: vegetation and landform habitats of Australia.
Ken Simpson, M.Sc. (*Honoris Causa*)
Species 4-17, 33-43, 89-93, 275-9, 392-8, 416-21, 441-50, 464-8, 514-17. Chukar, Common Turkey, Helmeted Guinea Fowl. Families Podicipedidae, Spheniscidae, Diomedeidae, Cuculidae, Aegothelidae, Caprimulgidae, Apodidae, Atrichornithidae, Muscicapidae, Nectariniidae.
Lance Williams, B.Sc.
Species 474-501, 687-9, 736-8. Families Muscicapidae, Zosteropidae, Corcoracidae.
John Woinarski, B.Sc.(Hons)
Species 682-6. Family Pardalotidae.
Richard Zann, B.Sc., Dip.Ed., Ph.D.
Species 690-715. Families Fringillidae, Passeridae, Ploceidae.

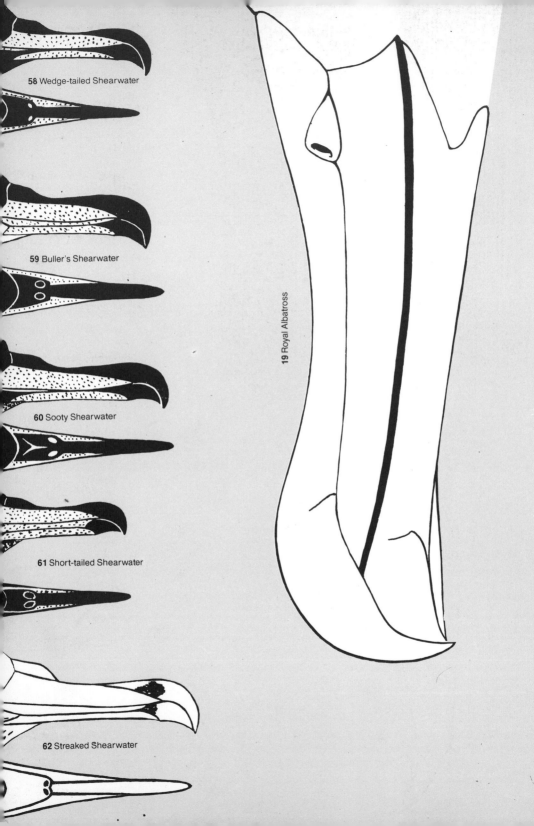

58 Wedge-tailed Shearwater

59 Buller's Shearwater

60 Sooty Shearwater

61 Short-tailed Shearwater

62 Streaked Shearwater

19 Royal Albatross